Preacher

Billy Sunday and
Big-Time American Evangelism

Preacher

Billy Sunday and
Big-Time American Evangelism

ROGER A. BRUNS

University of Illinois Press
Urbana and Chicago

First Illinois paperback, 2002
© 1992 by Roger A. Bruns
Reprinted by arrangement with the author
All rights reserved
Manufactured in the United States of America
P 5 4 3 2 1

♾ This book is printed on acid-free paper.

Library of Congress Cataloging-in-Publication Data
Bruns, Roger.
Preacher : Billy Sunday and big-time American evangelism /
Roger A. Bruns.
p.   cm.
Originally published: 1st ed. New York : W. W. Norton, c1992.
Includes bibliographical references and index.
ISBN 0-252-07075-5 (pbk. : alk. paper)
1. Sunday, Billy, 1862–1935. 2. Evangelists—United States—
Biography. 3. Revivals—United States—History—20th century. I.
Title.
BV3785.S8B75   2002
269'.2'092—dc21   2001054008
[B]

To My Parents
J. Donald and Margaret E. Bruns

Contents

Photographs appear following page 160.

Preface

It has been a long road from the crude tent meetings of early evangelists to the media drives of today's big-time preachers. Billy Sunday stands as the towering figure on that road.

He packed huge tabernacles across the country, gained hundreds of thousands of followers, made bitter enemies, honed the business of revivalism to near perfection, crusaded for an array of moral causes, entered the political arena, created controversies, and took on radicals, intellectuals, evolutionists, modernists, foreigners, birth-control advocates, liquor interests, and newfangled ologies and isms. The ex-ballplayer from Iowa brought fiery, zealous evangelism to dizzying heights early in this century. Standing four-square against the swirling changes wrought in American society by industrialization, immigration, and war, he became a symbol of old-fashioned, militant, fundamentalist Christianity.

Billy Sunday paved the revivalist road for a later generation. His spirit breathes still in the great crusades of Billy Graham and in the television evangelism and radio ministries of preachers across the country. The fundamentalist message which thundered from his pulpit many decades ago is a major force in American life today— the evangelical voice asserting the power of the gospel and of prayer, the supreme authority and inerrancy of the Bible, the need to eradicate vice and moral rot from society, and the duty to stand up for America and its values. This book examines the Sunday phenomenon in light of the evangelistic roots from which his career sprung as well as the later American religion industry which has powerfully moved into the country's politics and national affairs.

My appreciation goes to the Archives of the Billy Graham Center, Wheaton College, and its director, Robert Shuster. The Archives has done an exceptional job of organizing the Sunday Papers and informing researchers about related collections. The microfilm edition and its guide, prepared by Shuster and his colleagues several years ago and now available from Scholarly Resources, Inc., are invaluable in researching the life of the evangelist.

My thanks also go to Professor Lyle Dorsett of Wheaton College, who shared his insights on Billy. Professor Dorsett is the author of a recent volume on Sunday in Eerdman's new series of religious biographies. I am grateful to Professor Robert Seager, who kindly alerted me to numerous references; to Julie Nash and Carrie Bruns, who first read the manuscript and offered valuable suggestions; to Mary Giunta, who gave her usual excellent editorial help; to Martha Millard, who gave encouragement throughout the writing; and to Jim Mairs and Eve Picower at Norton, who guided the book to publication.

My appreciation also to Patricia Kelly and Russell McCall of the National Baseball Hall of Fame and Museum, Inc.; Mary Boccaccio, East Carolina University; Archie Motley and Eileen Flanagan, Chicago Historical Society; and William Darr, Grace College.

Preacher

Billy Sunday and
Big-Time American Evangelism

Prologue

Hallelujah!

s the preacher marched to the tabernacle pulpit, the vast throng cheered and clapped, most waving white handker-chiefs—a revival army ready to take on all that Satan could muster. From the swirling white sea of jubilant spectators and from the massive choir thundered "The Battle Hymn of the Republic." Ascending the tabernacle steps, the preacher waved amid the chorus of whoops and shouts. Like a fighter climbing into the ring, this greatest of God's warriors prepared for battle.

The thousands squirmed with anticipation, awaiting the Word. The preacher quickly lashed out with a vengeance, roaring at the crowd, "If you want to live in sin, all right, live in sin, and go to hell at the end." This "whiskey-soaked, harlot-ridden world," with its moral degeneration and putrid spiritual apathy, was in desperate need of a great infusion of religious enthusiasm. Religion in America, he said, was slumbering, hopelessly vulnerable to the devil's assaults. The whorehouses, drug dens, two-bit booze joints, and other iniquities could only be brought to their knees by a national spiritual rebirth.

The preacher moved around the stage waving his fists, banging them in his palms and on the pulpit. He challenged anyone in the crowd who sided with the forces of evil to fight him, here, now, right in the tabernacle, before thousands, before the devil, before God. "Come and fight me. Come on, and God bless you!"

Wildly tearing across the stage, thrashing his arms, kicking, shouting, he jumped on a chair and bent himself backward like a fencer's foil. The frenzied crowd gasped; some women fainted. He bounded to the front. Most of the human race was, he said, a "mean, contemptible, scurrilous" bunch. Only through repentance and conversion, only through a religious awakening, could they rise above the level of pigs.

"The hour is come for plain speech. Everything the devil's in favor of I'm against. I'm against the theatre, because the devil's in favor of it; I'm against booze and I'm against card parties because the devil's in favor of them." Here was the preacher and the devil facing off, square against each other, iron wills clashing. Resolutely, the preacher charged on. He railed against dancing, a "rotten, infernal, lustful, licentious" practice. The devil was for it; the preacher against. He assailed weak-kneed, pusilanimous ministers afraid to take on the tough issues, lacking strength of purpose and the assurance of faith. They were "poisoned pups," too pretty, too dainty, unfit soldiers for the Lord. They were the devil's playthings, his handmaidens. The devil was for 'em; the preacher against.

He fought on. He attacked the churches, institutions lolling in ceremony, isolated from human needs, concerned with membership rolls and donor lists and ceremony and tradition, and so oblivious to sin and salvation. The devil liked 'em; the preacher did not. He was reeling across the stage now, spitting, leering, his face twisting from one contorted grimace to another. He howled.

The audience, swept up by the raw animal vehemence, began to shout, "Hallelujah! Jesus Christ lives!"

He mocked millennium darwinism, Unitarianism, and Watch Tower nonsense. He scoffed at Christian Science, "the worst fal-de-rol of the lot; the worst tommy rot that ever came down the pike." He attacked the insipid isms and schisms infecting the world—Hinduism, Shintoism, Zorasters, followers of Confucius and Buddha. He attacked the evolutionist theory of creation, a theory of bastards, he said, of godless losers. He scoffed at something called Blavatskyism which taught that life is dreamlike, cosmic progress. The followers of such absurdities were all demented, silly, deluded fools, clouded by miserable, wistful philosophies dreamed up by shysters. They were all the devil's disciples. The devil loved them; the preacher did not.

Enemies lurked everywhere, threatening true religious values and American spirit—alien enemies. Attacking the criminal inclinations of many foreign-born Americans, he exploded, "If they don't like it here let 'em go back to the land where they were kennelled." If you walk the streets of New York or Philadelphia, he said, not one in three faces have in them the strains of pure Americanism.

Skipping across the stage, he shadowboxed the devil. He pretended to pick up giant boulders and hurl them into the crowd. He slid like a ballplayer crossing home plate with the winning run. Moving, always moving, darting with lithe, supple athletic agility, the preacher enraptured the crowd in a spellbinding display.

His words came easily, rhythmically. From retribution to righteousness, courage to pathos—the moods and themes rolled and shifted, sweeping the audience from near delirium to silence. You can't temporize with the devil. You can't bow to his whims and duck from his attacks. You can't compromise.

This was no dainty, sissified, lily-livered piety the crowd was hearing. This was hard-muscled, pickaxed religion, a religion from the gut, tough and resilient. Prayer here was a manly duty; faith was mountain-moving, galvanic. There was power in reverence, energy in belief. The tough guys were on the right side. This was not a place for weak-kneed, four-flushing boozers and sin-soaked infidels.

"If we have the sins of Babylon we must have the judgment of Babylon." Swinging his arms now in wide circles, stomping on the platform, he exhorted the crowd to "get a new vision." "Oh, it's a good thing for some fellows I'm not God for about 15 minutes. There would be something doing. I wonder that God lets some people live."

He attacked biblical scholars, those anemic, rank skeptics and their sneering, highbrow intellectualism. He attacked the social churchgoers and their indifference to God's truths. Religion was rooted, he said, in personal experience and emotion, in faith and action, not in punctilious rites and pointy-headed, self-serving dogma.

He was in stride now, the epithets and charges pounding into the audience like a sustained drumbeat, cadences rising and falling with searing emotional effect. The crowd, entranced, mouths agape, followed his every move, every violent gyration. Sometimes the drumbeat suddenly, eerily slowed, the voice lowering its pitch, the crowd hushed straining to hear every word. "Oh, the hour has come to believe what the Lord says and trust the blessing. The time has come to present yourselves before the Lord. Acknowledge your wrong and see what God will do for you. The hour has come to go out after the lost and bring them back to Jesus Christ."

To millions across the land as well as those in the tabernacle this night, the preacher was God's mouthpiece, ordained to drive the sin-stained multitudes out of their spiritual muck and grime, and into the fold of the Lord. At a time of dizzying change in society, a time of labor problems, crime, of monster cities choking in poverty, of masses of alien peoples pouring into the country, a time of attacks against capitalism, against religion, against tradition, the man was there, a voice harkening back to simpler times, to true moral values, fundamentalist theology, to the American way. To conservative politicians and businessmen, he was a powerful force against radical left-wing interests. Here was a man of truth and decency and all that remained good.

To others, however, this was a religious grafter, his Jesus spiel straight from savage, right-wing, conservative dogma, his words mind-numbing pabulum, fed to masses of middle-class followers— the words of a reactionary. Be loyal, patriotic, industrious, he was saying, and your reward waits in heaven. At this time of social and political upheaval, the preacher stood to some as a rock of assurance, a mighty figure of morality and righteousness; to others he loomed as a wretched symbol of right-wing oppression.

To the thousands packed into the tabernacle this night, he was prophet and teacher, an inspiration. His message was not grounded in sophisticated theological equation or subtle argument; it was simple, uncomplicated fundamentalist belief, the time-worn biblical stories told powerfully, coarsely, told in the language of the street and field. "I know no more about theology," he said almost proudly, "than a jackrabbit does about pingpong or an elephant does about crocheting." Religion was not study and discourse; it was courage, deep faith, a test of the will.

Against charges made by his enemies that he had accumulated a fortune in his evangelistic crusade, the preacher snapped at the audience, "I don't see why so many people are begging for the crumbs from God's table when He would rather give them the bakeshop . . . I could never understand why you wouldn't rather be a millionaire in grace than a hobo. God wants you to be a millionaire in grace." He quoted John 15:7: "If ye abide in me and my words abide in you, ye shall ask what ye will, and it shall be done unto you." For all willing to obey God, to serve God, a new world awaited.

Back and forth across the stage he strode, fighting on, even leading the crowd into historical fantasy. He pictured himself as Wellington at Waterloo, standing in ankle-deep mud, digging his nails into the flesh of his palms until they ran blood. Wellington had held fast. The preacher would also. He was Grant at Shiloh making a death stand. Grant triumphed. The preacher would also. He was good versus evil, right versus wrong, morality versus wickedness, salvation versus sin. He was here to make war. Against such an onslaught, against such daring and bravado, the devil must surely wilt.

Moving closer to the front of the stage, he quietly told how it had taken him over twenty-seven years to build his Christian character. Defying his critics to follow him around the country to find a flaw in any of his personal habits, he said, "Our virtues are best discerned when subjected to the serverest trials." He was not a philanderer, he said, not a boozer, a gambler. Once, a long time ago, he had cavorted in saloons, had drunk the devil's drink. Now, he stood as a foremost fighter against it.

Soon he was again pummeling the pulpit, perspiration streaming into his eyes, slashing out at the liquor menace, that despicable evil polluting the minds and spirits of Americans young and old, rich and poor. All people who called themselves Christians must take a stand. "If you sleep with dogs you must expect to get up with fleas and lice."

He decried the lack of moral principles in American society. The insipid high-society belle meandering from one dance to another was no better than the town loafer downing a quart of red-eye in a low-class suds parlor. The sins of all Americans could be remedied only by spiritual regeneration.

He was not a partisan in politics, he told the crowd; he was not in favor of the union of church and state. But he called for national moral reform in the name of Christ. "There is no reason why the politics of today should not become the communion of tomorrow." Any political party which would endorse a platform declaring a belief in the Almighty would prove a winner.

"I think it's a dirty, rotten shame that they took the Bible out of the public schools," he continued. "Schools used to teach discipline and obedience and morals not rebellion and anarchy. More children should be spanked and put to bed. The hickory stick should be in every home with the motto, "I need thee every hour."

Slowly, deliberately aiming a finger from side to side at the thousands of faces peering up, his own face with a contemptuous glare, he suddenly sneered, "All you do is to beat a little path through the church and keep a section of a pew warm on Sunday while this old world is going to hell so fast you can't see it for fog." Arms outstretched, body quivering, he wailed, "Oh God, may all Americans be stirred by the . . . revival. America needs a tidal wave of religion, a cyclone of redemption."

He was nearing the close now, shaking violently, color red-dening, muscles taut. And then he seemed to relax as if punctured. He looked sorrowfully at the crowd. "There stands Jesus Christ," the preacher cried softly, "with the thorn-crowned brow and the bleeding hands, pointing to the unsaved . . . 'They're lost! They're lost!' " He gazed heavenward and pleaded, "May the multitudes here accept Thee tonight. Make this a marvelous time. Lead us and guide us to Thy glory. Amen!"

Hundreds in the crowd sobbed and moaned. Some cried "Hal-lelujah!" Most sat stunned, drained, ground into emotional waste by the moment's passion.

Another minister came to the side of the exhausted preacher and helped him off the stage. Muttering, eyes half closed, lips tightly pursed, complexion pale, the preacher stumbled along. "Amen!" he managed to shout. "Glory to God!"

1

Prairie Days

Only a few soliders were there for the burial, bracing against the wind and a chilling drizzle in the early winter of 1862. Once again they played out the lonely ritual, this time on a small hill near a federal military camp in Missouri, a ritual acted out in so many places, so many thousands of times throughout the Civil War years. On this biting, frigid day, all emotion and spirit seemed drained from the occasion, all sentiment washed away in the weather and the routine: another dead young man, another family back home left grieving—routine.

As two soldiers carried the body from the hospital tent, the fife and drum corps, the rifle squad, and the chaplain marched slowly behind, preparing to enact the familiar ceremony. After the chaplain threw a soggy handful of dirt on the crude wooden box, the participants in the occasion quickly returned to cover.

The soldier's name was William Sunday. Born in Perry, Pennsylvania, in 1828 to German immigrant parents named Sonntag, Sunday was a poor farmer and sometime bricklayer who had enlisted in the service of the Union Army in August 1862, a private in the 23rd Iowa Volunteers Infantry, Company E. He was thirty-four, a man who could play the violin, a father of three, including an infant he had never seen. His wife, Mary Jane (or "Jennie"), had given birth to their third son, William Ashley, on November 19, shortly after her husband had left their little farm near Ames, Iowa.

After marching with his regiment from Jefferson Barracks over the Iron Mountains route to Camp Patterson in December, William had suffered from exposure and contracted disease, probably a virulent form of measles. The lack of sanitary conditions, medicine, and competent doctors usually made such cases hopeless. He died within a few days. With the new child and her other two sons, Albert Monroe, age four, and Howard Edwin (called Ed), age two, Jennie now faced the grim, daunting challenge of surviving the prairie by herself.[1]

Born in 1841 in Syracuse, Indiana, Jennie was the oldest in a family of eight children. Her father, Martin Corey, a Revolutionary War soldier from Ohio, moved to Storey County, Iowa, in 1848, a relatively wild, raw, unsettled land of rolling, wooded hills. To the resolute families who made homes in the area, Corey, one of its earliest settlers, became known as "Squire." As his youngest grandson, Billy, later remembered, Squire Corey "wore a coonskin cap, rawhide boots, blue jeans . . . drank coffee out of a saucer and ate peas with his knife." He was royalty in his domain.[2]

Jennie married William in 1857 and they built a small log cabin not far distant from her father's large farm. The cabin was austere, simple, with two rooms, a flagstone fireplace, log chimney, floor of rough boards, a typical home for poor prairie folk. The couple struggled, William taking odd jobs, the two acquiring a few farm animals, clearing the land, planting some crops. With the birth of the first two children the financial struggle became even more intense.

When he enlisted in the Union Army in 1862, William probably had more in mind that patriotic fervor. Perhaps a career in the military could help lift the family out of its increasingly racking poverty. Full-bearded, in his military uniform, he sat for a photograph with his wife shortly after enlisting. A few months later, Jennie had only the photograph, the little farm, and the personal possessions of her husband sent to her by the War Department—his clothes, a few papers, and ten cents.[3]

After her husband's death, Jennie grimly carried on. Young Billy was not yet two years old when she remarried in Nevada, Iowa, in August 1864. Leroy Heizer, age forty-three, a farmer who had relocated to Iowa from Indiana, moved into the log cabin near Ames and became the official guardian of Jennie's three sons. Shortly thereafter, a fourth son, Leroy, was born, followed a few years later by a girl, Elizabeth ("Libbie"). The family's financial dilemmas mounted.[4]

It didn't help that Billy was quite sickly, was scarcely able to walk at times, and often had to be carried around on a specially made pillow. According to a family story, an itinerant French country doctor stopped by the cabin when Billy was about three years old and told Jennie that he could cure the boy. Concocting a secret witches' brew from mulberry leaves, elderberries, and other wild fruits, the doctor administered the palliative and from that day forward the young boy seemed rejuvenated. Soon he was playing vigorously and running more swiftly than any other youngsters his age in the area. Into adulthood, Billy ate elderberries and mulberries, drank sassafras tea, and always claimed that nature had created a plant or herb to heal all maladies.[5]

Once in good health Billy was immersed into the plowboy life—milking night and morning, laboring in the wheat- and cornfields, chopping wood, boiling molasses. He remembered: "I wore a coonskin cap and rawhide boots and overalls and a hickory shirt, and had my hair cut once a year."[6]

Later, he would look back on those days with conflicting emotions—pride in his honest roots, a kinship with those who also faced the rigors of the prairie, embarrassment at his cornpone manners and deprived education, resentment and self-pity over the absence of his father, gratitude for the simple code of honor and hard work and religious values instilled by his mother. He would see himself as a battler who had confronted all the grime and misery and deprivation of the isolated farm and had come out on top, a survivor, a tough-in-the-gut fighter. "I am a rube of the rubes," he said, "I am a hayseed of the hayseeds, and the malodors of the barnyard are on me yet." At another time he said, "I have greased my hair with goose grease and blacked my boots with stove blacking. I have wiped my old proboscis with a gunny-sack towel . . . I have crept and crawled out from the university of poverty and hard knocks, and have taken postgraduate courses."[7] He would see his boyhood as a heroic climb out of the depths and would wear that early life like a medal.

His existence was indeed hard, but it was also hard for countless others on the prairie. Across an America recovering from the throes of the Civil War there were many children orphaned, families broken, fortunes lost, lives disrupted and overturned in unimagined ways and numbers. There were poverty, hardship, misery, and a war's worth of suffering and pain.

But Billy was right; he had in his youth much to overcome. In addition to the poverty there was grief. Billy's oldest brother, Albert, kicked by a horse when he was a young boy, was never mentally stable, suffering from seizures and other afflictions that demanded nearly constant attention his mother could not provide. He was later institutionalized. Billy's half-sister, Libbie, in a horrible, bizarre accident, caught her dress on fire and burned to death. Sudden death, loss, and tragedy for the young boy already plagued by uncertainty, illness, and fear made these early years haunting and traumatic.

And yet, there were the good times. Billy deeply admired his grandfather, later calling him the most versatile man he ever met. Squire constructed wagons, built houses, laid stone walls, and made waterwheels, looms, and even a cane mill. He taught Billy gymnastics tricks and to ride a horse bareback while standing up. Squire would parade into Ames on horseback with Billy proudly perched on his shoulders. So skilled at circus feats did Billy become under his grandfather's tutelege that a troupe visiting Ames once asked the boy to join.[8]

Leroy Heizer was never in Billy's eyes an adequate replacement for his lost father. Jealousy, resentment, the disbelief that his mother could entrust the well-being of the family to a stranger—all of it pressed on him. To love and respect his grandfather was right and honorable; to accept the interloper as a father substitute was impossible.

In 1871 Leroy, racked by alcoholism, abandoned the family. Once again, Jennie was alone with her children and in dire financial need. She was soon ready to make a fateful decision. She had endured much—the loss of one husband, the desertion of another; the death of one child, the permanently debilitating injury to another; a life of struggle and want. And she was still in her early thirties. The responsibility of providing and caring for the children finally seemed overwhelming. She was weary, worn down by the prairie and its unrelenting demands. Billy and his brother, restless, strong-willed, and short-tempered, often quarreled and fought with other boys. They needed, she knew, discipline and education. They needed more than she could give.

In Glenwood, Iowa, in the southwestern part of the state, approximately 150 miles from the Sunday home, was one of the branches of the Iowa State Orphans' Asylum, or more popularly called the "Soldiers' Home." This and the other branches of the Soldiers' Home were inspired by Mrs. Annie Wittenmyer who, while caring for soldiers on Civil War battlefields and hospitals, had listened to the pleas of dying men that someone, some agency, provide for their children. Under Wittenmyer's organizing zeal the homes opened in several states in the mid-1860s. The home at Glenwood began operations in November 1866. It would, for a time, beginning in 1872, be the home of young Billy and his brother.[9]

"One of the saddest memories of my life," Billy wrote, "is the recollection of the grief I felt when leaving the old farm to go to Ames to take the train for the trip to Glenwood." For a youngster who had never been farther away from home than Nevada, Iowa, eight miles east, the long trip to the orphans' home and the forced exile from his relatives were devastating. He later remembered the scene at the train station: "I looked into mother's face. Her eyes were red and her cheeks wet from weeping, her hair disheveled. While Ed and I slept she had prayed and wept. We went to the depot, and as the train pulled in she drew us to her heart, sobbing as if her heart would break."[10]

The forced separation left deep psychological marks in Billy that would last a lifetime. He often spoke of his childhood, remembering the long, agonizing train ride to Glenwood, the crushing feelings of rejection, the hours he and his brother cried, the incomprehensibility and uncertainty of their lives. Billy would react against the shocks and hurt with grit; the experience toughened him.

The Glenwood home was fairly isolated among the rolling hills and thick forests of southwestern Iowa, and the children had large fields and woods in which to romp. Billy hunted rabbits and squirrel, played baseball, and ran foot races against other boys in the home. It was there that Billy and others began to realize how fast a runner he was. Nobody could begin to match his speed.

The school offered a concentrated, formal education and some religious training, including close scriptural study. But to the Sunday boys it was imprisonment, a torture to be endured for untold indiscretions and sins. They were, nevertheless, fighters and angrily confronted this monstrous affront to their pride.

When the crowded Glenwood home later transferred a large number of its boys to the Soldiers' Home in Davenport, Iowa, in the far eastern part of the state, Billy and Ed prepared for another train ride, this one much longer than the first—the Burlington line from Council Bluffs to Des Moines, then the Rock Island to Davenport. Learning that the train would pass through Des Moines in the center of the state relatively close to their home, they plotted an escape. The superintendent off the Davenport institution, Mr. S. W. Pierce, had traveled across the state to Glenwood to escort the boys on their latest journey. When Ed foolishly confided to a friend on the train that he and his brother were planning to hop off at Des Moines and head home, the friend then confided to the superintendent and the planned escape was foiled. Billy soon went after the ratting kid and, as he said later, "cleaned up on him."[11]

The Davenport home, several buildings occupying sixty acres of land, was the province of Mr. Pierce and his wife, superintendent and assistance superintendent, respectively. The two made a polished team, he the enforcer and symbol of authority, she the understanding, caring shepherd dispensing comfort and warmth to the flock. The untiring Mr. Pierce was vigilant and demanding. Careful grooming, timeliness, respect, order—these were the hallmarks of the school and Mr. Pierce steadfastly enforced them. Runaways were his special challenge. A tenacious hunter who ultimately bagged his game, he would doggedly pursue them on foot, on horseback, or by train to any and all parts of the state. Upon their return to Davenport, the runaways suffered the chastening— a forced march around a cinder track in front of the school's administration building, eight hours a day for a week, with meals and periods of sleep offering the only interlude. Billy, not unexpectedly, tested the hunter's tracking skills and lost, thereby incurring the forced week of circling. He also endured occasional mild whippings for fighting, his punishment always ameliorated afterward by Mrs. Pierce's kindness.

For his regular chores, Billy made beds, scrubbed floors, toiled in the laundry, washed dishes, worked on the school's farm, and read aloud his required religious readings each night in front of the other boys. During their stay at Glenwood and Davenport, Billy and Ed received a decent grammar-school education, but because of the lack of much formal schooling while on the Ames farm they still faced a long educational trail ahead.

Although Billy had resented the regimen of the Soldiers' Home, he later recognized its profound impact not only on him but on most of his fellow classmates. Many successfully made their way in the world—as railroad men, farmers, millhands, even teachers. The Pierces ran a creditable institution, Billy concluded, thoroughly dedicated to the well-being of the children.[12]

Because of the Davenport home's age limitation, Ed was required to leave after turning sixteen in 1876. When Billy defiantly announced to the school's officials that he would not stay there without his brother, his mother and grandfather decided that he should leave also. Thus, for the fourteen-year-old youngster, it was homecoming.

Attempting to regain strength and confidence, Billy's mother had left the little log house and settled for a time at Squire Corey's. When Billy and Ed arrived at the Corey house, Jennie and her father welcomed two boys who had become even more fiercely independent. Their love for their mother and grandfather was still strong but both had braced themselves against their gnawing sense of rejection with tough emotional shells, and had developed a stubborn resistance to authority and a growing sense that they must, even in these early teenage years, make it on their own.

Ed didn't stay long at the Corey house; he was soon living with a neighbor. Several years later he returned to Davenport and worked at the orphans' home as one of the carpenters and watchmen. He married one of the girls from the school, moved to North Dakota, and took a job with the Northern Pacific Railroad Company.

Billy also grew restive on the farm. One day when he and his half-brother, Leroy, were hitching a team of horses, they clumsily pulled the rings out of the yoke, infuriating Squire, who was anxious to go to town. Angrily, their grandfather swore and hurled insults at them. Hurt and furious, Billy impulsively packed his bags. He was on the road, never to live again in Ames.[13]

The trepidation and loneliness which had enveloped the twelve-year-old two years earlier when he boarded the train for Glenwood had been drowned in a storm of rebellion, anger, and determination. The orphans' home had tested his resilience and strength of will, and he had left Davenport contemptuous of any individual or institution that threatened dominion over him. He left convinced that he could take on shocks and injuries, that he had cried enough. The incident with his grandfather was only the trigger; Billy was ready to leave behind the farm and its destitution, to try other places and other jobs, to make certain that the prairie did not drain from him, as it had drained from his mother, energy, spirit, and youth. Soon after Billy left the farm for good, Jennie married a man named George Stowell. This third marriage lasted until Stowell died in

1907. He left two-span of horses, some wagons, and some harnesses which were sold to pay off bills.[14]

Billy's inaugural journey on his own was hardly dramatic. After staying at the house of a family friend for a short period, he set off for Nevada, Iowa, about ten miles east of Ames. He worked at a hotel for a while and then returned to the Corey farm for a couple of days to ease family tension. Soon, however, he was back in Nevada, working as an errand boy for Colonel John Scott, a one-time lieutenant governor of Iowa. Billy lived on the Scott estate, caring for the twenty-one Shetland ponies, milking cows, and chopping wood.

Refined, educated, and of some wealth, John and Sophia Scott, living ten miles from Billy's birthplace, seemed from another world. Gone now for Billy was the constant specter of privation and worry. Here, the wolf was not at the door, as Billy often said of his life in Ames; the wolf was in the woods—the hunted, not the hunter. Here the concern was not over survival but over political affairs and reading and social events. Concerned about Billy's education, the Scotts arranged for him to enter public school.

Nevada High School in the 1870s was something of a scholastic oasis on the prairie. Run by Henry Christman, an imaginative educator from New York who had left his home there because of his health, Nevada High was so far advanced academically from many other schools in the area that it began to gain a reputation as a spawning ground for college students.

Billy made his own special impact on Nevada High. Fellow classmates and teachers remembered him especially for his practical jokes, his oratory, and his running speed. Never was there any waggery or high jinks at Nevada High, they said, that Billy did not create or of which he was not fully aware. Full of pep, vim, and pent-up mischief, that was Billy, they said. And all of this energy was at a time when he was working at the Scotts as well as holding down a part-time job as a janitor at the high school. Up at 2 A.M. in the winter months, Billy slogged through all kinds of weather to start the fires in the fourteen school stoves, to sweep floors, and to perform other janitorial duties long before beginning classes. Although often lapsing into sleep over his desk, he never seemed tired for very long, managing to keep up a herculean schedule that would have destroyed most. Stamina—he had it all his life. Moving, always moving, as if that wolf might be closing in. Ward off the fangs, keep up the banter, the good face; make those bad memories of death and separation vanish under a barrage of wit and humor; slug it out with the demons; keep moving.

He loved to speak before classes and even before larger assemblages at the school, even though he was always plagued by nervousness before appearing. Teachers and students remember him expounding on the poem "Parrhasius and the Captive" by Nathaniel Parker Willis. Grim and forbidding, the poem tells of the captive, tortured and killed so that the Greek artist might perpetuate on canvas the agony of the moment. A dramatic Billy, one teacher recalled, would hold the class spellbound with the ghastly sounds of clanking chains, the sadistic scheming of the artist, the cries of the anguished victim, and a thought or two about life and the hereafter. His rhetorical flourishes were, some said, like brushfires raging on the Iowa prairie. From "Horatius at the Bridge" to "Spartacus and the Gladiators," Billy's heroes took on towering dimensions. Whenever an announcement was made about upcoming student orations the first question at Nevada High was whether Billy was going to recite. If the answer was affirmative, a large audience swarmed into the auditorium or classroom.

Billy's classmates not only relished his oratory but were awed by his athletic prowess. From the circus and gymnastic stunts taught to him by his grandfather to his raw foot speed, the youngster was a physical marvel. Friends remembered a cocky fellow sauntering into town one day challenging anyone to a race. He and his pride soon limped away after running against the speedster of Nevada High. Over the years, Billy would leave many with track cinders splattering in their faces.[15]

The Fourth of July, midwestern style, Ames, Iowa. Bedecked in America's colors, the town basked in the summer heat and festivities. There was something for everyone—freshly made lemonade stirred in a large underground vat to keep it cool, a giant glass for a nickel; homemade, honest-to-goodness, down-on-the-farm, pure-cream ice cream; street vendors hawking fistfuls of firecrackers; slices of bologna and ham and a cornucopia of vegetables; booming cannon from the campus of Iowa State College in Ames; music and singing and playing. And games.

Folks in Ames took the hundred-yard dash seriously on the Fourth of July. Runners trained for the event—runners from Iowa State, former high school stars looking for one more moment of glory, and many others. Three dollars cash for the winner. The favorite this day, a professor from the college, reeked of seriousness, garbed in a rose-colored silk running suit and sleek running shoes. Fourteen contestants strode up to the starting line, thirteen men and one teenager. The boy removed his shirt and turned up his overalls to his knees; he was barefooted. At twenty-five yards the runners were fairly bunched; at fifty yards three surged ahead, the professor, a farmer named Bates, and the boy; at seventy-five yards Bates had dropped behind; at the finish bare feet crossed five yards ahead of running shoes. Billy's friends hoisted him on their shoulders and he treated his admirers from his winnings to lemonade and ice cream.

In Billy's boyhood days, the fire departments in the various counties and townships in Iowa were all volunteer, and all felt a strong indentification with their communities. Each year the fire brigades held a tournament offering prizes in such events as running, ladder-climbing, and hose-cart racing, a wild contest in which teams of twelve pulled giant, 500-pound, two-wheel carts that held drums wound with fire hoses. The finish line was a hydrant 300 yards away. The fire companies scoured nearby cities and counties for athletes to join their brigade teams. In the town of Nevada resided a prime recruit.[16] Billy would soon be on the road again.

Though Billy would travel extensively throughout his life, he would never forget his early days in Iowa. He often recalled those years in melodramatic literary effusions: "Shall I ever forget the home of my childhood?" he once wrote. "Yes; when the flowers forget the sun that kissed and warmed them. Yes; when the mountain peaks are incinerated into ashes. Yes; when love dies out in the human heart. Yes; when the desert sands grow cold."[17]

Those early days always remained for Billy a reference point, a measure of how much he had overcome, how far he had advanced.

Occasionally returning to the farms of his parents and grandparents, he remembered the little things that somehow kept appearing larger in his mind—his favorite tree that, like himself, had survived and grown; the places on the Corey farm where he had first ridden horses bareback, where he had learned tricks that no other boy in the area could match. Those days never seemed far distant no matter how far he traveled. The life on the prairie had demanded much of him. "I have battled and fought and struggled," he once wrote. "I know all about the dark and seamy side of life, and if ever a man fought hard, I have fought hard for everything I ever gained."[18]

But he was on the move now, keeping good distance from bad memories and lurking perils. Keep darting and dodging, turn on the speed, that's the secret!

2

From Sandlots
to Sawdust

Saturday, June 10, 1886. No one in Chicago could remember such an enormous baseball crowd in the city. The World Champion Chicago White Stockings were poised to take on the current National League leader, the Detroit Wolverines in a key game.

Youngsters and old-timers, Civil War veterans, politicians, entertainers, the rich as well as the lowly surged through the Chicago Ball Park's turnstiles or snuck into the park in myriad ways—over 16,000 eager spectators jockeying, scrambling to find a seat or place to stand. The crowd spilled onto the field, a rather fearsome spectacle for law-enforcement officials and ushers attempting to keep order. Some of the crowd sat down on the grass close to the infield and foul lines, much to the frustration of the police. In the outfield the fans formed a huge semicircle enclosing the playing area, a few lines of people sitting in the front, others standing behind. In nearby houses, apartments, and hotels, all windows, it seemed were filled, and folks lined up on rooftops like massive flocks of starlings.

Back in Detroit, as newspaper reporters waited for the wires to inform them and the eager Detroit fans of the game's progress, they heard that the Chicago crowd was so huge and boisterous that the game might not be played. But soon the hoopla began, the march of the heroes toward the diamond—following behind a sprightly stepping band, horse-drawn carriages rolled through nearby streets carrying the players. Fans along the route yelled and cheered and waved; the players doffed their hats. The White Stockings were decked out in their usual playing finery: sleek, pressed uniforms, dark bow ties, wide black belts, flat-top hats, and, of course, the distinctive white socks. Most of the players sported the traditional, neatly sculptured, waxed mustache common in the 1880s.

Waving and smiling as their carriages passed under a sweeping triumphal arch built at the entrance to the stadium, the players radiated to the fans a gladiatorial aura. They climbed down from the carriages and, like a finely tuned, disciplined regiment, lined up for the parade onto the playing field. Led by the incomparable team leader, Captain Adrian Anson, they strode forth toward the center of the field basking in a tremendous roar from the Chicago faithful. They were physically large men, many well over six feet and most with admirable physiques; Cap Anson always liked the physically intimidating type on the team, the type that drew gasps from women and respect from men, the type that looked the part of the World Champions they were.

The Detroit team, the White Stockings' principal National League adversary, had skilled players at most positions; they were swift, deft fielders and solid hitters at the plate, a collection of formidable athletes. And yet, most in the Chicago crowd that day would have put down heavy odds on the team in the pale socks to win it all again in 1886. As one of Chicago's sportswriters saw it, the team had coalesced into a fearsome machine against which most other teams blanched. The White Stockings had reached the pinnacle; the team was, the editorialist said, the Marshall Field and Co. of the baseball business.

From the opening pitch this day, the drama and excitement reached an intensity seldom achieved in sport. The crowd seemed strung taut, emotionally skying and plummeting with each play. The fans fed to both teams an extra degree of concentration and purpose, each player expectant, each ready to make the play that could decide the game. Infielders made wizard-like pickups of hot ground balls destined for the outfield; pitchers reached back for that bit of extra speed, that extra spin on the curve, nipping at the corners of the plate like maestros directing favored orchestrations. As the game progressed in the early innings, one newspaper reporter leaned to another and said that he had never seen baseball played at such a skillful level.

In the fifth inning, the White Stockings, behind the masterful pitching of ace John Clarkson, led 2 to 0. At the plate stood Detroit's hard-hitting Charlie Bennett. In right field, the extraordinarily fast kid name Billy Sunday waited nervously. Bennett, Clarkson knew, like the ball down in the strike zone and the Chicago pitcher was determined to keep the ball up. As Clarkson rocked into his windup, however, he stumbled slightly, his release having neither the velocity nor the direction he intended. As the pitch lamely sailed across the plate about knee high, Bennett swung ferociously and connected, the ball rocketing toward the huge crowd in right field. At the first sound of the thunderous crack of the bat most assumed the ball would land far into the right-field crowd.

But like a track sprinter at the sound of the starting gun, outfielder Sunday broke into full stride. He later remembered muttering a prayer for help as he raced into the crowd. The fans in right field leaped about, clearing a path, like an ocean of parting waters, and he ran with shouts of "Go, Billy" ringing in his ears. Looking back over his shoulder he now saw the ball whistling overhead. With a desperate, grasping effort, he flung his body high and extended his glove arm to its full length.[1]

Marshalltown, Iowa, a few years earlier. The fire brigade sought an exceptional runner to help them in their annual firefighting tournament against teams from surrounding counties. Word of Billy's marvelous speed had spread throughout the local communities and some of Marshalltown's civic leaders invited Billy to join the brigade, promising to find him work. For a youngster who had been through countless odd jobs, the offer from this fire brigade seemed indeed an honor, and he accepted.

When Billy left Nevada High School to join the hose team in Marshalltown, he gave up attending his school's graduation ceremonies. This opportunity, he thought, was more important. Billy participated in the July Fourth games, stayed in Marshalltown with the fire brigade team, and took a job with a furniture store, a position which included driving hearses to cemeteries, a chore Billy always found distasteful. "I couldn't stand the grief and sorrow of the people mourning over their departed loved ones," he wrote later, "and to this day I do not like to visit a cemetery or attend a funeral."[2]

During this time in Marshalltown, Billy joined the town's amateur baseball team. The game was almost entirely new to him but his extraordinary agility, coordination, and lightning quickness made the youngster a natural talent. Billy, Marshalltown wags noted, could track down and gobble up fly balls as no other performer they had ever seen. In an 1882 game against rival Des Moines to decide the state championship, Billy scored five runs and made several scintillating catches in the outfield as Marshalltown prevailed.

The town had few noteworthy distinctions to set it apart from other small farm communities in the hog and corn country of central Iowa. It did, nevertheless, boast a distinguished citizen, Henry Anson, one of the founders of the town; his son, Adrian (or "Cap" for Captain), was perhaps America's premier ballplayer in the 1880s. When Cap Anson visited his hometown in the winter of 1882, everybody around Marshalltown, it seemed, including his father and his Aunt Em, who had seen the game against Des Moines, talked about this homegrown kid Billy Sunday, his amazing speed, and his knack for flagging down drives to the outfield at which other players would have only gazed. Aunt Em and father Anson encouraged Cap to invite Billy to Chicago for a tryout with the White Stockings.

The following spring a telegram arrived for Billy, the first he had ever received in his life. It was from Anson in Chicago. The White Stockings wanted to take a look at the phenomenon from central Iowa. Although his brother Ed warned that Chicago would "be the ruin of you," Billy eagerly packed his bags.[3]

By the spring of 1883 baseball had already swept much of the country as the post–Civil War national game. Sandlots from New York to Illinois, Virginia to Iowa tested the skills of thousands of young men longing to reach the chosen land, the major leagues, the bigs. In cities like Providence, St. Louis, Indianapolis, and Detroit, followers of the sport jammed into large stadiums to urge on their charges. Fans could reel off batting averages and pitching statistics and describe in excruciating detail the fine elements of the game, from pitching technique to running the bases. So popular had the sport become by the late 1880s that a company called the McLoughlin Brothers in New York even found success selling a board game called "Game of Baseball," complete with a colorful playing field and miniature players.

The players who donned the uniforms in the majors began to assume the role of heroes to men, women, and children scrambling to put their lives together after the war. Local ball teams not only began to fill an emotional void in growing cities and towns, they helped give those communities a sense of identity. Immigrant groups cheered on their brothers and learned also to cheer on their teammates, whatever the nationality. Raw farm kids played next to the sons of miners and steelworkers and railroadmen. Kids brought up under revivalist tents in the Midwest played next to Italians, Irish, and Jews. They came together each looking for fame and glory and fortune, a way out of personal and economic situations and dilemmas grinding them and their families down, all trying to climb the baseball ladder to the top. They could make names for themselves playing a game, could take on new identities, could find public adulation, could even become idols. Michael Kelly, an Irish kid from Boston, became "King" Kelly. Describing Kelly and his battery mate, star pitcher Clarkson, a Pittsburgh reporter wrote, "But there they were, plain flesh and blood ball players, worshiped like heathen gods from the center to circumference of baseballdom. The people cheered and clapped their hands as these mighty men stripped off their extra coverings and got ready to practice."[4]

And it was all because of the public's thirst to escape the routine, the pulverizing hammer of day-to-day sameness—in factories, stores, and fields. Baseball was a vernal offering, a vicarious world of excitement and tension and personal identification. The people took these teams to their souls and the sport grew not only in dimension but in passion and loyalty. A *New York Times* reporter wrote of the fans who for much of their lives are confined in offices, shops, and factories; unleashed at the ballpark, they jumped "about like colts, stomped their feet, clapped their hands, threw their hats in the air, slapped their companions on the back, winked knowingly . . . and from a baseball standpoint, enjoyed themselves hugely."[5]

When Billy arrived in Chicago, he was about to join a team that had already taken on legendary proportions. The recently renovated White Stockings baseball field on the Lake Front at Randolph Street was a showplace, a palace—grandstands holding over 10,000 spectators, a bandstand pagoda where the First Cavalry Band and other musical groups held forth during the season, a private box for the Western Union Telegraph Company to receive up-to-date reports of other games in progress, a battery of ushers and policemen to maintain order, cushion renters, and, as one might have expected, a bust of the president of the Chicago White Stockings, Albert Goodwill Spaulding, a name that would live in baseball lore for generations. For Spaulding himself, a luxurious private box came equipped with a gong to call for assistance and a telephone to conduct outside business.[6]

Spaulding had assembled a group of superstars never before equaled. The White Stockings had rolled to National League pennants in 1880, 1881, and 1882. Led by the tough, accomplished Cap Anson, they not only dominated play on the field but did it with a raucous bravura and flair. Cap sometimes called the team his "Heroic Legion of Baseball."

A young Connie Mack saw the White Stockings play an exhibition game in his hometown of East Brookfield, Massachusetts, in 1883 and remembered the event as bigger than the inauguaration of a president. With an entourage of assistants and hangers-on, the team rode into towns like a conquering army in their handsome open carriages drawn by white horses. Cap delivered stirring orations to the townspeople.

At six feet two inches and about 220 pounds, the blond giant Anson looked and played like the leader he was. Consistently a top hitter, he was tough and aggressive and so were his players. He was also a man of baseball innovation—the first to coach from the baseline, to institute a pitching rotation, and to take a team to the South for "spring training." He was even idolized by sportswriter Eugene Field:

> *Lo! from the tribune on the bleachers*
> *comes a shout!*
> *Beseeching bold Ansonius to line 'em out.*

The infield was "the Stone Wall." Cap anchored first; Ned Williamson patrolled third and was, said Cap, "the greatest all around player the country ever saw"; slick-fielding Tommy Burns played short; and "Dandelion" Fred Pfeffer was at second. One of his teammates once claimed that Pfeffer could lay on the ground on his stomach and throw a ball a hundred yards.

The most flamboyant member of the team was catcher/outfielder King Kelly—fleet, hard-hitting, able to play after long bouts with women and the bottle. In Chicago's tenderloin of bars, whorehouses, and gambling dens, Kelly cut a rakish figure, twirling a walking stick, women on both arms, his ascot adorned by a giant jewel and his patent-leather shoes as gleaming as his jet-black hair.

It was Kelly who was always trailed by eager reporters ready to lap up a story and by droves of kids waiting for autographs and Kelly's next quip. Outrageous both on and off the field, he was a master base-runner. His base-stealing prowess gained immortality in the song "Slide, Kelly, Slide," popularized by famous songstress Maggie Cline. When the King reached first base, folks in the stands would break into song, imploring Kelly to make his move. He normally obliged with his patented "Kelly spread," the nineteenth-century version of the hook slide. Kelly was probably the first catcher who delivered signs to the pitcher, moving his tobacco chew from one side of his mouth to the other to indicate fastball or curve.

The King was imaginative. On one occasion, while not in the lineup, he leaped off the bench as a pop fly headed in his direction, quickly announced to the umpire that he was replacing another player in the game, and caught the ball. Kelly's antics caused several additions to baseball's rules. Half the game, one wag declared, was changed to keep Kelly from cheating.

Frank "Old Silver" Flint usually handled the catching chores and after several years behind the plate his gnarled, broken fingers and facial bones testified to the quality of baseball equipment used in his day. Pitchers included Larry Corcoran, who threw several no-hitters in his career, and John Clarkson, master of control. Kelly called the 1882 team the best of them all. "We wore silk stockings and the best uniforms money could buy. We had 'em whipped before we even threw a ball. We had 'em scared to death."[7]

It was this formidable collection of talent that Billy joined in 1883. He arrived in Chicago wearing a sage-green, six-dollar suit and carrying one dollar in pocket money. The kid from the prairie confronted a city of over half a million, from the manicured Gold Coast crowd to the gutter bums on West Madison: a concrete forest of monster buildings; the mad rush of big-city sidewalks and streets; and the strange sights and sounds of people recently arrived from Poland, Italy, Germany, and Ireland.

At Spaulding's office Billy met a number of players and that afternoon he worked out for the first time at the park. Anson decided right away to find out just how fast Billy was and asked him to race Pfeffer, the swiftest man on the team. Barefooted, the Iowa farmboy beat Pfeffer easily, much to the amazement and amusement of the other teammates. Billy had gained prompt respect.[8]

On Tuesday, May 22, 1883, 500 spectators braved a ferociously bitter Chicago day—thermometer reading 32 degrees, a hearty wind whipping from the Lake across the park—to see the White Stockings take on the Boston Beaneaters. It was on this day that Cap decided to insert his awestruck Iowa youngster in the lineup.

Here was Billy, playing left field and leading off, nineteen years old with no professional baseball experience, surrounded by Anson, Kelly, Pfeffer, and the other World Champions; on the mound for the Beaneaters, staring down with a menacing countenance, was "Grasshopper" Jim Whitney, ace of the Boston staff. Wily, experienced, Whitney was called by many the best control hurler in baseball.

There were no baseball miracles this cold day in Chicago. Offering up a dizzying array of curves and off-speed pitches to go along with respectable hard stuff, Grasshopper totally baffled the rookie. Billy struck out his first time at bat, and his second, third, and fourth. This was not the sandlots of Marshalltown, Iowa; this was the bigs and Billy was not quite ready.[9]

Cap stuck with his lightning-quick rookie through a succession of plate appearances in May and June, through an embarrassing string of thirteen consecutive strikeouts. Cap taught Billy how to choke up on the bat, to cut down on his swing, to make contact. Billy was benefitting from the instruction of one of the greatest hitters that would ever play the game and eventually he began to make bat meet ball. With Billy's blazing speed, any ball hit on the ground was a stiff challenge for the defense. Although hitting would never be a strong skill for Billy, Cap was at least making him respectable.

When Billy joined the White Stockings, Cap asked the youngster to take on a variety of chores in addition to his very limited playing time. He helped with the advance plans for trips, rounded up baggage, purchased hotel and train tickets, and performed other routine duties as he soaked up the exhilarating atmosphere of the White Stockings and the major leagues. Billy became so trustworthy in Cap's eyes that he sometimes carried in his satchel thousands of team dollars from town to town.[10]

In Billy's first few seasons he gained increasing confidence and, on the base paths, even daring. In the outfield his speed made most fly balls hit in his direction easy pickings. But he continued to struggle at the plate, hitting .241 in 1883, .222 in 1884, and .256 in 1885, all in a utility role. As frustrated Chicago fans, knowing of Billy's speed, suffered his hitting woes along with him, some were heard to quip, "If only he could steal first base!"

But the fans took him to heart. Many thought he was the best-looking player in all of baseball. A reporter noted, "Billy Sunday had his new uniform on, and when he came to bat the ladies in the stands all admired his handsome figure and voted him a real nice man when he popped a neat little single." The blond, clean-cut youngster refused to grow a mustache, as most major leaguers had done—in a mid-1880s photograph, Billy is the only one of the White Stockings not sporting facial hair.

Billy's name, as one might expect, became a source for puns and, sometimes, genuine confusion. During the 1880s some of the teams were playing ball on Sunday, a practice in which the White Stockings had not yet engaged. A reporter from the *Chicago Inter-Ocean* overheard a gentleman on a streetcar complaining as he peered over his Monday paper, "This Sunday ball playing is a shame and an outrage." A small boy seated nearby replied, "You don't know what yer talkin' about. Sunday is the best base runner in the hull league." As Billy became increasingly popular, his picture began to appear on the new sepia-toned, cardboard-backed baseball cards then being sold by Goodwin and Co. with their Old Judge and Gypsy Queen cigarettes and by D. Buchner and Co. with their Gold Coin chewing tobacco.[11]

The White Stockings began to showcase Billy's running speed in match races. Arlie Latham, the superb base-stealer of the rival league's St. Louis Browns, was reportedly the fastest man in baseball. When the White Stockings pitted Billy against him, club owners, players, and fans bet heavily on the race, some baseball writers estimating the total as high as $75,000. Billy won the hundred yard race by a full ten feet.

The White Stockings even arranged matches for their young gazelle with champion sprinters outside of baseball. A Canadian runner named Leon Lesser faced Billy in a match in August 1885. Several thousand spectators watched with curiosity as the ball-player beat the track star by a yard. The Iowa farm boy was not only the fastest in professional baseball; he was, many said, one of the fastest in America.[12]

A year later, Billy got a chance to face the best; for one day, at least, he officially stepped into the world of international track. He entered a meet in Chicago which featured world-class athletes. It was here he was finally beaten in a race, nipped by H. M. Johnson of Pittsburgh, called by sportswriters and track aficionados the "Champion of America." Many sprint coaches agreed, however, that the young Sunday, given a modicum of training, could have become even more formidable a competitor than he already was.[13]

Billy never quite seemed to fit the image of an 1880s ballplayer. Most were rowdy, hardened, inured to weeks on the road living in hotels and eating in diners; many were vigorous drinkers and womanizers. The game itself in these early years was rough and getting rougher with frequent fights, vicious umpire baiting, strong verbal abuse of opponents, and fans in many cities ready to pelt opposing teams not only with well-chosen epithets but with flying objects. Billy was too clean, neat, too seemingly naive and unseasoned. But his teammates were, from all indications, fond of the plucky kid from the plains. He strolled the seedy streets of the cities with them, touched the world of the lurid and clandestine. He drank, but not with same prodigious vigor achieved by some. On the field and off, a dedicated team man, a cheerleader on the bench, hard worker in practice, Billy gave total effort.

After his difficult youth, Billy was hardly the dependent youngster that many might have guessed. He could fight with the best of them in his Iowa days, some said, and he had a quick temper. But he had always been honest and forthright. Billy had learned and survived much in Iowa and the experiences there served him well when he was faced with the likes of King Kelly. And yet the life of boozing and gambling and carousing, which lured large numbers of players, never swallowed him. He also had religious inclinations, a rectitude and piety of plain roots. He remembered fondly the hymns sung by his mother and his friends at the old log-cabin church where he had gone to Sunday school. He remembered Mrs. Pierce at the Davenport orphanage telling Bible stories and leading the children in prayer. The simple, clear faith of these folks of the prairie was comforting to Billy.

And now, on a night in early June 1886, those stirrings of religious passion hit him like a tornado on the plains. Billy was in

Chicago during a series against the New York Giants. He was making the rounds of the bars with a number of the Giants and his own teammates, including Kelly and Ned Williamson. After getting tanked up, as Billy later put it, the group stopped at the corner of State and Van Buren and sat down on the curb. Nearby, a company of men and women sat on a horse-drawn "Gospel Wagon" and filled the tenderloin night with the sounds of horns, flutes, and a trombone—religious hymns, some of which Billy had sung as a child. The memories of those early days filled him with tears and he began to weep. One of the men with the troupe walked up to Billy, told him that he was from the Pacific Garden Mission close by, and asked the youngster to join them there is services. Billy left his teammates sitting on the curb and followed the gospel street missionaries.

Founded by Colonel George R. Clarke, a western miner and Chicago businessman, Pacific Garden Mission was established as a haven for those whose lives had been shattered by sin and circumstance. Clarke said that the mission represented his religious offering to the shrouded community in Chicago, the community of the lonely, hurting, and homeless.

Amidst assorted bars, whorehouses, hobo haunts, grimy dance halls, gambling dens, and cheap greasy spoons stood Pacific Garden. Over the door a lantern lit up the inscription "Strangers Welcome." Along the street sauntered hookers, booze-racked down-and-outs, safecrackers, pickpockets, and assorted men and boys on the lam and on the run, a netherworld of human miscellany. Inside on one of the walls was the verse "Christ came into the world to save sinners, among whom I am Chief." As Billy walked in, Harry Munroe, director of the mission, was introducing on the stage some burglars, second-story men, and drunkards who had accepted the Christian gospel and pledged to try to change their lives. Billy sat among the shabby audience listening to the testimony, singing the hymns, and was deeply touched. By the time the services had ended Billy said to some in the crowd, "Boys, I bid the old life goodby." This night among Chicago's red-light, transient world, among derelicts and thieves, changed Billy Sunday forever. Several nights later he was at the mission and returned again and again.

His pledge to alter his life was heartfelt, and gave him direction, conviction, and purpose. Many years later he wrote, "I have followed Jesus from that day to this every second, like the hound on the trail of the fox."[14]

The day following his conversion Billy showed up at the ballpark and told his teammates of his experience. Expecting some good-natured jibes and quips, he got, instead, some understanding words. Kelly said to him, "Bill, I'm proud of you! Religion is not my long suit, but I'll help you all I can." Anson came up, along with Pfeffer, Clarkson, Flint, and Williamson, all of them with gestures of encouragement. Billy never forgot the kindness and never felt more a part of the Chicago White Stockings.[15]

In Chicago, at the corner of Throop and Adams streets, stood the Jefferson Park Presbyterian Church, close to the hotel where Billy boarded. He began to attend services there and even joined a young people's Christian Endeavor group. It was at Jefferson Park Church that he met Helen Amelia Thompson. She was eighteen, black-haired, and dark-eyed, the daughter of William Thompson, a prominent wholesale milk and ice cream manufacturer, a Civil War veteran who had been badly wounded at the battle of Shiloh. Scotch Presbyterians, the Thompson family lived across the street from the church and were active members. The Thompsons had a son who was the mascot and bat boy for the Chicago White Stockings and the family often attended games.

Billy was immediately attracted to Helen, or "Nell." He wrote later, "The first time I saw those flashing black eyes and dark hair and white teeth, I said to myself 'There's a swell girl.' " Billy now began to attend prayer meetings and other activities at Jefferson Park church even more resolutely; he had strong motives, not entirely religious. At the prayer meetings he always positioned himself in a seat along a wall where he could keep one eye on Nell and the other on the preacher.

As the two began to see each other at the Thompson home, Nell's father became increasingly restive and uneasy. Although he enjoyed baseball and appreciated Billy's talents on the field, he knew of the rakish reputations of the players. For his young girl, a baseball player could, William Thompson assumed, bring nothing but trouble. Despite her father's protestations, Nell continued to see Billy and the two began a decorous courtship.[16]

Sportswriters called the catch miraculous, "seemingly impossible." Surrounded by screaming fans in right field, the Chicago speedster had flagged down in a dramatic leap Charlie Bennett's sizzling drive. "Nobody but Sunday could have ever got down the field in time to capture that fly of Bennett's," wrote a *Tribune* reporter. "The sprinter's brilliant work probably saved the game." This 1886 game with the Detroit Wolverines, played shortly after Billy's conversion experience at the Pacific Garden Mission, proved to be one of the most important of the season. Attributing his magnificent grab to divine intervention, Billy declared, "I believe the Lord helped me get the ball that day because I was trying to trot on the square for him."[17]

The White Stockings won the pennant again in 1886. This time, however, the magic escaped; they were nipped in the World Series by the St. Louis Browns. The defeat cast a pall over the proud team, a malaise of dissension between the owners and players. Spaulding was reportedly so upset by the team's defeat that he refused to pay their way back from St. Louis to Chicago. He blamed it all on the players' loose living, gambling, drinking, and skirt-chasing.

Before the 1887 season began Spaulding convulsed the baseball world by selling Kelly to the Boston Beaneaters, who had long lusted to have the Irishman in a hometown uniform. Boston paid an unprecedented price to get him—$10,000. Spaulding had hired Pinkerton detectives to follow Kelly and the snoops delivered an extensive file that read like an odyssey through a wonderland of vice. So drunk would the King sometimes be at game time that the trainers would be hard-pressed to get him on the field in a standing condition. And yet, he had performed splendidly and Chicago's fans loved him. One devotee was so inspired by the announcement of his sale to Boston that he composed something of an ode to the King for the *Sporting News*. Some of it read:

Ten Thousand clear in Puritanic gold.
We surely have the pity of every sister city,
In our loss of Kelly, the tricky and the bold.[18]

But Spaulding had reached his limit with Kelly, whose off-field antics, he thought, were not only reprehensible but a vile influence on the younger players and on the image of the White Stockings. Spaulding did follow through on a promise to help Kelly obtain a $5,000 salary from his new club, and the King thus became the highest-paid player in the game.

Spaulding wasn't finished. He traded off pitcher Jim McCormick and two other outfielders, George Gore and Abner Dalrymple. His champions had fallen from baseball's heights to complacency, Spaulding believed, had succumbed to the siren's snares of the flesh. He wanted a new team of clean-living men, men of sobriety and pure morals, "new blood." In a public announcement at the start of the 1887 season Spaulding proclaimed, "Our men this year do not drink, and they take pride in keeping up the reputation of the club."[19]

For the rebuilding White Stockings, the sales of the players brought the team a whitened public image more befitting their name (or so Spaulding assumed) but it brought an end to their reign as National League champions. It also, eventually, brought a new name. Cap's raw, young players were soon called the "Colts" and then the "Cubs." And later, especially when Joe Tinker, Johnny Evers, and Frank Chance arrived, there would be other Chicago heroes and champions. But never would they equal the legacy of the 1880s, the "Heroic Legion"—the conquering army entering the stadium in a magnificent carriage drawn by white horses.

For Billy the loss of Kelly and the others was of great regret; they were personally close to him, especially King. Although Kelly's life-style was now increasingly alien to Billy, King had always treated him with respect, especially after Billy's religious conversion. Decades later, Billy would speak fondly of Kelly and with much admiration.

The departure of many of the White Stockings did give Billy

more playing time and the 1887 season proved to be his best yet. In fifty games he hit nearly .300 and stole 34 bases.[20] However, Billy's conversion created an insatiable thirst for self-improvement. Some of it was undoubtedly a desire to please Nell's parents, especially her father, but it also seemed deeply rooted in his character, a sense of challenges faced, obstacles hurdled, the conviction to make it in the face of long odds.

Billy wanted some college training and he applied to Northwestern University in Evanston, Illinois. Although his early education was insufficient for him to enter as an accredited student, Billy agreed to coach students in baseball and other athletic training in return for permission to enroll as a special student at Evanston Academy, a prep school run by the university. In a course in rhetoric at Evanston, Billy again tackled, as he had done back in Nevada High School, such epics as "The Charge of the Light Brigade" and "Spartacus and the Gladiators," and began to learn finer points of oratory, to add some refinement and technique to his natural flair.

He began to take classes in elocution, physics, English, and other subjects at Chicago's YMCA, where he gave talks to young boys on religion and personal habits. To the youngsters at the YMCA, these lectures were nearly magical; here was a major-league hero right there in person speaking especially to them. No more attentive audience could a speaker ever hope to enjoy than the awed boys listening to Billy Sunday. One of his first talks was entitled "Earnestness in Christian Life." A reporter wrote, "If W. A. Sunday plays ball as well and as earnestly as he talked yesterday before a large body of young men in the hall of the Young Men's Christian Association, he ought to be in great demand among rival clubs." Eagerly, with serious purpose and a dose of theatrics, Billy was thus beginning the long struggle to make himself a public speaker.[21]

On New Year's Day 1888, Billy proposed marriage to Nell and she accepted. "I went home feeling as though I had wings on my feet," he wrote. "I didn't sleep that night. Visions of those black eyes stared at me from the darkness and turned night into day." William Thompson raged and fumed about the prospect of his daughter marrying a ballplayer, even if he happened to be a religiously converted one who now gave lectures at the YMCA on Christian earnestness. Nell refused to heed her father's warnings and the marriage was scheduled for the following September.[22]

Euphoric over the engagement, Billy and Nell began to make plans for the wedding and beyond. But the lives of baseball players have, from the earliest days of the sport, been subject to whim and dollar. President William Nimick of the Pittsburgh Alleghanies had always wanted the young speedster to be his regular center fielder. On February 3, 1888, Nimick and Spaulding of the White Stockings announced a proposed deal that would send Billy to the Pittsburgh club. After a meeting between Billy and the two executives, Nimick told a *Sporting News* reporter, "I wish we had more ball players like that young man." He praised Billy's off-field activities as well as his playing skills.[23]

Spaulding and Cap Anson soon told Billy that his sale to Pittsburgh was optional, that he could stay in Chicago if he wished. But they pointed out that Chicago would not pay him close to the salary offered by the Alleghanies. For a couple planning marriage with little money in hand, the offer presented a perplexing dilemma— to stay in Chicago near relatives and friends or to move to Pittsburgh and begin to save money. After much reflection, they finally decided that Billy should take the offer.[24]

The infant roots Billy had planted in Chicago were thus being pulled up, this time partially by his own hands. He was now leaving behind fellow players who had become his close friends, Chicago's baseball fans who had taken him to heart, his associates and mentors and classmates at the YMCA, and the youngsters he taught in his classes. And most important, he was leaving behind, at least for the coming months, his financée.

But this time was different. As he jumped aboard another train, Billy now had a greater measure of self-assurance. The psychological coping, the struggles, the deep anxieties had been softened, the pain eased. He now had his religion, a new faith that his God would see him through, a sense of mission and purpose. And he had his love for Nell. As he boarded a train headed east, he once again suffered the crush of separation, the apprehension and uncertainty. These were all old, ubiquitous companions, unrelenting, onerous. But now, he knew, there were other roots from which to draw strength.

The Pittsburgh baseball club was not the kind of superteam to which Billy had become accustomed, although the Alleghanies did have pitcher Jim McCormick and outfielder Abner Dalrymple, traded by Spaulding from the White Stockings a year earlier. A club formerly in the American Association, the team had joined the National League in 1887 and had limped home a disappointing sixth.

They played in Recreation Park, an old ball yard next to the Ft. Wayne Railroad tracks on the north side of Pittsburgh. The outfield actually ended with the tracks themselves. For the ex–White Stockings now playing under these raw conditions, Chicago's stadium must have seemed, in retrospect, like the magnificent Roman Colosseum. Recreation Park was later turned into a wooden saucer for motorbike racing.[25]

For the first time in his baseball career, Billy was now a starter. Roaming center field like a spirited deer, he began to draw raves from the Pittsburgh press. "Sunday's fielding . . . has stamped him as one of the finest in the country," one reporter wrote. "He covers a vast amount of territory, throws finely, and backs up bases well."[26]

He continued to struggle at the plate. But when he did reach base, he usually gave crowds exciting moments. In addition to his blazing speed, he was often crafty and cunning. In a game in Philadelphia, Billy was hit on the leg by a wicked fastball and limped pathetically to first base in apparent severe pain. Nursing the wound at first, Billy gave the impression that it might have been difficult for him to walk to second base. With the pitcher's motion to the plate, however, came the familiar flash down the base path. "Quick as a wink," a Pittsburgh paper reported, "the famous sprinter with the sabbatical name was on second base and, turning up his fingers at all, including the paralyzed pitcher, who still held the ball."[27]

Billy soon became a favorite of both fans and scribes in Pittsburgh, just as in Chicago. In assessing the skills of the various Pittsburgh players, the *Pittsburgh Dispatch* concluded, "Sunday will do. He is almost a sure catch, a great thrower, a fair hitter, and one of the finest base runners in the profession."[28] Although his batting average again hovered around .250, he stole 71 bases. Well over half the time the speedster reached base, either by hit or by base on balls, he stole another one. The crowds loved it.[29] Back in Chicago, the *Herald* reported, "Billy Sunday is a big man in Pittsburgh."[30]

Billy was still a very big man among some people in Chicago, especially a certain member of the Jefferson Park Presbyterian Church. He and Nell exchanged a flurry of long, lovesick letters filled with biblical references, hope, and expectation. "God knew all," wrote Billy, "knew who of all in this world would make me a true and loving Wife and how happy you will make a home."[31]

His search for love, for stability, and for a foundation on which he could rest his life was over, he told Nell. His God and his marriage would anchor his racking, battered soul, he said, and would give him serenity and devotion. He talked of his turbulent childhood, of his early rowdy days, of the powerful transformation in his life. "I leave myself in God's hands," he wrote to her; "I know that I am safe with God and Nell on my side."[32]

He talked of how she had become, even in these early days of their courtship, a mother figure to him, there to nurture, to care, to fill a great void. "Really you have been a mother to me," he wrote. "I hope you will let me call you Mother. I know you will." She had filled a profound emotional need, had given him companionship and psychological comfort as well as passion. He expressed his dependency and pledged total fidelity.

The kid who had roamed the sleazy big-city night spots with King Kelly and his other buddies was now so confirmed a teetotaler that he refused to step inside a bar. After a couple of his Pittsburgh teammates were arrested for fighting in a whorehouse, Billy wrote Nell, "Mama knows her darling is and always will be true to her. I would die before I would be untrue."[33] With all the womanizing and boozing and gambling around him every day, Billy wrote, "I do thank God that nothing can tempt me to be untrue to my darling even now."[34] He promised, "Soon our lives join forever. Our hearts have been linked together for a long time oh so strong that no earthly power could separate them . . . I never could live without your love and tender care . . . I have such childlike faith in you. I feel so dependent on your care."[35]

Billy soon began to teach Sunday school classes at a local Pittsburgh church. Even while on trips with the team, Billy sought out churches and YMCA headquarters in other cities. On a stop in New York, he took time to visit the skid-row district where he sat in Jerry McAuley's mission, with its motto on the wall proclaiming, "It's All Right," and cried along with the derelicts as the choir sang revival hymns.[36]

The Pittsburgh sportswriters, inured to trailing ballplayers through saloons and dives of one sort or another, found Billy Sunday marvelous copy. He was an odd contrast, refreshing. One reporter talked of his genuine dedication to his church activities, the way in which the young man piously, unobtrusively went about his business of volunteer work and self-improvement, all the while playing an exciting brand of center field. "He bears his honors so meekly that they pile in on him with unabated rapidity," said one writer. A baseball team for kids was named for Billy in Pittsburgh and a local councilman proposed that the city name a street after him.[37]

On September 4, 1888, one day before his marriage, Billy was with the Alleghanies in Indianapolis. "In the preliminary practice," the *Dispatch* noted, "Billy Sunday . . . scampered around out in the garden and frisked around like a young colt in a clover pasture. He is to be congratulated," the paper continued, "for Sunday is not only a fine ball player, but a gentleman in every sense of the word, against whose character not a word can be said. The profession needs more men like him."[38]

That evening after the game Billy left the team for Chicago. The following afternoon, September 5, 1888, at the Thompson home, Billy and Nell exchanged marriage vows. Dr. David Marquis of the McCormick Theological Seminary conducted the services. Fred Pfeffer, Billy's friend from the White Stockings, acted as best man.

Following the wedding, the couple quickly went to the Chicago ballpark where, in celebration of the event, Spaulding had arranged for a specially draped box for the two at the White Stockings' late-afternoon game. When the Sundays appeared, most in the grandstands and bleachers rose and cheered. Billy's old teammates lined up in front of the couple and doffed their hats. At five o'clock the two left Chicago on the Pennsylvania Limited.[39]

They began their married life on the road with the Pittsburgh Alleghanies. Indeed, the day after the marriage Billy was back in uniform, the leadoff hitter. Before the first pitch, his Pittsburgh teammates held a short ceremony and presented Billy with a bronze clock, some china, and silverware.[40]

After much misgiving, Nell's father accepted the marriage and became, in a short time, a loving and devoted supporter. The Thompsons provided money to Nell so that she could make some of the road trips with Billy and the two traveled the National League cities—Chicago, Boston, New York, Detroit, Philadelphia, Indianapolis, and Washington. To the newly married couple, the road together seemed invigorating with its assorted hotels, its foods offering new taste adventures, trains that proffered excitement and change down the tracks, the myriad sights, faces, and sounds. The two were constantly planning, arranging, always with an eye on the clock and on the calendar, always trying to keep ahead of the swirl, a kaleidoscope of time and meetings and commitments. They reveled in it.

Resourcefully, canny, and astute, Nell, from the first days of the marriage, took over much of the planning for the trips, paid the bills, and kept Billy's affairs in order. He put his complete trust in her judgment and insight. She was there to encourage, to raise his spirits, to mother and reassure, to give him emotional and psychological support. The two would be, Billy knew, a resilient, mighty team and he gave himself completely to her care.

The Pittsburgh club had a disappointing season in 1888, again finishing sixth in the league. During one of the team's long losing streaks Billy seemed frustrated and anxious, his biting, competitive spirit shackled by the team's ineptness and his own limitations. With the Alleghanies he was a key performer, not a part-timer, and Billy bristled over his continuing struggles as a hitter. But the edge in his temper gradually softened. He knew he was giving as much as he could, always hustling in the field, putting extra time in practice, concentrating, taking additional hitting instruction. The timing, the stroke, they just would not develop as he and his teammates and the team owners hoped. Although a valuable player because of his speed, fielding, base-running, and indomitable spirit, he seemed destined to be a consistently mediocre hitter. He wrote to Nell, "we would all much rather be first or among the first and no one does more as far as his ability than your boy, well baby dear we cant all be Kings."[41]

Gradually, inexorably, Billy's religion gained dominance over his baseball. Bob Allen, one of Billy's Pittsburgh teammates during the 1889 season and later president of two minor-league teams, recalled that practically everyone in the National League believed that Billy was destined to give up baseball for what he regarded as a higher calling—preaching. He remembered Billy on many days burying his head in his Bible on a railroad day coach crammed with rowdy teammates. He would sit there amidst the noise mouthing to himself over and over again those stirring biblical phrases and copying them in a notebook. Allen told of the day Billy purposefully strutted to the rear of a car to ask his buddies to quit playing poker; after all, it was the Sabbath. As soon as the boys spotted the fledgling preacher approaching, they scrambled to put up the cards. When Billy returned to his seat he said to Allen, "Well, Bob, I made 'em stop. But please don't go back there and see how long they remained stopped. I know that bunch. But they'll realize I'm right some day."[42]

Back in Chicago in the off-season, Billy took on additional study courses in the Bible at the YMCA with such a zealous spirit that the director urged him to consider a full-time position with the organization. The YMCA could not offer Billy nearly the salary he was making in professional baseball, which was itself modest; but working for the Lord, his friends there assured him, was a priceless contribution. Billy was not yet willing to make the move, but he was listening.

In 1890 major-league baseball suffered through a serious rupture between owners and players. Three years earlier the players had formed a union known as the National Brotherhood of Ball Players and has escalated their demands for a greater share of the burgeoning profits now being amassed by the organizations. With the collapse of negotiations with the owners and with the backing of a few moneyed promoters, many of the ballplayers broke from the established leagues and formed a new one—the Players League. New clubs, stocked by players who now abandoned their former teams, suddenly appeared in New York, Brooklyn, Boston, Philadelphia, Chicago, Cleveland, Buffalo, and Pittsburgh. Baseball thus experienced the unprecedented spectacle of a number of cities supporting two teams, the maverick teams and the old-line teams competing for the support of the fans and the gate receipts.

Every player on the Pittsburgh Alleghanies leapfrogged to the Players League with the exception of two, a seldom-used pitcher named Bill Sowders and Billy Sunday. Billy had agonized over whether to join the rest of his teammates but the whole issue seemed to rouse in him religious solicitudes, such irritating questions as loyalty and service and dedication. He feared that the revolt of the players would appear traitorous to the public, that it would paint the players with a black image of greed.[43]

Playing center field in 1890 for the established Pittsburgh team, Billy was joined by a collection of mediocre players rounded up by management from minor-league teams around the country. One historian of the Pittsburgh club once wrote, "What happened to the Pittsburgh National League club that season shouldn't happen to three skunks and a weasel." The team, he said, comprised the most bizarre assortment of older men, young boys, and "trolley leaguers that ever masqueraded as a major league ball club." The inept team sunk like a colossal deadweight to the depths of last place, swallowed up by a torrent of defeats, 113 of them including one losing streak of 23 consecutive games. The team won only 28 times. The hapless Alleghanies even had the dubious distinction of losing three games in one day to the pennant-winning Brooklyn Dodgers.

The team became so desperate in one game against Philadelphia in July that they asked Billy to pitch in relief in the fifth inning. Hitter number one against Billy walked, the second tripled, the third doubled, and the fourth was hit by a pitch. Billy returned to center field. So wretched were the Pittsburgh nine that at one game only about twenty faithful fans showed up. One reporter quipped that Billy Sunday could draw more people to hear one of his religious talks at a local YMCA than the Pittsburgh team could draw to one of its games.[44]

Although the Players League, boasting the better players, did well in attendance figures and offered, by all accounts, a better brand of baseball, it lost the war. The revolt was financially disastrous to both sides, but the big capital lay in the hands of the established leagues and those teams were able to hold out through the year. In November 1890, Spaulding could declare, "The Players League is dead. The warfare has been a costly one to both sides, and the patrons of the sport will be glad to know that hostilities are over."[45]

For the original Pittsburgh team, so woeful during the players' revolt, there was a legacy. When the players who had defected to the new league returned to the old one, a number of contract disputes erupted between teams. During a confrontation between Pittsburgh and Boston over a player named Harry Stovey, an American Association executive called the actions of the Pittsburgh club "piratical." The name stuck—the Pittsburgh Pirates.[46]

Billy never played for the Pirates. The 1890 season was his last in a Pittsburgh uniform; he was sold to Philadelphia. Billy signed a three-year contract with the Phillies covering the years 1891–1893. But from the moment he signed, he seemed uneasy, unable to reconcile his now overwhelming desire for religious service with his baseball career. He and Nell agonized and prayed hard about the dilemma over the winter. The couple now had a baby girl named Helen to care for and escalating debt, but they both agreed that Billy should follow his religious instincts, even if it meant taking a substantial cut in salary. Billy asked the Phillies to release him from the contract; he wanted to take a job with the YMCA. The Phillies executives refused and instructed him to report to spring training.

Billy continued to work and study at the YMCA. He told the Phillies that he would not join the team early in spring training but would report on April 1 in shape and ready to play. He again made known his desire to enter Christian work.

Billy later said that these winter months were some of the most troubling of his life. He still loved baseball, was captivated by the competition and camaraderie, prized the excitement, the chance to test again and again his skills and reaction under pressure, and was still consumed by the spirit and feeling of the game. And yet, he now grappled with a powerful religious need, an emotional drive which he couldn't explain, both compelling and distressing. Jumping a contract would not be an ethical move, especially for a man preparing to enter religious service. But three years seemed an impossible burden. He later remembered making a proposition in a prayer: "Lord, if I don't get my release by March twenty-fifth, I will take that as assurance you want me to continue to play ball; if I get it before that date I will accept that as evidence you want me to quit playing ball and go into Christian work."[47]

On March 17 Billy received word that he could have his release. Philadelphia's executive brass had undoubtedly concluded that Billy's contributions in the coming year would be compromised severely by his burning fervor to give up the game and they relented to his wishes.[48] Billy was joyous. The Lord, he believed, had spoken.

After word spread throughout the baseball community that Billy was no longer under contract with the Phillies, he soon received an offer from the Cincinnati club, an enticing offer that tested his resolve to its limits. The Reds promised Billy $5,000 to play in the 1891 season—five times what he could make in a year with the YMCA; that $5,000 loomed in his mind, he said later, like a gold mountain, like the Empire State Building. He couldn't sleep; everywhere he looked he saw that figure—$5,000.

For a young married couple in 1891, that kind of money could be a tremendous boost. Billy talked to his friends, to his associates at the YMCA, even to Cyrus McCormick, president of the McCormick Harvesting Machine Company and president of the YMCA, whom Billy had met through his religious work. Many advised him to play in Cincinnati in the summer, pocket the money, and join the YMCA in the fall. Nell counseled otherwise. 'There is nothing to consider," she told Billy; "you promised God to quit."

Billy began work as an assistant secretary of the Chicago YMCA at a salary of $83.33 a month. His baseball days were over; his career in the professional religious ministry was launched.[49]

Baseball had been a savior to Billy Sunday. It had taken him from crunching poverty and total anonymity to big cities, to the columns of newspapers, to the stadiums and the wildness of the crowds, to friendships never forgotten. He kept always his deep reverence for the game, followed the new teams and the new players through the years, talked about the old days, the memorable pennant races, the great times with King Kelly and Old Silver Flint and Cap and the others. He would outlive them all. Many of them died broke and dissipated and Billy lamented their passing with much sorrow. They had exerted special influences on his life, accepting his cornfield roots and innocence with magnanimity, making the green kid part of the team and their own lives, tolerating with patience and understanding his eccentricities. "Baseball is American to the core," he once wrote; "what other sport could so characteristically serve as the play outlet for the nervous, high-strung, third rail, double-barreled, greased-lightning, strenuous, hustling, bustling bunch of folks—bless 'em!—that inhabit this country today." Baseball, he went on, was magnetic, with the "power to stand you on your toes and tangle up your diaphragm and larynx in a carnival of noise that you never dreamed possible."[50] He would miss it, but he was content.

He takes his lead at first, poised on his toes for the first movement of the pitcher to the plate, total concentration—and then the flashing spikes churning toward second, fast, so fast, and the lithe slide hooking around the bag, and then the blast of sound from the stands. The kid could run.

3

Revivalist

In the Lord's service now—"secretary of religious work," Chicago YMCA, six days a week at $83.33 a month, $1,000 a year. The former major-league ballplayer often went without lunch, dyed some of his old clothes to make them look new, and even began wearing a celluloid collar to save on laundry bills.

He took over the saloon route in Chicago's tenderloin. In this area of cheap eateries, missions, and bars, the mecca for Big Chi's transient culture of the hobo and tramp, Billy wandered looking for converts. In the teeming hub of battered men and joy ladies he tried to change lives, to persuade lost souls to take the step he had taken not so many years earlier on these same streets. Give your life to Christ, folks; trade this hell and the next one for salvation and everlasting life. Just take the free ticket, march to Farwell Hall a few blocks away, lose your sins in gospel songs and find redemption.[1]

Billy said that he once stood on a corner and counted in one hour several hundred men entering one of the bars in Chicago's skid row. One of them happened to be an old friend of his from Iowa then working at a local theater. As his drunken childhood buddy downed another shot, Billy pointed out a shabby bum in threadbare coat, with torn pants and shoes that refused to cover his toes. Drinking creates tragedies such as this, Billy preached to his old Iowa friend. Less than eight months later, Billy was standing on another corner of the tenderloin and, shuffling along the street, face bloated, eyes blazing scarlet, came his old friend. He had lost his job and was, as Billy remembered, "on the toboggan slide hitting it for hell."[2]

As the secretary of religious work, Billy visited hospitals, charged around Chicago securing speakers for the YMCA services, sought donations from businessmen, led noon-day prayer meetings, helped down-and-outs get jobs, and counseled losers to be winners. His excursions took him to a gambling room on LaSalle Street, near the New York Life Building, where he found an old acquaintance in the process of losing much of his life savings to keno, faro, and draw poker. Billy's work put him in contact with embezzlers, forgers, dope pushers, and men and women slipping toward suicide. It took him back to Pacific Garden Mission on East Van Buren Street where his own life had been so profoundly changed.[3] And all of this on $83.33 a week. Billy and Nell now had two children, George and Helen, and the generous offers still coming in from several professional baseball teams were tempting. But he was in the Lord's service now—to stay.

"We never had a man on our staff who was more consecrated, more deeply spiritual, more self-sacrificing," declared L. W. Messer, an official of the YMCA. "He was especially strong in his personal effort among men who were strongly tempted and among those who had fallen by the way."[4] The work on the streets hustling for converts challenged Billy, gave him a broader perspective of the hidden world of vice, an understanding of the depths into which victims could quickly plunge. Although a rabid teetotaler since his days with the White Stockings and those forays with teammates on the streets he now patrolled, Billy's daily contact with winos and wasted vagrants convinced him even more that booze was the devil's most effective weapon, turning good men into brutes, sucking the lifeblood from families, leaving thousands of children in the fangs of broken homes. Whiskey, he believed, was an unmitigated evil from hell carrying misery, poverty, death, and damnation. Billy's enmity toward "John Barleycorn" would be a driving force in his religious work.

Although Billy's YMCA job fulfilled his need for religious service, it failed woefully to pay his bills. When a financial depression struck the country in 1893 it seriously hampered the YMCA's ability to attract donations and thus to maintain its own payments to workers. Billy often was not even given his salary check.

He also was increasingly restless. Ever since his early days in baseball, Billy had traveled from one city to another, and it had filled a craving to keep on the move. Although the YMCA job gave him an opportunity to wander Chicago's streets and to confront a mixture of people and situations, it also involved substantial time in the headquarters office. During those days, Billy recalled later, he felt penned, trapped, his robust energy shackled. He said that the sudden change from an athletic, outdoor life which he had known as a boy and a ballplayer to the YMCA job "nearly killed me."[5]

After less than three years in the job, he quit. In 1894, he accepted a position as an assistant to the nationally prominent evangelist John Wilbur Chapman. Billy had come to the attention of the revivalist through Chapman's gospel singer and writer, Peter Bilhorn, who knew of Billy's dedicated work in Chicago's tenderloin. Chapman came to Chicago, interviewed the young, eager religious worker, and hired him at $40 a week to put up tents, sell books, organize committees, and occasionally address meetings.[6] The offer, Billy knew immediately, was a ticket back to the excitement of the road, back to the crowds, back to a life in which the famous ex-ballplayer could dig in the spikes.

A graduate of Lake Forest College and Lane Seminary, pastor of a number of churches before he began conducting revival meetings around the country, Chapman was a pursed-lipped, solemn, austere-looking man, dignified at the pulpit as he stared authoritatively at his audiences through narrow-rimmed, stark eyeglasses. By the time Billy joined up with Chapman, the preacher had been called by some of his fellow revivalists "the greatest evangelist in the country."[7]

In his early evangelistic career, Chapman held modest-sized revivals in Philadelphia, Boston, and New York and made a revivalistic excursion around the world. Later, as head of a special committee of the Presbyterian church formed to stimulate evangelistic work, he became a master of organization, plotting strategies for drawing crowds, lining up financial support, coordinating schedules with churches and other organizations in revival towns, developing mailing lists, instituting publicity campaigns, and enlisting workers to handle myriad duties. In Chapman's years as a traveling evangelist, Billy became one of his most trusted and effective campaign confidants.[8]

Working as Chapman's advance man, Billy made local arrangements and helped select singers for the choruses, oversaw the erection of the massive tents, held meetings with local ministers to generate support, spoke to factory workers and other groups to spread the word about the revivals, and made contacts with newspapers. The job required most of Billy's peripatetic agility; it was grueling in effort and detail, a welter of chores and assignments and contacts, all with a monster deadline looming.

Although he missed his family, Billy loved the road. Scurrying from one town to another—Paris, Illinois; Terre Haute, Indiana; Oskaloosa, Iowa; Troy, New York; Gault, Canada; Huntington, Pennsylvania—he was again in dizzying motion, learning the revival business from the guyropes to the prayer breakfasts. Each town, each meeting presented unique problems, especially financial and logistical. Billy was expected to pave the way for the revival leader as he entered the city, create a thornless path, muster the troops, anticipate complications, arouse the citizenry. This was the primitive gathering of the Christian flocks exhorted to the truth by the gospel fire-eaters. Billy revelled in it, the frenetic pace, the throb and tremor of shaking souls.[9]

During one of Chapman's revivals in Indianapolis, former president Benjamin Harrison sat in the audience with his daughter. The revivalist dispatched Billy to ask Harrison if he would join them on the platform. Billy eagerly complied, telling the ex-president that his standing beside Chapman would induce others to take a stand for Christ. Harrison reluctantly agreed to the request and walked down the aisle on the arm of Billy while the crowd, now aware of the presence of the former president, rose and burst into cheers and then sang "My Country Tis of Thee." Billy later called that occasion one of the proudest moments of his life.[10]

While working as Chapman's assistant, Billy honed his own speaking skills. The high school oratorical champion and baseball evangelist was now a close lieutenant of one of the country's most respected revivalists and Billy capitalized on the opportunity. He intently studied Chapman's sermons, noted the effects of phrases and lines on the crowds, and watched closely the mannerisms of the revivalist. He studied Chapman's book, *Received Ye the Holy Ghost?*, a work which praised the all-encompassing power of prayer to heal the wounds of the world. To Billy the message made sense. And, Billy himself, all listeners agreed, could pray up a prairie storm.

On several occasions, when Chapman was unable to deliver his sermon, Billy preached. A few years earlier, when Billy had given one of his religious talks while a member of the Pittsburgh Pirates, a local newspaperman had raved about his drawing power. Ever since his schoolboy days at Nevada High, Billy's oratorical performances always generated crowds.[11] Although increasingly confident, he did, nevertheless, still suffer initial jitters and stage fright before walking out before the crowds. But a reporter wrote, "His sermon to men Sunday afternoon . . . was one of the best I have heard for a long time. He is earnest and full of life."[12] The adjective "earnest" never seemed distant from the name of Billy Sunday.

During the Christmas holidays in December 1895, Chapman, tired of the road, decided to give up temporarily his revivalistic career and return to a church where he was formerly pastor, Bethany Presbyterian in Philadelphia, the church attended by the department store magnate John Wanamaker. Shortly after Billy learned of Chapman's decision, he received a letter from Garner, Iowa, a small town about seventy-five miles north of Ames. Three churches in Garner wanted a revival meeting and had rented the opera house. At the suggestion of Chapman, they asked Billy to lead the revival. "You bet I wired them I'd be there," Billy wrote later. "We knew it as a direct answer to our prayers."[13] He prepared to open his first revival campaign, appropriately it seemed, in Iowa; he had joined the ranks of America's evangelists.

Theirs was a special legacy, these gospel preachers of the movable tent, trudging through the backwoods to clear ground for camp meetings, bringing the messages of the diety to wayward sinners, warning of the lurking serpent of hell, pointing the way to salvation. They were self-proclaiming messengers of God, missionaries of the frontier, answering a calling for Divine service. From the earliest days of the dense American wilderness, they were there, the Bible-clutching, indomitable warriors on mules and horseback sounding their warnings.

They spread the old Puritan notion about America's fate as a special nation holding a covenant with God and the responsibilities of God's elect to follow His will and laws. Some began to spread the word, heretical in some quarters, about religion being a personal matter between individuals and their God, with the Bible the authoritative source for understanding and belief; they talked about people communicating directly with God, active and vibrant participants in their own transformation and redemption. They talked of the power of the Holy Spirit entering the lives of believers just as in the day of Pentecost. No one was, they said, universally damned to hell or guaranteed salvation. Seek the Lord, they proclaimed. Give yourself to God and the Kingdom of Heaven awaits.

In the mid-1700s the so-called Great Awakening swept over the fledgling country, a mass psychological and emotional outburst enveloping thousands in religious ardor. Here were men and women shrieking; here was a breakdown of social and religious tradition, a convulsion of new freedom released by the conversion experience, God infusing spirit on the multitudes. Itinerant preachers exhorted the populace, provoking, berating, taking on much of the established clergy as out of step. The messages now were of the joy of salvation, the forceful effort of sinners to repent, to "get religion" and be saved.

There was Jonathan Edwards, the New Englander, barking terrifying truths, dangling men like spiders over the flames of hell, delivering learned but frightening disquisitions on good and evil, sin and punishment. There was George Whitefield, trudging up and down eighteenth-century America singing hymns, telling his vivid stories, slashing his biblical sword at thousands gathered in clearings and pastures and public squares.

In Jonathan Edwards's own parish, a contemporary observed, the religious awakening seemed spontaneous, mysterious, unrelated to any "sudden and distressing Calamity or publick Terror that might universally impress the Minds of the People." Fire, storms, pestilence, disease, war—all were absent, the religious enthusiasm marked by no apparent threat of impending doom. This was surely the work of the Holy Spirit.[14]

The fires of awakening burned in the incendiary exhortations of the preachers, God's mouthpieces. Benjamin Franklin once said that George Whitefield's voice could reach 30,000 people and set out to prove that hypothesis by standing half a mile away as the evangelist preached in Philadelphia. Franklin heard his words. The sage philosopher, of Deistic persuasion, was a little surprised to hear in his relatively cosmopolitan Philadelphia the sounds of hymns and psalms echoing from house to house. This was, Dr. Franklin concluded, an impressive phenomenon.[15]

As Edwards and Whitefield and other preachers such as Gilbert Tennent and Eleazer Wheelock fueled the religious awakening in the eighteenth century, there were other clergymen who saw in them evil and treachery. These dastardly preachers were wicked charlatans, they said, cutting into the fiber of religious orthodoxy. Religion must be left to the established churches and trained clergy. The work of these revivalists was pernicious, trading on the fears and hopes of susceptible Christians, using the gospel to incite public clamor, and precipitating social unrest and religious dissolution. "Come to the wharf this afternoon and see the Lord's will done,"

a revivalist passing through New London, Connecticut, proclaimed, urging all to bring their worldly possessions. Into the bon-
fire that night sailed rings and necklaces, gowns, wigs, and books
written by unconverted ministers, even men's suits—all the devil's
playthings, all fit for the flames.

To many traditional church leaders, such practices were alien
effronteries, blasphemous outrages to the Christian message and
religious spirit. They were barbaric and pagan and the blame lay
largely with the revivalist preachers. Menasseh Cutler, a Massachusetts Congregationalist clergymen, was outraged when he listened to the preacher John Leland: "Such a farrago, bawled with
stunning voice, horrid tone, frightful grimaces, and extravagant
gestures, I believe, was never heard by any decent auditory."
Leland's performance, said Cutler, was an affront to the Sabbath,
to religion, and to common decency.[16]

In the early years of the nineteenth century, hundreds of itinerant preachers rode horseback up and down frontier mountains
and valleys—Presbyterians, Baptists, Methodists, men with roots
in other sects and denominations, many with their different religious persuasions at war with one another, but all rousing the people to a new religious passion. The advent of the camp meeting at
the turn of the century enabled folks from many towns to travel to
the revival service and camp for the night, sometimes for several
days. At the meetings ministers mounted large platforms and
exhorted the people to repent; moans and cries and tears of anguish
and victory swept up the crowds in religious fervor as people gave
themselves to God, faced their sins, and changed their lives. This
was religious frenzy played out in moth-filled tents and ramshackle
buildings. Some people fell so violently under the revivalists'
preaching that they lay on the ground rigid, as if frozen in a trance,
uncommunicative, barely breathing; others sang and prayed and
confessed and cried. These were scenes, observers reported, of
mass psychological torment and joy. The preachers challenged
common people to trust their own religious instincts, and thus offered
a powerful democratizing impulse to thousands. At a camp meeting
on an island in the Chesapeake Bay, the revivalist Lorenzo Dow
was nearly shouted down by a woman screaming "Glory! Glory!"

To Dow this was not an interruption. "The Lord is here!" Dow proclaimed. "He is with that sister!"[17]

The battles flared among Christians themselves and among Christians and infidels concerning the validity of revivals and revivalists in American society. The battles would rage through generations.

But in each generation there were the special men of God, the towering religious figures around whom masses of people rallied. In the early part of the nineteenth century there was Lyman Beecher, son of a prosperous Connecticut farmer, educated at Yale, who took up the mission to beat back the Deists, the Unitarians, and other false prophets, to fight off those who would destroy true Christian value and morality. Beecher saw himself as an instrument of God in a mighty struggle for redemption. "I was made for action," he said. "The Lord drove me, but I was ready." From pulpits in New England and in assorted revival meetings, Beecher talked of the mighty sword of God's retribution ready to strike down the gamblers, fornicators, drunkards, murderers, and all those who violate God's code of honor. Terrible plagues, earthquakes, and conflagrations await the offenders as God's lightning vengeance would cleanse the land with blood. He battled for temperance, organized societies for the suppression of vice, and immersed himself in political campaigns, all in an attempt to kindle the fires of reform and moral improvement, to lay waste the hosts of darkness through revealed religion.[18]

There was Charles Grandison Finney. Passionate and graceful, he rode on horseback through western New York in the decade of the 1820s drawing masses to his claim that their destinies lay in their own hands, that God gave them free will to choose, to play a vital part in their own salvation. His most famous sermon, "Sinners Bound to Change Their Own Hearts," put the responsibility squarely on the people. This speared hard the old Calvinist doctrine of predestination and shook the religious inhabitants of western New York violently. But they flocked to his banner. "If I had had a sword in my hand," Finney said, "I could not have cut them off . . . as fast as they fell."[19]

Some say his eyes had a hypnotic effect, that no man's soul

ever shone more vividly through a glare as did Charles Finney's. He was bombastic, unconventional, often using colloquialisms for shock effect. He was also dramatic, sometimes in an almost bizarre fashion. At Andover, Massachusetts, a theology student remembered the preacher's performance: "He fixed his glaring eyes upon the gallery at his right hand, and gave all the signs of a man who was frightened by a sudden interruption of the divine worship. With a stentorian voice he cried out: 'What is this I see? What means that *rabble-rout* of men coming up here? Hark! Hear them shout! . . . Thanks to hell-fire!' "[20]

Like no other preacher before him, Finney tried to speak to the people individually, often pointing out sinners in the audience, confronting them openly, challenging them personally to forsake their evil ways and to follow Christ. Like no other, he spoke language that was from the street and the fields, the language of the mechanics and artisans and farmers. "So it always is when men are entirely in earnest," he said. "Their language is in point direct and simple. Their sentences are short, cogent, powerful. The appeal is made directly for action."[21]

Both Finney and Beecher preached that the Christian faith commanded the converted, like a moral army, to reform society, to promote the public good. Finney preached that the covenant with God required that His people, those anointed with the Holy Spirit, work to promote "holiness" in society or "universal good-willing." The Christian and the church are, therefore, to lift up their voices against evil and corruption, "to reform individuals, communities, and government, and never rest until the kingdom . . . shall be given to the people . . . until every form of iniquity shall be driven from the earth."

By the 1830s all sorts of voluntary organizations and societies were formed to combat scores of civic and personal evils, from the use of alcohol to Sabbath-breaking, from the brutal treatment of children and the mentally ill to the denial to women of an education. There was even a "National Truss Society for the Relief of the Ruptured Poor."

Evangelists were often at the vanguard of these movements,

moral warriors leading their troops against iniquitous, anti-Christ enemies. As Finney explained, this combined force of aroused Christians, although not a tool of government, would be an ally, emboldening the reform impulse. "By this auxiliary bond the hands of the magistrate are strengthened, the laws are rescued from contempt, the land is purified, the anger of the Lord is turned away, and his blessing and protection restored."[22]

Finney's vision of a mighty force of reformed Christians purifying the nation of sin and sordidness would be a vision shared by evangelical Christians through the generations. A century and a half later, this vision of an army of morality and Christian principles smiting down the fiends of slime and filth, the works of the devil and his handmaidens, would remain alive. From Moral Rearmament to the Moral Majority, the organized Christian army of reform has been a dream never lost or abandoned.

Charles Finney took the revivalist impulse and mass conversion efforts from rural settings into the cities. Finney conducted interdenominational meetings sponsored by various churches and invited the populace to attend en masse. The revivalist was now a media attraction, with newspapers promoting and reporting his wanderings, with government and civic and church activities arranged to assist the revival. Finney recruited workers to help in the advance planning, distributed posters in public squares and on storefronts, arranged prayer meetings to prepare the city for his coming, trained pastors to work with converted sinners after their awakening, and hired assistants to lead the choirs and the brethren in the musical offerings. Finney's wife held special meetings for women, where she talked with them about their own special concerns and problems.[23]

The revival was often the biggest attraction around, the gathering place of much of the city's leaders, ministers, and citizens. It was becoming a carefully planned, orchestrated civic affair melding religious purpose with almost circus hype.

But always there were the detractors, questioning motives and religious doctrine, attacking the preachers as godless promoters perverting Christian values. The evangelists managed to alienate editorialists, politicians, ministers, and, naturally, such entrenched business interests as whiskey producers. But the crusades rolled on; the tradition survived.

From the time of the so-called first Great Awakening in Jonathan Edwards's day, there were other periods that evangelicals saw as special manifestations of God's power, other periods of awakenings which seemed to come in cycles, sweeping across America like storms and tempests. Once again, there were the mass conversions, the same kind of spontaneous religious hysteria and spiritual rebirth seemingly unrelated to wars, disease, or natural disasters, the same unexplainable intensity displayed by thousands of the converted. The awakenings were moral and religious happenings which believers knew could only be explained by the power of God's spirit working immediately in the affairs of humans, a sign that Americans were again infused with the understanding and power to honor the covenant with God.

After the Civil War the horseback-riding evangelist, armed with his stock sermons and his invitations from towns along the way, was a familiar figure in America. Many of them were conscious disciples of Charles Finney; some had even read his handbook on revivalism. Most were zealous, committed, intent on winning as many souls for Christ as possible. They vied for space in newspapers, spent extraordinary amounts of energy attempting to draw crowds, warmed in the devotion of their converts, and rode off again in search of other conquests. All to the Glory of God. Each generation had produced great revivalist figures—Edwards, Whitefield, Beecher, Finney. In the late nineteenth century it was Dwight L. Moody.

In his early years as a street evangelist and later as president of the Chicago YMCA, Moody was a familiar figure to church leaders, not only in his home base of Chicago, but around the country and in England where he had visited leading evangelical leaders in 1867. A man who had given up a promising shoe business to enter Christian ministry, Moody was relatively uneducated but a man of perception, extraordinary organizational acumen, and tremendous vigor, a man who easily drew to his side dedicated followers who transferred to others his sense of mission. He became one of the country's most beloved religious figures.

The bearded, 250-pound evangelist was a cyclone of determination, his large barrel-chested frame darting from one religious activity to another, acting as chaplain to military troops, carrying on regular churchwork, giving lectures and prayer meetings at an exhausting pace. "I never saw such high pressure," remarked a man who had just witnessed one of Moody's breathless days. "He made me think of those breathing steamboats on the Mississippi that must go fast or bust."[24]

He was not a terrorizing orator like many of the earlier revivalists and some of his own contemporaries. For example, one preacher, James McGready, was so forceful that audiences seemed to bend under his barrages like thin reeds in a hurricane. After witnessing one of McGready's inspired performances, one wilted observer wrote that the evangelist "could so array hell before the wicked that they trembled and quaked, seeing before them a lake of fire and brimstone yawning to overwhelm them while the hand of the Almighty is visible thrusting them down to the horrible abyss."[25] Moody was not of the same temperament. His deep sense of religious urgency was tempered with tolerance and an uncensorious manner.

Moody, along with a singing partner named Ira Sankey, teamed up in the early 1870s to create one of the most effective revivalistic organizations ever built. In Scotland and England they drew thousands of listeners to their services, most from the lower, uneducated classes. When they returned to America, newspapers and magazines had heralded their way, lauding the amazing successes of these American evangelists abroad. On their return the two launched a revival crusade in America. Beginning in Brooklyn before 5,000 spectators, holding three sermons a day, they then toured Philadelphia and Manhattan, winning thousands of converts. Before his career ended, Moody, some say, converted over one million people. After one of Moody's services in 1877, the young J. Wilbur Chapman sat in a back prayer room and spoke at length with the renowned evangelist. This was the meeting that changed Chapman's life and made him a Moody protégé.

Under Moody's driving impulse the revival began to have a

significant impact not only in small towns but in major cities. Moody showed the way to mass-produce religious conversion. At the same time that American industry and business enterprise were transforming the United States from an agrarian to an industrial society, Moody was transforming American revivalism from a small-town, rural phenomenon to the urban revivalism of the twentieth century. The old-time religion needed modern methods and approaches and Moody charted a course later revivalists would follow.

An exacting businessman, he delicately plotted every detail of the revivals, from scheduling to advertising to tent construction. As no revival team before them, Moody and Sankey placed great emphasis on the musical service, carefully selecting and performing the hymns, and recruiting trained singers for the choirs. They published and sold millions of hymnals. Moody worked diligently to establish support for each revival from various city elements, including churches, civic leaders, fraternal groups, labor organizations, and social relief agencies. The revival became a united religious campaign geared to reach masses of individuals.

Moody swore allegiance to no religious denomination or sect and, like the YMCA which he had served with distinction years earlier, he built an independent organization geared to serve the masses. Not a deep theological student, he avoided sectarian disputes and controversies; indeed, he seemed convinced that such commotion and infighting detracted from the real work of saving souls. His message was informal and simple—renounce sin; accept redemption by Christ.

In one important respect, Moody did hold theological views contrary to the beliefs of many of his immediate revivalist forebears. He was a premillennialist. Millennialism, in its broadest terms, is the Christian belief that sometime in the future a long period of peace and righteousness will occur, closely related to the second coming of Jesus Christ. Revelation XX told of Satan being bound and cast into a bottomless pit for a thousand years, of the reign of the returned Christ, of the eventual freeing of Satan from his prison, the gathering to battle of the forces of Satan against those of God, Satan's defeat, and God's judgment of souls. The biblical story is not elaborately detailed and has generated over the centuries a probing search for meaning by scholars as well as lay readers.

To revivalists such as Beecher and Finney, the story of the millennium was a call for social action and reform. Christ would return to rule, they believed, after gospel ministers and the church had established conditions through their own labors. Christ's return would come after the establishment of the millennium through Christian teaching and preaching, through social reform, and through the ascendancy of Christian morality and power. Those who accepted this belief, like Beecher and Finney, were known as "postmillennialists."

The postmillennialist revivalists were filled with the driving commitment to clean up society's evils, to make the world fit for Christ's return—hence the extraordinary efforts to create organizations and societies for the betterment of suffering groups in society, the powerful push to cleanse, to reform, to sweep away the vices so long infecting the world.

Moody and his followers held different views of the millennium. They believed that Christ would return at any time to a hopelessly corrupt, depraved world, a world drowning in apostasy and sin; He would come to establish the millennium amidst the ruins. Efforts to cleanse the social and moral foundation of the nation were thus futile; that would be accomplished through Christ's own might and power. For these "premillennialists," the reform impulse was muted. If the present civilization was a crumbling, wretched, doomed place and if attempts to redeem it through human efforts were folly, the mission of the preacher, then, was to save individuals from the fire, not to save society's decaying institutions. Moody declared, "I look upon this world as a wrecked vessel. God has given me a life-boat, and said to me, 'Moody, save all you can.' God will come in judgment and burn up this world, but the children of God don't belong to this world; they are in it, but not of it, like a ship in water." Darkness and ruin were imminent but so was the second coming of Christ. For those who repented and gave their lives in Christian faith, personal salvation awaited.

Moody was neither inhumane nor uncaring about the social ills and dissipation he saw rampant in the land—the vices, the poverty, the cities now beginning to choke as masses of immigrants clustered in ghettos, the unemployment, the financial depressions that seemed to strike with intolerable regularity, the excesses of robber baron capitalists, the horrors of child labor. But he saw religion as insular, personal, not as an agent for social experimentation. His tabernacles and auditoriums and other places of worship were refuges from the decay, places where individuals could find new hope, could overcome spiritually the chaos on the outside. Moody could mount the evangelist stage and warn that Jesus Christ might return that very night to purify the world. Of what use were the insignificant efforts of men to reform the world? Most of the evangelists following Moody, including Billy Sunday, accepted his premillennialist beliefs.[26]

A long history of evangelical revivalism was thus rooted in America's past as the young preacher named Sunday packed his bags, copied sermons he had learned from one of Dwight Moody's protégés, and headed to a small town in northern Iowa. The names of Edwards, Whitefield, Beecher, Finney, Moody, and Chapman loomed large in the revivalist tradition. They and their associates had carried the torch, sought converts in the wilderness. Seeing their calling and mission differently at times, often disagreeing on theological doctrine, they still combined to establish a tradition that carried into the twentieth century, a tradition inherited by the ex-baseball player now ready to take on his own mission.

Billy's predecessors had made revivalism a significant element in religious history, had developed tactics, techniques, and organizational patterns, and had moved from the backwoods to the big cities. Mostly from the lay ranks, they spoke the language of the farm and the city square. Theology was important to most of them, especially the belief in the inerrancy of the Scriptures. But theology was not their contribution; what they gave to American Protestantism was a fighting spirit, a rousing emotionalism that reached from the barnyards to the boardrooms. If religious learning, dignity, and tradition were often trampled in their religious stampedes, the revivalist preachers, nevertheless, made a deep and permanent impact on American society.

Garner, Iowa, seat of Hancock County, population about 1,000.
When Garner's churches invited Billy Sunday to take charge of
their revival they did so after Chapman had told them of the young
man's religious conviction and determination. Nervous at the prospect of attempting to conduct a revival on his own, even if it were
in a town the size of Garner, Billy nevertheless plunged ahead,
hustling around town enlisting from local churches twenty singers
for a choir and doing his best to promote the event. The Garner
newspaper and others nearby carried short items on the revival.
Billy had enough sermons organized to last about a week and that
was fortunately the scheduled length of the Garner revival, January
8–15, 1896. With no musical assistant, Billy had to lead the singing, an arduous job for someone who, he admitted, didn't "know a
note from a horsefly." He did know the tunes, however, and "supplied the vim, ginger and tobasco sauce."

From all accounts, the revival went as well as he could have
hoped. The services drew good crowds and Billy later claimed that
many people came forward to give their lives to Christ. A local
paper, the *Hancock Signal*, reported, "These meetings have been
well attended and much good has been accomplished."

Before the Garner revival closed, Billy received another invitation from another small town in Iowa—Sigourney, located in the
southeastern part of the state. For the young evangelist the offers
would never cease. "From that day to this," he wrote, "I have
never had to seek a call to do evangelistic work. I have just gone
along entering the doors that the Lord has opened one after
another."[27] In Sigourney, Billy began to stimulate some of the
enthusiastic newspaper coverage and editorial praise that would mark
his career. "Packed Houses and Great Interest Manifested" ran a
headline in the *Sigourney News* on January 23.

When Billy arrived for the first meeting in the town, he was
astonished to see all the chairs and standing room occupied; even
many women were on their feet, midwestern chivalry notwith-
standing. By this time, Billy had managed to find a musical director, John Van Winkle, from Keota, Iowa, a small town about fifteen
miles from Sigourney. Van Winkle thus became the first in a line

of Sunday campaign musical leaders, some of whom would achieve
national reputations in their own right. Opening the Sigourney
revival, Billy pulled from his coat a sermon entitled "Whatsoever
Ye Sow, That Shall Ye Reap." He spoke effectively, directly, and
to the approval of all at the meeting, declared a local editorialist.
Billy Sunday "keeps up the reputation that preceded him to this
city." The folks in Garner had obviously spread the word. [28]

Billy carried on the practice employed by Chapman in asking
converts to fill out cards which read, "I have an honest desire
henceforth to live a Christian life. I am willing to follow any light
God may give me. I ask the people of God to pray for me . . .
Name . . . Residence . . . Church or pastor preferred . . . Usher's
name." Hundreds of people in Sigourney signed these cards. "People like Sunday's preaching," a reporter said, "and it is wonderful
how the people continue to go to hear him." The reporter compared the contents of his sermons, not surprisingly, to those of
Dwight Moody. [29]

Billy closed the Sigourney revival to plaudits about his earnestness (always that adjective) and his rallying spirit. The *Sigourney News* called him a "powerful speaker" who knew the hearts of
men, a man of insight who captured in "vivid pictures" the emotions and yearnings for the Christian life. Billy "sent many a man
thinking as he had not for months." The Sigourney congregation
at the last meeting expressed through a unanimous vote the desire
of the townspeople for Billy to stay longer. He could not. Another
revival, in Pawnee, Nebraska, awaited. [30]

Remembering much later these early months and years of his
evangelistic career, Billy told of the many instances in which town
officials pleaded for him to remain a while longer. "I would 'stall'
and tell them I had to hurry to the next town, which was true, but
they would have allowed me a week longer." The real reason he
skipped out of those revivals on schedule, Billy admitted later, was
that he had run out of sermons. [31]

Billy began to immerse himself in the Bible in a frantic scramble to enlarge his repertoire. Often staying up all night vigorously
jotting down scriptural passages, Billy read other religious books
and tracts and began to prepare new sermons in small notebooks,

filling page after page with quotes, biblical sayings, and his own thoughts. Doggedly, he worked on the sermons and they began to take on a more personal touch with some of his own stories and reflections, especially about his life on the baseball diamond.

As Billy hit the new towns in these early years of his evangelistic career, his campaign was still nearly a one-man show. To ensure adequate space for the crowds he purchased equipment and supplies for his own tent, which he put up himself. During rainstorms he would sometimes spend hours wrestling with the ropes and canvas so that the structure would not collapse. Working in such towns as Oneida, Illinois, and Emerson, Iowa, Billy made collections that were barely enough to pay expenses and to get to the next town. He later remembered working in one "whiskey-soaked, gambling-cursed, jay-rube town out in the short grass country on the kerosene circuit" for two weeks, convincing 127 people to sign his conversion cards, and making only $33.

In addition to leading the revival services, Billy addressed YMCA meetings in the towns, conducted local prayer meetings, and spoke before various civic and fraternal groups. He sometimes held meetings for women only, for men only, and for the elderly. Many of the towns were in Iowa and increasing numbers of people across the state were soon praising their native son and making plans to invite the young preacher to their own communities.

Reporters in Malvern, Iowa, talked about the initial skepticism of many church and civic leaders when they first heard of Billy's revivals and how those doubts and misgivings had been swept away as people rallied behind the rising religious star. "The hearts of old and young were touched, and the desire for a higher and purer plane of living became general," said one observer who had attended a service. At the closing Malvern gathering a thousand people crammed into a rickety building meant for far fewer and many disappointed worshippers were left outside.

From the town of Humboldt: "His manner is magnetic and his smile so winsome that the heart of a misanthrope would go out toward him." From Sibley: "The revival meetings which have been held here for three weeks under the direction of W. A. Sunday, closed on Sunday evening with the largest congregation ever assembled under one roof here." And from Tabor came the word that Billy Sunday had stirred up the citizens, had fanned a religious brushfire that made the community "vastly better for his having been with us."[32]

He worked the towns with that effervescent, infectious zeal, that childlike, innocent, determined air; he reached citizens personally just as he had reached teammates on the White Stockings; he sparked a kind of euphoric emotionalism among those who listened to his sermons. Although the content of his message was pedestrian and simple, he had begun to turn loose on the platform the kind of fury and force that moved people elementally. He was now demonstrating the qualities which would propel him into the national limelight.

Billy understood these people from the small prairie towns, identified with their rural instincts, shared their aspirations, understood their trials. When he rolled up his sleeves to help set up his tents, when he talked knowingly about hedgehogs and turkey buzzards, he fit comfortably into their communities.

To large churches, auditoriums, and opera houses, Billy charged around Iowa and neighboring states. He related stories of the prairie, about his White Stockings days, about the evils of liquor and other vices he saw in the Chicago tenderloin. He began to recount biblical events in a homespun, earthy jargon, much like the talk of a midwestern storyteller spinning tales around a country store's hot stove.

But, unlike the storyteller, Billy was always in motion. It seemed impossible for him to stay in a position of repose even for a few seconds. He was like a top strung to its limits and set loose on the floor whirling with exaggerated speed, darting in quick flashes. He pumped his arms, gestured with every phrase, the pitch of his voice rising and falling with emotional moments. He seemed bursting with kinetic energy. The man had a presence under those lights, held audiences in a captivating fire. Some said his performances were crude, vulgar, even sacrilegious, yet most who walked into a Sunday rally in these early years walked out convinced that they had just seen a budding evangelical hero. With verve and style, Billy now faced his Lucifer demons with emboldened presence.

"You have been missed very much by a great many people," wrote one woman to Billy several weeks after a rally. "Your enthusiasm was an inspiration to us." Reverend S. T. Davis of Alton, Illinois, added, "Your work here seems very deep, thorough, and lasting."[33] The news of the stirring Sunday rallies was now drawing farmers and their families from adjacent towns and counties, many camping out before the next day's service to get a good seat. Often hundreds of people had no place to view the services.

By 1900 Billy was able to hire an ex–iron molder named Fred Fisher to become a permanent "choir master." Born in Mendota, Illinois, to German parents, Fisher was a nephew of Peter Bilhorn, Chapman's singer who had introduced Billy to the evangelist. Fisher had been involved in choir and revival work for several years after leaving a job in Wyoming. Joining Billy at a revival in Bedford, Iowa, he was dressed in a once-black, torn coat with ancient trousers barely reaching shoes that were sewed up on the side with black flax thread. Explaining his sartorial disgrace, Fisher said that evangelistic work had netted him only about $4 a week. While swinging his arms conducting his first choir in a Sunday rally, Fisher ripped one arm of the threadbare coat almost loose. Billy saw to it that Fisher was attired in a wardrobe more appropriate for a worker in the Lord's service. He soon sported fine clothes, pince-nez glasses, and a curled, waxed mustache. Fisher brought exuberance, indefatigable energy, and a deep respect for Billy and his work.[34]

For now, Billy was still a relatively obscure evangelist trudging through the corn and hog circuit of the Midwest. But the young preacher was beginning to assemble a team. No two-bit, mud-daubing, turkey-buzzard bunch would this team be, no rank, second-division club like the old Pirates. This would be the White Stockings of evangelism, the best in the world, riding proudly under the stadium arch in a magnificent carriage drawn by white horses, dressed in their fine uniforms, trim, athletic, intimidating; the Sunday team—World Champions.

4

The Man, the Method, the Team

From Billy's early courting days when he was sending letters to Nell from baseball towns, he had spent much of his life on the road. Now it was Rochester, Minnesota; Salida, Colorado; and Prophetstown, Illinois—more towns, more revivals, more planning and traveling, days and nights on the platform, new seas of faces, more outstretched hands, unceasing work for the Lord—Sharon, Pennsylvania; Ottumwa, Iowa.

For a decade Billy ground out a Spartan revivalist career, gradually muscling his way into prominence. He was moving from the minor to the major leagues. His colorful baseball career had made the young evangelist great newspaper copy, had propelled him to the nation's attention, and his riveting stage performances had brought out the crowds in uncommon numbers. Ahead were big cities—Pittsburgh, Columbus, Philadelphia, Boston. In the period 1896–1906, 90 percent of the towns in which he held revivals had populations under 10,000. By 1915 the average city visited by Sunday was home to over half a million people. His early campaigns had been almost exclusively in the midwestern corn belt. After 1910, the evangelist traveled to states across the country, from Colorado to Washington, from Texas to Massachusetts.

He was rolling. With his early successes some said that Billy was the dean of a "virile evangelism school" of which earlier preachers such as John S. Culpepper and Sam Jones had been forerunners, the fire and hellfire, spit in their eye, punch 'em out, rugged revivalists, the men for whom Christianity was a roll on the ground, a fighting business. Picturesque and witty, Culpepper and Jones had been dashing figures in the South and had drawn big followings. But if Billy was in their mold he was destined for something far greater. He would not simply be the dean of any one school; he would define a profession.

Newspaper reports of Billy's successes in the Midwest gave him constant injections of emotional fuel, revved the engine to greater speed and efficiency. Even if some of the newspaper reports were biased against the evangelist and his techniques, the copy was never dull because Billy was never dull.

The *Truth Seeker*, a national left-wing periodical, snidely talked about a baseball player turned preacher who was entrancing thousands of Protestant evangelicals, the kind of people who would cheer on noisy hoodlums at the ballpark. But the *American Magazine* featured in 1907 a long, illustrated article on Billy's Fairfield, Iowa, revival entitled "The Reverend Billy Sunday and His War on the Devil." Here was the rising star of the revival world, here was dynamism, flair, a touch of electricity from the cornfields. Here was a religious hero making converts by the bushels, turning the heathen and the tainted into the saintly, searing the devil with hot invective. Here was somebody for the nation to watch.[1]

But behind the national publicity, behind the headlines about God's super-warrior, were the personal lives of the evangelist and his family. In the early years of his ministry, Billy spent long periods of time separated from Nell and the children. By 1907 they had four—Helen, George, Billy, and Paul—and Billy missed them all greatly while on the road. He would spend hours in hotel rooms writing homesick letters back to Nell and the others in the rented Chicago flat.

After Helen enrolled at DePauw University in Greencastle, Indiana, and George began attending a college prep school, Billy and Nell made a critical decision; she would spend more time on the road. She would be at his side handling finances, directing prayer services, speaking at women's meetings, assisting the choir, and acting as a buffer between Billy and his critics. Through the years friends, admirers, and Billy would call her "Ma." Charming and persuasive, she helped charge up the publicity machine, convincing small-city editors to include stories and pictures of the rising evangelical star. She buoyed Billy's spirits and confidence and her companionship was an enormous element of his success.[2]

Across the country, revival crowds now talked about the relentless energy of the man on the stage. They talked about the kind of spell that seemed to capture his crowds and hold all individuals in them like so many bits of steel clinging to a magnet. Pacing about the tabernacle platform, he seemed bursting with pressure, the veins of his neck and forehead swelling, the face reddening, the voice growing hoarse, great drops of perspiration coursing down his face and body until he looked as if he had just emerged from the sea. He was utterly lost in the moment, so absorbed in the sermons that he seemed to live the biblical tales, to experience personally the joy and anguish.[3]

From the whirling dervish buffoonery to the sobering, quiet reflections on the hereafter, Billy's sermons and stage manner were becoming uniquely inspiring. Part actor, gymnast, theologian, comedian, and stump orator, he could take an audience through a galaxy of emotions. When he spoke occasionally on the Chautauqua circuit, as he sometimes did in his early years as a revivalist, he vied with ventriloquists, opera singers, and hypnotists for attention and always emerged a decided winner. Chautauqua crowds, just as revival crowds, loved him. The rhythmic, alliterative phrasing, the rising and falling inflection, the voice that overcame a raspiness to reach falsetto, the quickening and slowing of pace, Billy captured crowds in an emotional net, played with their minds, built excruciating tension. Watching a revival crowd, you could see the fingers gripping the benches, the eyes cavernously wide awaiting Billy's next burst of energy. A superb mimic, he often acted out several parts in a sermon, some of the skits lasting five minutes or more. Many stage experts testified that he could have been a scintillating vaudevillian performer or actor. Many compared him in stage presence to George M. Cohan; some said he was much better.

Although most of his sermon material was borrowed from or inspired by other evangelists such as Chapman, B. Fay Mills, "Gypsy" Smith, Moody, and others, Billy gave the material fresh spark, anecdotal garnishing, vernacular changes, and, above all, his commanding delivery. Dr. Glenn Frank, later president of the University of Wisconsin, supplied Billy with much early sermon material. Also, Billy on occasion worked with a southern evangelist named M. B. Williams who sometimes toured the Midwest. Williams was a salty, roll-up-your-sleeves dynamo who shouted and gesticulated wildly on the revival platform and fired off slangy idioms. Billy learned much from Williams.

He also learned much from Sam Jones of Georgia, a folksy, homespun preacher who mixed wit with biting satire and whose showmanship and spirited manner attracted large crowds from Memphis to Toledo. Some compared his storytelling to that of Mark Twain. Billy had heard Jones preach, had visited him at his home, and he used much of his sermon material. Billy's stringing of series of compound adjectives, such as "hog-jowled," was undoubtedly inspired by Jones.

Billy was not blessed with the booming, stentorian voice of a classical orator like Daniel Webster, who could reach audiences over great distances by sheer force of delivery. Billy's range was weak by comparison. Nevertheless, he could mesmerize a crowd with as great a power as any speaker America had ever produced. He was the ultimate spellbinder, a man who could sweep up an audience in a rollicking, emotional ride; he was big show and center stage; he was energy; he was ignition and sparks firing off into pantomime and acrobatics, ranting, raging, laughing, yelling, reeling off those complicated tongue twisters, blending in jokes and witticisms, bounding along at a breathless clip. People in the first row could swear he was about to tumble in their laps. "Say, are you riding a blind baggage or a gospel train? I'll know in a minute whether you're men or mutts . . . I'll know whether you've got gasoline or dishwater in your veins, whether you're real or a four-flusher."

He had a prodigious memory. Although he usually carried a manuscript or notes of a sermon to the pulpit, he rarely glanced down. The material was now becoming second-nature, the delivery rapid-fire, a torrent of words and phrases. He could dish out long quotes without a slip, could reel off those adjective configurations with unerring deftness and speed: "Bull-necked, infamous, black-hearted, godforsaken, hell-bound gang."

One observer of a Billy Sunday sermon in Boston in 1916 came away still hearing the musketry of the Boston massacre, the voice of Longfellow reciting the song of "Evangeline," the oratory of Wendell Phillips expounding on liberty, and the cheers of Red Sox fans all wrapped up in a sublime package that had brought down the house. When you sat in the audience before Billy, he said, you saw every art of the platform that any performer could ever bring to bear—vivid language, perfect staging, dramatic effect, and all of it made more magical by the inspiring music of the choir. A master of pathos as well as invective, Billy could entertain, shock, and play every passionate chord. As another listener said after leaving the Boston tabernacle, "Well, he raised Hell with me!" And he could do it day after day, over and over again; he could hold a crowd as could no other performer.[4]

He had a certain infantile, boyish effervescence, an impetuosity that never cooled. It aroused others, this ebullience, caught them up in his religion, his causes. One writer called him "the world's spiritual Tom Sawyer," earnest (as always), slightly mischievous, one who would work his fool self to death because he downright enjoyed it. The slang, the gymnastic moves, all of it had a high-jinks character, like a cheerleader at a school rally. And his religious and social views seemed almost as boyish, rooted in a trusting, adolescent innocence. He was the red-blooded, rough-

and-tumble young gang leader for the Lord, chip on his shoulder, taunting the bully devil and his thugs.

In an interview with a Detroit reporter, Billy attributed his success and popularity to that unstoppable, youthful enthusiasm. He looked at life, he said, as a kid. The challenges still seemed fresh, the excitement of the crowds still intense; he still had "punch." He couldn't explain it, that burning drive inside, that heady exhilaration every time he walked out on the tabernacle platform and saw those faces peering up. But the drive to turn on the juice, to conquer the moment, never eased. "Enthusiasm, that's youth's big stuff. Enthusiasm keeps me awake, alive, tingling."[5]

Billy once said that he had a warm feeling under the vest when he saw pictures or heard stories of Civil War soldiers, the men who had marched through the wilderness, slept under torn blankets in sub-zero weather, made thanksgiving cheer with coffee and hardtack. He said he had inherited from his family and the memory of his father's fate the thrill that comes with the sight of a worn, weary figure who had given his best. When Billy Sunday, clothes wrinkled and wet after a sermon, body drained, exhaustively made his way off the tabernacle platform night after night, he was himself filling that image of the soldier in the trenches sacrificing his whole self to a cause.

His appearance on the platform at the beginning of a service was certainly not that of a typical minister or, for that matter, a soldier; it was snappy, jazzy, fashionably man-about-town, with delicately creased suits, flashing patent-leather shoes, a diamond stickpin, and the highest-quality silk necktie that seemed to sparkle under the tabernacle lights. It was vaudeville and new-car showroom and Saturday night on the town. With Billy Sunday there was never the look of austerity.

But it was also the look of an athlete, a prizefighter maybe, to those who didn't know his background, with stern, square jaw, supple muscles, quick movements, always ready for jabs or hooks or uppercuts. This was Billy's look of a Christian—neat, groomed, fit, classy, ready for all comers. And no athlete ever subjected himself to such a physically rigorous and demanding regimen. The two and sometimes three appearances a day took incredible stamina. The moment he stepped off the platform after a sermon, Billy headed to a room nearby for a bath and rubdown by a masseur.

The preacher napped often, changed clothes frequently. The scene was repeated month after month, year after grueling year in city after city. For the ten months a year he was usually on the road, he ate sparingly and often slept fitfully. Because he hated the changes in the water in the various cities, he ordered bottled water from the Poland Springs Company in Maine. He kept going, never missing sermons, taxing his strength, his nerves, and his voice to their limits. On occasion the pace seemed to catch up with him and he became increasingly testy and unpredictable. But his endurance, which he credited to his earlier training, was extraordinary.

At times he seemed almost a prisoner to his calling. He and Nell took few vacations. The revival trail was a frantic race around the country—arranging, organizing, preaching; it was all constantly changing, the new people, new towns, new sights, and yet it was also agonizingly routine. He relied on Nell to handle much of the press and to delegate organizational responsibility to the staff. She made it possible for Billy to concentrate almost completely on his preaching. The man to whom millions looked for inspiration and guidance, whom they saw as a kind of family friend, was in many ways isolated and lonely, spending much time in rooms writing and memorizing and rehearsing and trying to retain strength for yet another series of appearances in other tabernacles in other towns, again and again and again.

Physicians warned Billy repeatedly to slow down. During the Wichita campaign in 1911, he admitted that a doctor had warned him of inviting a nervous breakdown and suggested he take several weeks off. Billy refused. "I'll not quit preaching till I am compelled to do so. I'll preach till I break down. As long as I can get on the platform and talk I'll give the devil a run for his money." On many occasions he remarked that his life would likely be short. "I don't expect to live to be an old man," he said. "I burn up too much energy."

While on the road he found it almost impossible to relax, to quit fidgeting and moving about. He couldn't, he said, "turn off the gas." It had been that way since he was a young boy. In 1917, on a train heading for Atlanta, a reporter asked Billy, then fifty-five, when he was going to stop the frenetic pace. Both he and Nell shook their heads. "We have been talking about stopping for the last five years," said Nell, "and I guess we will be talking about it for five years more, and then some." There was so much to do, they both agreed, how could they stop?

It was not only at the tabernacles in the various cities and towns that Billy held forth from a speaker's platform over the years. He spoke at YMCA banquets, at prayer meetings, at high schools, in private homes, at debutante balls, even in tobacco warehouses and movie theaters. He also ventured out from the revival cities to make appearances in neighboring towns.

On the train rides, thousands turned out at every stop to see the evangelist. On his way to the Columbus campaign in 1911 the citizens of Dunkirk, Ohio, were ready. At the train station an automobile whisked him off to the town's largest church for a quick sermon. Church bells mixed sounds with fire bells, whistles, and the shouts of the crowds; stores and schools and offices temporarily closed down; people lined the streets. Reporters later estimated that half of the town's citizens had shaken hands with the evangelist.[6]

In one small town in Indiana, Billy did try in his own way to slow down. At Winona Lake, where Billy and Nell took up residence, a visitor could sometimes see a man in a tattered Panama hat puttering around the garden of a pretty but modest house. Many of the bungalows nearby were somewhat larger and more lavish. The visitor could hardly guess that the unimposing gentleman in the hat was one of the most prominent religious figures in the country. Sometimes Billy and Nell would "hitch up" the automobile and drive out into the beautiful northern Indiana countryside, along its narrow, winding roads through the green valleys. This was a time for rejuvenation, for cooling down, to leave for a time the rush of the revival assault. But even here the notion of rest just didn't seem to be in his nature. On those automobile rides, Billy confessed, he had a heavy shoe on the accelerator.

Winona Lake was a small town nestled on the shores of the

water for which it was named, amidst brilliant groves of towering oaks, willows, and sycamores. It was built on soil that was at one time a Pottowatomie Indian reservation. In this same area men such as James Whitcomb Riley, Ambrose Bierce, and Theodore Dreiser romped as children after the Civil War.

At the turn of the century Winona Lake became the scene of the most famous annual Bible conference in the United States. The idea for the summer conference grew out of conversations between Moody and Chapman. One of the founders of the conference, Dr. Sol C. Dickey, superintendent of home missions for the Presbyterian church of Indiana, called it a "kind of religious chautauqua where ministers and church workers could assemble for Bible study and the discussion of church problems." Built with the help of such financial backers as John M. Studebaker and H. J. Heinz, the Winona Lake sanctuary became in the summer months a mecca for Protestant ministers, teachers, lecturers, business and professional leaders, and evangelists from around the country who streamed into this glorious area for a series of religious activities. Chapman became director of the conference and led the institution for many years.

Winona Lake provided a place where Christians could gather in a wholesome environment, dedicated to the promotion of Christian life, and, as the *Winona Lake Year Book* said, "to shut out everything of doubtful tinge." During the summer months the giant auditorium, the girls' school, and the boys' college bristled with prayer meetings, Bible study, symposia, and lectures. The dozens of neat houses became filled with students who took classes at the agricultural institute, the conservancy of music, and the Bible school. Visitors could also attend a Sunday School Workers' Training School, a Christian Citizenship Institute, or a National Purity Federation Conference. No place could have been more suitable for Billy Sunday.

From the outside the Sunday house was mostly indistinguishable from the others around it; inside, however, it told a remarkable story. On the walls were photographs from some of the revivals and paintings given to the Sundays by friends around the country; there was a photo of the White Stockings with only one clean-shaven

player among them; there was a sofa from the old days when Billy
and Nell first started seeing each other; there was a pillow deco-
rated with a drawing of the face of Teddy Roosevelt.[7]

In addition to the bungalow at Winona Lake, Billy also bought
a small ranch and apple orchard in Hood River, Oregon, where his
brother Ed lived. Billy's mother stayed in Hood River some of the
time, along with Leroy Heizer, Billy's half-brother, who operated
the orchard. Jennie Sunday at last was living a life of relative ease.
Billy spent many summer months at the ranch.[8]

Billy and Nell remained deeply committed to each other and
to their religious cause. The extraordinary pressures of the limelight, the constant, unrelenting demands on their time and energies, did not shake their mutual devotion. And they both held great
hope that their children would follow in the religious path blazed
by the Sunday revivals. For a time, George, the eldest son, did
work as one of Billy's closest assistants. But George eventually left
the revival trail. For all of the Sunday children there were great
pressures—the daunting need to achieve, to fulfill expectations, to
play the proper roles. Those pressures, those grinding pressures,
would eventually take a sorrowful toll.

But these early years of success and fame were soul-stirring for
the Sundays and their followers. To people across the country, to
his neighbors at Winona Lake, to the people who knew him closely,
Billy aroused comradeship. His daughter, Helen wrote to her mother
in 1911 that a garbage man had stopped by the house and left a box
of peaches for the Sundays from his small garden. "It almost made
the tears come," said Helen. "He was so simple and shy about it.
It made me love old daddy the more, because the old garbage man
loved him."[9]

Billy always felt common roots with such people. As his own
fortunes arched skyward, he always remembered the early years on
the farm, the days of cleaning schoolhouses and driving hearses,
always told the stories of the prairie with nostalgia and a genuine
respect for those who faced hard times. Still, he remained self-
conscious about his relative lack of formal education, especially
religious training.

In 1903 he did achieve the title "Reverend" before an esteemed

board of ministers of the Chicago presbytery. In answering various
questions on church history asked by the board, Billy typically
responded: "That's too deep for me" or "I'll have to pass that up."
But the evangelist, who had spent long nights in hotel rooms and
trains immersing himself in the Scriptures, demonstrated a considerable grasp of conservative theology. The ordination examination
quickly ended when one of the board members observed that God
had used Billy Sunday to win more souls to Christ than had all of
the members of the board combined and that God Himself must
have ordained the former ballplayer.

Billy liked to tell a story about Mel Trotter, another evangelist
who had a similar experience in an ordination examination. When
beset with a number of puzzling queries on religious history, Trotter scratched his head and muttered, "Gentlemen, you can search
me, but I believe in the redeeming power of the blood of Jesus
Christ." For Billy that was enough.[10]

By 1909 Billy had in his oratorical arsenal the basic sermons he
would use for all of his evangelistic career. Through the years he
would add some new material, hone the old, refine the dramatic
techniques of his movements and gestures, improve his cadence
and delivery, spice the repertoire with more dashes of humor, and,
most of all, as he gained increasing confidence, intensify the power
of his rhetoric. But the foundation had already been solidly laid.
There were sermons on morality, on the home and family, on
motherhood, attacks on evolution and a call to old-time religion,
and on the necessity of being born again in the spirit of God. There
were sermons on the power of prayer, an assault on booze, a warning against alien political philosophies, a catalogue of evil amusements in which people indulge and that inevitably lead to ruination
of human character, and an appeal to young people to abandon the
lures of the flesh and, like the biblical hero David, to slay the Goli-
aths of their own lives.

One observer concluded that a large portion of Billy Sunday's
audience was made up of people who could be considered poten-
tially religious. Here were decent, hard-working folk sharing the
same fears common to all, leaning toward belief yet only lukewarm
in religious practice. They came to the tabernacle for a kind of

religious freshening up, for reassurance that, indeed, there is something to all of this talk of gospel miracles, that there is some hope of the life beyond. Billy offered comfort, was there to tell them how to live confidently, civilly, soberly, how to cope; he was to them a friend whom they trusted and admired and who represented in his rollicking ride up from poverty the true Christian champion. In trying to explain Billy's popularity, John D. Rockefeller, Jr., remarked, "Mr. Sunday is a rally center around whom all people interested in good things may gather."[11]

Although chastising them for their misdeeds and small faith, Billy never towered over them intellectually, never ridiculed their station in life whether they were shoemakers or carpenters, newspaper carriers or butchers. He was conversant in their language and knowledgeable about their trades. A livery-stable man in Fairfield, Iowa, told a reporter during the revival there that Billy was a good judge of a horse. A shoe salesman nodded. "He certainly gave me some new ideas about shoe stock."[12]

In Spokane, Washington, in 1909 Billy held his first revival in a city of over 100,000 people. The stops in towns such as Redwood Falls, Minnesota, and Maryville, Missouri, were less frequent. He would still take the revival team to small cities but the focus was now on places where Billy could reach the masses, garner national publicity, and make the big impact. The drive was to win souls for the Lord and to prove he had done it.

The method was trailhitting, or marching "down the sawdust trail." In the logging camps of the Pacific Northwest, the term had been used for years. Loggers would scatter handfuls of sawdust in their path to mark their way out of the dense forests into which they ventured. Later, they would follow the sawdust trail home. When Billy first held revivals in the Northwest, the term caught on in the newspapers as reporters described those who marched down the aisles at Billy's call to come home to Christ.

Down the sawdust aisles they stream, older men and women leaning on canes, young people, the prosperous banker in line behind the calloused laborer, the high school athlete with the bank clerk, the stenographer and the down-and-out alcoholic—an amalgam of humanity led arm after arm by the Sunday campaign workers. To the refrains of the choir softly singing "Almost Persuaded," they come forward, many with tears streaming down their faces, come to the evangelist to shake his hand, come to the Lord to join the revival list of the saved.

During the trailhitting service, Billy would leap down to a lower platform closer to the crowd and there call for the people to come to him, to join the army of the Lord. The song changes to "I Am Coming Home" and then to "Ring the Bells of Heaven, There Is Joy Today." They come forward, united in religious fervor and shared experience, united in a single emotional cause.

Billy's most famous convert was a man named Albert Saunders. An alcoholic working in the liquor business in Scranton, Pennsylvania, Saunders, on a dare from his friends, went to a tabernacle service one night in 1916. Billy and Saunders exchanged angry words during the service as the inebriated Saunders staggered in the aisle. At one point, Billy called him an "old scruff" who was racing to hell. The embarrassing encounter somehow touched Saunders deeply and he later went back to the tabernacle to hear the evangelist preach.

Saunders followed Sunday to Trenton, New Jersey. After a service there, he went to Sunday's room behind the tabernacle platform to make his peace with the famed evangelist. "I've come to apologize to you for hard things I've said," Saunders began. Billy, dressed in his bathrobe, quickly grabbed Saunders's arm and said, "Let's tell it to the Lord." The two knelt together, the alcoholic and the preacher, and prayed.

Saunders gave up drink and began to give talks to groups in various cities about his own conversion and the greatness of Billy Sunday. In Boston, Philadelphia, Chicago, and New York, Saunders traveled to tell his story. So effective was Saunders in giving public testimony that the Sunday organization used him to help persuade civic leaders in various cities to support the evangelist. After Saunders spoke to a committee of Wall Street leaders, George Perkins, a Morgan Company partner, later said that there hadn't been a dry eye in the room that night. Saunders proved to be an invaluable promoter of the Sunday campaign. He said of Billy, "He spoke to me in language I understood . . . he knew human nature as few men ever did."

In 1916 five New York Yankee ballplayers, including later Hall of Famer Frank "Home Run" Baker, marched down the sawdust trail. An excited Billy clutched each of their hands as if he and they had just won the seventh game of the World Series. Later asked about the incident, Baker said that no umpire had ever received such a verbal slashing as that meted out to the devil by the powerful evangelist. Billy made religion understandable, said Home Run Baker, just like eating, sleeping, and playing baseball.[13]

As Billy traveled from city to city, the daily results of his work began to appear in the papers, highlighted like baseball box scores. Here were figures on collections, attendance, and the numbers of individuals who had walked down the sawdust trail to proclaim their allegiance to Christ. The convert cards signed by the trailhitters became in Billy's mind like runs scored, as if every time an individual affixed his or her signature the statistic would ring up on the Great Scoreboard in Paradise.

Billy could reel off amazing numbers to show the public that his revivals were bringing forth converts as no other religious machine in history. Indeed, the Sunday campaigns dwarfed previous evangelistic crusades in most cities and those cities began to vie with one another over monies raised and numbers of trailhitters. After the Paterson, New Jersey, revival, the *New York Times* reported that Paterson had far eclipsed Philadelphia in proportionate generosity.[14]

Religious writers, editorialists, church officials—all seemed caught in the numbers games. One article which cheered the Sunday camp presented a table showing the results from eighteen cities where Billy had held revivals. The final figures showed that the evangelist had gained 167,036 converts and had received for his efforts $267,917.22. That added up to $1.60 for each convert, a statistic which brought joy to Billy's supporters.[15]

On the other hand, the statistics also opened up Billy to the inevitable question of what it meant to be saved. Mass conversion achieved by advertising, manipulation, and temporary fervor, the critics charged, was artificial and the statistics woefully unreliable. Over the years several investigators conducted follow-up studies to determine what permanent effect Billy had made in the lives of those who walked the sawdust trail and in the religious lives of the communities in which he conducted revivals. Many of the studies found that most "converts" did not actually join churches. Although Billy and his defenders laid the responsibility for backsliding on the churches themselves, on their failure to build on the spiritual uplift sparked by the revivals, the question of the degree of religious impact produced by the crusades always plagued the evangelist.

In calling for the spirit of revival to sweep into a community, Billy was inevitably rough on organized religion and its practitioners. One major reason that revival was necessary, presumably, was the failure of local clergy to arouse their congregations, to sustain religious passion and commitment. Although Billy's criticisms stung the ministers deeply, most publicly praised his work and testified to his power.

The Reverend Pearse Pinch, pastor of the Fairfield, Iowa, Congregationalist Church, candidly remarked that Billy had trampled all over him and his theology, had kicked his work and that of his fellow pastors around like footballs, had performed in the pulpit in a manner sometimes outrageous and alien to his own ideals of how religion should be brought to the people. "But what does that count, as against the results he has accomplished?" remarked Reverend Pinch, admitting that his congregation would be increased as a result of the Sunday revival. "I didn't do it. Sunday did it! It is for me to humble myself and thank God for his help. He is doing God's work."

Even certain religious teachers and scholars felt that Sunday's positive impact far eclipsed in importance his theological shortcomings. J. Gresham Machen of Princeton Theological Seminary first heard Billy from the back of a packed tabernacle in Philadelphia, standing in a passageway. Twenty thousand people had waited in the rain to wedge themselves into the tabernacle to hear the evangelist and, to Machen, the whole scene was inspiring. The power of Billy Sunday to attract such gatherings day after day and the incredible force his work had upon the religious intensity of the community made him in Machen's mind a great leader.

But others recoiled; they were too revolted by Billy's image, style, and message. Joseph F. Newton, a pastor in Dixon, Illinois, was one of two ministers who refused to cooperate in the Sunday revival in that city. Newton did attend some of Billy's rallies as a reporter for a local newspaper and wrote several editorials. After watching the evangelist in action, Newton charged that the tabernacle message was not of divine truth and inspiration, but a hyperbolic orgy which appealed to the most primitive fears of Divine vengeance. Beyond Billy's vanity and bigotry, said Newton, there was nothing but a void and, far from a revitalizing influence, Billy left communities like so much burned-over forest singed by the fires of fanaticism.

Newton and other opponents saw Billy as an untrained religious showman and huckster treating sacred matters like high-wire acts. When Billy came to Pittsburgh in 1912 a reporter for the *Post* named George Seldes was assigned to the story. Describing the revival as a three-ring circus replete with parades and singing and hysteria, Seldes also noticed something else. During the trailhitting service, the people who rose immediately at the preacher's call were good church members, officers of the YMCA, members of the Epworth League and other religiously affiliated organizations. There were no new converts at all, claimed Seldes; they were what circus types call "shills," people who buy the goods after the fakir's spiel so that others would follow. To George Seldes, Billy was something akin to a traveling snake-oil salesman.

Other detractors were revolted by what they saw as Sunday's avaricious money-grabbing. The *Philadelphia Public Ledger* ran a headline: "Sunday Gets Pans Filled with Money." The talk here was of collection plates brimming with crisp bills and checks; of ushers hugging the plates close to their bodies so that the loot would not spill on the sawdust; of a giant, galvanized bucket near the pulpit also stuffed with cash and so heavy that the Sunday aides could barely lift it; of a squadron of policemen escorting an official of the Land Title and Trust Company, speeding across town with several heavy leather bags crammed with U.S. currency and many four-figure checks; of more, much more money to come. Everybody in Philadelphia, the *Ledger* supposed, was anticipating the great question: How much will he get? And later there was in the paper a picture of a beaming Billy, the caption reading, "Naturally, the Evangelist Smiled." With all the pans and buckets and bags, who wouldn't? A day after Billy's departure from Philadelphia, the paper ran a picture of the check for the last offering of the campaign made out to William Ashley Sunday in the amount of $51,136.85.[16]

From the earliest revivals of his evangelistic career, Billy was fiercely determined that his work be financially solvent. Many traveling preachers over the years had seen their careers shattered by debt and Billy struggled mightily to avoid this menacing trap. Conducting a religious revival was an expensive proposition—the costs of constructing tabernacles, paying workers, publicity, and all of it could quickly drown a fiscally careless revival team in a rushing stream of bills. To build confidence in the revivals, Billy knew he needed to assure the public that the books were balanced, that this was one revivalist who paid his way. An agent for the Lord, after all, should be able to stay out of the red, to keep his accounts straight.

Moody's campaigns were most often underwritten by large donations from wealthy backers. Although Billy relied on gifts and other support from prominent individuals, he refused to allow campaigns to be financed solely by such gifts. In Philadelphia the department store magnate John Wanamaker, who was an outspoken evangelical, offered to pay for the entire costs of the campaign himself. Billy refused, saying that the revival would mean considerably more if one million folks gave a dollar each rather than a single individual giving a million dollars.

Wealthy backers supporting the Sunday revivals did, however, provide to banks promissory notes or pledges of money to guarantee that expenses for labor, equipment, promotion, and other campaign requirements would be underwritten. Collections at the tabernacles during the revivals were deposited and the amount of the pledges gradually liquidated. Once the campaign expenses were made and the pledges taken off the books, collections were suspended. Only on the last day of each campaign was a collection taken for Billy's own services, what he called the "freewill offering," and some of those funds were used to help pay his staff.[17]

Throughout his career Billy fought to shake the charge that he was a shyster and grafter. It is true that, as his fame and success swelled, he took on many of the personal trappings of wealth— expensive suits, shoes, and cars, even an expensive dog. He soon held sizable amounts in savings and invested heavily. On the trains, he now rode on the plush, not in coach as before. The money, he believed, was a reward for services rendered; God takes care of His workers. As the money flowed into the Sunday campaign and as the family succumbed to some of its lures, Billy and Nell became increasingly defensive, somewhat guilt-ridden, and worried about the bad press. The issue would never die.

Before throwing his open support to the evangelist, John D. Rockefeller, Jr., hired private investigators to examine Billy's financial dealings. Instead of finding a charlatan, Rockefeller's investigators found a civic-minded, charitable citizen who contributed such donations as $100,000 to the Winona Lake Bible Conference and who, after a series of meetings in Ocean Grove, New Jersey, donated the entire sum of the freewill offering, more than $5,000, to provide for the maintenance of a home for super-annuated and needy clergymen. Later, after the New York crusade in 1917, Billy gave the freewill offering of about $120,000 to the Red Cross and the YMCA and after the Chicago campaign he gave $67,000 to the Pacific Garden Mission. Billy even began to provide money to several young men studying for the ministry.

No one who examined Billy's finances closely could fail to see two things: (1) that he had risen from the poverty of the Iowa cornfields to a position of financial security and (2) that he contributed to charitable enterprises and especially, as the years went by, gave away much of his money to his four children. On several occasions he turned down offers from Chautauqua bureaus which would have netted him substantially more than the revival circuit. Over the years, he refused financial offers to endorse everything from books and hair tonics to pianos and automobiles.

Throughout Billy's career, the various industrial and business giants close to the evangelist, such as Rockefeller and Wanamaker, played active roles in convincing other civic and religious leaders in their communities to promote the revivals. It was generally accepted by both Billy's supporters and his detractors that the evangelist was good for business. His message of civic uplift and pride, religious duty and patriotism, and personal sobriety and industry was healthy for the economy of the cities. Businessmen wanted their names connected to the country's most visible religious figure—it was good for their image; it was good for their financial enterprises; it was good, they hoped, for their souls. The names of John Studebaker, S. S. Kresge, H. J. Heinz, Henry Clay Frick, Louis F. Swift, and many others dotted the lists of committees associated with Sunday revivals. In some cases Billy was invited to their homes to give talks and often stayed with them during the revivals.

But even though much of Billy's public support came from these prominent businessmen and financial moguls, Billy tried to pitch his religious appeal in his sermons to the struggling American. "They play no favors in Heaven," he said. "They shout and yell for joy just as loud in Heaven for the hobo convert as they do for the millionaire conversion. They don't keep a Dun or a Bradstreet on tap up there."[18]

Controversial, beloved, feared, and admired, Billy Sunday was now a national figure and his revival team a growing force. So popular was the evangelist that he could make strong demands on the communities which sought his revival team. He asked that churches close their doors for the duration of the revival so that religious intensity be focused on the campaign. Large percentages of Protestant ministers across the country complied with this request.

Billy also began to require that all communities hosting a Sunday revival erect wooden tabernacles built to his own specifications for the services. He decided to give up tents after a heavy storm dumped three feet of snow on his tent in Salida, Colorado, in 1905, cracking the center and side poles and tearing the walls to shreds. Although no one was injured seriously in the storm, Billy was ready to give up on the rickety, dangerous contraptions and move on to tabernacles.

Perry, Iowa, holds the distinction of erecting in 1901 the first Billy Sunday tabernacle. The Perry edifice became a model for others Billy used throughout his career. Curved and squat, the pine building looked like the shell of a giant turtle. Inside, backless pine benches surrounded a five-foot-high platform with a pulpit in the center. Sawdust and wood shavings covered the floor to muffle noise. So proficient did the tabernacle builders become at directing the construction of the huge buildings that they could tell just how far the evangelist's voice would carry inside and could plan the construction so that the maximum number of people could hear. The buildings were constructed with lumber in full lengths so that the pieces could be easily reused and were also specially designed so that the side walls could be torn away to allow escape in case of fire. As the size of the revivals grew so did the size of the tabernacles, but they all resembled the one in Perry.[19]

In addition to the support of the Protestant clergy and the construction of a tabernacle, Sunday also made another requirement of a community before committing himself to a revival. He insisted that the financial arrangements made in advance guarantee that the revival not finish in the red. This was a demand that most of the cities met, although some fell short. The fact that established churches and ministers in America came to terms with these kinds of arrangements testified to the impact that Billy Sunday was making in the religious life of the country.

What made it all work, this Sunday phenomenon? Organization! By the time of the Spokane campaign in 1909, Billy had on his revival team a variety of specialists. He had advance workers who arrived before the revivals to line up local support. He had people to oversee the construction of the tabernacle. He had specialists in Bible work, specialists in speaking to men's groups, to women's groups, individuals to visit factories, to work with students, to contact business executives, and to organize the musical services. The Sunday organization also helped set up local committees in the revival cities. When Billy arrived, there awaited an array of local officers prepared to make the evangelist's visit a success—finance committees, building committees, secretarial committees, publicity committees, and nursery committees. Ushers were organized and drilled like military companies and the officers proudly bore titles of "Captain" and "Lieutenant."

Billy had learned much about organization from his early days on the road keeping some of the books for the Chicago White Stockings. He had also learned much from the Chapman organization. He had read about and talked with other evangelists, had studied their methods. He was now building the most formidable revival machine ever put together, a carefully orchestrated, trained team, fine-tuned, ready to take the Lord's message to the people.

In 1905 Billy hired his first advance man, Fred Siebert, known in the Midwest as "the Cowboy Evangelist." A decade later, at the Boston revival, the local committee was told eight months before the evangelist arrived that the following numbers of volunteer workers would be needed for a successful campaign: 2,000 ushers; 700 secretaries; 200 doorkeepers; 5,000 workers to lead local prayer meetings and to engage in other personal work; 1,000 women to approach businessmen; another 1,000 women to approach women in factories, hospitals, and hotels; 500 women to act as day-care assistants in nurseries; and 8,000 to sing in the choir. This was a total of nearly 20,000 individuals. Following the revival, the campaign reported that Boston had more than achieved its mission; nearly 35,000 individuals had actively participated. They had, the campaign reported, brought more than 60,000 folks down the sawdust aisles to accept Christ.

Organization! So primed were the revival cities before the evangelist's arrival that newspapers usually ran stories days, even weeks, in advance. Prayer meetings were assembled; donors were lined up; and meetings for various delegations were arranged, from fraternal lodges to factories. In Spokane the three major dailies printed numerous stories about the evangelist, his background, style, and the influence he had made in other communities. From curbsides to boardrooms, the talk was Billy Sunday. Someone took the trouble to calculate that during the Spokane campaign the evangelist generated from the newspaper print shops 1,242,000 seven-column pages that were read in several states.

The Sunday team sold the evangelist better than major corporations sold tires or breakfast cereal; its instinct for promotion was uncanny, its effort intense. There were posed publicity shots for the press showing the evangelist in various contorted stage positions; there were advance copies of sermons so that reporters would not have to cope with Billy's machine-gun delivery, his torrent of words; and there were campaign souvenirs, hymnbooks, pamphlets, posters, and "authorized" biographies of the preacher for sale. When Billy hit town, the town moved.

He played every publicity card he could deal out. In Fairfield, Iowa, in 1907 he organized a baseball game on the town square between various downtown shop owners. Driving with Nell to the game in a wagon pulled by a yoke of oxen and driven by the oldest white male in the country, Billy played in the game for both teams.

In the Boston campaign, the tabernacle was a stage for some of the chorus girls from Al Jolson's Winter Garden troupe. Because of the generous publicity given by Billy to Jolson at the tabernacle, the entertainer dropped his burlesque routine of the evangelist he had been using in his musical *Robinson Crusoe, Jr.* To those who criticized him for treating religion as a circus, Billy gave additional ammunition. He hired for a time a former Barnum and Bailey "giant" to act as an usher.[20]

Billy's advance workers were, for the most part, excellent speakers in their own right and they warmed up the cities before the main attraction hit the scene. In Buffalo, for example, advance man James E. Walker stormed around the town for four weeks speaking in such places as the Delaware Baptist Church on "What the Sunday Campaign Will Mean to Buffalo," to the Railroad YMCA on "Billy Sunday as a Railroader," and to a group of businessmen on "Sunday's Methods Appeal to Businessmen."[21]

When the revival team reached the cities, Grace Saxe, director of Bible study, set up classes in neighborhood schools and churches, delivered talks to civic and religious groups, and spread the word about the revival activities. Mrs. William Asher, in charge of reaching women, assigned teams of workers to hold meetings in offices, factories, YWCA branches, and stores. She dispatched nurses and wives of physicians to organize Bible study in the hospitals, assigned high school and college girls to set up meetings in churches scattered throughout the communities, and recruited women to lead downtown prayer groups. She later organized "Virginia Asher Councils," permanent groups to engage in follow-up work after the revivals. [22]

Dr. Isaac Ward, leader of the "men's work" of the Sunday campaigns, toured railroad shops, industrial plants, prisons and jails, trolley barns, and businesses—wherever he could assemble large groups. The sight of Ward, accompanied by a Salvation Army cornetist, leading crowds of factory hands in "Brighten the Corner" and "Since Jesus Came into My Heart" defied claims by some of Sunday's enemies that lunch-bucket factory men were mostly skeptical of the revivals. "We never touch the labor question," Ward once said, "but when we have been where there were labor troubles, we have been told that our meetings eliminated them." One job of the Sunday revivals, Ward said, was to tell the workers that it was a man's job to be a Christian. [23]

Billy had his own postmaster, Fred Buse, who established at each of the tabernacles a revival post office with boxes marked with the names of various churches in the communities. Into the boxes Buse sorted thousands of convert cards by location. The ministers of the churches could then contact the converts and attempt to persuade them to join the individual churches. Postmaster Buse also handled the great volume of mail that came into the Sunday team. When Billy Sunday arrived in a community, many observers noted, it was as if he brought another small-town mailroom with him. [24]

Bob Matthews held the title in the organization of secretary-pianist. The son of a Kentucky Presbyterian minister, Matthews had been organist and choir director of the Fullerton Avenue Presbyterian Church of Chicago. While in Chicago, he also worked as a writer on the staff of the *Tribune*. With the Sunday organization, Matthews composed numerous gospel hymns and teamed with Nell as revival organizer, diplomat, press agent, and general protector of the evangelist.

George Brewster, Billy's chief soloist and pianist, was a fellow Iowan who had started out as a printer working for $2 a week. He soon discovered his singing voice, however, and launched a brief theatrical career in New York, appearing in several musicals. Later,

Brewster left New York and returned to Iowa. Billy found him teaching vocal lessons in Des Moines.[25]

Frances Miller from North Dakota had studied at a Bible institute in Chicago and worked with two evangelists before joining Billy. She held Bible classes at the tabernacle in the afternoons. Annie MacLaren, a native of Scotland, had worked for the Moody Bible Institute in Chicago, sung in evangelistic revivals under the auspices of the Congregational church in Iowa, and tried social settlement work in Scranton, Pennsylvania, before she met Billy. She joined the Sunday party at the Springfield, Illinois, meetings and was often assigned to teach classes for children.[26]

The chief lieutenant was Homer Rodeheaver. Tall, cherubic, his dark hair set against a white suit, the musical director would twitch the smallest finger of his left hand and ignite a huge choir. In city after city Rody warmed up the tabernacle crowds, preparing the way for the evangelist. In his soft Tennessee accent, the good-natured, former coal miner could put almost anyone at ease and the glorious Rodeheaver trombone was a weapon of the Lord, marshaling the troops in song. Rody played, sang, chatted, gave announcements, told stories, and his feel for the crowds seemed uncanny—always the right tone, always able to whip up enthusiasm and spirit.

Born in Ohio, Rodeheaver grew up in Jellico, Tennessee, where his father was in the lumber business. As a boy he learned to play the cornet. At Ohio Wesleyan University where he enrolled in 1896, he took music courses, played in the band, and also learned to play the trombone. During the Spanish-American War, Rodeheaver played for the 4th Tennessee Band which traveled to Cuba. When he first entered college, he intended to pursue a law degree but his music eventually ruled. In 1904 Rody worked for the evangelist William E. Biederwolf and for five years traveled with the preacher, eventually becoming his chorister. Rody was an extraordinarily affable stage performer, anxious to try new musical directions. He could even perform magic tricks, a considerable asset in meetings for children.

Billy offered him a job in 1909, after seeing him at a Chautauqua program in Winfield, Kansas, and the two immediately shared

a great deal of mutual respect. "While I was at Chautauqua," Rody
remembered, "one man wanted to give Sunday $500 to speak an
hour and a half and he offered me $150 for 10 days. And that man
knew the value of service, too."

Starting a Billy Sunday revival without Rody, one observer
once quipped, would be like starting a minstrel show without a
brass band. Rody lugs the trombone around the stages as if it were
glued to him; he points it, twirls it, tucks it under his arm, and, at
last, plays it. He sometimes sings a solo in a sweet baritone; he
sings duets; he leads the band.

The song service by itself could have attracted large crowds.
Mighty choirs since the days of Martin Luther and the Reformation
had stirred religious passion. But Billy's choirs, led by the indomitable Rody, brought musical power to modern evangelism as never
before. From Luther's own great hymn written in prison, "Ein feste
Berg ist unser Gott," to Cardinal Newman's "Lead, Kindly Light"
to the modern gospel songs of Charles Gabriel and B. D. Ackley of
the Sunday team, the splendid choirs did more than warm up a
revival; they gave it fire and spirit and life.

Upbeat and confident, like the evangelist himself, the musical
service was aggressive—hymns of battles won, of the armies of the
Lord on the march to Zion, of spiritual triumph. Because of the
large platforms constructed for the tabernacles, Rody could assemble enormous choirs, as many as 2,000 voices. Under the chorister's
artful direction, the great hymns such as "Hallelujah, What a Savior" jolted audiences as never before—resounding, powerful music,
music made dramatic by the contrasts of volume and tempo, by the
harmonies of altos and tenors, great crescendos of sound. When
2,000 voices filled the tabernacle with "Stand Up for Jesus" or
"Onward, Christian Soldiers" it was a musical experience almost
shocking to the senses.

So effective was the chorister in stimulating popular interest
in many of the new songs and in rejuvenating the old standard
hymns that he established a successful phonograph recording business in 1916 and sold over a million copies of his recording of "The
Old Rugged Cross." Also, thousands of copies of his hymnbook,

Songs for Service, issued and reissued over the years, found their way into churches and Christian homes.

The great choruses of the Billy Sunday revivals led many young people into a career in music. The Metropolitan Opera Company star Marion Talley, when she was a young girl, first started singing from the Rodeheaver songbook her mother bought for her at a Sunday rally in Kansas City. Other Met stars such as Gladys Swarthout and Grace Moore also traced their singing careers to the influence of the Sunday campaigns. The orchestra leader Ted Weems first decided to take up the slide trombone after seeing Rody in action.[27]

But Rody was never Billy's main ally. A reporter once said that Nell was the general, the adjutant, the orderly, commissary, treasury, censor, and press agent of the team and a master at all of them. She had a marvelous knack of recognizing which newspapers in the various towns to court and which to avoid; what civic leaders to woo; whom to allow near her husband and whom to drive away. When the liberal journalist John Reed tried to interview Billy in Philadelphia he found the wall between himself and the famed evangelist nearly impregnable; the wall was Nell. Rodeheaver told him, "I can't help you. You'll have to see Mrs. Sunday. She runs everything around here." Reed did talk to Nell. She probed his background, assessed his politics, evaded some of his questions, tried to ascertain whether he was a Christian, and finally left him for a delegation of ministers from Richmond, Virginia. Only after Reed was able to inveigle information out of another campaign aide was he able to see the evangelist. He conducted the interview in Billy's bedroom with the evangelist in his bathrobe.[28]

Seemingly indefatigable like Billy, Nell led Bible meetings, prayer meetings, and meetings for women. She spoke at various civic functions. She was a formidable religious figure in her own right.

But the star was always Billy. Thousands streamed to tabernacles in city after city to see the famed preacher in action, trembling at the power of his sermons, inspired by his intensity and passion, startled at the anger and vehemence, cheered by the humor and soft touch. Billy cajoling a crowd for donations: "What's the matter with you Masons? You've got the finest building in the world, why don't you make a subscription? Now, you Odd Fellows come across! Where's the country club? Why can't it come across with ten dollars? Good. There's the Rock Island. Guess I'll have to go home on that road." Exhorting the crowd to hand over their pledges to the assistants wandering down the aisles, he played one company delegation against another, one railroad against another, singling out the lodges, the various church organizations, and civic groups. He pranced and tore and hopped around the stage. "Where are the Eagle men? Where are the Beacon crowd?" He played on various emotions—pride, charity, competition, the desire to belong to a group. Get in on the giving, folks! Get right in the world and with the Lord. Open up your hearts, give, join the crusade. Under Billy's withering pressure, they all dug into their pockets.

Often he was impatient and could suddenly stop in the middle of a sermon and glare at a child who acted up or a person who was coughing. A drugstore in Wichita reported a run on throat lozenges, cough drops, and hard candy, not because of an increase of colds in the city but because of the desire of tabernacle visitors not to disturb the services. Nobody, said a reporter, wanted to take a chance on a "tannic call down" from the Reverend Billy.[29]

Those in the tabernacle all seemed to have stories of the great power and influence of the evangelist, in ways both far-reaching and very personal. George Whitney, a teller at the Fourth National Bank of Wichita, testified to his impact. In the mail one day came $1.75, restitution paid by a customer who had accidentally been given extra change by the bank in a bygone transaction. During the Sunday campaign, conscience had struck. "You must give Billy Sunday and a heart that wants to do right the credit," said a letter accompanying the $1.75.[30]

Friend and inspiration to his workers, he was at the center of a great religious and moral movement to which they were deeply committed. But they also felt his rebukes. In Paterson, New Jersey, Billy gruffly admonished his campaign aides after one of the services. "You're not doing enough work," he railed. "If you think I'm going to wear out my life for a lot of dead ones you're very much mistaken." Flushed, exhausted after a night's labor that brought far fewer converts than expected, the evangelist complained about his workers' lack of effort, about high expenses, about the lethargy of the church people of the city. Following his florid denunciation, delivered to good effect with reporters standing nearby, the campaign picked up smartly in the days following. Temper storms from Billy brought results.[31]

But sometimes the temper flared in frightening dimensions. Wielding a hammer, he once stormed the offices of the W. B. Conkey Publishing Company in Hammond, Indiana, and smashed the plates of an edition of his sermons, protesting that his words had been grossly garbled. "My reputation is at stake," the evangelist bellowed at the thunderstruck Mr. Conkey. "I will never allow that edition . . . to get into circulation. It's an outrage." Billy wrote the publisher a check for $3,500, bought the copyright, and had 4,000 books cast to the flames.[32]

Although Billy claimed to be free of political party ties, he readily affirmed his Republican leanings. And even though he often said that politics and religion should remain separate, his evangelical campaigns for morality, decency, and the prohibition of alcohol often included a healthy number of Republican officials and businessmen. Billy doled out as much scorn for modern politicians as he did for modern preachers. The politicos of the old school, he once said, the rock-ribbed, genuine, civic-minded, honest, pure leaders (Theodore Roosevelt for one), had given way to "little, wart-spittle, rat-hole ward healers who are ruining our politics now." Those rat-hole ward healers Billy had in mind were in the large cities and they were, of course, Democrats.[33]

The only political job he would ever take, Billy once said, was that of school administrator. (Billy later let it be known that he might be willing to take on the job of president of the United States.) But as school administrator the first thing he would do would be to raise teachers' salaries. Teachers earn less then bootblacks in most cities, said the evangelist, and they should be paid in proportion to their value to society. "Teachers have thankless jobs. They go into the schools at the beginning of the term, cheeks like roses, and come out in the spring with cheeks like lilies." Teachers, said the preacher, are one of the best classes of people in society and should be recognized as such. In the Sunday hierarchy of civil service, they were at the summit and the politicians were mired far down in the direction of hell.[34]

In the crowds that journeyed to the tabernacles there were teachers as well as politicians. Although predominately middle-class white Protestants, the crowds were, nevertheless, from many segments of American life—businessmen and workers, young and old, people from isolated farm regions and inner-city residents. The diversity could be seen in the various delegations that visited the tabernacles en masse—firemen, bankers, railroad workers, policemen, factory workers, college students, fraternal lodges such as the Odd Fellows, the Masons, and the Knights of Pythias, civic groups, political clubs, member of town councils and state legislatures, and especially veterans' groups such as the American Legion who came sporting their own uniforms and flags. The Sunday organization also paid particular attention to various nationalities and held special nights at the tabernacle during which the groups were encouraged to wear native costumes and to speak and sing in their native languages.

Rody carefully acknowledged all of the delegations at the beginning of the services and whipped up cheers and salutes. When 100 laundry workers visited the Wichita tabernacle, the crowd sang, appropriately, "Wash Me as White as Snow." Employees of the Massey Iron Company came armed with their own poetic message emblazoned on a massive banner: "Iron is strong and lasts long, but God's love is stronger and lasts longer."[35]

Transfixed, staring up at the famous speaker, the thousands in the giant tabernacle seemed as one, noted a writer for the *New Republic* in 1915. Common threads were woven among these people; many perused the *Ladies' Home Journal* and the *Saturday Evening Post*, shopped at Woolworth's, spent their extra nickels on bars of Hershey's chocolate or glasses of beer. These were "domestic" Americans, people who led simple, commonsense, traditional lives, people from sewing circles and YMCA classes, people who knew the price of eggs. Some of them were destined at the Sunday revivals to "catch religion," a spiritual passion, for the moment; others were merely there to enjoy a great day's worth of entertainment.

But, for some, the tabernacle would be the place where their lives would be turned around.

In Billy they found common ground, a balm to their elemental fears, a grandstander for their patriotism and prejudices, a model for sincerity and dedication and purpose. Instinctively they felt that he cared for them, that he understood their lives, respected their work, felt he was truly going to bat for them with the Lord, interceding on their behalf. In the middle of a sermon, Billy might suddenly stop, remembering someone he had recently met. "O yes Lord; bless Bill and his family and the boys at the foundry. Don't let them get hurt." The message was often this personal. And the message was for morality, sacrifice, a yielding to God's power and might, the finding of grace and salvation through "born-again" religion.[36]

For others, for the detractors, Billy was a rank peddler of ignorance and bigotry. Some of his most bitter critics saw the Sunday crowds as ignorant sheep stumbling blindly into the lair of the raving Christian wolf. The irascible Baltimore journalist, H. L. Mencken, proud foe of Christianity and its proselytizers, wrote to a friend, the novelist Theodore Dreiser, about the "adolescent, chloratic girls; silly-looking middle-aged women; men with blank eyes and no chins" whom he saw at a Sunday rally. It was, he said, a "convention of masturbators." To most liberal pundits and the intelligentsia, Billy's success was an example of mass human folly and the dangers of a skillful, fanatic leader.

Men like Mencken pointed out that the Sunday message was filled with much more than morality and religious sacrifice; it was also filled with militancy and hate. At several rallies Billy said that if he were God he'd immediately fill the papers with obituaries and fill many freight cars with the dead. He would command a moral purge, a slaughter of the atheists, the worshippers of pagan religions, and the ungodly. And when Billy began to list actual individuals he would consign to hell, the message became almost grotesque, especially considering the euphoric atmosphere of the tabernacle. Here was the other side of Billy Sunday, the bigoted grim reaper, slaying the devil's disciples, those Unitarians, atheists, Christian Scientists, left-wing radicals, booze merchants. They were all fair game to Billy the executioner. This was the Billy of the Crusades, Billy the Avenger, willing to sink to the most gruesome means to make the land the Lord's.

It was all too much for many religious leaders and editorialists. An editor for the *Philadelphia Ledger* called Billy's rhetorical outbursts comparable to "the blood lust of the worst of the Middle Ages." The baseball evangelist had, as no other preacher, brought bleacher-crazy, frenzied aggression to religion. What Hearst did for journalism, Billy had done for evangelism—made it yellow. Adrip with gutter slang, the blackguard of the tabernacle had swept up Protestantism in incendiary and blasphemous passion and sensationalism. He was, some said, a prophet for the gasping crowd. Billy never paid much attention to the critics, never backed off, never moderated, never allowed himself to be swayed by the harsh rebukes. All of it merely fueled the engine.[37]

As Billy's public notoriety swelled, as his career increasingly swirled in controversy, he faced physical threats. Police in numerous cities arrested anti-Sunday hecklers in the crowds and provided guards to protect the evangelist from possible assault. Many hate letters came into the Sunday campaign headquarters, some threatening Billy's life. At the homes and hotels where Billy stayed during revivals several bluecoats could be seen patrolling nearby, and even his principal financial backers in the revival cities would often receive protection.

In Springfield, Illinois, he was attacked. On February 26, 1909, as he began his sermon, a dark, hefty assailant flailing a horsewhip leaped off the front bench, charged at the evangelist, and screamed, "I have a commission from God to horsewhip you." He lashed the preacher twice. Never intimidated, Billy, swinging his fists, lunged at the attacker and screamed just as loudly, "I have a commission from God to knock the tar out of you, you lobster."

Billy fought off the assault but in the scuffle he severely wrenched his ankle. He did manage to finish the sermon but the performance lacked the usual acrobatics, and physicians later placed the ankle in a cast. Of the confrontation, Billy remarked, "I guess it is well I didn't get down to the fellow when I wanted to. I believe

I would have enacted baseball days with little trouble." The attacker's name was Sherman Potts, described by Springfield newspapers as a "religious fanatic." There would be other similar attacks in Billy's career by others on their own private missions to punish the evangelist.[38]

But the formidable Sunday revival machine rolled on, oblivious to attacks and threats of attack. As city after city gave witness to Billy's extraordinary influences and growing fame, other influential figures appeared at his side. At one of the services in Pittsburgh in 1913, Secretary of State William Jennings Bryan sat in the crowd with his wife and listened intently. Impressed by the vigor of the sermon and the compelling effect it had on those around him in the audience, Bryan wrote to Billy, "I can not conceive of your surpassing that effort in effectiveness. Do not allow yourself to be disturbed by critics—God is giving you 'souls for hire' and that is sufficient answer." The two great orators could meet many times in the coming years. On some occasions the legendary Bryan would deliver speeches from Sunday tabernacles and they would be fellow warriors for God and temperance.[39]

On January 18, 1915, Billy was in Washington, D.C., where he met President Wilson, had tea with Secretary of State Bryan, and spoke to a crowd of 5,000 occupying every seat in Convention Hall. U.S. senators, members of the House of Representatives, Supreme Court justices, members of the cabinet, representatives of government departments, diplomats—all listened attentively as the evangelist expounded on the topic "If Christ Came to Washington." If Christ came to Washington, Billy said, he would be sorely disappointed. It was up to the people in this audience, with God's help, to change direction, away from sin and corruption to healing and love. The platform gymnastics, the attacking style, the slang, the power—it was all there for the nation's leaders to see personally, and the elite seemed as enthralled with the preacher as the folks had been back in Marshalltown, Iowa, and Prophetstown, Illinois. They were on their feet cheering at the end. "It was the greatest day I ever spent," Billy said later. "I enjoyed every moment of it, and I look forward to being able to take God's message to

Washington and stay longer." He would, indeed, return.[40]

Much of the nation now knew of Billy Sunday: thousands had seen his cosmic jousts with the satanic darkness, had thrilled to his sweeping oratory and religious extravaganza. On March 9, 1915, he made his first foray into New York, appearing at Carnegie Hall. It was the first time Billy had been in the city since he played ball for Pittsburgh over twenty years earlier. Billy swept up Carnegie's crowd in a frenzy remarkable even for New York. A "besieging" mob, the *New York Times* called it, so dense that Mr. and Mrs. Andrew Carnegie couldn't get into the hall that bore their name.

In his Carnegie address Billy charged that churches in American were more like dainty social organizations than serious religious institutions and that many church members seemed to think they had a free Pullman ticket to heaven. "If church members did their duty," declared Billy, "hell would be for rent."

Billy had tested the waters in the great metropolis and found them to his liking. As would be the case with Washington, he would be back in New York. The Reverend J. K. McClurkin of Pittsburgh, who introduced the evangelist at Carnegie, said of Billy, "As a preacher I can compare him only to John the Baptist."[41]

Much of the nation shared the effusions of Reverend McClurkin. In 1914 the *American Magazine* had conducted a poll on the question "Who is the greatest man in the United States?" In eighth place, tied with Andrew Carnegie and Judge Ben Lindsey, was William Ashley Sunday.[42]

One observer concluded that Sunday was easily the most compelling figure in America. There was a time, said the writer, when a Teddy Roosevelt or a William Jennings Bryan or a William Howard Taft could pack a stadium or auditorium, could rally 20,000 for a night. But who in the United States now, except Billy, could gather those kinds of crowds day after day for several weeks? No politician or entertainer, no Chautauqua performer or religious figure, was his equal.[43]

"The Boss" most of his staff called him; the term was apt for all the world of American revivalism. He had indeed assembled a mighty team, the White Stockings of evangelism—skilled, well trained, organized, and disciplined, team players all. As they entered the campaign cities, newspapers heralded their coming, posters on walls announced their events, crowds lined the streets to cheer them on. The glory days for Billy were back. But there was a difference. As baseball hero, Billy had been a minor star; as evangelist he was king.

5

Furies of Change

Faith of our Fathers! Holy faith!
We will be true to thee till death!

—Traditional hymn[1]

When Billy Sunday was a boy growing up in rural Iowa, folks in towns such as Marshalltown and Ames were pretty certain about the major things affecting their lives. Most believed that America was a Christian nation favored by the Creator. Most believed in heaven and hell, in reward and punishment, in the Protestant values of hard work, thrift, sobriety, and good citizenship, in family life, honesty, justice, and Christian duty. Billy and his fellow students had read in their *McGuffey's Reader*s about these moral demands and had been warned from church pulpits about such evils as Sabbath-breaking and liquor. Their parents taught them that the Bible was divinely inspired, that it held the basic truths about their lives and destinies, that its stories were completely true. They believed that virtue would be rewarded, that American economic free enterprise was consonant with scriptural teaching and Christian morality. If times were often hard, riddled with the uncertainties of health, weather, prices, and war, life was at least understandable, ordered, subject to natural forces. Traditions and values had not changed dramatically from one generation to another; the fears and challenges and hopes of fathers and mothers were those shared by their children.

As people in Marshalltown and Ames and in other small towns and cities across the country faced the new century, however, simplicity had somehow vanished. New forces of industrialization, urbanization, and scientific discovery had swept aside much of what individuals such as Billy had for so long taken for granted. The world of yeoman farmers and village artisans had yielded to one of vast business combinations, of masses of industrial workers crowding into factories, of labor disputes, of increasingly depressed conditions for small farmers on the prairie, of large cities filling with alien people. This was a new age of exhilarating invention, of machines and consumer items that dazzled the imagination. It was also a time of corrupt political organizations, of robber barons, of furious finance capitalism, of land being sucked up by railroads and corporate interests, of socialism and populism and other political movements that attempted to gain credence and power.

As Americans in every area of life sought to adapt to a swirl of change, nowhere were the tensions and conflicts of these years more evident than in religious life and thought. In this new age, the old-time religion was under assault. In many quarters the old Bible stories now seemed antiquated, tired, and suspect. Such philosophers as F. C. Bauer and D. F. Strauss in Germany and J. E. Renan in France marshaled formidable attacks on the historical accuracy of Gospel accounts. In each book of the Bible, chapter by chapter, verse by verse, the scholars scrutinized, dissected, and analyzed the scriptural account, subjecting the text to what became known as "the higher criticism." They pored over church doctrine and biblical tenets, these "modernists," assessing the accuracy and consistency of scriptural passages through objective, "scientific" processes.

The "higher criticism" was not the only force battering the walls of tradition. The question of Darwinism also reared mightily in the faces of evangelicals. What seemed a remote theory when *On the Origin of Species* appeared in 1859, Darwinism now seemed ubiquitous, appearing in books, articles, and even sermons. Its theories and assertions brazenly amoral, ascribing to humans the same kind of doctrine of survival as for other beasts, Darwinism was an explicit challenge to traditional Christian faith, and it was frightening to most evangelicals, suggesting that the survival of humankind was dependent on the same forces that determined the fate of herbivorous sauropods.

But some theologians openly applauded the application of scientific principles to Christian belief, attempting, usually clumsily, to reconcile evolutionary theory with Gospel accounts. At a meeting of evangelical teachers, writers, and missionaries in 1873 a Princeton College professor proudly showed off detailed charts elucidating how the events told in the book of Genesis neatly squared with the latest discoveries of science. Scientific discovery need not be antithetical to scriptural doctrine, he asserted boldly, but was merely a manifestation of God's handiwork.

Other religious leaders resorted to a kind of wistful philosophical speculation that seemed to acknowledge the force of argument on both the side of science and that of traditional religion. One theologian reached the hazy conclusion that the infallibility of the Bible is the infallibility of common sense, that the experimental "triumph" is within all of us, and that the Bible had a "living power" beyond scientific explanation.

Henry Ward Beecher, son of the renowned revivalist Lyman Beecher and widely respected as one of the most exciting preachers of the late nineteenth century, counseled toleration of new theories and a fresh examination of the Scriptures employing new scientific ideas. In 1885 he published *Evolution and Religion*, considered by many the first straightforward work of American theology that adopted evolution as both scientific and religious fact. Here, God was the master builder and the Scriptures revealed His wonders. See the Lord, implored Beecher, "when He is at work in natural laws, when He is living in philosophical atmospheres, when He is shining in great scientific disclosures." Beecher saw God as the Divine gardener, germinating the seeds, tenderly cultivating His worldly crops.

With mixed enthusiasm and acumen, religious thinkers of all denominations challenged biblical authority, and for the evangelicals the debate became particularly intense. In earlier generations many religious believers had little difficulty in lauding scientific inquiry and the findings of such eminences as Francis Bacon and Isaac Newton, calling their discoveries further proof of God's intricate, marvelous universe, testimony to His omnipotent creativity. Science, here, operated in its own sphere, not impinging seriously on standard Christian belief. With Darwinism, however, the discoveries and theories had taken on especially threatening, ominous implications. Too much of this rationalistic inquiry clashed with scriptural purity; too many of the old truths now appeared vulnerable.

Many evangelicals fiercely fought back, rebelling against the modernists and the scientists and some of their own religious brethren who had embraced the new scientific notions. Charging that the scientists had ventured much too far into speculative theory, had extrapolated figures and experiments into new realms of fantasy, had made scientific exploration a plunge into blasphemy, the evangelicals scorned the idea that frogs and fish and primeval forests and slime and creatures of ions past, brainless and senseless, could have any concrete meaning in challenging the biblical story of creation. Darwinian natural processes of selection had galloped far beyond biology into a world of romantic fiction, they charged. One religious writer maintained that the Bible, far from being open to speculation, far from being a creation of writers who used hyperbole or imagery, was an "absolute transcript of God's mind." Another referred to the Bible as a work literally "dropped out of Heaven."[2]

Still other evangelicals embraced the hope that somehow all the controversy would just evaporate, and they clung to the view that theology had its insular world beyond the reach of the probing questions posed by the higher critics and by the scientists. The things of the spirit were greater than the understanding of science, beyond the equations, microscopes, and mathematical theorums;

faith was the blessed assurance of the Creator, science merely the deductive reasoning of the laboratory. Religion was sensibility and inspiration; science was material and mechanical. Keep the worlds apart!

But the religious controversies intensified. In theological seminaries, in public debates, in essays of sectarian journals, and from pulpits across the country religious leaders staked out philosophical ground. In some churches and seminaries individuals lost their pastorates or professorships because of their views on biblical issues. As the issues sharpened and patience wore thin, religious communities bristled with acrimony and bitterness.

One adherent of the new theology left a meeting of conservative Alleghany County, New York, ministers convinced that he had just been back in the Middle ages: "Such archaic ideas of religion, such hopeless notions of biblical interpretations I never before encountered. Why if I should have told them what I believe, I think they would have hanged me to a gas light."[3]

The intense debate over the complete accuracy and authority of the Bible as evangelical orthodoxy would carry into the new century. Indeed, the issue would reverberate into the age of televangelism, the age of Oral Roberts, Jerry Falwell, Jimmy Swaggart, and Pat Robertson—the Bible versus science, creationism versus natural selection, faith versus empiricism, Adam and Eve versus the primeval soup of organic chemicals.

Dwight Moody was one of those who would have preferred to see all the controversies, all the arguments, debates, and bickering, and all the antagonism dividing religious groups mercifully end. At one point an exasperated Moody asked innocently and sincerely whether the fighting sides could agree to a truce, whether all the contention could be postponed for ten years while the work of saving souls progressed. Dabbling in intricate theological detail, said Moody, only disrupted the practical labor in the Lord's vineyard.[4]

Relatively unlettered, Moody had extraordinary gifts of leadership and organization but an almost defiant lack of interest in theological analysis. Preaching a simple faith of personal salvation, unmoved by proofs or challenges of biblical texts, Moody said simply that the Bible was the Holy Word; it was the truth, every word of it; it was man's guide to life and redemption. Though he avoided as best he could most of the theological warfare over the Bible, Moody did grimly warn his congregations to be wary of the atheistic teachings of evolution. "New Theology" professors, he explained, were like balloons which went "whizzing above the heads of the people." To the renowned preacher, all this scientific inquiry seemed nettlesome, annoying, and especially puzzling. "You call it metaphysics," he remarked, "but I don't know what it is."[5]

Some of Moody's lieutenants slashed on the offensive against the modernists. Reuben Torrey reminded his audiences that Christ in his own life attacked those who stood for evil and error. The theologians playing with the Scriptures, meddlers in elemental questions of existence, deserved stern rebuke and censure. The so-called higher criticism was religiously nefarious, a sniveling capitulation to forces of the anti-Christ. Torrey remained uncompromising.

So did William Jennings Bryan. The "Great Commoner," the most popular evangelical politician of his time, saw this contest, as he saw most things, in unadorned terms. This was a battle between atheists and Christians, between materialists and believers. Let the godless produce a "better Bible than ours, if they can," Bryan challenged.[6]

For Billy, the attacks on the complete accuracy and authority of the Scriptures were a direct assault against a way of life, against a heritage of his evangelical forebears on the frontier, against the simple, Christian message to which he had given his life in a Chicago mission decades before. For Billy religion was not intellectual process, not doctrine or dogma or history or philosophy; it was personal, spiritual, and experiential. Salvation had nothing to do with a study of texts or theory or the differences in denominational teaching.

Admittedly, he knew little of the fine distinctions of theology or the origins of doctrinal positions; indeed, even many religious terms were puzzling to him. Thus, the world did not get from Billy Sunday a theoretical defense of old-time religious belief. It did, on the other hand, get a rousing condemnation of all those who had the effrontery and gall to challenge the Holy Word with their punctilious theological scribblings and their academic snobbery. It got from him a vigorous, hellfire affirmation of what he saw as traditional, American, Christian positions.

In the hymns through which Billy's mighty choirs roused congregations, there were always the great struggles between two sides—on the one side stood sin, hell, slavery, death, sorrow, pain, bitterness, and grief; on the other, mercy, victory, peace, blessing, love, redemption, and joy. The two sides were always at war, God and Satan; there was always the battle, always the threats, always adversaries hacking away at truth and right. For Billy, the egghead philosophers challenging his Bible were just other enemies to smite. The Christian life, the revivalist preached, was always a struggle to preserve basic, fundamental values. The slackers and trimmers, the skeptics and philosophers attacking the truths of the Bible were all agents of the devil. They should not be dealt with through reason or compromise but must be pummeled. As the old hymn "Sound the Battle Cry" had commanded:

> *Gird your armor on,*
> *Stand firm every one . . .*[7]

Temperamentally very different from Moody, Billy brought a strident militancy to the forces of American revivalism at a time when it was under siege. He saw no ambiguities in this struggle, saw no room for accommodation. A sharp instinct to retaliate at detractors, a boundless confidence that he could win all confrontations, an infectious enthusiasm for controversy—he brought it all to the tabernacles and engaged his huge crowds in the warfare. He roused his army. Fight the godless, strike back at those who threatened Christian values.

All of this theological controversy at the time of Billy's emergence as a national revival leader gave him burning issues on which to wage his aggressive battles. He skillfully placed himself at the front of a war to preserve tradition and old-time Christian ethics and morality, to rescue the simple, plain truths that millions of Americans understood, to ensure that the Bible, God's Holy Word, remain undefiled by small men.

When Billy looked at the religious convulsions of the day, he detected conspiracy. Many of the "Liberal Protestants," those "higher critics," were, after all, foreigners, largely from Europe, especially Germany. Many of their godforsaken theories, Billy said, had been dreamed up over mugs of beer in Leipzig and Heidelberg. The rationalists and behaviorists, the loyal lapdogs of Freud and Nietzsche, were bent on destroying the sacred beliefs and values of millions of Americans not connected to academic institutions.

At one point Billy claimed that the German kaiser, in outlining a scheme for world conquest, had instructed his minions to change the predominant religion of the German nation. Down with Martin Luther; up with the higher criticism! Billy later claimed that the suffering inflicted on Germany during the First World War was God's punishment for its religious heresies.

What made Billy especially indignant was the capitulation of many Protestant ministers to this scurrilous, un-American scientific barrage. To Billy, much of the modern clergy had become fools. The devil was going out of fashion among this bunch as they congenially stuffed him with "fried oysters and toast and tea" to make him more palatable. Sissified, lily-livered, these so-called clergymen had wilted under attack; they were not fit to stand at church pulpits to explain their sin-laundered religion. They were "fudge-eating mollycoddles" who should be stood on their heads in mud puddles. They were all hypocrites and Billy loved to take on hypocrites: "I can skin a hypocrite, salt his hide, and tack it on a barn door to dry before you are puckering your old mouth to spit on your whetstone to start to sharpen your jack knife to begin the operation."

With scientists and philosophers now referring to God as the "First Cause" or the "Prime Mover," with writers such as Herbert Spencer referring to God as "the Great Unknown," with biblical scholars explaining that man had evolved from an amoeba-like cell into a hairy quadruped, with the very nature of man being reduced to microscopic organisms in a bacterial horror, these weasel, spineless preachers, Billy charged, were going along with it all, some hailing it as divinely inspired revelation. He stormed: "Some preachers in every denomination and many professors in many universities are teaching blatant infidelity and with their false discordant doctrines are trying to lead the symphonies of immortal souls." They were shackling Christians with handcuffs of speculation and linking man to the "rotting, vile, shriveled, stenchful corpse of unbelief." They have, Billy roared, "unchained the passions of Hell." From their vicious work would emerge libertines and athiests.

Billy engaged in free-form verse:

> *Take your evolution theory*
> *Take your gland grab bank*
> *Take your protoplasm chop suey*
> *Take your bloodless religion*
> *Take your "Mental disease" crime*
> *Take your non-existence of body and soul*
> *Take your "mortal thought" instead of reality.*

Billy would, instead, take the Bible. He would take light not darkness, would take God's balm and salvation, and would take heaven as his home.

The modernists and rationalists, said Billy, were attempting to take God out of religion and to elevate man's intellect to the level of the Deity. Such philosophy, Billy charged, led to anarchy and irresponsibility, led to men recognizing no law other than their own desires. The intellectual and theological engineers, if allowed to chart man's directions through a sin-cursed world, would "dissolve the atoning blood of Jesus into mist and vapor."[8]

Most ministers remained on the side of Billy Sunday throughout these years. Some genuinely agreed with most of the religious beliefs of the evangelist; others were fearful of losing the support of their congregations and of fellow ministers if they edged too close to the liberal camp. Whatever their motives, most Protestant clergymen openly backed the Sunday revivals.

One disgruntled liberal, the Reverend Charles Aked, minister of the First Congregational Church of San Francisco, lamented that fellow ministers in his city wallowed along with Billy in "an apotheosis of ignorance." Aked confessed astonishment over "these decent friends of my own in the ministry of various denominations who can lend their countenance to what is so obviously calamitous." Another liberal, Reverend George Merrill, minister of the Congregational Church of Burton, Ohio, wrote of Billy, "I suppose he can only be left to the refining influences of time and death and the expectation that Dante . . will be greedily waiting for him in the other environment to set him off right personally, but he will do a lot of mischief in the meantime."[9]

If Billy's campaigns were mischief to the liberals, they were to his followers a crusade, a call to return to God, to return to the basic fiber of Christian religion. The evangelist became on the tabernacle platform God's fighting general, sword unbuckled, spirit on fire, flailing at the infidels, men like Charles Aked and George Merrill, who were storming His temple. If the nitpickers and academics were wedging themselves through the Christian gate, Billy would unload cannon shot at them.

The whole controversy gave to Billy and his campaigns extra zeal, an air of excitement as if tabernacle worshippers were filling giant arenas to see gladiatorial combat. The more enemies Billy collected, the more animated and vicious his attacks. He had Satan to assault, he had a host of sins and worldly vices, and he had godless ideology and its practitioners, the thinkers and tinkerers. As no other preacher, Billy militantly took on all those who challenged his simple, unadorned vision of Christian faith.

His contempt for the modernists was total. In Chicago in 1893, about the time Billy began his religious work, 4,000 religious figures from all over the world had wedged into the Hall of Columbus to open a World's Parliament of Religious. Here, amidst the fluttering of flags from many nations, consorted representatives of faiths of all kinds—followers of Brahma and Buddha and Muhammad, Hindu theists, Parsi ecclesiastics, Taoists, Shintoists, and others, all aglow in brightly colored robes and tunics. On speaker announced that Christianity must broaden its horizons, must avoid bigoted orthodoxy. This era would be a new time of cosmopolitanism and wide vision, of understanding, and a march of civilization toward "the nearness of man to man, the Fatherhood of God and the brother of the human race."

Years later, looking back at the 1893 event, Billy said it was one of the biggest curses that ever came to America. The "Fatherhood of God and Brotherhood of the Human Race," said the evangelist, was a notion from hell. Those religious figures who were participating in such events, those teachers and pastors who were parading around with representatives of heathen faiths, who were sacrificing the truths of the Bible for "international cooperation," were traitors. The exponents of universalism were "turning men to hell by . . . false teachings."[10]

In a sermon in Marshalltown, Iowa, his old stomping grounds, Billy swept into a foreboding vision of the real hell, a forlorn pilgrimage into the depths of torment: the sobs of the suffering, the bellowing of beasts, the thorny, unfathomed depths of pain—a real place, yes, not some literary allusion. Hell was the madhouse of the universe. The rationalists, Billy said, were now trying to obscure the truth about the existence of hell, about its torments, by describing biblical texts as mere devices of theoretical imagery.

All of this was dangerous, hiding basic truths with soft-sounding tripe meant to ease the fear of death. A best friend, Billy said, is one who warns you of danger, not one who obscures its existence. Billy was there to present God's word and "God says it's either heaven or hell for every one." He declared, "I have no objection to a new theology if its newness consists in making old truths more clearly understood, but if its newness consists in trying to take the old truths out of our hearts, then to hell with their theology!"[11]

One of the modernists, George Harris, a faculty member at Andover Seminary in Massachusetts, smugly remarked in 1914 that it would be difficult to find an intelligent individual who still believed in the inerrancy of all texts of the Bible. The Reverend George Gordon of Boston's Old South Church said much the same thing. Among Boston's intelligent, sophisticated people, said Gordon, the Bible could never again be what it was in the past. The higher criticism and scientific processes have thrown aside moldering superstitions and misguided ignorance. William Rainey Harper, founding president of the University of Chicago, called the work of the modernists a mission to clear away the rubbish of the past. Harper later founded a journal called *The Biblical World*, a work for educated, thinking students of biblical inquiry.[12]

It was this kind of intellectual snobbery that so rankled Billy. Over 150 years earlier the revivalist Gilbert Tennent viciously attacked many in the established church who had characterized the Great Awakening as nothing but a wild fit of superstition. Tennent called these ministers "Hirelings; Caterpillars; Letter-Learned Pharisees; Men of the craft of Foxes, and the Cruelty of Wolves; plastered Hypocrites . . . foolish Builders whom the Devil drives into the Ministry," and a host of other epithets.[13]

And now, to the "Letter-Learned Pharisees" at Andover Seminary and at numerous other academic institutions in his own time, Billy spat the same kind of anti-intellectual venom. They were "walking theological mummies" spewing out their isms and schisms and ologies. When scholarship says one thing and the Bible says another, "scholarship can go to hell."[14] The "chile con carne" beliefs of these so-called thinkers were asinine, poppycock rantings of intellectual sissies. "We are as good as we are now not because of these new fads but because of the impetus of the old belief of our grandmothers and grandfathers in God and the Bible that has carried into our day."[15]

Billy did try in his own fashion to take on the intellectuals on the question of evolution. He denied that species ever change ("It's the same old hog even if you put gold bills in his ears and pink ribbons around his side," and "Old Burbank has developed the potato, but he hasn't made an orange out of it!"). He asserted that Spencer wasn't present when God created the world. He ridiculed the notion that man came from a monkey (a monkey never used a tool, was never gifted with speech, and never said his prayers at night). He asserted that Jonah, indeed, took the first ride in a submarine. He did allow that the word "evolution" was acceptable if used to describe progress; it was unacceptable, however, in explaining creation.

Not from a fortuitous concurrence of atoms did man arise but from the hand of God. "I do not believe that my great, great grandfather was a monkey with a tail wrapped around a coconut tree. If you believe your great, great grand-daddy was a monkey, then you take your daddy and go to hell with him."

Billy compared the creation of the world to the making of a watch. The watch's case, its mainspring, jewels, the stem—all were the products of someone's labor. Imagine, Billy said, if he were to go before a revival crowd or Chautauqua audience and try to explain that the watch had not been made but that endless years ago, with innumerable atoms dancing in chaos, a fortuitous concurrence in some unexplained way had shaped those atoms into what we now call a watch. Those audiences, Billy said, would not call him a philosopher for propounding such ideas; they would call him a "foolsopher."[16]

Science is not a god, Billy declared; rationalism and pragmatism and biology are not gods. Far from omnipotent they are riddled with error, confusion, and controversy; they are only the playthings of the intellect. Even the scientists and thinkers, Billy said, must admit that there are many things even they do not understand. "Why is it that what a cow eats turns to hair, what a chicken eats turns to feathers, and what a sheep eats turns to wool?" Billy asked. The world was not made by happenstance, was not an accident of chemicals; it was made by a designer with a plan. So much for those "evolutionary hot-air merchants!"

The great evil in all of this, he said, was that many children's minds were being poisoned by the theories of evolution. He envisioned the day when most public schools would dole out such nonsense as fact, would undermine Christian faith with theory masquerading as science. Keep such speculation out of the schools, Billy warned. "Don't allow them to turn the faith of my children one iota from the fact that the old world is just as God almighty made it." Billy's fears in these years about the teaching of evolution and his battle cry against Darwinism would become an evangelical crusade a decade later, the time of a mighty confrontation in a small town in Tennessee.[17]

When Billy stood against the academicians and philosophers and theorists he was allying himself with the masses of evangelical Christians who were relatively unsophisticated, accepting the simple, old biblical stories on faith, who could not have understood much of the technical treatises on higher criticism even if they had been inclined to tackle them. In this intellectual arena the battle lines were sharp and Billy was solidly entrenched on the side of the majority.

His anti-intellectual rantings were refreshing and welcome to most of the tabernacle worshippers; he was their ally against an aristocracy of the educated who often seemed culturally distant, intimidating, and hostile. This was a time when higher education for most Americans seemed far removed from everyday life and academic professors seemed mostly pretentious and isolated from events and people who mattered. For most in the tabernacle crowds, the academics were easy targets, those with their D.D.s and their L.L.D.s, sitting around theorizing about obscure doctrines, challenging beliefs held sacred by so many Americans. The evangelist's scorn of these intellectuals drew riotous cheers from his crowds.

The liberal clergy, Billy charged, were fighting sham battles, sinking in "fal-da-rol and tommyrot," their obligations as religious leaders left unfilled. They knew something about Jesus but they did not know Jesus.[18]

Vehemently defensive about his own intellectual limitations and prairie beginnings, Billy had a profound disgust and resentment of seminarians and academic types who, as Billy put it, tried to tickle the palates of the giraffes with their high-sounding rhetoric while their sheep starved. The seminaries, he said, were turning out little bottle-fed preachers stuffed in theological molds.

Many of these men had, of course, attacked Billy as a cheap religious charlatan and grafter. Slashing back at those who belittled his background, laughed at his cornpone philosophy, ridiculed his methods, charged him with money-grabbing, and lamented his popularity, Billy said they were all in a sink of intellectual putty. "I want to say that I believe the Bible is the Word of God from cover to cover. Not because I understand its philosophy, speculation, or theory. I cannot; wouldn't attempt it; and I would be a fool if I tried. I believe it because it is from the mouth of God." The philosophers who questioned the Bible were iniquitous and spiritually doomed. "I know my doctrine is all right," he quipped, "and

I know that I do not need to have some doctor to doctor my doctrine."

To the doubters and skeptics of some of the old Bible stories, Billy told of an incident involving a modern-day sailor as related in a magazine article. While harpooning a whale off the Mediterranean coast, a vessel capsized. One of the men was presumed drowned. Later, when the dead whale was cut up, the sailor was discovered in the stomach of the beast, unconscious but still alive. He later told of how horrifying it had been as he slipped down into the whale's belly, the realization he was doomed and so on. For the unbelievers, Billy now had his nineteenth-century Jonah.[19]

Often the evangelist's anti-intellectual fury seemed completely unrestrained. At one meeting he said that any minister who believes and teaches evolution is a "stinking skunk, a fraud, a hypocrite and a liar." At another service he saw a liberal theologian in the audience, turned toward the man's direction, shook a clenched fist at him, and exploded. "Stand up, you bastard evolutionist; stand up with the infidels and atheists, the whoremongers and adulterers."[20]

Biblical criticism, liberal theology, modernism, new philosophies—for Billy Sunday it meant an attack on cherished beliefs by infidels and he continued to blast them with his formidable arsenal of mockery. But the attacks on the inerrancy of Scripture and the march of evolutionary theory were not the only threats Billy saw rumbling down the theological highway in these years. There was also something called the "Social Gospel."

In 1907 Walter Rauschenbusch, a faculty member of the Rochester Theological Seminary, published a book entitled *Christianity and the Social Crisis*. Concerned that the contemporary American economic and political system was unprepared and unfit to deal with the burgeoning problems created by industrialization, Rauschenbusch asserted that preachers had concentrated too long on individual salvation while ignoring the social and economic distress rampant among their parishoners. He urged Christians to answer the true call of Christ, to care for the poor and the hungry, to relieve suffering. Advocating "socialistic" reforms—charitable work, support for labor, better business ethics—Rauschenbusch declared that the church, instead of being isolated from society's concerns, should be out front leading the way in solving these problems, should be the "swiftest to awaken to every undeserved suffering, bravest to speak against wrong, and strongest to rally the moral forces."[21]

Many influential and respected clergymen rallied to Rauschenbusch's call—men such as Washington Gladden, pastor of the First Congregational Church of Columbus, Ohio; Herbert Newton, rector at All Souls Church in New York; Francis Peabody, professor at Harvard; and W. S. Rainsford, a man who called himself a "Christian Communist."

The Social Gospel movement encouraged upper- and middle-class religious Americans to respond to broad moral and social responsibilities. In these days of municipal graft and spoils, whiskey rings, white slave traffic, fetid tenements, child labor, impure food, high infant mortality, and increasing street crime, the seminary professors and Protestant pastors who formed the vanguard of the movement were determined to move beyond the isolated individualism of the church, its concentration on personal salvation and the winning of souls, to a broad restructuring of society based on a Christian social order. For Rauschenbusch the idea of Christianity was not merely getting individuals into heaven but dramatically "transforming the life on earth into the harmony of heaven."[22]

Gladden, one of the most influential and active of the Social Gospel leaders, created community organizations to teach employees and employers that ethical business practices must be based on the Golden Rule; he advocated profit-sharing and unionization and fought gambling interests and prostitution. The government can be made to work for the good of the social order, Gladden believed, and he waged a sometimes lonely struggle to push such solutions as muncipal ownership of public-service corporations. He established in Columbus an associated charities organization and was active in a host of other charitable enterprises, from the YMCA's Men and Religion Forward Movement to the National Conference on Charities and Corrections. The causes of much of society's dislocations and poverty, said Gladden, arise from a distressed environment, from economic and social forces—cutthroat competition, unemployment, drunkenness, and poverty. It was the duty of the church to help ameliorate these conditions.[23]

The Social Gospel went further than the old postmillennialist urge to cleanse society through personal charitable enterprises. Rauschenbusch and other Social Gospelers instead saw the need to overhaul the country's economic and social order in the light of Christian ideals. Although most Social Gospel leaders stood apart from socialism and the Socialist party movement and most feared its "radical" politics, they favored a vague "cooperativism" between government and the private sector. Abhorring socialism's tendency to stimulate class conflict, they looked instead for national fellowship, a partnership under Christian ethics. To the Social Gospel leaders, the movement represented a recapturing of primitive Christian ideals of justice, fair play, love, and charity. As the engines of modern industrial capitalism ground many men and women to economic and social despair, Christians must push vigorously to confront those forces, to relieve suffering, and to make religion a powerful force for social change.[24]

To Billy, the Social Gospel was yet another liberal, modernist upsurge against orthodox, conservative American values and Christian tradition. It was a drive to move Christianity away from its principal mission—to save souls; it was dominated by intellectual religious meddlers; it was antithetical to the American capitalist system; it promoted alien political philosophies such as socialism; it relegated Christianity to a social reform agency; it was sacrilegious quackery; it was, the evangelist said, "godless social service nonsense." So disdainful did Billy become over the Social Gospel movement and its proponents that he once called Gladden a "bald-headed old mutt."

It was one thing for a Christian to give a person on the skids a bath and bed for the night, Billy said; he had done that many times in his own work, had walked those back streets, those dim alleys of sin, and had helped many a man through a hopeless night. But the road into the kingdom of God is not by the bathtub, or the gymnasium, or the university, but by the "blood red hand of the cross of Christ." Gladden and his cohorts were not paying enough attention to individual salvation, were getting their priorities skewed.[25]

How should religion take on society's problems? Billy's views on the labor question are typical of his approach to many other issues. He had always considered himself a friend of the working-man, the "dinner-pail" American. And yet, he mistrusted organized labor and ridiculed the pro-labor efforts of left-wing political groups. They were, he said, unnecessarily interfering with traditional American institutions. The answers for the laboring man were not in agitation and striking but in finding God.

During his revivals, Billy's special labor team toured the factories and held meetings to enlist workers in the crusades, an effort which, not surprisingly drew the condemnation of leftist and labor spokesmen. The Sunday organization, they charged, was a tool being used by big business to quell the spirit of reform in the labor ranks. But Billy insisted that the only true reform could be in the personal salvation of both employer and employee.

Down with modernism; down with evolution; down with fuzzy liberal theology; down with the higher criticism; down with the Social Gospel; down with the furies of change pounding against old-time religion. Billy Sunday, this relatively uneducated, uncultured, simple evangelist from rural Iowa, had assumed unto himself the mantle of defender of the faith. Much of the controversy and intellectual wrestling was beyond his understanding, yet millions of Americans trusted him to make some sense out of the chaos and uncertainties of their time.

In his own way, Billy considered himself as much a reformer as the most ardent progressive. He deplored the poverty, the crime, the graft, and the corruption. He lashed out at the abuses of moneyed interests. He knew about the debased, wretched lives of people on skid row, had confronted the misery and degradation personally in his days with the YMCA. He knew drifters and whores and bums and winos and wanted desperately to help change their lives.[26]

But Billy's vision was rooted in premillennialist Protestantism, the belief that the Lord would return to wash away the sins of the world. In his sermon "The Second Coming of Christ," Billy scoffed at the notion that the world will "grow better and better" preparing the way for Christ's coming. No, the Bible teaches no such thing. Lawlessness will increase, vice and adultery, divorce and graft, unitarianism and all kinds of "tommyrot" will sweep the land until the Lord returns to bind Satan. Most social and governmental experimentation was, therefore, futile and misguided. Only through the rescuing of individual souls, the changing of individual lives, could there be lasting reform.[27]

Billy's vision was also focused strictly through the lens of conservative Protestant ethics and an unquestioning respect for the American economic system. The vision was clouded by dark fears of impending doom, the specter of forces which imperiled the American way, of alien philosophies and religious heresies and intellectual gibberish and smug, mean, contemptible enemies all striking at the things he and his fellow Americans held precious.

For Billy the revival tabernacle was the site of a holy war. His crusades sought to give refuge from the onslaught of those people and ideas that would destroy an Americanism he believed divinely guided. In his set of beliefs—the need for personal salvation, traditional Protestant ethics and values, the inerrancy of biblical Scripture, the rejection of modernism and secular philosophies, respect for American democracy and capitalism, and the preservation of American society on Christian principles—Billy had staked out a position very close to what would be called in the 1920s "fundamentalism."

For now, he was in full stride in his own battle to reform America. Behind all the corruption and poverty and waste plaguing the nation, Billy saw instruments of the devil. Society needed to be clean again, needed moral awakening. In the power of the Holy Word was the answer. For the nation there would be no cures for its ills until, as a people, it returned to "the old and sure paths that in other days have been the highways of our progress, our prosperity, and our peace."[28]

He would run his own reform campaign. He would tackle sin

and vice and personal corruption and moral dissolution. From the pulpit he would thunder the old truths, would strike out at people's failings and foibles, take on the liquor interests, the sin merchants, the decrepit habits that infected society, would beat down the anti-Christ with his huge biblical club. In these matters, the premillennialist preacher was perhaps the country's most ardent reformer.

6

Up with the Dukes, Devil!

You may barter your hope of eternity's morn,
For a moment of joy at the most;
For the glitter of sin and the things it will win—
Have you counted, have you counted the cost?

 —"Have You Counted the Cost," Sunday revival hymn[1]

The glitter of sin—humankind was awash in it, the "pleasure-mad throng" hurrying along a trail of degradation and shame, oblivious to the Cross, rejecting salvation, ignoring the final price that must surely be paid. The hymn told the ageless story of man's folly. For Billy Sunday this was the heart of the Christian message. In tabernacles across the country the evangelist charged into battle against sin; he was the moral spear-carrier of the Lord.

From the earliest days of American Protestantism, revivalists held fast to the belief that the universe was neatly divided between God and Satan, the elect and the damned, the pure and the despoiled. From Jonathan Edwards to Charles Finney to Lyman Beecher to Dwight Moody, Bible-clutching evangelists preached the complete authority of the Scriptures, the necessity of personal conversion, and a life free of vice. Personal and individualistic, evangelical Protestantism taught a close relationship between men and women and their God, challenging the sinner to renounce the ways of the devil and to repent. Personal salvation and moral responsibility—these were the demands on the faithful. "The Gospel is free as the air you breathe, and every man has an invitation to come and take of it," Moody exclaimed. "It is the sinner that God wants. There will be no peace for a man until his sin is put away."[2] For the wealthy as well as the poor, for the uprooted, the uneducated, the despairing, the unemployed, the sick, the underfed—the fields of plenty awaited, the rebirth, the salvation. It was all a matter of personal choice, of commitment, faith, and prayer.

The Keswick Movement, a religious program of spiritual renewal that began in England in the 1870s, emphasized strongly the toll that moral degeneracy had taken among Christians and the necessity of purifying religious life. Sanctification could only be achieved by breaking the gripping bonds of sin's slavery. The Keswicks had profoundly influenced Chapman, Billy's mentor. And Billy himself once said that it was his job to make it easier for sinners to do right and to make it more difficult for them to do wrong. "I will try," he said, "to disgust you with your sin until you turn away from it."[3] From the tabernacle stage the firecracker evangelist totally engaged audiences, locking them in awe and suspense as he wove his chilling tales of the devil's treachery, of the frailty of humankind, of torment and death to those who strayed.

Billy begins a story. The devil walks at the elbow of a husband on a downtown street on a Saturday night. A family man, temperate, industrious, a model father, he's entitled, says the wily Satan, to a little fun. Look over there at the grogshops, look at the alluring ladies, look at all the laughing and playing. He deserves that. The devil takes him into the bar and leads him through a rowdy night on the town. About midnight, delirious, broke, the man stumbles through his front door. His wife, tired from worrying and waiting, has gone to bed but has placed a chair in front of the door so that the noise would wake her when the husband returned. She planned to make him a late dinner. As he reels through the door into the living room, the good citizen and family man has taken on a fearful Hydian aspect—the beast has surfaced, the sense of right and wrong has evaporated, the spirit of the fiend is now dominant. Tripping over the chair, he explodes in a mad frenzy. As the wife rushes into the room, he strikes her a fearsome blow with his fist across her face. As she lay in her white nightgown on the floor, with his small child screaming "Papa! Papa! Don't hurt Mama!" the beast viciously kicks his wife with his heavy boots, cracking her ribs. Crazed, inflamed with the satanic fires, he then seizes the small girl and dashes her head against the stove. (At this point the preacher grabs a chair on the platform, swings it over his head, and smashes it to the floor, splintering the legs.) "And she lay there," the preacher howls, "with the blood and brains oozing through her golden curls." The police take the murderer away. From the scaffold where the executioner fits the noose around his neck and covers his head with a black hood, the man shrieks, "I'm coming to you, Devil, to thank you for your *fun*."

Billy believed in the devil and his power. To those modern preachers who shifted away from espousing the literal truth of the Bible, to the skeptics, philosophers, journalists, and teachers who suggested that the devil was merely some poetic personification of the idea of sin, Billy bristled. They were all rank, thieving hypocrites and they were all going to find out firsthand how literal, how real the devil really was because they were all going to hell.

In Billy's sermons, the devil became the arch-foe, the black villian against whom the evangelist pitted his own strength and resolve. Billy boxed him, taunted him, cursed him, spat at him, called him names—"cloven-hoofed, forked-tailed, blazing-eyed Old Devil." Billy's mood as he went after his super-enemy seemed to oscillate from an almost jocular, sporting tone to sobering, ominous warnings to sinners facing a hellish fall. Satan was smooth, cunning, slippery, unscrupulous, and totally evil. For Billy to face such an enemy was in itself an act of courage. But the evangelist was the gladiator of the Lord, carrying the great weapon of truth and righteousness—the Bible.

To the thousands who jammed the tabernacles, this preacher,

as none other, brought the old stories of heaven and hell, of God and the devil, and of man's duty to resist evil to a new vividness and intensity. They loved his show. He simply went further than other preachers, and did it with imagination and incredible energy. His stories of horror were shocking, his language salty, his impersonations skillful, his stage presence electrifying.

And, at all times, Billy exuded an aggressive, militant masculinity. To be a Christian was to be tough, a swashbuckler like Theodore Roosevelt—Teddy, hero of San Juan Hill, the president who fought prizefighters in the White House, the man who stalked wild beasts in foreign lands, rough, big stick, a battler. Billy's biblical hero was, naturally, David, conqueror of the mighty ogre, victor at long odds. His favorite hymn was "Onward, Christian Soldiers"—the army of the Lord marching to wipe out the enemies of God. Billy's sermons sounded the rough-hewn phrases of the prairie, told the stories of his own life as a young man struggling to make it on his own, stories of the glory days on the base paths, the crucial games, the pressure, the victories in the clutch, reminiscences about races won, about enemies challenged and humiliated, about rippling muscle and steely nerves. He carried his audiences on a panoramic sweep through a land of heroism—mythical heroes, biblical heroes, American heroes. The world sorely needed the fighters with giant hearts and unrestrained courage; it needed a leader, to confront sin with heavy guns. Billy was the man.

One writer who witnessed one of Billy's assaults on sin fairly gushed about the evangelist's masculinity: "He stands up like a man in the pulpit and out of it. He speaks like a man. He works like a man. . . . He is manly with God, and with everyone who comes to hear him. No matter how much you disagree with him, he treats you after a manly fashion. He is not an imitation, but a manly man giving to all a square deal."

During a Sunday foray into Philadelphia, Charles Trumbull, editor of the *Sunday School Times*, marveled at the heroic specimen on the platform, the taut muscles, the lightning flashes across the stage like a lithe Indian scout, the thrusts of the arms, the bodily grace. "I had realized," said Trumbull, "that here was a supernatural physical strength, given and used by God as the earthly vehicle of the supernatural spiritual strength that was overflowing."[4]

A reporter for the Spokane *Spokesman Review* remembered the evangelist, his collar wilted, voice hoarse, face scarlet, smashing the sides of the pulpit with thundering blows, exhorting the crowd, standing there with a defiant, almost contorted expression, completely absorbed in a fantasy world of combat. Tough. In one of his sermons, Billy contrasted the manliness of workingmen with their oppressive white-collar employers: "Men are feeding their muscles and bone and sinew into the commercial mill that grinds out the dividends . . . and the men who get the dividends sit by and watch it." These slackers riding the backs of others were pitiful excuses for men, said the evangelist; they were "big, fat, hog-jowled, weasel-eyed, pussy lobsters."

As Billy stood at the pulpit, the spokesman for the rough and fit and the gallant champion of strong Christians, he derided the mushy and lily-livered who had no place in the tabernacle; religion in here was no "dish-rag" proposition. "We've got to be more aggressive," he said. "Christianity is a battle and not a dream. . . . If many armies were officered like some of our churches, they would be defeated at the first pop of a gun." Moral warfare, this struggle against sin, needs disciplined troops, dedicated and aggressive. "Too much of the preaching of today," he said, "is too nice; too pretty; too dainty." It did not, he said, kill. In the tabernacle, this Christian knight with muscle was in charge. "Lord save us from off-handed, flabby-cheeked, brittle-boned, weak-kneed, thin-skinned, pliable, plastic, spineless, effeminate, ossified three-karat Christianity."[5]

As we have seen, when Billy began his religious ministry in the last years of the nineteenth century, evangelicals faced growing tensions. The dominant American culture now seemed to most evangelicals less ordered, less under control; individuals were more threatened. As the world drew menacingly closer, evangelicals needed someone to stand up for the traditional, old-time religion of sin and salvation.

To the thousands who flocked to Billy's revivals in cities and towns across the country and accepted him as their Christian moral warrior, he seemed close to God, knew God's wishes and commands, was God's messenger. People felt safer around Billy. Somehow he made the world seem a more familiar, predictable place, more distant from the distress and dislocation affecting society. If Billy pounded at them from the pulpit about the consequences of forsaking the Lord, if he rained down on them horrible stories of suffering and death caused by their sins, if he castigated them and ridiculed their foibles, he nevertheless made it easier for them. The evils in the world, in Billy's eyes, were uncomplicated and could be dealt with; they were the same ones their fathers and grandfathers had faced. War, poverty, disease—all of it was wrapped up simply in the evil of the devil and in man's own sin. And the answer was so simple, so available, so comforting. Give yourselves to the Lord, sinners, and all will be well. In the tabernacle this "giant for God" had the truths and the answers and the people listened.

As Billy, the Christian soldier, marched to war against sin, the campaign carried a sense of mythic and epic dimensions, as if his calling was to resurrect past and glorious values, to stand as the great defender at the wall of righteousness. He started with the Ten Commandments. At a rally in Toledo, Ohio, he opened a meeting talking at length about those fundamental biblical laws and asked all in the crowd who had broken any of them to stand up. Most everyone in the massive audience rose in unison and pleaded guilty. Billy prayed for them, prayed for the city of Toledo, for its mayor and city officials, for firemen, policemen, lawyers, just about everybody in all walks of life. One group of people Billy said he couldn't pray for were those engaged in the white slave traffic. He said he couldn't muster enough grace to ask for the redemption of these creatures but left it up to the Lord: "but Lord, save them, or if you can't save them, kill them."[6]

But the Ten Commandments were only the beginning. Billy's entire philosophical orientation revolved around nineteenth-century, rural, middle-class, Protestant ethics—thrift, perseverance, hard work, kindness, frugality, piety, decency, family responsibility, courtesy. America had been extraordinarily kind to Billy Sunday; it could be kind to all who gave themselves to the Lord and who followed His moral code. But such a code, aside from specific biblical injunctions such as murder, theft, and adultery, had not been laid out in explicit detail in the Scriptures. It was, therefore, the responsibility of the preacher to interpret God's will and to teach it to the multitudes. Billy had no difficulty understanding the truth, no hesitancy in revealing it to his flocks.

He called one of his early sermons "Moral Lepers." After describing how the insidious disease of leprosy spread over a sufferer's entire body destroying tissue, the evangelist declared, "So it is with sin." The growth of evil habits will surely infect the sinner like leprosy, he said, until the individual is no longer free but captive to its horrible effects. A life of sin begins with minor transgressions and with each new offense the degeneration races apace; the sinner plummets to the depths. "If you want to know why it doesn't rain when you want rain," Billy mused simply, "it's because you are too devilish."[7]

The disease of moral leprosy can only be cleansed by the act of repentance. The way to the Cross is not strewn with theological axioms or discourse or analysis but is a simple act of releasing one's self to the Lord's care. And the path is open for anyone to walk. A dwarf, Billy said, can as easily turn on an electric light in a room as can a giant. And to turn on heaven's light, a dwarf, as anyone else, must simply repent.

Although evangelists of earlier generations had fulminated mightily about numerous human failings and disgrace, from gambling and tobacco chewing to fornicating and drinking, none had ever matched the roar of Billy's moral cannon. As he marched his followers into the great war for morality, it was as if he saw before him a dreadful, disgusting sin monster, like a giant centipede with scores of wriggling legs, each representing an element of moral disgrace. So many sins! There were dancing and cardplaying and smoking and gossping and telling off-color jokes and billiard playing and birth control and undue attention to pets, especially dogs, and novel reading and licentious music and slander and selfishness and the theater and premarital sex and cursing and idleness and lust and greed and vanity—all these wriggling legs and a very large tail, LIQUOR. Billy went after those slimy legs and hideous tail with a ferociousness only he could bring to the kill. "I loaded my old muzzle-loading Gospel gun with ipecac, buttermilk, rough on rats, rock salt, and whatever else came handy, and the gang has been ducking and the feathers flying ever since."[8]

In one of his sermons in McKeesport, Pennsylvania, Billy told listeners to imagine they were inviting Jesus to their home and were making him a member of the family for a time. Jesus, said Billy, would have been a most irritating house guest. He would find beer in the refrigerator and throw it out and find cards on the dining room table and throw them out also. The nasty music on the piano would be cast away, as would the cigarettes and the novels. And how could Jesus tolerate a husband who cursed, played poker, and spent time with other women, who abused his wife and beat his children; how could He tolerate a wife who spent the family's money on "fool hats and card parties," who spent hours patting and smearing her face with rouge and lipstick, who gossiped and wasted time, who enrolled her children in dance schools and allowed them to associate with undesirable friends "whose character would make a black mark on some piece of tar paper?" How could Jesus tolerate a young boy who flipped pennies for money, read dime novels, and played marbles for keeps: how could He tolerate young girls who played jacks rather than dolls?

Billy saw in these early childhood diversions ominous trends toward other vices and a retreat from lofty ideals of decency and hard work. When Billy opened his Wichita, Kansas, revival in November 1911, the local newspaper, the *Beacon*, ran a story which seemed to capture the spirit of the times in which Billy found himself embroiled, the changing moral climate that made him so uneasy and defensive. In a public restaurant at the Bellevue-Stratford Hotel in Philadelphia, Mrs. Craig Biddle, of the illustrious Biddle family of Pennsylvania, bluebloods of the bluebloods, had drawn from a gold case a tiny roll of scented tobacco and had lit up. The world was tilting. Lop off those wriggling legs![9]

Before Billy Sunday, the most entertaining evangelist in the war for moral uplift had unquestionably been Sam Jones of Georgia. Like Billy, Jones saw religious denominations turning into "crocheting societies." Like Billy, he preached a militant brand of Christianity, attacking sinners on sundry dalliances from "high sawciety" dancing to "adulteress drama." Jones also attacked as a sin a certain sport. "There is not a more corrupting thing this side of Hell," said Jones, "than baseball."[10] Not surprisingly, Billy refused to include baseball in his own long litany of sins, except to say that it shouldn't be played on Sunday. But Billy's catalogue of moral crimes was indeed formidable and no one could go on the offensive like the ex–center fielder.

He especially liked to turn his firepower on dancing. The dance hall or even the ballroom was in Billy's eyes the next thing to a brothel, a place nurturing all the sensuous passions. Every woman who gave herself over to close dancing was edging very seriously toward whoring. "The dance is the dry-rot of society," he declared. To those who claimed that dancing was innocent and healthy exercise, Billy retorted: "If it's only a question of exercise let men dance with men and the women with the women and in two weeks every dance hall from New York to Frisco would be closed up." Such dances as the kangaroo, the jelly wabble, the snuggle, the kitchen sink, and "hell only knows what" were corrupting American youth. That low-necked, décolleté dress of the ballroom was, he noted, the invention of a prostitute in a Paris bordello.[11]

Billy was joined in his crusade against vice and sin by a formidable ally—his wife. Nell began to publish in newspapers across the country a series of essays directed at vulnerable young women. In this column called "Sisters of Folly," she published such musings as "The Girls Who Loved Actors," "The Woman Who Wore Low-Necked Dresses," and "The Woman Who Believed in Birth Control."

In an essay entitled "Hugging Alias Dancing," she described Gladys, a spirited young women entranced on the dance floor: "There was a pliant yielding to the man's embraces, a pressing closer and closer of her young body to his, a drooping of her red lips and a filling of her eyes, all of which told their own story."

Billy also tried his hand at capturing the essence of dancing. A man brings his wife to a dance, another man claims her hand, the husband watches as they two-step out on the dance floor, and, lost in a "voluptuous, sensual embrace, their bodies swaying one against the other, their limbs twining and intertwining, her head resting on his breast, they breathe the vitiated air beneath the glittering candelabra, and the spell of the music . . ."

It's no wonder that Billy began to suggest the virtue of a possible law prohibiting unmarried girls from engaging in dancing. He went even further; he objected to square dancing. "The swinging of corners in the square dancing," he reminded his listeners, "brings the position of the bodies in such attitude that it isn't tolerated in decent society." To those who considered his objections to square dancing somewhat extreme, Billy retorted: "They all look alike to me! There's many a short-cut, my friends, to round one."[12]

On the subject of swearing, Billy claimed that no man who wanted to be a good husband, a respectable citizen, or a gentleman should use gutter language. It was vile, disgusting, demeaning, and some of it was blasphemous. Cussing robs old men and young boys of both their public and private esteem, he said. God loathes it. Decent towns become Babylons infected with a "dirty, cussing, swearing gang of blacklegs on the street." Billy asked men in the tabernacles how they would feel if their wives or sisters suddenly began to curse. He said he knew a wife who once tried it out on her own husband, gave him some of his own medicine. "Why you old blankety, blank, blank, bald-headed blankety, blankety blank . . ." The husband was, Billy said, astonished.[13]

On the matter of the modern theater, Billy scored the playwrights who chose themes and language appealing to prurient interests. In times past, popular plays and their songs used to glorify the marriage relation, he said. Now, we hear songs in the theater as "My Wife Has Gone to the Country, Hurrah!, Hurrah!" and "I Love My Wife, But, Oh, You Kid!" Most plays were immoral, things of the devil, things driving audiences to sin and hell. He excluded Lew Wallace's *Ben-Hur* from his general indictment, citing this particular play's own moral spirit—a conscience-stirring testimony to the power of the Lord, a chariot race symbolic of the race of life, a victory over the lash of the tyrant. A hundred million people should see *Ben-Hur*, Billy exclaimed. But almost all other theater productions, nevertheless, were sordid.

The evangelist's attitude toward the theater elicited various counterassaults from members of the profession, especially the actor

Raymond Hitchcock. At the Detroit Opera House in March 1917, Hitchcock was starring in an English musical comedy called *Miss Betty*. During the curtain calls Hitchcock began to include a special twenty-minute, rollicking parody of Billy Sunday, a burlesque on the evangelist who would be Moral King. Billy was the P. T. Barnum of religion, said Hitchcock; Billy was the greatest showman on earth, the top actor on the Lord's stage, saving souls at $4 a head. Night after night Hitchcock mocked the evangelist. On one occasion a group of Sunday supporters heckled the actor during his remarks and their spokesman railed: "Your pleasantries don't conceal the fact that you are brazenly blaspheming." The hecklers then defiantly marched out of the opera house.

Hitchcock first decided to take on the evangelist publicly when he learned that Billy had asked 200 children at a rally in Boston to raise their right hands and pledge never to enter a theater. The actor ridiculed the proposition that men and women who attended the theater, even women who wore fashionable gowns, were going to hell for that reason. His mother had attended the theater, said Hitchcock, even in expensive gowns, and "I don't know who gave Billy Sunday any patent to say that my mother is in hell."[14]

Billy went after dog pamperers with special zeal, heaping scorn on women who spent inordinate time and effort and loving care in training, feeding, dressing, photographing, and playing with the creatures while many young children across the country went to bed hungry each night. "I like a good dog," said Billy, "but its place is in the kennel, not in your arms. It makes me sick to see a woman hugging a dog." "You women," Billy ordered, "do not waste the affection which God gave you on a spitz!" A husband's lack of affection to his wife, his cooling ardor, may be the result of his ignominious position as second fiddle to a crooked-nose pug. Too many women of wealth live vacuous lives, passing their time in a meaningless succession of inane pursuits, especially dog worship. "There are multitudes," said the evangelist, "whose horizon is bounded by pink teas and frappes."[15]

The cursed vices and sins are like vampires sucking the life-blood from America's youth, he said. Boys barely out of long breeches and frizzle-topped girls know more about evil today than their great-grandmothers did when they turned seventy years old. The street gutters, asylums, and hospitals are filled with the pathetic losers.

Often, when Billy had groups of children and teenagers in the tabernacle crowds, he would enlist Rodeheaver in the assault on sin and the devil. Rody relished the opportunity and he would tell gentle homilies on bad habits using little boy dolls named "Willie" and "Jimmie." All kinds of bad habits, Rody would explain, form themselves into a chain of character qualities that can strangle. Smoking, idleness, sloth—hideous sins lurked. He would then display a chain. Only Jesus could break the chain of sin, he would say, as he ripped it apart. For the children, for all of God's people, the road of sin into hell can only be avoided through repentance and saving grace.[16]

More sins. Birth control especially agitated Billy. Physicians, he pointed out, are known by the designation "M.D." In the case of those physicians who redden their hands with the blood of the unborn the designation, said Billy, should be changed to "D.M." or "Damnable Murderers." Birth control was unnatural, irreligious, sinful, another device of the devil. Women who lowered themselves to the use of pessaries had on them the mark of Cain. This godforsaken birth control destroyed life and encouraged prostitution. He quoted his hero Teddy Roosevelt to the effect that a woman so selfish as to refuse to have children was a criminal. Roosevelt was concerned that if respectable middle- and upper-class families began to practice birth control in great numbers, the country was in danger of a kind of "race suicide." The great increases in population, in other words, would not be from traditional, Protestant Americans but from the immigrant masses in the cities.

Billy was particularly acrimonious toward childless women who abandoned the responsibilities of motherhood and instead went about touring in automobiles, cruising in yachts, and hitting golf balls. "Society has put maternity out of fashion," he declared, and went so far as to charge that women who avoided motherhood through "the crime of murder committed to avoid maternity" were as much murderesses as if they had choked to death twelve-year-old children.[17]

Billy lamented the fall of young girls into prostitution. At times, he focused on the wayward transgressions that lured the girls into such a state in the first place—broken homes, suggestive movies, dance halls, an obsession with rouge and powder, alcohol. But he slashed especially hard at the pimps and so-called respectable businessmen who owned the whosehouses and saloons and dance halls. They were vipers, "despicable beasts," merchandising human beings for filthy lucre. "Some men are so rotten and vile that they ought to be disinfected and made to take a bath in carbolic acid and formaldehyde." To those who advocated segregated vice districts in cities, Billy had nothing but scorn. The business of vice is no different than the business of theft or the business of murder; the government should have no authority to sanction evil.

In many of his sermons, Billy lectured openly about venereal disease and the dangers of succumbing to pleasure of the flesh. Billy acknowledged that many preachers and editorialists had expressed shock and disgust over the evangelist's frank discussion of sexual practices from the revivalist pulpit. Talk of syphilis and whorehouses, some suggested, should not be subjects freely and explicitly flaunted from the tabernacle. Billy blasted back. He had read extensively the works of medical authorities, he said, and had reduced the scientific evidence to language understandable to average men and women. Physicians had told Billy that his advice given publicly from the pulpit could not have been better than the advice they could have given in a doctor's office. Somebody has to run the risk of incurring criticism from some "rattle-headed man or woman," he said, and predicted that there would be a time when sex hygiene would actually become part of high school curricula across the country. "I would rather have my children taught sex hygiene," said Billy, "than Greek and Latin."[18]

On and on the evangelist railed, from one moral failing to another, from seemingly innocuous practices to wretched crime. To Billy, they were all part of a terrible grab bag of snares and traps in society strangling unwary humans, all part of a hellish system of evil, the anti-Christ. This moral leprosy, this infectious disease and its ubiquitous germs, these sins inherited by sons from fathers, by daughters from mothers, sins of government and business, of individual weakness and passion—all of them were out there lurking. Lop off those wriggling legs!

Many in the tabernacles might have chuckled nervously when Billy carried on at length about cigarettes and slow dances and dog pampering. At the same time, they recognized his principal argument—that the relatively benign offenses were all part of a larger pattern, a matter of degree. What the sinner needed was discipline, rigorous conditioning in moral orthodoxy. A cigarette habit, a bit of social drinking, some swearing—they were all revealing of character in disintegration, those germs taking hold in the body, infecting, destroying. The tabernacle worshippers may have taken lightly some of the evangelist's admonitions but the sum of his assaults on sin took its toll. Most who left the revival meetings undoubtedly thought a little harder about their behavior; many tried to change. They and their sins always took a pounding from the preacher. In Fairfield, Iowa, Billy ended a prayer by giving the Almighty a pointer on how to save certain sinners: "Lord, wear rubber gloves."[19]

Billy's catalogue of acceptable moral conduct often sounded more like a lesson in good citizenship and decency than a call for spiritual rebirth. Some of his dictums, for example, are similar in spirit, if not in tone, to ones written nearly two centuries earlier, in 1746, in a work entitled "Rules of Civility." This document, whose origins of thought have been traced to a Jesuit essay written in Latin and to a popular English translation of a French book on conduct, prescribed such rules as the following: "Let your Recreations be Manfull not Sinfull" and "Labor to keep alive in your Breast that little Spark of Celestial fire called Conscience." There are many others in the work, including an injunction against cursing, all designed to turn society into a respectable, clean-living, decent, courteous, orderly, virtuous place, precisely the vision behind the Billy Sunday crusades many years later. If Billy had seen these rules of conduct (there is no evidence he did), he would have applauded the expressed sentiments; he was preaching many of the same things. He also would have been surprised at the authorship. The "Rules of Civility" were written by George Washington at the age of fourteen.[20]

In city after city, newspaper reporters, civic officials, and religious leaders reported new moral breezes in the air following Sunday revivals. In Spokane, an editor praised the zealous preacher who had held thousands of tabernacle visitors in his spell. "Mr. Sunday wages splendid warfare upon vice and evil, and at the same time is exalting righteousness in the home, in business, and in public service." The Spokane *Spokesman-Review* ran the headline: "Beer Sales Fall: Bibles in Demand."[21]

In Scranton, Pennsylvania, the Reverend Joseph Odell, pastor of the Second Presbyterian Church, talked of multitudes of people turning again to the Bible, of thieves repenting, of drunkards sobering, of a community growing brave against gambling and other vices.[22]

In Des Moines, Iowa, one minister waxed mightily on the effect Sunday's preaching had on individual behavior: employers seemed to treat employees a little better, wives and husbands seemed to act a little more civilly toward each other and their families. Billy Sunday, said the minister, is a "scourge for morality."[23]

In Fargo, North Dakota, the Sunday revival sparked a movement to curb the city's notorious "devil's half acre" of vice. The city passed a red-light abatement act penalizing owners of brothels and the police padlocked over seventy establishments within a year. One reporter wrote, "There is no gainsaying Sunday's influence upon community life, upon the family, and upon sobriety." Following the Pittsburgh revival in 1914 a newspaper proclaimed, "What Years of Reform Work Could Not Do, He Has Wrought in a Few Weeks." A few months after the Detroit revival, the Billy Sunday Club of Detroit announced that members would launch an evangelistic campaign among some of the nation's prisons, an effort to prepare inmates for reentering society again, to live moral lives, to give themselves to Christ.[24]

From Philadelphia to Columbus, from small towns to large cities came the stories of reformed lives. Charles Hesselgrove, pastor of the Central Congregational Church of South Manchester, Connecticut, wrote of Billy's tremendous effect on communities across the country. "His power as a leader in such moral reforms inspires both hatred and fear in those who fatten on the weaknesses and vices of their fellow men." Thousands of individuals who had lost their grip on basic moral values, said Hesselgrove, had been given new strength and resolve by the Sunday crusades.[25]

Three years after a Sunday revival in Decatur, Illinois, a religious writer returned to the city to measure, as best he could, the lingering effects. His conclusion: "The civic life of Decatur is still on a plane appreciably higher than that of its sisters." There was still in Decatur, he said, much of the civic uplift and righteousness that had pervaded the city during the Sunday revival.[26]

Another religious writer compared Billy to the Roman poet Juvenal, who had fearlessly attacked the vices of imperial Rome eighteen centuries earlier. As in Rome, vast riches had accumulated in the United States, much of the wealth unscrupulously raked in through corruption and fraud. Just as Rome had sunk morally into a cesspool of sin, the United States faced the same danger. Billy, like Juvenal, was a voice of censure and warning.[27]

Although impressionistic, such reports of Billy's influence on the moral tone of cities and towns in which he conducted crusades drove many local officials and business leaders to form committees, gather petitions, and solicit funds to encourage the revivalist to add their own communities to his schedule. When the journalist John Reed traveled to Philadelphia to cover the Sunday revival for *Metropolitan Magazine*, he interviewed a man named Alba B. Johnson, president of the Baldwin Locomotive Works. Johnson, who had the most "businesslike set of cold eyes" Reed had ever seen staring through spectacles, was one of the civic and industrial leaders who had combined their forces to lure Billy to Philadelphia.

Reed asked Johnson why these city leaders were so anxious to get Billy Sunday to their hometown. Johnson replied that he and the others had long believed that the country desperately needed a "moral awakening," a resurgence of purity, thrift, and those virtues which the American people had always treasured but which had been crumbling in an avalanche of extravagance and a whirl of corruption. The laboring classes were now filling low-class saloons and dance halls and the fashionable elements of society were drowning in ostentation and indolence. The moral standard of the American people was at stake. Immoral plays, immoral clothes, immoral talk—immorality was sapping the strength of the people and Americans needed an injection of old-fashioned religious values. "What we need in this country," Johnson told Reed, "is a Moral Influence." Philadelphia called for Billy Sunday.[28]

Ministers in Spokane had said almost exactly the same thing a few years earlier. Spokane then was in a crisis, said Dr. E. L. House, pastor of Westminster Congregational Church. The young men of the city seemed especially hellbent on moral decay—drinking, carousing, gambling, fornicating, swearing. C. Ross Baker of Spokane's Emmanuel Baptist Church announced that the city needed a "mighty moral upheaval"; it needed purification of its social mores, its business ethics, and its open vices of gambling, drinking, and prostitution. Spokane also called for Billy Sunday.[29]

This call for the moral crusader was, of course, not universal. Many liberal religious leaders of various sects and denominations, some labor spokesmen, left-wing political philosophers and politicians, editorialists, pundits, and scores of skeptics and individuals whose businesses were hurt by the evangelist all denounced the Sunday revival as a circus, a fraud, a religious charade.

The staff of Princeton University, bastion of evangelical Christian tradition, voted in 1915 not to invite the evangelist to their hallowed institution. Professor Andrew F. West, acting as spokesman for the university, cited Billy Sunday's "travesties of the teaching of Christ" as the central reason Princeton refused to give him its imprimatur. If Billy was in some ways a positive moral force in the community, that force was, said West, overwhelmed by his vulgarity and perversion of the Bible and his downright bad taste. West told of a case in which Billy pictured Christ in prayer, lamenting the foibles of women: "Ladies," said Christ, "Do you want to look pretty. If some of you women would spend less on dope, pazaza, and cold cream, and get down on your knees and pray, God would make you prettier." Very funny, said West, and very blasphemous.[30]

Princeton's rebuke of Billy was not surprising. The religious scholars and theologians of the institution could not be expected to condone Billy's irreverence, his slick salesmanship, or his impieties. West and his colleagues were understandably aghast at some of the evangelist's slang, vituperation, and fanciful depictions of biblical stories and his liturgical outrages. They also were totally repulsed by the evangelist's attacks against liberal theologians and the established clergy. Who was this vulgar barbarian to assail respected teachers and pastors with his outrageous, coarse insults and billingsgate? One minister, calling the Sunday revival a "vaudeville extravaganza," suggested that Billy needed the traditional treatment meted out to children who used vulgarisms—to have his mouth washed out.[31]

Billy's fiery manner and style, his lack of sound theological grounding, his brash militancy and anti-intellectualism, the whole essence of his revival approach seemed a colossal affront to almost everything for which they stood. For the theologians, the black irony of it all was the evangelist's enormous popularity, not only with vast numbers of tabernacle worshippers but with other religious figures.

From a poll of editors of religious periodicals of various denominations in 1915, the *Literary Digest* announced these results: Out of 127 editors interviewed, 56 gave Billy Sunday an unqualified endorsement; 43 favored the evangelist with some reservations; and 28 flatly opposed his work. The principal reasons for the support of Billy, concluded the *Literary Digest*, were the beliefs that that evangelist was earnest and sincere, and that he was on a mission for spiritual and moral uplift. Most of all, the cities and towns which had experienced a Sunday revival seemed the better for it. Saloons and vice dens immediately appeared on the run when Billy hit town, said most of the religious journalists.[32]

It was not just the support of those editors polled by the magazine that Billy enjoyed but the adoration of thousands of clergymen across the country, pastors who closed down their own churches during Sunday revivals, who worked on local arrangement committees for the revivals, who enthusiastically praised Billy's work. When Billy arrived with his troops, it was as if a mighty force of religious euphoria had taken over the community—the extraordinary press coverage, the excited crowds, the massive tabernacle, almost eerie in its shape and size, the air of expectancy, the sense of change, of new beginnings. When Billy came to town much of everything else seemed to pause or stop.

When Washington Gladden, a Columbus, Ohio, minister and prominent Social Gospel leader, refused to endorse Billy's Columbus campaign, some local religious leaders defended the evangelist. Alfred Isaac, minister of the Tenth Avenue Baptist Church, wrote, "I have talked with men of intelligence and sanity, and they all have the highest regard and warmest admiration for him." The moral and ethical results of Billy's work, said Isaac, were "overwhelming." Another friend of Gladden heard Billy speak in Wheeling, West Virginia, and had also been amazed by the evangelist's power. "He is stirring the hearts of the people of all classes as no man ever has."[33]

Billy totally lacked the theological training Professor West and his Princeton colleagues were instilling in their own students; he lacked doctrinal consistency, philosophical insight, an understanding of social and cultural forces at work in society, a knowledge of history, an appreciation of any intellectual pursuit. And yet, he had, as no other religious figure, drawn close to millions of Americans. A visitor to the tabernacle, packed together with thousands of others, gained at least for the moment a sense of community. The evangelist in action on the platform seemed instinctively to understand the crowd's fears and emotions, their longings, and the pressures they all felt to survive, to cope. "I know men," Billy said, "I know their trials, their temptations, and I know there are men in Hell tonight who never meant to be there, any more than you do."[34]

Whatever his failings, Billy believed he was fulfilling a Divine mission, believed he was helping folks in the tabernacle face the ultimate truths in their lives. America had lost her way, Billy said. Thirty years ago, he said, you couldn't find many boys on the streets drinking, running in gangs, and uttering obscenities. Thirty years ago families were more stable. There is now much Sodom in America, he said, and he was there to take it on. He was the messenger sent to fight sin, to point the way to salvation; he was there to lead the way to a moral awakening, to forge a common religious cause and ethical foundation.

"When is a revival needed?" Billy asked. It is needed when the forces of evil overwhelm the power of the church; when the people slumber in degradation; when amusements and alliances and vice gain allegiance over the souls of men; when Christians lose the power of prayer; when the great weight of wickedness bears heavily on individuals and they feel lost and desperate; when it's time to fight back.[35]

Billy was there to take on the devil, to bolster faith in the wayward, inspire the slumbering, lead the aimless; he was there to rock the tabernacle with spirit, to offer hope to people that it was now possible to change direction and face the threats and the fears, possible for them to charge back into life with resurgent energy. "So you people are being choked to death trying to gulp down the forbidden things of the world. It may take some of the good hard clapboard raps of the gospel to dislodge it, but I have come as your friend to help you and I hope I might."[36]

The moral crusade thundered on, all those wriggling legs of sin and vice slashed and ripped by the Lord's warrior. But the biggest vice of all, the infamous evil that threatened the moral underpinnings of society, loomed ahead for the crusader—the centipede's giant tail, alcohol. For this disgusting enemy the evangelist was ready with all his weapons.

7

Away, John Barleycorn!

One that hath wine as a chain about his wits,
such an one lives no life at all.

—Alcaeus, *c.* 620–*c.* 580 B.C., from *Demetrius: On Poems*

O thou invisible spirit of wine! If thou has no
name to be known by, let us call thee devil!

—William Shakespeare, 1564–1616, from *Othello*

Liquor is the bloodsucker of humanity; it is God's
worst enemy and hell's best friend.

—William Ashley Sunday, 1862–1935, from speech in Atlanta

Billy Sunday had ole John Barleycorn in his sights. Rum, the preacher believed, was indeed a demon. Spirituous liquors were the devil's most vile instruments of torture and death, sinking good men and women into perdition, destroying their souls, corrupting and wrecking their lives. The brewers and distillers and saloon owners were no less than handmaidens of hell, sucking the lifeblood from American moral and social institutions as they filled their filthy pockets.

Billy saw the saloon as the most insidious evil in America, the "parent of crimes and the mother of sins." It fathered violence and broke families apart; it harbored prostitution and filled insane asylums; it wrapped its hideous tentacles around American institutions and economic systems; it perverted religion; it filled the land with "misery, and poverty, and wretchedness, and disease, and death, and damnation." Billy had no greater foe than John Barleycorn and he and John B. were in for a long, heavy-hitting battle.

Legions of warriors had marched into combat against the demon over the centuries. They had pleaded and preached, appealed to reason and religion, fired off volleys of morality, knifed at the beast with laws, tried to scare and intimidate his followers. John B. lived; he prospered, glass upraised.

From the earliest days of American society the consumption of alcoholic beverages was deeply ingrained in the culture. Most Americans considered drinking neither dangerous nor evil. Indeed, some of the colonial laws referred to liquor as "the good creature of God." Men, women, and children of all ages swilled great quantities of the creature almost with abandon. Physicians prescribed various alcoholic mixtures, tonics, tinctures, elixirs, and the like for toothaches, broken limbs, colds, and snakebite. Toddies of rum and water, for example, were just the thing to quiet unruly babies. For any and all health and psychological disorders, alcohol was the answer.

The Pilgrims found their "aqua vitae" (probably Hollands gin) a most effective device in negotiating Indian treaties. The great Indian chief Massasoit, colonial historians reported, seemed much more cooperative after downing "great draughts" that "made him sweate all the while after."

Even the Puritans, so careful to forbid many pleasurable activities, allowed liquor to go relatively unregulated, aside from ordinances against public drunkenness. When the good ship *Arabella* sailed into Massachusetts Bay the holds sloshed with 42 tons of beer and 10,000 gallons of wine. Hard drinkers, the Puritans were the first distillers of rum in America. As an old colonial verse recounted:

> *It was often said, that their only care,*
> *And their only wish, and only prayer,*
> *For the present world, and the world to come,*
> *Was a string of eels and a jug of rum.*[1]

The colonial clergy inbibed heartily along with the other members of society. Indeed, bottles of whiskey were often encased in the cornerstones of newly built churches as symbols of thanksgiving for God's blessings. At the ordination ceremonies of the Reverend Edwin Jackson of Woburn, Massachusetts, in 1729 the celebration required six and a half barrels of hard cider, two gallons of brandy, four gallons of rum, and twenty-five gallons of wine.[2]

For the clergy as well as other Americans, liquor was plentiful. From applejack or "Jersey Lightning" to a gin sometimes called "Blue Rum" or "Strip and Go Naked," the potables were cheap and very potent. From a tumbler of rum or whiskey in the morning as an "eye-opener" to breakfasts which might include whiskey, fruit cordials, Dutch-brewed beer, gin, or hard cider to "leven o'clock bitters" in late morning to lunches spiced with assorted concoctions made with rum and brandy and beer to dinners with wine and whiskey and brandy to bedtime nightcaps, Americans drank.

The most famous drink of early America was probably the rum flip, a mind-numbing combination of rum, beer, and sugar stirred with an iron poker called a loggerhead. Bitter, with a slightly burnt taste, the drink was extraordinarily potent. Too much of the stuff could easily drive individuals to disagreements and brawls, sometimes with the loggerheads used as weapons—thus the expression "at loggerheads."

In 1792 the United States could boast over 2,500 registered distilleries to serve a population of around four million. According to tax assessors, the per-capita consumption for every man, woman, and child came to 2½ gallons per year. In the next several decades that figure nearly doubled.[3] From rural farmhouses to city taverns, from isolated mountain cabins to the fine tables of Washington's Mt. Vernon, they drank.

A few lonely voices cried out in protest. Increase Mather and his son, Cotton Mather, eminent Puritan clergymen, preached often against intemperance, warning that the fabric of New England society seemed vulnerable to the excesses of drinking. In his private journal and from his pulpit, Cotton Mather lamented that the flood of spirituous liquor threatened to drown Christian society, that intemperance was driving men and women from the folds of the church, that the colonial government must more adequately deal with the problem of drunkenness, must regulate taverns and tippling houses, must somehow deal with the unquenchable thirst before it became an unsolvable national vice.

In 1774 the Quaker school teacher and abolitionist Anthony Benezet published anonymously America's first temperance pamphlet. It was called *The Mighty Destroyer Displaced, In some Account of the Dredful Havock made by the mistaken Use as well as Abuse of Distilled Spirituous Liquors*. Personally gentle, deeply religious, the Philadelphia Quaker was an ardent reformer, carrying on an indefatigable crusade not only against liquor but against slavery, against violations of the rights of Indians, and against other vices he believed were infecting American society. Benezet saw intemperance as a moral and religious plague, an evil, menacing and destructive.[4]

As various temperance leaders and organizations emerged in the coming decades, they would sound the same kinds of urgent calls for reform as did Benezet, would marshal, as he did, moral and religious arguments, would strike the same uncompromising posture. The liquor traffic was a horrible affront to religious dictates and a despoiler of human dignity and must be obliterated. Billy Sunday would later sound the same alarm.

In 1785 Dr. Benjamin Rush, a friend of Benezet and also an abolitionist, authored a pamphlet entitled *An Inquiry into the Effects of Ardent Spirits on the Human Body and Mind*. Rush brought to this long essay of nearly forty pages a scientific attack of devastating intensity: liquor was the cause of many diseases and aggravated others; it had no value as a source of food; it caused psychological disorders; it caused crime. Published many times over the next twenty years, Rush's hefty essay was welcome ammunition to fledgling reformers. The essay added a frightening dimension to the religious and moral arguments marshaled earlier by Benezet, the Mathers, and others. Intoxication was not only religiously reprehensible and morally debasing, it was dangerous. With Rush's essay, the drive to ameliorate the terrible effects of hard drinking would gain momentum. A succession of associations, reformers, church leaders, preachers, circuit riders, and civic officials would build on Rush's work.[5]

In the small timberland town of Moreau in upstate New York, a twenty-three-year-old physician named Billy James Clark had read Rush's pamphlet. For the millworkers and loggers of Moreau, the rugged days on the job gave way to the nights in the town's six taverns, one of which was close to Clark's house. As he read, Clark recognized in many of his neighbors the symptoms of alcohol abuse. The favorite libation in Moreau, consumed not only by lumberjacks but by their wives and children, was a rum fustian, a devastating combination of rum, sherry, gin, beer, egg yolks, and nutmeg. The entire town, Clark concluded, was in a dazed stupor.

On April 30, 1808, forty-three men led by Clark met at a schoolhouse to form the first formal temperance organization in the United States—the Union Temperance Society of Moreau and Northumberland. The members pledged to fight in their community not only against hard liquor but also against wine. They pledged personal abstinence—if caught drunk they were fined and made to take oaths of reformation.

After the founding of the Moreau society, other groups formed in the next decades, some branching out from their own small communities to include neighboring counties. In Connecticut, Massachusetts, Rhode Island, New York, Vermont, New Hampshire, Maine, and Pennsylvania temperance organizations followed on the trail carved by Clark. The members drew up articles of intemperance detailing the economic and moral outrages of alcohol, and many articles written by society members began appearing in religious periodicals. The leaders of the reform groups grew increasingly confident that a mighty national war was imminent, pitting the forces of morality and decency and religious truth against the forces of evil.

It wasn't. Most of the organizers of the societies had little or no political experience or influence. Instead of drawing to their lofty banner streams of converts, they often drew ridicule. And when some of the societies did gain strength they also gained political opposition. In 1823 the *Boston Recorder* reported that the temperance reform effort was woefully feeble, drowned in apathy and failure. "Their influence was gone," declared the paper, "even sooner than their names."[6]

Into the breach charged a revivalist preacher. Lyman Beecher, fiery and humorless, was an orator who could fashion images so terrifying that congregations would drop to their knees wailing and shuddering in fear, whose frowning brow and icy-gray hair slinking down to his collar framed a countenance that warned of doom. To Beecher the fight for temperance was not merely a wistful stab at modifying some people's habits; it was not merely a matter of medical consideration; it was not just statistics and science and an alteration of social behavior—it was an injunction from the Almighty, a matter of personal salvation, rescuing lost wayfarers from the bottomless pit, of opening the gates locked by an unmitigated evil.

Beecher's postmillennialist inclinations made his attack on liquor a driving cause. Just as he had assailed infidelity and gambling and other social ills, he attacked drunkenness as a violation of God's law, an offense that had to be cleansed from the land with vengeance. It was the role of the preacher to prepare the way for the Lord's coming, to rid humankind of vice and darkness.

In a blistering series of six sermons delivered in Connecticut and later published in 1826, Beecher lashed out at the liquor menace, urged abstinence, and called for "the banishment of ardent spirits from the list of lawful articles of commerce." To sell liquor, Beecher proclaimed, was unlawful in the eyes of God. Beecher's words would later be the words of Billy Sunday.[7]

At the same time that Beecher's sermons circulated in New England, the Reverend Justin Edwards, pastor of the Congregational Church in Andover, Massachusetts, rallied several friends and fellow ministers and on February 13, 1826, they founded in Boston the first national temperance organization—the American Society for the Promotion of Temperance. The organizers hoped to gather recruits for a national effort to drive the stake through John Barleycorn—no compromises, no retreat, no backsliding, no mercy for the devil's brew.

The national temperance drive, fueled mostly by the energies of evangelical Protestants, grew during a period when other reform efforts were being launched, many under the leadership of religious figures and organizations. The welfare of women and children, the question of slavery, the condition of paupers and the insane—all were targets of humanitarian reform. All these reform efforts were grounded in the belief that society must be cleansed. [8]

Through the Civil War years the movement waned. The temperance forces, nevertheless, regrouped and began to wage war on a new front. At a convention in Chicago in September 1869, leaders from such temperance organizations as the Independent Order of Good Templars, the Sons of Temperance, and the Temple of Honor met to form the Prohibition party. Temperance leaders thus entered the political world riding a dominant moral cause.

American women also played a significant role in the movement. In November 1874, 135 women representing 17 states met in Cleveland to form the National Woman's Christian Temperance Union (WCTU). Begun as a religious and moral movement to guard families against the terrible effects of alcoholism, the Union developed sophisticated techniques of lobbying and strove to secure a national constitutional amendment, a drive to which Billy Sunday would later become strongly committed.

During the 1880s and 1890s, a number of states and communities enacted prohibition and local-option laws allowing individual districts to ban the sale of alcohol. The wets were now on the run, at least in scattered communities. For thirsty teetotalers there was now instead of the rum demon Dr. Samuel F. Stowe's "magic fluid," his "Ambrosial Nectar," a fragrant, wholesome brew extracted from medicinal roots and berries. The good doctor from Providence called the beverage "The Great Temperance Drink." America's saloon-keepers did not rush to stock the magic in great quantities. [9]

In 1893, at the same time Billy Sunday was trading the life of baseball for that of religious service, the most powerful temperance organization ever assembled joined the great cause—the Anti-Saloon League. One of the League's founders, the Reverend Francis Scott McBride, wrote, "The League was born of God."

Formed largely by affiliations of Methodists, Congregationalists, and other evangelical denominations, the League was a potent force; its fight, in the words of one of its leaders, Ernest Cherrington, was "the fight of the organized church forces against the organized liquor forces." The League established local organizations

Billy Sunday, an Iowa teenager, 1884. (Grace College Library, Winona Lake, Indiana)

The fastest man in baseball: Billy Sunday in his early days with the Chicago White Stockings. (National Baseball Hall of Fame Library, Cooperstown, New York)

The rising evangelist star: Billy Sunday in 1906. (Grace College Library, Winona Lake, Indiana)

MOTHER EARTH

VOL. X.   MAY, 1915   No. 3

BILLY
SUNDAY
TANGO

Ridicule from the Left: Billy's Tango. (*Mother Earth*, Vol. 10 [May 1915], copy in Library of Congress, Washington, D.C.)

The evangelist as portrayed by the artist George Bellows
at the Philadelphia Revival of 1915. (National Portrait Gallery,
Smithsonian Institution, Washington, D.C.)

Inside a Sunday tabernacle. (Grace College Library, Winona Lake, Indiana)

As powerful on the outdoor stump as in the tabernacle, New York, 1917. (Grace College Library, Winona Lake, Indiana)

Practicing his moves in a hotel room. (Library of Congress, Washington, D.C.)

On the Pullman Plush: The ex–White Stocking returns to Chicago, ca. 1918. (#000565; Chicago Historical Society, Chicago, Illinois)

The Lord's master of ceremonies: Homer Rodeheaver.
(Archives of the Billy Graham Center, Wheaton College,
Wheaton, Illinois)

across the country to agitate for local-option and statewide prohibition laws.[10]

If the prohibition movement had powerful organizations to attack the liquor interests, it also had colorful warriors: Frances Willard, independent, resourceful leader of the WCTU; Carry Nation, tireless agitator, hatchet wielder, wrecker of saloons for the glory of the Lord; William E. ("Pussyfoot") Johnson, master orator and publicist for the Anti-Saloon League; Wayne Wheeler, general counsel of the Anti-Saloon League, a man who promised, "We'll make them believe in punishment after death!"[11] And out in Nebraska a noted teetotaling politician declared his support for local option. His name was William Jennings Bryan. "The Great Commoner" and Billy Sunday would later march side by side.[12]

The temperance movement had many of its roots in evangelical Protestantism and many of its titans and their followers were zealous crusaders marching behind a banner of righteousness. Liquor became the personification of evil; to make war against it was Christian duty, to defeat it a panacea.

If cities were choking in industrial smoke and shameful immorality, if strange, new peoples and alien languages and political philosophies cast an eerie cloud over traditional America, there had to be reasons. If economic misery strangled the nation, if families split apart, if crime increased and suicides were on the rise, there had to be answers. For many, the greatest of the reasons was liquor; the most urgent of the answers was to wipe it out. Liquor became, as Billy said, "the sum of all villanies."

Since the beginnings of his evangelistic work, Billy, as any good premillennialist, had always emphasized that saving souls was his great calling. From midwestern towns to eastern cities, from one revivalist tent to another wooden tabernacle, the sinners strode down the sawdust trail, the pledge cards multiplied, souls were saved. And Billy was counting.

But especially in the case of the prohibition movement, Billy, despite his premillennialist leanings, was out to change society, at least the behavior of individuals in it. To Billy, the temperance movement was merely a part of the mission to save souls; the preacher's duty was to get out into the world, to attack this kind of institution that stood in the way of Christian ideals. If men and women were sinking into a moral abyss, Billy would try to lift them up, change their ways, bring them to the Lord.

But Billy's range of reform was narrowly focused. As the many reform efforts of the Progressive era such as child welfare and various workers'-rights legislation were debated in the state legislatures and in the halls of Congress, Billy stood aside. He was honing in on John Barleycorn, the curse, he believed, of all curses. The preacher on several occasions did publicly declare himself in favor of women's suffrage but his support on that issue arose directly from the prohibition fight. Women, as defenders of the family, of purity, and of moral uplift, would, Billy concluded, be a key to enacting the prohibition legislation he so passionately supported. Billy was firmly convinced that abolishing liquor would melt away many of the ills destroying traditional America, and especially the family.

Billy stood for the protection of an American way of life he saw under assault, the way of sentimental, commonsense, middle-class values, of rigid Protestant ethics, of respectability and dependability and moral courage, of individual initiative, of the family. One temperance poster proclaimed, "Defective Children Increased with Alcoholization of Fathers." Fighting for prohibition was fighting for the purity of the family, fighting to preserve the most treasured of America's institutions.[13]

From his days with the Chicago White Stockings and his romps in the tenderloin, Billy had seen firsthand what alcohol could do. It had robbed men like Mike "King" Kelly of their youth, their careers, and their lives. A number of the players on that great team had succumbed to alcoholism and died from its complications and Billy had seen a few of them shortly before their deaths. The strapping athletes he had known had degenerated into wheezing, coughing wrecks of men. In his missionary work with the YMCA, Billy had counseled gutter bums and tramps and winos, had watched men squander savings in two-bit dives, had seen the squalor and licentiousness and vice in the red-light districts, had been to hospitals and asylums and listened to the wretched stories of souls lost to alcohol.

In the early years of his evangelistic career, Billy made temperance a common theme in his sermons. Increasingly, he became more strident, more politically aware of the wet versus dry battles in whatever cities or towns his crusade had reached. Always suspicious and mistrustful of the masses of foreigners crowding into America, Billy often warned of "the foreign vote" that threatened prohibition fights across the country. He once declared, "It will take a great Anglo-Saxon majority to overcome this foreign influence." The outsiders, Billy believed, were easily susceptible to alcoholism and to the political muscle of the liquor business interests.

In early revivals in Iowa he encouraged city leaders to enforce laws regulating saloons. Later, he began to work with temperance officials in using his meetings as forums for local-option movements. In all the meetings the crowds eagerly flocked to hear his "Booze Sermon."[14]

The "Booze Sermon"—actually it was called "Get on the Water Wagon," but over the years friend and foe began calling it by the more popular title, sometimes with the adjective "famous" attached: the "Famous Booze Sermon." It changed only slightly over the years, its whip-cracking message just as effective in New York in 1917 as in Spokane. The sermon was copyrighted, printed numerous times, and published in newspapers and periodicals.

The long exposition was filled with almost every argument, assertion, charge, and insult on which the preacher could lay his hands. Attacking biblically, morally, and economically, gliding from statistical compilations to homilies to pleading to old-fashioned character assassination, Billy bore in with his full arsenal, sprucing up the pejorative adjectives, intensifying the visions of gloom awaiting transgressors, spicing the delivery with quotes, allusions, quips, and barnyard slang.

The liquor traffic is, he said, the "most damnable, corrupt institution that ever wriggled out of Hell and fastened itself on the public." Fighting the accursed beast is a matter of decency and manhood; it is beyond political parties or ideology; it is goodness and right against poverty, evil, and crime.

And then a barrage of figures gleaned by the evangelist and his team from scores of early-twentieth-century publications—75 percent of all idiots come from intemperate parents; 82 percent of all poverty can be attributed to the same menacing influence. The annual drink bill for New York City is six times the value of all the silver mined in the country in one year, and four times the annual output of gold. The approximately 250,000 saloons in the United States, allowing for fifty feet of frontage for each, would stretch from New York to Chicago. If the statistics were suspect and even peculiar, plucked from snippets of newspaper articles, books, speeches, and offhand remarks, the total assault was formidable, mashing and grinding everything in its path.

End the nefarious liquor business, Billy argued, and the states would have far fewer mental incompetents for whom to care, far fewer criminals to prosecute. End the business and fewer families would disintegrate. Out of the shadow of drink we must ascend, beyond the prostrate bodies of the sick and dying, the purple-faced drunkards who crawl away to face the jaws of doom. Walk to the sunlight of reform of Christian renewal.

Story after pitiful story he recounted: a young man from a good family falls under liquor's spell and in a drunken rage kills his best friend on a public street; another man of sound background gets tanked, takes up with a prostitute, quarrels, chases her with a gun, and accidentally shoots a mother holding her baby; another young man, delirious, demands money from his mother for more booze, seizes a hatchet when she refuses, and kills her. On and on the sordidness and filth and misery march, a parade of suffering and woe orchestrated by the strutting, smirking maestro, the evil one, alcohol.

God's most sacred institution, Billy asserted, is the home. Here is the haven to protect against the arrows of life, a harbor in the storm. Here are nurtured purity, fellowship, and religious spirit. Alcohol, rearing its obscene form from the scalding sewers of hell, attacks the home insidiously, strikes at the foundation of American values. See the father stopping at the infernal saloon on his way home, dropping his wages into alcohol's rat hole of disease and damnation. See the wife and children, penniless, forlorn, driven to despair by the father's addiction. The saloon: assassin!

But the awful thing will perish, will shrink under the withering retribution of the Almighty. It will die from the forces of decent society, God's messengers, an army of righteousness hacking down the liquor enemies infesting society. Of all his sermons, this was the most violent. The wicked form of liquor must be put to the sword, slain with vengeance, executed. "I have no interest," Billy once said, "in a God who does not smite."[15]

Join the booze fighters on the water wagon, join the crusade, trade in the sordid habits for the clean, take those dollars and buy pork or calico or homes and keep the money from the whiskey gang; do something for yourself and your God.

The shameful stories would rain down again as Billy wound up his attack. A little boy on crutches pounds at a minister's door screaming that his father had just murdered his mother. At the jail the confessed killer declares, "I don't blame the law, but it breaks my heart to think that my children must be left in a cold and heartless world. Oh, sir, whiskey did it." At the funeral, the orphans of the executed man shriek in agony. The police bury their faces in their hands. The preacher in the story falls on his knees, clenches his fist, and swears before God and the whiskey-ruined family that he will fight the liquor menace for the rest of his days.

Billy then plunged into a nauseating recitation of the effects of alcohol on the human body, about blood corpuscles withering, about rotten tissue, about strawberry noses and vile stomachs and paralyzed nerves and dead livers and even bad breath. Rise from the pit of drunkenness, he would say, reach above the slime to the light. Billy called for men to show their strength of will. Throw off your slavery, show your manhood, stand up to the curse. "In the name of your pure mother, in the name of all that is good and noble fight the ogre." Act, you men, act with your ballots, vote out the legislators who support the whiskey crowd, defeat the swine, act before the saloons spew out husbands and their sons "and send them home maudlin, brutish, devilish, vomiting, stinking, bear-eyed, bloated-faced drunkards."

Like a thunderous, roaring freight, Billy rolled over the land-scape of American values, morals, economics, and religion, whack-ing at the liquor devil. If America was mired in poverty, crime, family disintegration, and moral decay, the greatest nemesis was liquor. Stamp out the dastardly evil or lose American society and your very souls.[16]

The "Famous Booze Sermon"! Over and over again through the years, the speech electrified, seared, and shocked audiences. Billy's virulence, stirring invective, zeal, and pathos were all there, packaged to great effect. Temperance leaders and civil officials praised the evangelist at every stop, testifying that the speech and his other efforts against liquor had breathed life into the dry army, had aroused public sentiment. Pro-liquor spokesmen attacked the preacher as a demented, misguided lout, a demagogue peddling lies. Billy never backed off. "When I go into the ring with old John Barleycorn," he declared, "they will find me on my feet, my wind good and ready to go the limit."[17]

In Ohio in 1910, the brewers and distillers were on the run. Not only were the temperance crusaders at their throats; so was buttermilk. The *American Issue,* the periodical of the Anti-Saloon League, hailed the drink from the churn as the new national bev-erage. So popular was buttermilk that even saloons began to dis-pense the stuff. In Columbus, a buttermilk store opened its doors and became so popular that others appeared across the city. It was sold at soda fountains and at restaurants; even some dry-goods stores set up buttermilk stands. The ads for the drink compared it favor-ably to alcohol: it was cool instead of hot; it had friendly germs that waged war on unfriendly germs while alcohol was poison; it did not, as did alcohol, cause its drinkers to beat their wives and ter-rorize their children.[18]

Unfortunately for temperance supporters, buttermilk did not ultimately drive liquor from Ohio. As Billy's revival party arrived in Lima, Ohio, in 1911, temperance forces needed help and they got it. The preacher declared from the tabernacle, "If Jesus Christ were in Lima tonight, he would be against every brewer, every distiller, and every saloon, and if you are not, you are an insult to him."[19]

Billy walloped liquor hard in Ohio. In Canton the following year and in East Liverpool and Columbus he worked with an aggressiveness and force that rallied temperance workers and brought scorn from pro-saloon papers such as the *Liberal Advocate*. They called him a grafter, a mountebank, a false prophet, and a fake. His religion was perverted and, above all, he was dead wrong on the liquor question. Before the Columbus revival, temperance leaders countered by importing an editor from one of the McKeesport, Pennsylvania, dailies to address a large crowd in Ohio's capital. The editor claimed that, as a result of Billy's earlier crackling, brushfire campaign in McKeesport, saloon business had dramatically dwindled, many bartenders had lost their jobs, and even barmaids went looking for honest work. Billy's influence in the industrial town, said the editor, had been astonishing. Many of the tough millworkers who had usually spent hours after work congregating in the taverns had been persuaded to change their ways.

Billy did not disappoint temperance forces in Columbus. Day after day thousands were turned away from the jammed 12,000-seat tabernacle and temperance organizers reported that the saloon doors in the city were swinging less often, that old topers were not coming in for their swills, that even social drinking was falling off during the Sunday crusade, that beer orders were plummeting.

Billy flailed at the saloon in the Columbus revival with special fury. Comparing it to the despicable, traitorous, left-wing alien politicos and philosophers slinking around the country, he called liquor a menace whose "red flag is dyed with the blood of women and children." It was, he said, "hellsoaked." The rhetoric soared: "The saloon will take off the shirt from the back of a shivering man. It will take the coffin from under the dead. It will take the milk from the breast of the poor mother who is the wife of a drinking man. It will take the crust of bread from the hand of the hungry child. It cares for nothing but itself—for its dirty profits. It will keep your boy out of college. It will make your daughter a prostitute. It will bury your wife in the potter's field. It will send you to hell."

When the Columbus campaign ended in February 1913 after seven weeks of meetings, Billy could cite attendance figures of nearly 850,000, and those were only the ones who were able to get inside the tabernacle. On most nights, the building was ringed with people crowding the walls to hear the message. "Old King Booze received a solar plexus punch," reported the *American Issue.* "In almost every sermon, as well as in his special addresses devoted to the subject, the liquor business was given blow after blow." Another magazine reported that during one lunchtime hour at one of the popular cafés in the city, a place usually mobbed, five men were inside—two employees, a man drinking at the bar, and two standing away from the bar discussing Billy Sunday and his work.[20]

He was never on the payroll of the Anti-Saloon League and he tried to avoid the appearance of overt political partisanship. Nevertheless, wherever he went the dry cause was a foremost consideration in his plans. Officials of the Anti-Saloon League in various states sent him reports of dry successes and failures. Following state and local political activity intently, Billy acceded to the wishes of civic and political leaders to speak at various forums on the temperance question, and was even persuaded in some instances to extend revivals in order to help mobilize prohibition forces for imminent elections.

Despite Billy's hard campaigning in Ohio, voters continued to reject statewide prohibition. But a number of midwestern towns such as Mason City, Iowa; Decatur, Illinois; and Steubenville, Ohio, voted dry shortly after Sunday revivals. In West Virginia during the Wheeling campaign the Anti-Saloon League shuttled Billy by train to other towns to help influence rural voters. The state went dry. During the Spokane campaign, 112 businessmen and pastors chartered a train for a 425-mile jaunt around the state of Washington to boost a local-option bill. Billy was their star attraction, flaring out the "Booze Sermon" in Olympia at the state capitol and at the opera house and all along the route at various train depots where fevered crowds gathered cheering and waving white handkerchiefs. Although there were legions of booze fighters and powerful organizations aligned against the liquor interests, Billy was now being hailed nationally as one of the prominent spear-carriers for prohibition.

The liquor interests intensified their fight against the evangelist in the press and on the lecture platform. Billy wrote to Nell,

"The whiskey gang seems to lie awake nights hatching out schemes to attack me." The extensive assaults on Billy by wet interests in the *Liberal Advocate* and other papers such as the *Iconoclast* were a measure of the animosity and fear that the evangelist had struck within the camps of his enemies. Before the Pittsburgh crusade opened in December 1913, about 200 saloonkeepers and liquor dealers met to discuss the Sunday threat. As the meeting opened, an agitated speaker characterized the Sunday revival as a "movement of gigantic character" threatening the entire liquor industry in Pennsylvania. Billy was poisoning the minds of citizens, the speaker continued, by his "clownish antics and lying tirades of abuse and vituperation." The preacher had them worried.[21]

Billy could, from the revival pulpit, draw crowds that other temperance orators could not. He carried the authority of God, many of his listeners believed; he spoke the truth of the Scriptures and powerfully connected the reform impulse with the religious message. To forsake one was to forsake the other. He literally terrified many avid churchgoers into abstinence.

Anecdotal stories abound of the evangelist's influence in converting lieutenants for the temperance fight. In Wilkes-Barre, Pennsylvania, for example, a local sheriff walked into a Sunday rally, heard the "Booze Sermon," and became a convert to Christianity and to the anti-liquor cause. His zealous enforcement of all local ordinances relating to saloons and drunkenness, temperance leaders reported, "caused widespread terror among liquor dealers."[22]

From Burlington, Iowa: J. S. Caster, mayor, issued a proclamation closing the saloons on Sunday. He wrote to Billy, "Your great work here has reached its culmination . . . this result was brought about by your work in Burlington." From Canton, Ohio: F. M. Vagan wrote to Billy of his new life: "God knows that I climbed on and fell off the wagon and fell overboard . . . but now I'm in the Chariot, with the MASTER DRIVER." From Johnstown, Pennsylvania: Following a Sunday revival, local citizens formed a group called the "Billy Sunday Anti-Liquor Association." The group continued to hold meetings long after Sunday's departure and its membership steadily rose. From Philadelphia: The president of the Franklin Reformatory for Inebriates reported that over the entire existence of the institution, about half a century, between six and eight new alcoholics had been admitted every week. Following a Sunday revival, not one individual had applied for admission for over two weeks. From New York: "An Admirer" wrote to the evangelist that while having lunch at a downtown restaurant he or she overheard that the employees of breweries, distilleries, and liquor dealers were forced to contribute to a fund to fight Billy Sunday. From Pittsburgh: A group of politicians who had for years worked the wards of Alleghany County for candidates favoring the liquor interests changed their allegiance. They told a writer that the reason for their political conversion to temperance was their religious conversion in Billy's tabernacle.

In Decatur, Illinois, Billy closed a six-week revival on the eve of a local-option election. The day following the triumphant victory of the drys, there appeared a sign in the front window of a well-known saloon:

CLOSED UNTIL FURTHER NOTICE
By order of
BILLY SUNDAY

And there was a poem, copyrighted in 1915, by Isabel Stiles Lynch in which she proclaimed that Uncle Sam himself had joined the Sunday war on liquor:

He's proud of Billy Sunday and of his wagon proud,
He will shout for prohibition and shout it long and loud.[23]

Businessmen loved the Sunday crusades. Numerous industrialists, plant foremen, and supervisors from all sorts of business and industry raved about the effects that Billy's revivals had in sobering up their employees and making them more productive. An official of the Cambria ironworks in Pittsburgh once estimated that the Sunday revival in his city dramatically increased his company's earnings by a quarter of a million dollars. Why? "Because of the increased efficiency of the men. They were steadier . . . they produced enough additional steel to make their work worth the quarter million additional."[24] From Billy's perspective the prohibition effort helped both employer and employee. If the employer could reap the full rewards of higher productivity, the employee, at the same time, saved his money, his family, and his soul.

The prohibition drive was a highly organized, mass movement of many societies and organizations and thousands of local leaders and foot soldiers. Its successes and failures from state to state and city to city were the result of varied influences. But the Sunday revivals, with their extensive press coverage, hoopla, and cadre of workers, buoyed temperance forces in communities across the country.

Statewide prohibition and local-option legislation created many dry communities prior to World War I. And in 1913 Congress passed the Webb-Kenyon Act prohibiting the shipping of hard liquor into any state opposed to its entry. Nevertheless, along with successes, there had been numerous failures at the state and local levels. The reform engine needed new spark. Temperance leaders therefore began a bold, vigorous campaign for a national solution—an amendment to the United States Constitution. Purley A. Baker, national superintendent of the Anti-Saloon League, declared, "We shall do in this national contest what we do in that of the towns, counties, and states—fight; and if we are defeated one season we shall appear fresher and more ready for the fight when the next year begins."[25]

On December 22, 1914, in Washington, D.C., over 1,000 prohibition supporters marched down Pennsylvania Avenue from the Willard Hotel to the Capitol. In a biting wind on the Capitol steps, officials of the Anti-Saloon League presented a draft of a prohibition resolution to Congressman Richard P. Hobson of Alabama. A slender, Spanish-American War hero and temperance speaker, Hobson introduced the resolution on the floor of the House of Representatives, calling for a constitutional amendment to prohibit the manufacture and sale of alcoholic beverages. The liquor trust, Hobson declared, debauched the youth of the land through tens of thousands of saloons, through a business network worth millions of dollars in capital. The enactment of constitutional prohibition would destroy the liquor trust. "The youth would grow up sober," the congressman said, carefully presenting a litany of prohibitionist arguments and rhetoric that had echoed from temperance halls, pulpits, civic meetings, state legislatures, and newspaper editorials for over half a century.

After intense lobbying efforts over the succeeding months, the Hobson resolution garnered a majority of votes but fell thirteen short of the required two-thirds necessary to submit an amendment to the states for ratification. But the vote inspired temperance leaders. By 1914 West Virginia became the ninth completely dry state, and many other states were dotted with local-option counties. The drive for prohibition, many reformers now believed, was ready to steamroll. Baker's resolve to fight across the land was shared by thousands and Billy was staunchly in their number.[26]

During some of his revival stops, the evangelist seemed as much a politician as a preacher. In Philadelphia in 1915, Billy leaped into a Pennsylvania local-option fray like an unleashed tiger. Dull, thunderous thuds sounded from the sides of the pulpit at one meeting as the evangelist's clenched fists pounded away. "Get this into your heads," he hollered, ordering his startled audience to add their names to prohibition petitions. "Sign them!" He stomped across the platform, raced at top speed, swung his lithe frame completely in a circle, and clapped his hands. All in favor of temperance and opposed to the liquor devils stand up! Everyone in the great tabernacle at Nineteenth and Vine leaped up in unison as if the seats had delivered a shot of electricity. Some stood on the rough pine benches, others kicked and whipped up the sawdust; many jubilantly waved handkerchiefs. "Now, boys, it may be there'll be a demonstration in Harrisburg. It may be they'll want 4,000 or 5,000 men to go up there and show those lawmakers . . . if they do, get into it!" Many in the crowd that day would have gone almost anywhere for the evangelist. Here was Billy the commander, armed with the authority of God, leading the sinners against a putrid evil, assuring the faithful that the Almighty wanted prohibition. The crowd exploded in cheers.

This was martial fury, Billy's battle against booze, hell-for-leather bravado and militancy. One of the Sunday team's rallying songs was "De Brewer's Big Horses Can't Run Over Me." During

the "Booze Sermon" the evangelist often directed the choir to blast
out a version of the piece accompanied by Klaxon horns, automobile whistles, and bells. The effect, one listener said, "is fairly
thrilling," this march to holy war. As the old victory hymn "Sound
the Battle Cry" proclaimed:

> *Strong to meet the foe, Marching as we go,*
> *While our cause, we know, must prevail . . .*[27]

On Sunday afternoon, March 7, 1915, at the request of local temperance leaders, Billy turned the Philadelphia tabernacle over to a
mass demonstration called "The Men of Philadelphia for the Man
of Galilee and Local Option." Scores of students from Central High
waved a large banner overhead and sang "Hang all the booze shops
on a sour apple tree." Billy proclaimed, "The whiskey barrel's more
dangerous than the gun barrel. It's better to be a signpost than a
tombstone. Don't be a moral tramp." The tabernacle was, the *Philadelphia Ledger* reported, like a dynamo.[28]

Billy postponed a scheduled revival in Paterson, New Jersey,
to stay another week in Philadelphia for the Cause. "God won't let
me go to smash," he said when asked about possible exhaustion.
"I've just got to stay a week longer. There are thousands of people
who haven't been able to get inside the tabernacle yet. I'd be a
piker to quit when I'm needed."

As the seemingly indefatigable Billy carried on the fight, there
was another famed orator on the anti-liquor trail and he was nearby.
On March 15 two of the greatest spellbinders in American history
were in action, one in Philadelphia and the other in nearby Trenton, New Jersey. At the tabernacle in Philadelphia built for the
Billy Sunday revival a crowd of more than 25,000 greeted William
Jennings Bryan. The one-time boy orator from the plains had been
through a long, dizzying political career but his searing thirst for
reform still raged. He was here in Philadelphia to launch another
personal odyssey. Billy, on the road for a separate appearance in
Trenton, had loaned Bryan his tabernacle and his male chorus.

Bryan opened at the tabernacle a series of rallies to be held
across the country, a continent-embracing assault to pummel the

liquor interests, to expose the waste of human life at the hands of John Barleycorn, to rally the nation to pass prohibition legislation and elect to office political leaders who would fight for the temperance cause.

The Bryan campaign was formed under the auspices of the National Abstainer's Union, an organization begun by the Federal Council of the Churches of Christ in America. With the indomitable Bryan on the rally tour, the sponsors hoped to draw huge crowds like those massing to hear his friend Billy Sunday. They hoped to mobilize various church and temperance organizations and to attract formidible publicity.

At the March 15 rally Billy's chorus opened with a stirring hymn. The still fiery Bryan, the old Chautauqua orator and presidential candidate and champion of world peace and Christianity, rammed the liquor devils with a stinging succession of blows—liquor is an economic waste and drain to the country; it is the direct cause of crime, poverty, and human degradation; it threatens property and life; it is morally debasing. In contrast to Billy, who wildly moved about the stage during his sermons, Bryan stood almost motionless at the pulpit, a tightly clenched fist sometimes cutting the air or a forefinger shaking at the crowd. Yet the old power, the gripping, dramatic quality of his intonation, still held the crowd. "Oh God," he implored, "we pray that Thou wilt hasten the day when our land shall be free of the curse of strong drink, when we may cut the hands of our thraldom." At one point the chorus and crowd united in a deafening yell:

> *William, William Jennings Bryan*
> *William, William Jennings Bryan*
> *William, William Jennings Bryan*
> *We'll all drink grape juice yet.*

"I believe in the gospel that Billy Sunday preaches," Bryan declared, and the crowd cheered even more wildly.

At the conclusion of the rally, Bryan asked that the crowd sign cards pledging abstinence. Thousands responded. On the platform's edge, Bryan kneeled, his collar wilted, his face reddened, and his hands shaking. He leaned over the edge grasping card after card on which to add his own signature to the signed cards of his supporters. For fully half an hour Bryan's fountain pen swirled, while the crowd became more boisterous, eager to meet the famous speaker up close and get his autograph. With the crowd completely engulfing Bryan, the rally organizers finally called in the police to escort him out of the crush. The Bryan temperance war was thus under way.[29]

That same afternoon, Billy carried the fight in Trenton. At the assembly chamber of the state capitol, he addressed a joint session of the legislature. For the first time in the state's history, according to the *Philadelphia Ledger,* a preacher was speaking before the lawmakers in their official home.

The galleries were overflowing. Outside, thousands of onlookers waited to catch a glimpse of the evangelist. Cameramen jockeyed for position. Arriving hours early to get a seat, some women knitted. There was Rody with his trombone ready to play "Brighten the Corner"; there was Ma Sunday glowing. Except for the lack of sawdust, the legislative chamber was now a tabernacle and Billy gave them his breath-stopping business. At one point, he wove a story about the angels intervening when Abraham Lincoln was discouraged. "Abe, don't cash in!" said the angels. "Buck up!" Then one day, Billy said, "the world knocked at Abe's door and the house fell to pieces and he stepped out and up." To emphasize the point, Billy suddenly leaped up himself and clambered atop the desk of the House Speaker. This was unquestionably another first in New Jersey history. The audience gasped and laughed and then began to clap. Billy had mesmerized the state representatives of New Jersey and others in the legislative chamber as he had mesmerized euphoric tabernacle crowds across the country.

At another point, Billy recounted the biblical story of David and Goliath in his own unique fashion. "The slinger of Israel," declared Billy, had overcome his adversary by hitting him "square in the middle of the coco and putting out his lamps."

An assemblyman from Camden, Charles Wolverton, thanked

Billy for addressing the legislature, calling him the foremost Christian worker in the world, and the assembly presented the preacher with a large red-and-white floral horseshoe surrounding the New Jersey state seal. Leaving the capitol through a massive crowd outside, Billy stopped and told the people he would be back in Trenton later with his evangelistic team. He returned to Philadelphia.[30]

Bryan and Sunday—the two evangelical warriors charged ahead on their respective missions, Bryan on his temperance tour, Billy on his own revival campaign. The larger movement for prohibition had numerous streams of support, some not directly tied to religion—business, civic organizations, nonsectarian reformers, an amalgam of interests, organizations, and leaders, the combined force of which had sustained a drumbeat of reform against the liquor goblins over many decades. From the national leaders of the major organizations to grass-roots soldiers the movement had grown despite setbacks and frustration. This combined force was now on the verge of major successes and Bryan and Sunday added much weight to the cause.

What they offered to the burgeoning temperance army was national exposure, excitement, great crowds stirred by volcanic oratory, celebrity figures who drew press coverage not only in the local papers but in national periodicals and newspapers such as the *New York Times*. They had great followings, people who, respecting the careers and work of their heroes over the years, would listen to them on an issue such as temperance.

Billy was now making spectacular news on the temperance front across the country. When his revival team entered Paterson, New Jersey, over 100 men immediately volunteered for a temperance canvass. In Baltimore, Maryland, a group called the "Personal Liberty League" attempted to counteract the effects of Billy's temperance lectures by importing several speakers from out of state. Their meeting drew a half column of space in one of the Baltimore dailies; Billy's revival earned eighteen columns. The anti-Sunday meeting drew 2,400; Billy attracted 100,000 in rallies on the last Sunday of the revival. In Portland, Oregon, Billy addressed a mass meeting said to have been the largest assemblage ever gathered at one place in the state. For two hours, 10,000 listened to the evangelist, half of them standing throughout. Political managers, according to a prohibition publication, were later fearful that any candidate they might book for that hall in Portland would suffer in comparison to Billy Sunday—his drawing power made that of other speakers appear anemic.[31]

By September 1916 dry forces could boast that 51 percent of the American people lived in dry areas. Both prohibition leaders and their foes, however, agreed that the country was heading for a showdown and the state of Michigan was the prime battleground. No vote on prohibition in states across the country had generated such fervor and strategic maneuvering as the upcoming vote in Michigan scheduled for November 7, 1916. But even though half the country was now under dry control, the prohibition forces had not been victorious in a statewide election in a single large manufacturing state east of the Mississippi River. Also, if Michigan went dry in 1916, Detroit would be the first American city with a population over 250,000 to shut down the liquor business. The city was the fifth largest in the United States.

Nervous wet forces feared that a major loss of a city the size of Detroit would signal the beginning of a precipitous disintegration of support for their interests, that investors in the liquor business would soon lose heart not only in Michigan but across the country, that momentum would rally the prohibitionists to new intensity, and that the rocky road to total prohibition would be paved.[32] At this critical juncture, at a time when wet supporters counted on a strong vote from Detroit to defeat statewide prohibition, at this time of political tension and struggle, a hated foe arrived in September. Into Detroit came Billy Sunday.

Awaiting the evangelist was the Gridley Field tabernacle, seating capacity 16,000, the largest structure ever built up to that time in America for a religious revival. One hundred twenty of Detroit's churches decided to suspend their Sunday morning services so that their faithful could attend the evangelist's meetings.

When he stepped off the train, Billy met a crowd of 3,000— larger than the one that had greeted President Wilson in his visit to Detroit that summer. Billy had not made a public appearance in Detroit since the 1890s when he had played ball at old Recreation

Park at Brady and Bush, and a few of the old Detroit Wolverine players were in the crowd on September 9 as well as many old-time fans. Several people remarked that the center fielder had not changed much in appearance, and his manner, they would soon find out, hadn't changed much either. This was a new game in 1916 but the razzle-dazzle and gusto Billy had exhibited years before on the playing field were still there in the tabernacle. He ached to win and would go after the wets with everything he had. "Now you bull-neck degenerates," he declared, "I defy you in the name of Jesus Christ."[33]

There had never been a show in Detroit quite like Billy's. High above the crowd packing the tabernacle, Billy opened the revival in top form. He made them laugh, shiver, cry, shout, and sing; he treated them to the full epigrammatic arsenal, the body gyrations, the platitudes somehow made adventuresome, the slangy, salty phrases, the hysteria, the moments of solemnity and introspection. "Help old Detroit," he implored the Almighty. "Throw your arms around her. Go into the barber shops, Lord, into the hotels, factories and saloons. Help the man on the street, the floater, and drunkard. The devil has him almost out. He's on the ropes and groggy, Lord. One more stiff uppercut will finish him. Help him, Lord, to square his shoulders, raise his dukes and cry, 'Yes, Lord, I'll come when Bill gives the call.' " Billy and the Lord, the Lord and Billy, on the march in Detroit! Billy's huge choir filled the tabernacle with a rousing rendition of "Down in the Licensed Saloon," an anti-booze song which answered the question posed by the old hobo song "Where Is My Wandering Boy Tonight?" The wandering boy was

Ruined and wrecked by the drink appetite,
Down in the licensed saloon.[34]

On September 17, 1916, the *Detroit News* suggested that Billy might someday take over the White House. On page one of the paper is a cartoon of "Prohibition President Sunday" addressing Congress in 1921, giving the national legislature the same kind of hell about the prohibition issue he was now giving the liquor interests. Leaning off the edge of the platform, fist shaking, Billy declares in the cartoon, "You boneheaded hog jowled old geeks. Pass this bill instead of the buck and give the Fool Killer a vacation."[35]

From the moment he hit Detroit in 1916, Billy made inroads in most areas of society. He visited the polite estate of John S. Newberry in Grosse Point and spoke to 300 exclusive members of the city's social elite, an assemblage whose names dotted the Social Register. Rody and his trombone led the group in "Brighten the Corner." Mrs. Truman Newberry and her fashionable friends agreed to host additional Billy Sunday "home meetings" with other acquaintances.

At the same time that Billy was courting the higher strata of Detroit society (he was, incidentally, staying throughout the revival at the elegant home of S. S. Kresge), he also seemed to be making an extraordinary impact on Detroit's workers. At a men-only service on September 21, the tabernacle, built to hold 16,000, was the scene of near bedlam. An estimated 29,000 men, mostly from Detroit plants, swarmed into and about the structure. Many of the industrial factories sent organized delegations and when Billy or another speaker mentioned their occupation or trade, groups of men would erupt from a section of the building. It was all riotous yet good-natured, an assemblage thirsting to see a celebrated performer. They got that night a version of the Booze Sermon, those thousands of industrial workers, many of whom regularly tipped steins in neighborhood beer joints, and they cheered the evangelist on. To those who criticized the prohibition movement on the grounds that it violated personal liberties and freedoms, Billy exclaimed, "It's everybody's business what you do. I have no right to exercise my liberty to injure others . . . the personal liberty that Godforsaken whiskey bunch wants is the personal liberty of the jungle." When he closed and asked the men to hit the trail, they came toward the preacher by the hundreds, like a "flood bursting through a door," said one reporter. Booze and the devil had taken a terrible beating.[36]

Alcoholic rehabilitation clinics such as the Detroit Neal Institute published large advertisements encouraging the public to hear Billy, "the implacable foe of booze." Church leaders, civic officials, and temperance organizations all persuaded their members to head to the tabernacle. There they could see a master performer of many faces—fire-eating preacher, hometown philosopher, righteous leader, even comedian. Only one liquor owner in history ever told the truth about liquor, Billy said. His name was Stormy Jordan and he lived in Ottumwa, Iowa. Yes, old Stormy told the truth about booze; he called his saloon "The Sure Road to Hell." And right under the main sign of Stormy's bar was a smaller sign which read "Nose paint."[37]

The wets needed ammunition to fight this kind of impresario and they countered with an especially heavy gun. The eminent attorney Clarence Darrow, burning with visceral antipathy for all evangelical moralizers, arrived in Detroit and on October 15 he addressed a gathering of labor union members at the opera house. Liquor was not the main cause of crime and insanity and poverty, Darrow said. These claims were fanatical and were made by fanatics. Prohibitionists such as Billy, he charged, were opposed to the one thing that made life worth living—liberty. Darrow declared, "Liberty is the only thing worth fighting for, and they are attempting to deprive us of our liberty."[38]

To Billy, Darrow's liberty was nothing but abhorrent license. The preacher assailed the notion that in the name of freedom individuals could engage in practices antithetical to religious dictates, morality, and the public good. Moral lepers, he called them, that was the whiskey gang, and their thugs like Darrow were nothing but the devil's disciples.

Billy left Detroit briefly and took his prohibition fight to Saginaw and Ypsilanti and then to Ann Arbor. Addressing a boisterous crowd of students at the University of Michigan, he enlisted nearly a thousand students and faculty to canvass in the upcoming election. He appeared in Ann Arbor one day after Bryan had warmed them up. Billy promised the students that he would never let up his assault on the wets: "I will fight them till Hell freezes over then I'll buy a pair of skates and fight 'em on the ice."[39]

Back in Detroit the evangelist scheduled special noonday talks at the opera house to convert businessmen to the cause of God and prohibition. "I'll chase the devil of alcohol from the moneybags of

Griswold Street," he quipped, "and shake it to death in the busy streets of commerce." He visited the Ford plant, shook hands with the workers, and asked for their prohibition vote. This was Billy working the crowd, speaking the language, as comfortable among socialites as among pipe fitters, helping his prohibition friends forge a coalition.[40]

Wrapping up the Detroit crusade on Sunday, November 5, 1916, with four meetings, Billy drew enormous crowds, approximately 50,000 counting those who got within the sound of the evangelist's voice. The *Detroit News* pointed out that, according to Holy Scripture, the Apostle Peter converted 3,000 on the great day of Pentecost. Billy's figure for November 5, of those who marched down the sawdust trail, stood at 3,103.

At an afternoon service, Billy sounded the political bugle, serving notice on both Democrats and Republicans that prohibition would be the major issue in the coming years, that American citizens would elect to Congress men who stood four-square against the whiskey gang. America would be completely dry, he prophesied, in eight to ten years. "God wills that every wrong shall cease. The saloon is going to hell in God's good time."

At the final service, with the incredible crowd singing, shouting, and waving, Billy stood next to two old ballplayers from the Detroit Wolverine days—Sam Thompson and Charlie Bennett. Now physically disabled, Bennett was the Detroit catcher who had hit the towering drive to the outfield that Billy had flagged down during a crucial game thirty years earlier, shortly after his conversion experience at Pacific Garden Mission. Bennett had later lost both legs when he fell under a train.

Billy's farewell words to Detroit: "My message is all delivered. I leave you with God." One writer called the last day of the Detroit crusade "the greatest ingathering of souls in the history of the church in America." Another wrote, "Great evangelists have preceded him throughout the land and in foreign countries, but never has one of them secured such a vast array of converts."[41]

Billy left Detroit but he didn't immediately leave Michigan. In Grand Rapids, a day before the election, Billy stood on a platform waving an American flag before 7,000 people, urging them to flood to the polls with prohibition votes. Billy the politician was campaigning to the last minute.

The following day the state of Michigan voted for prohibition—353,378 in favor, 284,754 against. Anti-prohibition forces had counted on carrying the city of Detroit and surrounding Wayne County by 25,000; they carried it instead by only 1,368. Grand Rapids, the second-largest city in the state, went dry, 14,998 to 12,073. The Detroit vote, most analysts said, was the wets' greatest shock and disappointment.

Billy's zealous campaign for prohibition rolled on. He and Bryan spoke at a mass meeting in Madison, Wisconsin. The evangelist poured on the vituperation at King Alcohol in New York and other states. So effective was Billy in mobilizing support that the Anti-Saloon League decided to work with local Bible classes, prayer groups, and other Billy Sunday organizations remaining in the cities and towns where the evangelist had preached.[42]

Prohibition eventually prevailed. In December 1917, the House of Representatives, following a previous favorable vote in the Senate, approved a national prohibition amendment to submit to the states for ratification. The amendment would make illegal the manufacture, transport, and sale of alcohol for drinking purposes in the United States. By January 16, 1919, legislatures in the necessary three-fourths of the states had completed the process. The U.S. Constitution had its Eighteenth Amendment. Prohibition officially began one year later.

The national victory by the prohibition army resulted from many forces and the efforts of many leaders. To Billy it represented a national movement toward righteousness and purity, a victory to uphold American moral standards, family stability, and economic common sense, a triumph of God over Satan, patriotism over the alien influences infiltrating the country's moral and ethical fabric.

Billy's personal role in the prohibition fight, an effort in which he invested so much of his astonishing energy and drive, illustrated much about his character, beliefs, and motivation. It demonstrated his deep hungering for political battle, like a slavering wolf on the trail, fangs bared, out for the kill. He marked his enemies, stalked them feverishly, relentlessly, and attacked, ripping and tearing. He was the Lord's Lancelot, slaying the demon of hell, confident he was the agent of God, that he understood His will. "There is no one that will reach down lower, or reach higher or wider to help you out of the pit of drunkenness than I." Night after night, in city after city, he and ole John Barleycorn punched it out. In the eyes of those who packed the tabernacles the demon never had a chance. "I want," Billy said, "to be a giant for God."

Billy once said that the toughest Christian injunction for him personally to follow was to turn the other cheek. His entire evangelistic career, in fact, seemed a rejection of that precept. As the moral general, he was out to slay the enemies of God, not to humor or pacify them. That belligerence seemed to infect some of his followers during a parade in Scranton, Pennsylvania. With the crowd singing "De Brewer's Big Horses Can't Run Over Me," a few of Billy's more exuberant marchers overturned a beer wagon, launching the kegs on a roll down the street. "Onward, Christian Soldiers . . ."[43]

The prohibition battle was an extension of Billy's war to change the personal morals of God's children. If liquor, the most insidious moral rot of all, was threatening American institutions, Billy was out to lop off its head. His aggressive, masculine brand of evangelism made prohibition seem a test of will and manhood. Christ was tough and demonstrated in His own life tough discipline; He expected the same from His followers.

Strutting about the revival platforms, Sunday was a reassuring figure, facing the forces of Satan with defiance, a gritty, heroic battler, barking instructions to the sinners gathered about him. He told an audience of students at the University of Pennsylvania, "If your manhood is buried in doubt and cheap booze, dig it out. You have to sign your own Declaration of Independence and fight your own Revolutionary wars."[44] Resist the devil, you manly Americans, resist the plague threatening your health, your family, your country. Give your soul to God, give up the devil's brew. Many times

Billy pronounced, "I'm going to make this place so dry they'll have to prime a man to spit."[45]

By infusing furious anti-liquor rhetoric in his evangelistic campaigns, Billy strengthened his national prominence. The revivals gained burgeoning attention as friends and enemies responded to the preacher's anti-booze pronouncements and antics. His showmanship, his knack for capturing the phrase newspapermen craved, his rapport with the crowds, his organizational acumen—all of it reached unparalleled heights in these years, and Billy seemed fueled by the fight. His principal message was still the Christian word, his principal goal the saving of souls. But in the prohibition struggle Billy found a devisive, passionate issue toward which to direct his considerable stamina and energy. His commitment to the cause bolstered his own revival army and that of the prohibitionists as well.

For Billy prohibition was an inviting, convenient target. It was a vice upon which he could throw much of the culpability for a disillusioned, increasingly complicated American society. If American values and families were ripping asunder under the barrage of forces unleashed by modern industrialism, there was a simple solution. The answer was not in changing American economic systems, not in following godless ideologies or experimenting with untried government schemes; the answer was the same as it always had been—give your hearts to God, assert your moral will, resist evil. Alcohol was the devil's tool to disrupt and destroy; fight it! This was a cause which people understood, around which they could rally.

In attacking the demon liquor, the evangelist was not only wrapping himself in simple, traditional American evangelical values; he was wrapping himself in the flag. Several years before the Detroit revival, Billy had conducted a campaign in Marshalltown, Iowa, the place where he had come as a boy to play baseball. Here in Marshalltown, he again thrilled crowds, this time not on the base paths but in the pulpit. At the end of one of his sermons on the nemesis of drinking, he pulled from behind the altar a large red flag. "It's an anarchist!" he cried, dropping the flag to the ground and stomping on it. He then pulled out an American flag and began waving it vigorously, much to the delight of his audience. "Every plot against the old flag and our government has been hatched in some saloon!" he declared. At another stop he likened the liquor traffic to a snake winding its coils around the nation, its fangs injecting poisonous venom. "I am a sworn enemy to everything that is an enemy of my country," Billy said. "I say our enemy is the grog-shop."[46] Simple issues of right and wrong, simple definitions of friends and enemies, patriots and traitors—a simple solution. Liquor was anti-God, anti-human, anti-American. Wipe it out and preserve that which is good.

The war for prohibition did not abate with the adoption of the Eighteenth Amendment. In many respects it had just begun. Ahead were the days of speakeasies, bathtub gin, hip flasks, smuggling, near beer, moonshine, raids by federal agents, mob violence, and a continuous political fight over repeal. But for Billy the enactment of the amendment was a signal victory for God, country, and his own personal evangelistic career. He felt he had made a difference. William Anderson, an Anti-Saloon League official from New York, agreed. "It is not true," he said, "that every city where Mr. Sunday has held a meeting has voted dry . . . but most of them have." Billy's influence, said Anderson, had frequently turned the tide in elections, had been the single most significant factor in winning where the vote had been close. For Anderson and other prohibition leaders, Billy had been an invaluable ally. "I am shouting happy to think that I am going to live long enough to preach the funeral services of the liquor business in America," Billy said excitedly. "Whiskey is all right in its place, but its place is in Hell."[47] Ole John Barleycorn had been nailed to the door, at least for now, and there was no more deserving a villain.

As the evil menace made its comeback over the years, Billy would be there to hammer body blows, would be there to attack, attack, attack. "And don't you know I take more vile remarks, more damnable slurs, more infamous, rotten, stinking lies sent around by a lot of lying imps and pimps of hell who are subsidized by that dirty, rotten, stinking gang of moral assassins that will do anything to ruin the character of a man that they can't damn and that they can't debauch and that they can't drag down. . . . I will reach down lower, I will reach up higher, I will reach out farther, I will preach harder, I will preach longer, I will work more to save one poor staggering, hopeless, helpless drunkard from a drunkard's grave and a drunkard's hell than all of those damnable, infamous, vile, rotten, black-hearted, white-livered, beetle-browed, hog-jowled, weasel-eyed, good-for-nothing, dirty imps of hell and damnation, and I will fight them to hell and back again."[48]

8

Red Emma Et Al.

The devil's priestess of anarchism was on the trail of Billy Sunday. Emma Goldman, flaunter of convention, desecrater of patriotism, blasphemer of things religious, traveled to Paterson, New Jersey, in April 1915 to slash at the evangelist king, to confront firsthand the enemy.

Emma and Billy—the radical and the preacher. The two did share certain characteristics. Both had emerged from underprivileged backgrounds to become stirring orators, able through blazing invective to move massive crowds to fury; both were leaders of mass movements who, with stormy, magnetic personalities and unrelenting aggressiveness, had made legions of friends as well as enemies; both were uncompromising, intensely committed, totally convinced of the validity of their beliefs; both were seemingly indefatigable, traveling the country year after year in punishing, grueling speaking campaigns; both generated extensive press coverage, even though neither held public office. Emma and Billy— leaders who, by force of personality, will, and energy, had achieved fame, notoriety, and devoted followings. And yet, it is difficult to imagine two individuals holding such disparate worldviews, preaching so diametrically opposed philosophies.

At the same time Billy was beginning his evangelistic career in the early 1890s, Emma, a Russian immigrant, was immersing herself deeply in radical, left-wing politics. Influenced by the anarchist writings of the Russian scientist and philosopher Pyotr Kroptkin and by her friendships with Johann Most, fiery editor of the radical paper *Die Freiheit,* and Alexander Berkman, a passionate, young radical, Emma launched her career as a revolutionary orator, preaching a vague idealistic vision of absolute freedom and the evils of coercive government. The philosophy of anarchism set forth no political programs but held forth ideas of unrestricted human liberty, unbound by laws or convention. Emma and other anarchists called for direct action against and open defiance of all governmental dictums and external restraints on human activity—economic, social, and moral. She called for the uplifting of the masses from grinding poverty, from governmental repression, and from religious bigotry, and she pushed for the overthrow of capitalistic exploitation and economic tyranny. Down with government, down with religion, down with all restraints against individual liberty. She was for equality of the sexes, in the workplace as well as in the bedroom; she called for the international solidarity of the working classes; she spoke for free speech, participated in labor strikes, and preached the right of women to practice birth control. She was brilliant, compassionate, and deeply committed to the rights of the underclasses.[1]

And she was defiant. Some called her "Red Emma." "Tell all friends that we will not waver . . . that we will not compromise, and that if the worst comes we shall go to prison in the proud consciousness that we have remained faithful to the spirit of internationalism and to the solidarity of all the people of the world."[2]

Emma did go to prison—many times. Her firebrand radicalism would later lead to her deportation. As she traveled across the country speaking to large crowds, her name was emblazoned in newspaper stories usually linking her to civil unrest, assassination plots, subversion, and all things un-American. But the socialist Eugene V. Debs once wrote of Emma: "During all her years of service in this country, Emma Goldman stood staunchly always on the side of the struggling workers in every battle and for this she was hated, feared, and persecuted by the exploiting capitalists, and their prostituted newspaper scribblers, their tools in public office, and all the rest of their minions and mercenaries."[3]

Emma despised Billy. As did other radical leaders, she saw the evangelist as a dangerous tool of capitalists and industrialists to stem the reform impulse in America, to fill the minds of the workers with religious rubbish and hysterical obsessions. Every exploited worker who stumbled down the sawdust trail and accepted Billy's line that salvation lay in Christian duty and in obedience to established laws and morality was, Emma believed, a loss, a blow to the revolutionary fervor necessary to overthrow oppression. Billy and other religious grafters, she declared, were duping the ignorant masses, subduing, taming, and dulling their senses, making them intellectual slaves to custom and convention. Billy, she said, was a "frothing, howling huckster," a mouthpiece of established and entrenched interests. Religion, Emma believed, was an insidious poison and Billy Sunday the arch-poisoner. On the cover of one of the issues of Emma's magazine *Mother Earth* is a drawing by the left-wing artist Robert Minor of a sprightly, laughing Billy Sunday dancing a tango with a very forlorn, bleeding Jesus Christ.[4]

In the spring of 1915, Emma and a coterie of radicals arrived in Paterson, New Jersey, to protest Billy's revival. To radical leaders Paterson held a special symbolism. Two years earlier the city had been the scene of a bloody silkworkers strike. Led by Big Bill Haywood and Elizabeth Gurley Flynn, leaders of the Industrial Workers of the World (IWW, or "Wobblies"), nearly 25,000 workers had shut down the silk mills there demanding better working conditions and higher pay. The silk manufacturers responded with an army of private detectives to muscle the strikers. Beaten, arrested,

faced with increasing food shortages, the silkworkers gradually succumbed after several months and returned to the looms under very
much the same conditions they had left. Disheartened by the out-
come, many radical leaders, nevertheless, believed that the ordeal
had instilled in the Paterson workers a greater sense of class solidarity and belief in their own power. Flynn said afterward, "They
are not giving any more faith to the ministers."[5]

But now, two years later, the radicals saw Billy Sunday, the
Christian ringmaster, dragging his salvation circus into Paterson.
This city, symbol to the radicals of capitalist repression, was now
being invaded by a symbol of religious slavery. Emma Goldman
decided to fight back. She planned to gather various radical leaders
in Paterson and hold an anti–Billy Sunday rally.

When word of radical stirrings reached Washington, a Justice
Department official dispatched two agents to Paterson to protect
Billy from possible assault. The two posed as newspapermen and
Billy himself never knew they were there.

On April 16, Emma's advance man and lover, Dr. Ben Reitman, the notorious "Hobo King," defender of the rights of tramps
and whores, misfits and ne'er-do-wells, confronted one of Sunday's
personal representatives, Reverend Edward Emmett, at the Paterson tabernacle. Reitman asked Emmett, "Has any man who has
been converted ever bettered himself in any way?" "Yes," answered
Emmett, "they have increased their efficiency as employees." "Ah,
that is just what I wanted you to say," Reitman fired back. "They
have been able to give more to the bosses."[6]

On the following night Emma, escorted by Reitman, sat in
the audience to observe Billy firsthand. After the sermon a *New
York Times* reporter asked Emma about the evangelist. "He is a
good clown," Emma remarked, "but has ability."[7]

On April 20, Billy addressed 9,000 cheering followers at the
tabernacle on the subject of "Repentance." In Turn Hall across
town, in an Italian section of the city on the corner of Ellison and
Cross streets, a building that had rocked with exuberant labor rallies during the 1913 silkworkers strike, the anti–Billy Sunday rally
drew about 1,000. There, Emma held forth, labeling the evangelist
an "empty barrel," a screeching fraud preaching hell when the true

hell was right there in the workers' ghettos of Paterson, a hell built and nurtured by the kind of depraved hypocrisy and cant so characteristic of Billy Sunday and his cohorts. The workers needed better wages, better housing, better food, and better medical treatment; they didn't need maniacal claptrap about redemption and repentance.

Emma was followed to the platform by Carlo Tresca, the country's most celebrated Italian radical, who spoke to his many comrades in the audience in their own language. And Reitman delivered his own stinging rebuke of Sundayism and its evils in the form of a prayer which concluded:

> *Now, Mr. God, I don't want to make you tired by asking too much. Some of us who do not want to meet you face to face and walk on the golden streets want to get the full product of our labor. We want to build a world where we can live in beauty, harmony, and freedom. If you can help us, Mr. God, we will be much obliged and if you don't we will help ourselves and you can devote more of your time to Billy Sunday. Amen.*[8]

That night after the protest meeting, Turn Hall burned to the ground. "The judgment of God, surely," concluded John Callahan, chaplain of the Toombs Prison.[9] A sign? Retribution? God's wrath? Reverend A. Lincoln Moore, pastor of the Park Avenue Baptist Church, had no doubts. "It gave God His opportunity and He answered by showering His fire on the scene of the blasphemy." Mrs. Garret A. Hobart, widow of the former vice-president and an enthusiastic Billy Sunday admirer, concurred: "I believe God has shown that He is pleased with the work Mr. Sunday is doing."[10]

At the tabernacle Billy had warned sinners against defying God's authority, had admonished the flock against the evils of the world, against temporal excesses. Repent, he had said, or face the fires. On the question of the ashes heaped at the corner of Ellison and Cross, Billy had no comment.

Emma quietly left Paterson, her rally smoldering in the ruins of Turn Hall and in the snickers from pundits and respectable town officials and religious leaders alike that she and her followers had been struck by the wrathful vengeance of God. She wrote later that Billy had divested Christianity of meaning and decency. "Billy Sunday's vulgar manner, his coarse suggestiveness, erotic flagellation, and disgusting lasciviousness, clad in theological phraseology, stripped religion of the least spiritual significance."[11]

A month later Billy closed his Paterson revival on the anniversary of the great day of Pentecost and more than 12,000 jammed inside the tabernacle that May night in 1915; another 5,000 were turned away. Greeting the preacher with the old Chautauqua salute of waving handkerchiefs, the vast assemblage thrilled to the sweeping power of his oratory, gasped at his acrobatics, and joined the choir in bidding farewell with "Bless Be the Ties that Bind." In the sermon that night Billy spoke on the theme "Do It Tomorrow." The world, he explained, was composed of two classes, "the nows" and "the tomorrows." The former, he said, always won.[12]

This was the world of Billy Sunday—winners and losers, good and evil, the godly and the satanic, Americans and aliens, we and they. Life embodied the constant struggle against powers and forces and movements that threatened to break the lock of control which would unleash hellish, fiendish demons. The world was a besieged battleground and to flinch was to empower those evil forces.

Locked into this perception of moral and spiritual warfare, the evangelist saw a panoply of bewildering philosophies attacking from all sides—Darwinism, flying in the face of biblical creation; Freud, sinking man in a lowly muck of ego and id; anarchism and socialism, political philosophies reeking with the stench of anti-Americanism; free thinkers, free lovers, and assorted pusillanimous intellectuals cavorting in their Greenwich Village hovels; artists and writers and dancers and playwrights vilifying things sacred. It was a fearful onslaught, an ominous uprising of paganism, and Billy's simple, fundamentalist, midwestern Protestant heritage collided full-square against intellectual and philosophical movements which he did not understand and which represented to him a formidable threat.

The intellectuals, academics, poets, and philosophers who struggled to come to grips with the profound changes of urbanization and industrialization in the early twentieth century seemed to

Billy a single barbarous force, poised to strike down an America of simple but true values, an America of Christian faith and ethics. Socialists and anarchists, Bolsheviks and Wobblies—they were all the same, all part of an undifferentiated, alien menace, an army of single purpose: to destroy traditional America.

Through it all, he must remain steadfast and tough, must face the accursed enemies with disarming pluck and bravado, must disgrace and humiliate and conquer them in the name of God and country. To the intellectual snob he could say: "Thousands of college graduates are going as fast as they can straight to hell. If I had a million dollars I'd give $999,999 to the church and $1 to education."[13] To those advocating free love, such as Emma the Red, they were "poison peddlers," giving way to carnal natures driving them to "mentally and physically warped" personalities. They were immoral animals, drowning in sin and degradation.[14]

Billy hated the "Reds." The term itself began to take on a kind of generic quality defining a melange of individuals and movements for which he had no use, from Emma and the anarchists to socialists and even vegetarians, strange folk who, for some insidious, unfathomable reason, refused to partake of red meat, God's bounteous gift. All these people were menacingly mysterious, the enemy. They mocked and parodied him; accused him of greed, perfidy, and ignorance; called him a puppet and clown; questioned his sincerity and honesty and motives; and, most of all, stood squarely against just about everything in which he believed and to which he had devoted his life. Who were these intellectuals armed with their barbs and quips to attack Billy Sunday? To the attackers he would deal out bone-crushing counterpunches, would show them the kind of militant aggressiveness that he had always displayed from his early days on the base paths to these days in the Christian pulpit. "I have no use for these intellectual engineers who try to chart man's pathway through the sin-cursed world by the compass of their opinions."[15] They were all Reds; they were all pathetically lost.

Reds. In 1915 a young socialist writer named Carl Sandburg published a poem entitled "To a Contemporary Bunkshooter," a polemic attacking Billy as a grafter and fraud, a "bughouse peddler of second-hand gospel . . . tearing your shirt . . . yelling about

Jesus."[16] First published by the leftist magazine *The Masses* and reprinted in the New York *Call*, it was banned by police in two cities—New Haven, Connecticut, and Lynn, Massachusetts. Sandburg later said that this was the only time any of his work was censored.

In a highly charged letter to the publisher Alfred Harcourt, Sandburg painted a blistering picture of why the radicals despised Billy so vehemently. Sandburg told Harcourt that he knew several men who had worked in the Sunday campaigns, including a booking manager named Harry Holbrook. Sandburg claimed that Holbrook and the others told him that the poem was right on the mark, that Sandburg had "nailed his hide to the barn door and fixed him in the correct historic perspective." This man was no messenger from God, no prophet; he was a "crowd operative who uses jungle methods, stark voodoo stage effects, to play hell with democracy." Sandburg wrote that his fundamental hatred of Billy was rooted in the treachery of the evangelist, dabbling with people's elemental fears, invoking "terrors of the unknown." Years later, Sandburg asked a New York University professor to send a copy of the poem to Billy for his reaction. Upon receiving the poem Billy reportedly asked: "Who is this Sandburg? Isn't he a Red? He sounds to me like a Red."[17]

Henry M. Tichenor was a Red. The son of a prominent New Jersey judge, Tichenor had been a reporter for the *Chicago Daily Tribune*, a founder of the Omaha *Evening News*, and an editor of the Springfield, Missouri, *Leader Democrat*. With the onset of World War I Tichenor began to move into the field of left-wing journalism, joining the staff of the militant *National Rip-Saw*, a St. Louis socialist publication which featured writings by Eugene Debs, Kate Richards O'Hare, and other leftist notables. Tichenor was also a poet, whose revolutionary verses were sometimes compared to those of John Reed. In 1913 Philip Wagner, publisher of the *Rip-Saw*, decided to start a new monthly called the *Melting Pot* and asked Tichenor to become its editor. The journal was notable for its slashing attacks against Puritanism, superstition, and quacks of all stripes. Henry Tichenor considered Billy Sunday a ripe subject on all three counts.

On the front page of the August 1914 *Melting Pot* is a cartoon of Billy, pockets bulging with cash. Draped on the pulpit is an altar cloth sporting a drawing of a dollar sign. A bloated "Big Biz" sits in the background, money at his feet, halo above his head, and wearing a tag proclaiming him saved. Tichenor accompanied the cartoon with a scathing article on Billy's big-money evangelistic carnival. He told Wagner that he considered Billy, screeching his hell and damnation threats in the ears of women and children for big pay, worse than "the dope dealers of hop alley." In subsequent issues of the magazine, Tichenor sustained his blistering attack.

In late February 1915 a federal grand jury indicted Tichenor and Wagner for their editorial raking of the evangelist. The charge was circulating defamatory and scurrilous literature through the mails and it prompted a quip from Kate Richards O'Hare, Socialist party activist and reformer, that it was impossible to libel Billy Sunday. After much legal maneuvering the two defendants decided to plead guilty and throw themselves on the mercy of the court. A sympathetic judge treated them kindly, fining each $100 and court costs. Eugene Debs, who assisted the defendants in the case, declared, "We look upon Billy Sunday as a vulgar harlequin, a ranting mountebank who, in the pay of the plutocracy, prostitutes religion to perpetuate hell on earth."[18]

Reds. Charles Erskine Scott Wood. Graduate of the United States Military Academy at West Point in 1874, aide-de-camp to General O. O. Howard in the campaign against Chief Joseph's Nez Perce tribe and then against the Bannocks and Paiutes, Wood later earned a law degree at Columbia University. Wood's years of chasing and destroying Indians and his first years in corporation law soured him on the glories of the American capitalist system. From the red men slaughtered by white invaders to factory workers exploited by entreprenurial slavemasters, Wood saw corruption and evil polluting the nation. He became very Red-like, indeed, working for numerous social causes and befriending muckrackers such as Lincoln Steffens and radicals such as Emma.

The tall, bearded Wood channeled his ever-increasing restlessness with American values into poems, articles, and short stories which appeared in such periodicals as *Century Magazine, Pacific*

Monthly, and *The Masses*. Wood saw Billy as a fake, a prophet of false religion, distorting the real Christ of purity and justice into something tyrannical. In one of the most devastating satires ever directed at the evangelist, Wood pictured Billy entering the Kingdom of Heaven and meeting God. Swaggering, cocksure, Billy bounds through the Heavenly Gates as if expecting huzzahs and autograph seekers. Instead, a slightly puzzled God doesn't know who he is. "It's me, God. Your pardner, Billy Sunday. You know my holler." Billy reminds God that he, Billy, the world's greatest evangelist, had sent up more souls to heaven than anyone since Peter. God turns to Jesus; Jesus doesn't know him either.

A startled Billy finds heaven an eerie place, filled with very strange beings, folks such as Voltaire, Tom Paine, Confucius, Mark Twain, Buddha, even Billy's old target, the agnostic Robert Ingersoll. Billy also sees a man named Herman Morgenstern who had run a beer garden on Fourth Avenue in New York. When Billy protests that a beer-garden owner shouldn't be in heaven, Jesus replies, "I liked him. He was a gentle, charitable soul." Jesus also reminds Billy, "I lived with Publicans and Sinners." As Billy howls, God and the other Heavenly Hosts detect a disagreeable odor; it is Billy's soul. God orders the soul to be cleaned, bleached, fumigated, and sent to a part of heaven reserved for African medicine men.

Billy later returns, boasting that he has converted most of the African medicine men and proposing that he hold an old-fashioned, slam-bang revival in heaven. "I want to bring this old, played-out bunkhouse of yours right up to date. . . . I'll make it a regular Coney Island." Disgusted, God kicks him out of heaven.[19]

Behind the biting satirical assault, from which Billy's many liberal detractors drew much mirth, was Wood's deep conviction that peddlers of homespun Christian ethics and morality were distorting the teachings of Christ, turning religion into an orgy of patriotism, militarism, censorship, and greed.

More Reds. In 1915, when *Metropolitan Magazine* sent John Reed to Philadelphia to write an article on Billy Sunday, the artist George Bellows went with him to illustrate the piece. Bellows, who grew up in a Methodist camp meeting family in Columbus, Ohio, had since migrated philosophically to social anarchism leanings. He still revered what he regarded as genuine religious passion but he now espoused the beliefs of those such as Emma Goldman and Big Bill Haywood. Bellows harbored deep antagonism for Billy Sunday, whom he considered a phony huckster, "the worst thing that ever happened to America."

Billy, said Bellows, stood for authoritative Prussianism, was a force pitted against beauty, imagination, art, and freedom. Down Billy's sawdust trail was religious autocracy and stifling rigidity; down the trail was the ruination of individualism and creativity. So fascinated did Bellows become with the evangelist that he depicted him on four separate occasions. In the most familiar of Bellows's paintings of Billy, the preacher straddles the tabernacle press box, face in a contorted grimace, right arm slashing forward pointing in an incriminating gesture at the open-mouthed crowd. Here, in the tabernacle, were not peace and love and Christian goodness but darkness, evil, and hysteria. To George Bellows, Billy was a poisoner of minds.[20]

Reds. The accursed Reds. Infidel journalists, poets, orators, militant activists—they seemed to crawl and slink about everywhere. Against the denunciations and ridicule, the vicious slanders and hysterical atheistic rantings, Billy marshaled all his energy and combativeness. "This twentieth-century bunk—making the gland the seat of final authority, foisted on the public by alleged intellectuals . . . is nothing but an attempt to dethrone God and put man in his place."[21]

Some radicals, such as Wood, even claimed that Jesus Christ was one of their own, an assertion that especially rankled Billy. Unlike such violently anti-religious radicals as Emma, some of the novelists, essayists, and poets writing for leftist magazines sought to embrace the figure of Christ as a pacifist and rebel workman, at the same time attacking the established churches and religious dogma. In Jesus, they preferred to see a figure of brotherly love, the "first Socialist," and emphasized his virtuous human traits while rejecting his divinity—Jesus the reformer, Jesus the despoiler of the countinghouse, Jesus the humanitarian. Authors and philosophers devised and debunked contrasting theories and hypotheses, tested new approaches, all the time assaulting conventional mores and time-worn religious beliefs.

Some intellectuals applied Christ's teachings to the social order. The prophets, then, were the first muckrakers. Bouck White in 1912 wrote a book, *The Call of the Carpenter*, in which he claimed that Jesus' years of work as a day laborer caused him to identify with the working classes and ally himself against the despotism of their masters. Christ, in other words, was a revolutionary figure around whom workers could rally. [22]

To the intellectuals of the period all of this was invigorating. To Billy it was blasphemous, these so-called free thinkers, toying with Scripture, meddling with things sacred. "This is a day of isms and schisms and ologies," he lamented. "The devil has transformed himself into an angel of light." Billy had read some of these writings, had heard the attacks against his own ministry. These were evil men and women propounding vile doctrines, individuals who needed cleansing by the spirit of God. Their warped theories and newfangled notions were bunk; there "isn't religion enough in them to float their dirty fallacies!"[23] In a speech to a group of women in Buffalo, Billy remarked that he was not familiar with art or science or music but was just a preacher of the old-time religion that had endured for 2,000 years. "Ladies," he joked, "excuse me from talking about pragmatism, transcendentalism, or esoteric synthesis."[24]

The rancor and vitriolic volleys between Billy and the radicals did not abate in these years, especially as hostilities between European nations threatened to intensify into a world war that would envelop the United States. As the conflict in Europe and on the seas seemed to be inevitably gripping its hands around the throat of America, dragging her closer, Billy's evangelism took on a more strident, patriotic sound. Individuals like Emma, parading around the country tearing down its fundamental ideals, its religious heritage, its values, were not only immoral and ungodly but traitors. For any radical soapboxer or writer spewing out anti-American tripe, calling for class war, he had only scorn: "There are yet a lot of the blatant reformers who will stand out and damn Jesus Christ . . . cuss and damn the principles that have made them as decent as they are. Oh, I have no sympathy on a mutt like that—no sir!"[25]

All of the reform movements of any consequence, Billy claimed, from child labor laws to mothers' pensions, were tributes not to the work of radicals and revolutionaries, but to Christianity. "If you will name one thousand reforms, one thousand laws, that have benefited and blessed humanity, nine hundred and ninety-nine of them will go to the credit of Jesus Christ." Through spiritual exaltation, through the saving power of the Christian message, are society's ills overcome, not by the "God-forsaken anarchists, those agitators that spew out and stir up trouble."[26]

All of this ranting about personal liberties and free speech, Billy declared, was nothing more than a grasping for personal license. The personal liberty coveted by the "red-handed, black-hearted anarchist" is the liberty of the tiger, the liberty to prowl and tear and rip society apart. The betterment of society, Billy believed, was simply the sum of saved individual souls.[27]

Billy was hardly a solitary voice crying out against the leftists. Soon America's radicals, caught up in a national wartime mania of Red phobia, found themselves stalked by federal agents, arrested and jailed on new sedition and espionage laws, beaten, harassed, hounded, spied upon, their organizations outlawed, newspapers shut down, offices ransacked, documents destroyed. The Great Red Purge was at hand. Socialists, Wobblies, anarchists—they were all fair game. Debs, before being imprisoned, sorrowed over an America gone berserk, snuggled in the folds of the American flag: "In every age it has been the tyrant, the oppressor and the exploiter, who has wrapped himself in the cloak of patriotism or religion or both."

In Debs's hometown of Terre Haute, Indiana, a vigilante group attacked German-Americans on the streets, publicly burned German-language books, and lynched a socialist coal miner for refusing to buy a Liberty Bond. One observer in Cleveland told of another vigilante band: "The American Protective League are holding up everybody, regardless of age, throwing them into jail, and taking them to the federal building the following day to put them through the 'third degree' . . . they arrest street speakers . . . they are waging an unremitting war."[28]

The suspension of basic freedoms of conscience, speech,

assembly, and other guarantees of liberty is not unusual in times of war. Bolstered by inflamed, highly colored stories of plots, treasonous activities, atrocities, and other notions of impending doom, governments at such times, with the populace usually at their backs, have often rendered null such guarantees with swift, almost blithe workmanship. And in times of social upheaval the onset of war often brings choice opportunities for those in positions of power, both inside and outside of government, to enforce greater social control on rival groups. For Billy the war brought a welcome opportunity. His power was the pulpit club and he wielded it with crushing force. Defiant, emboldened by the war fever in the land, Billy lashed out fiercely at his hated tormentors with a kind of lynch-mob fury. He reportedly remarked, for example, that Christian pacifists should be fed the same medicine as that meted out in Butte, Montana, years earlier to Frank Little, an IWW organizer. Little had been brutally hung by vigilantes.[29]

To Billy the purge of the Reds seemed a ringing affirmation that America belonged to the Americans, not to muddled-thinking intellectuals.[30] Billy was the Roosevelt of the preachers, the tough, manly Rough Rider of religion, charging into the enemy lines sword drawn, slashing at those who would tear down his America or blaspheme his God. As Rody's own hymn proclaimed, "Heart and hand we'll pledge to starry banner / Staunch and strong we'll stand to colors true."[31]

In battling the moral assassins, God's vengeance, Billy knew, would be sure. The devil's serpents lose their heads. "Moral warfare," Billy declared, "makes a man hard. Superficial peace makes a man mushy. The prophets all carried the Big Stick."[32] Only a religion of rippling muscle could prevail. "If any cut-throat anarchists think they can come over and put our flag beneath their feet, there will be something doing before they get through! If they want to live in this country that belongs to us, they can. If they don't want to, they can hike back across the sea where they came from."[33] America is for Christians, rests on Christian traditions and values, forwards Christian goals. The territory was now staked, terms issued. No compromise! No retreat! Rippling muscle!

Billy's attacks on the Reds would get even harsher. Through

the war years and into the 1920s, his tolerance for left-wing political dissent of any kind evaporated entirely. Stung through the years by the barbs and insults of Emma and the others, those arrogant agents of the devil with their sniveling atheistic philosophies, Billy's contempt for the Reds remained powerful. On this issue he was bitter, vindictive, and increasingly hysterical. At times it seemed as if he were being trapped in a closed, shrinking room with the disciples of hell, the Reds, on the outside, surrounding him.

Long after Emma and 249 other radicals had been loaded onto a transport ship at Ellis Island and sent off to Russia, Billy would still be railing against the anarchist menace: "They tell me I am a marked man by these God-forsaken anarchists and cutthroats. All right, let me be a marked man, and if there are any of them here tonight they had just as well begin right now. I'll shoot the first one of them that starts anything as full of holes that he'd pass for a sieve anywhere."[34]

9

Of Rubicons and Waterloos: Billy in New York

A head loomed the great dragon, the monster city, destroyer of evangelists, the city that smote the sacred and flaunted its evils, city of hustlers and whores, cynics and sinners, of aliens and atheists, leering, sneering, the ultimate challenge. Billy Sunday was heading for New York.

Easter 1917 approached. On April 2, after several U.S. merchant ships had been sunk by German submarines in European waters, President Wilson asked Congress for a declaration of war, saying that the "world must be made safe for democracy." Several days later the United States officially entered World War I. Billy's battle for New York thus took on added dimension. For God, for country, the evangelical warrior stepped forth to slay the dragon.

This could be, he knew, the greatest achievement in the history of American evangelism, the culmination of his preaching crusade begun in the midwestern cornfields. He would face down the critics, silence the doubters and smirkers, disarm his enemies, overcome the odds. He would slash out at the devil's disciples—the kaiser-loving Huns, the Communists, socialists, and anarchists, the purveyors of godless ideology and intellectual filth. Nowhere else in America were the enemies so concentrated, so powerful as in New York. The enormity of the task ahead pressed hard at him. But to God's warrior the imminent battle stood as the purest test between the forces of good and evil, the struggle that he must endure and in which he must prevail. As the beloved old Scottish hymn "Soldiers of the Cross" that Rody played so often proclaimed:

Seize your armor, gird it on:
Now the battle will be won.[1]

As the preacher's train headed east from Indiana, reporters noticed a particular tension in Billy's voice and manner. The evangelist admitted he was nervous. The pre-revival hoopla surrounding the New York invasion was unprecedented and Billy keenly felt the pressure building.

Somehow New York, with its bevy of popular satirists and burlesque gagsters, with its corps of eager reporters digging for stories, seemed more intimidating than any challenge he had ever faced. Ridicule, always painful for Billy, would face him in New York in magnitudes unprecedented in his career. Fighting the banter and taunts of his enemies with his own verbal abuse, Billy's most prominent and potent weapon, could never be truly effective against the kind of onslaught he expected in New York. He could already see in his mind Satan's marksmen taking aim. But as the fears and doubts welled, so did his resolve. He had God on his side.

He also had his friends. John D. Rockefeller, Jr., offered special encouragement to Billy as the evangelist prepared for the New York revival. Governor Charles Whitman, also an ardent supporter, declared, "From my heart I wish this movement Godspeed."[2] And

Theodore Roosevelt, the public figure whom Billy admired over all others, the towering symbol of rugged, bully Americanism and honorable frontier values so revered by the preacher, wrote to Billy, "There is not a man in this country for whom I have greater respect and admiration than I have for you, and there is no man, in recent years, who has done better work than you, in this country!"[3]

But, most of all, Billy had his superbly organized, well-drilled army of revival workers. Incorporating all of the tactics and organizational acumen gained from earlier revivals, the Sunday team exerted herculean efforts to pave the General's march into the city. Nearly 50,000 individuals, hundreds of committees, mapped strategy. Like an enormous machine, pistons rhythmically firing, synchronized, the organization hummed. Prayer meetings, choir rehearsals, advertising and promotional ploys, fund-raising drives, volunteer recruiting—it all came together, raising to a feverish pitch the excitement and anticipation of a revival boldly announcing its determination to "Save New York."[4]

The Washington Heights tabernacle itself symbolized the hopes and ambitions that Billy and his lieutenants held for the revival. It was big. Some began to call it the "Glory Barn." Extending for 344 feet along 168th Street and 247 feet along Broadway, the tabernacle held 400,000 feet of lumber and 250 barrels of nails. There were 38 doors, nearly 18,000 seats. The building was also equipped with a post office; numerous telephone booths; a telegraph department; an emergency hospital care facility equipped with six beds; a small operating table and surgical supplies; and many rooms for ushers, the press, custodians, and other workers of all kinds. Library rooms awaited, filled with spiritual volumes and pamphlets. There was also a retiring room for the evangelist equipped with a rubdown table. So that all visitors to the tabernacle could hear the preacher's voice, a huge sounding board, looking something like an umbrella turned inside out, towered above the pulpit, its brilliant incandescent lamp inside enclosed by a sheet of heavy glass to shield Billy from its heat. It took two train carloads of red-cedar sawdust to cover the vast tabernacle floor. Perhaps most impressive in the cavernous edifice stood the immense platform on which over 2,000 chairs were placed for the great choir.

The city granted permission to the Fifth Avenue bus line to run buses every fifty seconds on a route to 168th Street and Broadway. Subways nearby planned to increase the number of cars in service. New York and the tabernacle awaited Billy's coming.[5]

So did his volunteers. Billy envisioned the crusade as a war for the soul of New York and his revival team treated the event in full military style. The usher's unit, charged with keeping order among the throngs of expected tabernacle visitors, organized itself into a veritable military command, 2,000 strong, complete with captains, lieutenants, and noncommissioned officers. They drilled, barked commands, and prepared for the onslaught of the masses of people. The usher's unit asked for and received the hearty cooperation of the New York City police force. Billy's army was poised for the battle, his own "Soldiers of the Cross."

> *Gird ye on the armor bright,*
> *Warriors of the King of light.*

The martial spirit surrounding the beginning of Billy's New York crusade thus mirrored the international turmoil that had inexorably dragged the United States into world war. As the thousands of Billy's enlisted volunteers prepared for the New York campaign, the war against the devil was taking on an especially strident spirit against the devil's main man—the German kaiser. For months, as world tensions mounted, as pressures intensified against President Wilson to lead the United States into war, Billy Sunday trumpeted his own call, spewing racial and nationalistic slurs at Kaiser Wilhelm as if Germany itself had signed a treaty with hell. Prussian militarism, Billy declared, was a "thousand-footed, thousand-headed, thousand-fanged demon."[6]

The web of world issues entangling nation after nation, the subtle diplomatic claims and counterclaims so puzzling and confounding to heads of state and their negotiators, had not at all clouded Billy's vision. The picture seemed simple, clear. This was good versus evil, God against Satan, the forces of righteousness and peace in battle with damnable powers of wickedness and evil. Against the tyrants of hell stood the mighty rock. This was Billy against the devil and his works; Billy against the Germans.

Next to the great tabernacle, workers set up recruiting stations for both the army and navy. In the Buffalo campaign a few months earlier, Billy had ended one sermon with a Bible in one hand and an American flag in the other. He was forging a symbolic, indissoluble link between Americanism and Christianity, tying Christian faith to patriotism.

Racing through a late-afternoon Hudson River mist on April 7, the Pennsylvania Limited streaked into the tunnel that led the renowned evangelist to Manhattan and his greatest challenge. A reporter on the train saw Billy press his face against the window and heard him mutter a short prayer. When the train glided to a stop at Pennsylvania Station, Billy became suddenly animated: "New York! By jingo. New York, here it is. . . . Come on Ma Sunday! Trail along here, boys! Let's see what a turnout they've got here in honor of Jesus Christ."[7]

Nearly sprinting through the opening door like a panther released from a cage, Billy bolted onto the platform where hundreds of well-wishers, including his son George who had handled much of the advance planning, shouted encouragement. Through the station the Sunday party streamed, out into the New York sunlight where a throng of thousands, many waving American flags, whooped and yelled, straining to glimpse the famed celebrity. Suddenly a chorus of thousands broke into a verse of "Brighten the Corner Where You Are." One reporter noticed Nell's eyes moistening. Billy charged through the rollicking crowd, slapping backs, pumping hands. At one point in his exuberation he nearly knocked down his wife and a few other women nearby. John D. Rockefeller, Jr., pressed through the crowd to shake Billy's hand. "Isn't this fine, isn't this wonderful," Rockefeller exclaimed to a reporter. "It seems to me that everything points to a splendid success for Mr. Sunday. It seems as though New York wants him and will be glad to hear his message."[8]

Against the backdrop of the noble stone arches of Penn Station, to the accompaniment of a contingent of cornetists, the thousands now joined in singing a selection of Billy's favorite hymns—"Since Jesus Came into My Heart," "Onward, Christian Soldiers," and "Beulah Land." They also sang the national anthem. "Never," wrote an editorialist of the *New York American*, had Penn Station "been so glorified."

From the station, a motorcade led by police escort headed to a home on Northern Avenue where Billy would reside during the campaign. Asked about the possible impact on the revival of the war fever abroad in the land, Billy declared, "Patriotism? Of course I shall preach patriotism. I have no more use for a man who is not loyal to his country than I have for a man who is not loyal to his religion." The United States had not wanted war, he said. But Germany "kept spitting in our faces." With national honor and pride at stake, with right and justice endangered, America must respond with great vigor. War, he said, would make people think of spiritual things.[9] Let the New York crusade begin!

> *Now the fight of faith begin!*
> *Be no more the slaves of sin.*

Easter Sunday, April 18, 1917. At two o'clock every chair, every possible standing-room vantage point on the outer perimeter of the tremendous tabernacle was filled, thousands of people straining to view the platform where 2,000 choir singers took seats. When Rody walked on stage, sparks of applause, starting in the front rows, crackled and grew like a brushfire throughout the building until the sound welled in the ears of the 20,000. Rody nodded, bowed, and introduced the Reverend Charles Goodell, pastor of St. Paul's Methodist Episcopal church, who would open the service with a prayer. But first the immense choir broke into "Come Thou Almighty King." Outside the tabernacle the sound could be heard for blocks; inside, it seemed to pierce into the walls and rafters of the building. It wrenched tears from the eyes of many, this almost otherworldly sensory experience, stirring and invigorating. After a few other hymns, the crowd of thousands began to jostle expectantly and strain for a view. They knew what was next.

From the rear of the platform the smallish, fifty-four-year-old former baseball player from Iowa moved forward. This was perhaps the greatest moment in his life. Stepping to the front, he raised his right arm in salute to the enormous assemblage and the people arose as one, cheering, clapping, many waving white handkerchiefs. Billy nervously leaned over to a friend on the platform and asked, "Do you ever pray?" "Well, sometimes," the friend answered. "All right, then, say a prayer for me now. I mean it. I need it."[10]

He stood there amidst this spectacle of sight and sound, a tense-looking, stark figure beneath the great, curved sounding board, a man who with grit, energy, and ingenuity had reached the heights. These thousands here on this day in this building, the many other thousands around New York and the country, had accepted this plain-speaking preacher as a figure around whom they could rally, a man who represented the virtues of soberness and discipline, who reaffirmed and solidified their old-time religious precepts and emotions, who stood for the ethics and the faith and sensibilities of generations before them. If the pace of modern America was racing uncontrolled with mounting confusion and bewilderment, Billy Sunday stood as a defender of the faith and of simpler and humbler times, as a solidifying force of certitude against the frantic changes and dilemmas plaguing the spirit.

After a thunderous version of "When the Roll Is Called Up Yonder," the Reverend Goodell delivered his prayer for the success of Billy Sunday's work in New York. "May this be the crowning hour in his experience," implored Goodell. "Oh, God, amen!" Billy muttered softly.[11] Following a few more preliminaries, Billy stood to deliver the opening sermon of his New York crusade. From the old log cabin in Ames to the mammouth "Glory Barn" in Manhattan had been a long, grueling, sensational road and he had arrived on top.

The sins of New York and the troubles of New York were the sins and troubles of men and women everywhere, he began. "To the average mind New York is built around the Great White Way, Broadway, but what of the six million? The society queen all decked out in her jewels has her troubles, but they are the same as those of the wash-woman who manicures her nails over her washboard."[12] To those six million, all groping, all searching for ways to cope, to come to grips with their own mortality, Billy offered nothing new. "I'm an old fashioned preacher of the old time religion."

But that religion, he believed, remained the bedrock, the hope and salvation for the pedigreed as well as the destitute.

Warming to the crowd, his voice gaining power, Billy wheeled and paced across the stage, flailing his arms, hurling invective against sin and the devil, turning 168th and Broadway into familiar Sunday ground. Pointing and gesturing wildly at the crowd, leaping about the stage, face reddening, Billy took on the heathen, the vices, the corruptions which, he said, were afflicting the nation's soul. Regeneration, rebirth, conversion, salvation—the answers awaited those willing to forsake evil. Swept up in the passion and frenzy, the electrified crowd shook and cried and whooped with every utterance, every trembling, shaking convulsion. This was New York but it could have been Dixon, Illinois, in 1905, Boulder, Colorado, in 1909, Columbus, Ohio, in 1913, or Omaha, Nebraska, in 1915. He had them in his clutches, carrying them on a roller-coaster spiritual ride, twisting and bolting along from one demon-infested sin and vice and evil to another, attacking, always attacking.

Then, suddenly, he had an announcement. In the press and from many platforms he had been called a grafter and a chiseler, had been charged with exploiting religion for personal gain, of commercializing and packaging the Gospel to make millions. Billy had never shrunk from the issue; indeed, he had often said that the Lord rewarded his servants. He pointed out that he had been offered a million dollars to be in motion pictures and had declined. Many thousands of dollars, he said, had been dangled before him to speak a sermon into a "talking machine." He had declined that offer also.

For this New York crusade, nevertheless, Billy attempted to diffuse the money issue altogether. He was prepared, he said, to donate all of the funds raised in the offerings, in excess of expenses, to the American Red Cross and the YMCA for their work among United States soldiers and sailors. "I don't want your money," he declared, "I want you; I want to win your soul to Jesus."[13] The crowd erupted into wild applause.

Billy concluded his opening New York service that afternoon with some of his usual flourishes—sliding across the floor, shadowboxing Satan, hopping on chairs. One reporter described the

crowd's response as like "an Alpine avalanche."[14] The evangelist beamed. As he left the stage, Rockefeller grasped his hand
and clapped him on the back. Billy left the tabernacle uplifted in
spirit. He said to some friends about the coming campaign, "It's
going to be all right. When she once gets going here in New
York she's going to go so fast you won't be able to see her for the
dust.[15]

That evening the tabernacle was again jammed with spectators. Billy slammed his Gatling-like verbal bolts at Prussian militarism. He called for loyalty, service, for an outpouring of patriotic
fervor from "God's Grenadiers" against the kaiser and his fiendish
murderers and torturers. Blindly led by unscrupulous, bloodsuck-
ing generals and drillmasters, the German people were slaves, "a
legacy bequeathed to them from the dark ages."[16] The American
soldier who "breaks every regulation, yet is found on the firing line
in the hour of battle, is better than the God-forsaken mutt who
won't enlist, and does all he can to keep others from enlisting."
"In these days," he declared, "all are patriots or traitors to your
country and the cause of Jesus Christ."[17] No subtleties here, no
hedging or debating of fine points; just black and white; one side
or the other—God and country or Satan and his servants. Choose!
Act! Patriots front and center! Spineless, lily-livered swine into their
holes!

Banging his feet, slamming his fists, tearing at his clothes,
shouting—it was still not enough! Billy climbed upon the great oak
pulpit, outstretched his arms and legs, the sweat pouring into his
eyes, his collar drenched and ripped, and waved an American flag
back and forth in great sweeps. Led by the thousands in the choir,
the crowd and the evangelist sang "America" and "The Battle Hymn
of the Republic." "Mine eyes have seen the glory of the coming of
the Lord." Men openly wept. Hard-bitten reporters shook their
heads in disbelief. The massive crowd seemed completely under
Billy's command, the verses of music swelling to an incredible cre-
scendo, the evangelist all the while waving his flag. After the last
tremendous note had faded, Billy leaped from the pulpit, mopped
his face, and said, "That's all." God's greatest lieutenant strode off
in triumph.

In the days following these opening sermons, Billy plunged into the New York revival with his usual gusto and effervescence. He dined with Rockefeller; entertained Theodore Roosevelt and General Leonard Wood; met with clergymen; spoke to a large gathering of newspaper carriers; appeared at a recruiting rally; hosted a group of high school girls who were to carry the campaign message to their friends; and entertained the press. He gushed, "If the President of the United States were to call me up on the phone tonight and say 'Bill, let's change jobs,' I'd answer him, 'Nothing doing, Woodrow!' "[18]

The crowds of well-wishers, the press of reporters, the elaborate media coverage—all of it was heady stuff. When asked about his impression of New York, Billy was effusive: "Gosh, I wish the dictionary had one million words, and then a million more words, most of them adjectives, that could express my new ideas of New York. I could say that it am delighted beyond expression." Billy seemed almost stunned by these early days of the New York campaign. "In my mind were months of doubt, months of misgiving," he admitted. But they had been washed away by the city's enthusiasm and hospitality.[19]

Operating like a refined political organization, the Sunday revival had achieved a level of sophistication unmatched in the history of American revivalism. Across the city its tentacles reached, canvassing, telephoning, mailing, deploying. From its central headquarters in a dozen rooms of the Metropolitan Building, the Sunday machine monitored committee work; set up prayer meetings; signed up organizations, fraternal groups, and businesses to visit the tabernacle en masse; worked with local church leaders; fed stories to the press; arranged Bible classes at various sites around the city; approached women's and labor groups for support; and dispatched various speakers, including Nell, to selected audiences. The behemoth organization included a secretarial pool of over 1,100. Both in size and savvy, the Sunday team in New York stood as a model for later evangelistic crusades.[20]

But if the organization delivered, so did the preacher. His sermons on patriotism, prohibition, and morality drew enormous crowds and sensational headlines:

Sunday and the Flag Give Crowd a Thrill
Billy Pillories War Slackers
A Dry Manhattan Billy's Fond Hope
Broadway to Lose the Devil
What Jesus Would Do in Visit to New York
Sunday Flays Bad Mothers
Sunday Takes 15,000 on Trip to "Fiery Lake"
5,000 People Make Revival Look Like a Football Game
Episcopalians, with Fifes, March to Billy's Service
Drones in Churches Scored Again by Evangelist

Around Manhattan people repeated many of Billy's epigrammatic slings and arrows. They exchanged stories about his onstage antics. In one performance early in the crusade, the preacher acted out a play called "Selling Gold Bricks to God" in which he performed all nine parts, including the duke of Wellington, a hog-jowled bartender, Benjamin Franklin, and a woman of the street.

Alf T. Ringling, master showman and one of the proprietors of the Barnum and Bailey Circus, had recently given his own poetical assessment of Billy:

Providence was prodigal in producing
this pre-eminent pattern of persuasive
power. She gave him strength, speed, skill,
virility, variety, venturesomeness, brawn,
bravery, brilliancy, brains, breath,
bronchia—she made him of flame and
fire, deft and dextrous, devout
and daring—danger-defying and
devil-defying.[21]

Seemingly indefatigable, Billy maintained his incredible enthusiasm and intensity and the campaign rolled along.

His detractors tried their best to strike down the Sunday aura. Stephen S. Wise, perhaps New York's leading Reform rabbi, attacked Billy as a moral terrorist and a charlatan who cowed obsequious church leaders into sniveling obedience. Wise saw Sundayism as a worse threat to religion than atheism.

A Methodist bishop called Billy "grotesque." Other church leaders called him a menace to Christ's teachings, a huckster perverting the spirit of religious solemnity, a rogue spiritual bandit on the loose. Labor spokesmen lambasted his close ties to capitalist bankers and industrialists. And two New York doctors cautioned parents not to expose children to the evangelist's histrionics, lest their impressionable minds be corrupted by vulgarity. One psychiatrist characterized Billy as suffering from intellectual and emotional "infantilism."[22]

Priests from the Roman Catholic church of St. Rose of Lima, West 165th Street, between Amsterdam and St. Nicholas avenues, struck at the evangelist with special vengeance. They announced to their parishioners that it was a mortal sin to hear Billy Sunday, that no absolution would be given to those who confessed they had been to that dreaded tabernacle nearby.[23]

The noted newspaper cartoonist and artist Boardman Robinson, who had with John Reed been to the war zone in Europe and had seen the horrors of trench fighting, attacked the evangelist, the Liberty Bond hustler, in *The Masses*. Robinson's cartoon: A jubilant Billy Sunday, dressed in a military cap, has bagged a downcast recruit. As he pulls the unfortunate gentleman by a rope circling his neck, Billy declares, "I got him! He's Plum Dippy over Going to War." The new recruit was Jesus Christ.[24]

Billy seemed unfazed by the heated assaults. He had heard it all before and had expected the New York crusade to generate the most concentrated inflammatory rhetoric he had yet encountered. The criticism had, indeed, been intense; yet the support had been overwhelming and Billy was buoyant. At one evening service 22,000 wedged inside the tabernacle three-quarters of an hour before the start. By the time Billy arrived, another 15,000, by police estimates, surrounded the huge pine building. At another evening service, police and firemen had a difficult time dispersing an even larger crowd.

Thousands gathered at the Washington Heights revival site night after night in the spring of 1917 for a host of reasons. Some visitors were avid Sunday followers; some sought religious experience; others were merely seeking diversion. But the numbers surprised even the most optimistic in the Sunday camp.

The unfolding war drama searing the nation's consciousness in these days undoubtedly played a major part in the campaign's spectacular impact. In late April Congress passed the Liberty Loan Act providing for the sale of lands to the public to finance the war effort, and in early May the United States Navy began convoy duty in the North Atlantic for troop transports and merchant ships. Congress soon passed the Selective Service Act. And the composer and entertainer George M. Cohan, who, like Sunday, would rouse audiences with patriotic, flag-waving performances, wrote a little ditty that Americans would hum for generations—"Over there, over there / Send the word, send the word over there . . ." Cohan was one of America's most demonstrative patriots. But those Yanks who were going over there to Europe had no greater booster than the preacher holding forth in New York.

In early June, Billy spoke before a thousand sailors from the Brooklyn Navy Yard and asked God to "strike down in his tracks" any man failing to register for the draft. Billy, financially flush in these times, also announced his own purchase of $25,000 worth of Liberty Bonds and declared that if "hell could be turned upside down, you would find stamped on its bottom 'Made in Germany.' "[25]

In a time of mounting tensions and uncertainties, the tabernacle seemed to many a refuge and Billy Sunday the chief steward, a man who could inspire and protect. Those thousands that pressed together to sing, shout, and thrill to the harangues thundering inside the giant wooden building found camaraderie, allegiance, and purpose. The gatherings were like enormous pep rallies for God and country, uplifting, stimulating, breathing new life and emotion into flagging spirits. The Sunday invective had always emphasized war and battle and Christian struggle.

Soon, your enemies all slain,
Crowns of glory you shall gain.

But now the similes and allusions portended threats much more immediate. If the devil's onslaughts seemed often distant and ephemeral, Germany's were not. Billy saw the New York revival as fostering a new surge of patriotism in the country.[26]

The organizers of a "Wake Up America" celebration, intent on infusing as much spirit and punch into the event as possible, asked Billy to deliver a talk at Carnegie Hall. The evangelist took on the assignment with characteristic gusto. He talked about his forebears who fought in the Revolutionary War and about his father, killed in the Civil War before he ever saw his son's face. The defense of freedom and liberty was a Christian responsibility, he said. Germany, emboldened by what it thought was American weakness and lack of resolve, had taken a murderous course of destruction and conquest and must be stopped. "I am a 24 karat, one hundred cents on the dollar, twelve inches to the foot, sixteen ounces to the pound, two thousand pounds to the ton, major league rooter and booster for preparedness." America's fight was God's fight. "I don't believe, like some people, that there is in the country a lack of patriotism."[27]

And he was out to prove it. At the tabernacle, in speeches to groups around the city, in interviews, he spewed venom at the mad-dog Prussians and appealed to America's nationalistic fervor. He praised a judge who jailed a pacifist for six months for distributing literature advising men not to enlist. True to his open, gushing admiration for heroic figures, for virile, guts-and-glory fighters, Billy embraced Moses, Joshua, and David as Christian examples of courage and fortitude, a kind of rough-and-tumble Hall of Fame. Combative and intractable, these biblical heroes didn't flinch. Neither should the United States in its own crisis. "The flag has been unfurled," he declared, "and we have been assaulted by the enemy . . . and damned us to our teeth, sir, and the country that gives you your clothes, your bread and your butter, and your home, surely—surely! when we unfurl the flag we are not going to deny fidelity and loyalty to it."[28]

To the slackers and trimmers, to those who would hide and slink and cower to avoid the draft, he had nothing but ridicule and contempt. They were, he said, as loathsome as traitors. Show your manhood, show your mettle, unite behind God's warriors for "Jesus Christ has raised the blood-stained banner." Wild applause inevitably followed such declarations. Billy rode the patriotic warhorse hard throughout the campaign.

But he also sounded the other familiar themes: lamenting the ills of modern life and its materialism, graft, corruption, greed, and fatally hectic pace; castigating alien political philosophies and religious cults, those vile beliefs slinking their carcasses out of the pit of hell; sorrowing over the outrages and misery caused by liquor, "the worst enemy to humankind"; warning about moral failings, about the putrid vices and black deeds so infecting society—strip joints, tango halls, cardplaying, close dancing, infidelity, apathetic preachers, and a host of other human and social shortcomings.

Against these corruptions and ills Billy sketched the other side, an image of Victorian responsibility straight out of the nineteenth century. Cleanliness, godliness, trust, honor, service, purity—these were the keys to salvation, the tickets to heaven, attributes and traits raised by the evangelist to cosmic dimension. All the woes and pain bombarding humanity could be traced to one monumental fact—sin. And the only answer, the answer dodged and evaded, ignored and repressed, was salvation through Christ. This was the reason for the New York revival. Billy meant to awaken the slumbering, to arouse and annoy and badger, to stir the populace from lethargy. "Oh Lord, Revive Thy work!"[29]

As in every Sunday campaign, the New York revival featured moments of the bizarre. During one of his brimstone, damnation orations called "No Second Chance," in which he declared that sinners consigned to hell must remain eternally, he preceeded, as he had done many times before, to name several historical figures undoubtedly in residence there. Among the damned selected by the preacher were Voltaire, Rousseau, Catherine the Great, Jezebel, Ivan the Terrible, and other kings, queens, and philosophers. A few days later one newspaper headline read, "Dancer Says Billy Should Go to Hell." The dancer was Isadora Duncan, performing at the Metropolitan Opera House. In a speech following her performance, the belligerent, leftist-leaning Duncan, draped appropriately in red, took issue with Billy's list of those in hell. "I am a spiritual and intellectual daughter of Sophocles, Plato, Euripides, Aristophanes, Galileo and Walt Whitman," Isadora bristled, referring to other notable figures listed by Billy as inhabitants of the Great Below. "If Mr. Sunday believes there is a hell, I advise him to go there, where he may speak with more authority."[30]

In late April Billy made his first New York call for his flock to hit the sawdust trail, to come forth and publicly join the recruits for Christ. His voice rasping and broken after an hour's hellfire preaching, Billy managed to leap to the top of a table to make the trailhitter appeal. Large numbers of sailors, soldiers, businessmen, and students from New York Bible classes began to shuffle through the carpeting of wood shavings to the sounds of "The Star Spangled Banner" to clasp hands with America's greatest preacher, to profess their will to join Christ's crusade and to lead better lives. The first call in New York for trailhitters set an all-time record for Sunday rallies, approximately 2,400 individuals.

One of the first recruits to make his way to the front was Patrick F. McQuade, one of the trainers and "rubbers" with old Cap Anson's Chicago White Stockings of the 1880s. "Many's the time I helped you get into shape to play baseball," McQuade said to the evangelist. "Now, Bill, get me into shape to meet God."[31]

They came to the pulpit in two lines to profess their faith and to meet God's celebrated servant. To greet them and shake their hands Billy swayed back and forth like a pendulum in a dugout portion of the platform specially built for the trailhitting services. Billy spoke briefly with nearly fifty individuals a minute, the ushers gently pushing and steering, keeping the growing lines moving, and the secretaries taking care of the card signing.

Exhausted, his clothes drenched and ripped, the evangelist grasped hand after hand: "Thank you, thank you, God be praised. God bless you. Thank you. God bless you. Thank you. Jesus is with you. Jesus greets you, son. Hallelujah. Amen. Amen. God speed you. Watch us now, Devil, watch us now. Glory to God. Jesus lives. Good luck. God is your father."[32] The choir sang softly "When the Roll Is Called Up Yonder," "Hold the Fort for I Am Coming," "Since Jesus Came into My Heart," and "Jesus, Lover of My Soul."

Two thousand four hundred. Record-breaking. More trailhitters in one night than in any night of his more than twenty years on the road. New York, fearful, alien, sin-stained, was responding. When the evangelist finally stumbled back to the dressing room, rubbing his aching right hand, tortured by endless handshaking, he slumped in a chair and weakly shouted, "Wonderful! Marvellous!" New York, he muttered, was not cold to God.

Night after night they came. They responded to one of the preaching giants, with his supreme gift of moving and molding crowds, of instilling powerful images, of psychologically kneading and leavening the audience, playing emotional symphonies like a master.

But most in the crowds were his from the start. Many observers noted the relative homogeneity in appearance—the starched shirts; the clean, sober demeanors; the look of small-town churchgoers on a Sunday morning. The dapper and dandy types were not here, nor were the young rebels, the poor, the unkempt and destitute, the immigrants, the blacks. Billy had brought old-time Protestant gospel to a hugh metropolitan area and had extracted from it the very people who might have arrived only a few years or weeks earlier from Joplin, Missouri, or Terre Haute, Indiana. They were mostly folks who were used to Wednesday night prayer meetings and Saturday bake-offs, folks who had migrated from farms and small towns, for whom Billy's message evoked powerful memories and emotions. This revival, this outpouring, was a demonstration of support and commitment by a segment of the big city wedded to midwestern religious virtue.

They came; service after service they came, renewing their faith, congregating with their people, paying homage to their Lord and honoring His most famous promoter. In subways, buses, private cars, and on foot they streamed to Washington Heights. So densely packed were the crowds on April 22 that the Sunday team held overflow services outside the tabernacle along Broadway. Over 3,000 trailhitters signed cards on that day alone. Billy's appearances drew such multitudes that, for blocks around the tabernacle, concessionaires found business so brisk that it seemed they had found a heaven of a different sort. Soon there were no longer two military recruiting stations nearby; there were six. Much of New York's action had, it seemed, moved north from Times Square about 125 blocks.

On April 25, Billy welcomed to the tabernacle his old mentor, J. Wilbur Chapman, to give the opening prayer. "I knew Mr. Sunday before he knew how to preach," said Chapman. "If, in the providence of God, I did anything to start Mr. Sunday on his mission, it is about the greatest thing that God could have permitted me to do." There was sometimes jealousy and fierce competition between evangelists. Between Chapman and Billy there was mutual respect.[33]

From a renowned evangelist of one generation to the greatest evangelist of another, this poignant testimony could not have come, in Billy's mind, from a more respected, admired friend. In sermon after sermon, Billy credited Chapman with being the principal influence in launching his career and a constant source of strength and support.

Billy's ebullition and joy over the progress of the New York crusade were nearly obliterated in early may as Nell fell ill. Never during their entire married life had she had serious health problems and at almost every service in his two decades of preaching she had been at his side. Nell was rushed to the hospital and underwent surgery for acute appendicitis. This was another of the devil's onslaughts against God's warrior. But he would trust in the power of the Lord. Billy gamely carried on his schedule, receiving frequent reports on his wife's condition from his son George. As she recovered, Billy made announcements at each service and the crowd cheered heartily in each instance. Billy had never underestimated his profound psychological dependence on his wife, his reliance on her care, strength of purpose, dedication, and organizational skill. In these days in early May, 1917, at the height of his evangelistic career, he came face-to-face with the haunting specter of loss. Nell recovered, but dark fears plagued Billy Sunday.

The New York crusade rolled through the last days of May into June. At the invitation of several civic and political leaders such as Jimmy Kelly and Jack Sirocco, Billy gave a stirring address on June 13 at Hadley Rescue Hall in the Bowery. It had been many years since Billy had paced the streets and hit the dives of big-city tenderloins. From those early years of wandering on the road from town to town and city to city on team buses, Billy knew well the world of the 5¢ beer halls, the gutter bums, and the joy ladies. Many of his early teammates had not survived that world.

Except for his early work with the YMCA, Billy's religious ministry had not taken him back to the inner-city netherworlds. It had taken him to the small towns of his midwestern youth, back to a new beginning among the people with whom he shared common roots. But as his revivals left the small towns and marched into the large cities, Billy was again coming close to the world which, he knew, had nearly engulfed him some three decades earlier.

When Billy spoke that night at Hadley Hall it was not as if he had come face-to-face with some strange, alien culture, some hellish jungle out of the pages of Maxim Gorky or Victor Hugo. He had been there himself. The preacher who now dined with the Rockefellers, who now toasted in drawing rooms of the Plaza Hotel, who now appeared at banquet halls and ballrooms, had beaten the long odds. He came back at least for this night to tell his story, to speak the language, to offer an example. Tonight he was not with the Rockefellers or the Roosevelts; he was with Utica Mickey, ShortChange Abe, Morris the Newsboy, Tubbo, and Loo Fook. A few in the audience came from a damp, underground passage under Doyers Street where men slept huddled like cargo in slave ships. The fetidly perfumed air of bad whiskey and stale tobacco, the sounds of persistent coughs and sniffles, the five-day beards and faces of purplish scarlet, the dubious, furtive expressions of mistrust and scorn, the dazed and hollow eyes—Hadley Mission greeted Billy Sunday.

With his voice even more hoarse than usual and his face showing the weariness that the long New York revival had inflicted, Billy leaned forward on the mission's lectern to the hundreds who had jammed into the stuffy, low-ceilinged hall. "Boys," he said, "I want to tell you this. God thinks just as much of the souls of the fellows down here as He does of the fellows on Fifth Avenue."[34]

The weathered audience—this collection of young toughs, hard-bitten labor skates, nearly delirious alcoholics, and needle-marked junkies—didn't hoot or jeer. Some of the men were bandaged, others wore eye patches, and some walked with pronounced limps. They had been through human wars known only through vague rumors by those in the Plaza Hotel.

They all listened. Billy talked about his own life, his early days mixing in the street life, his conversion. He talked about the evil effects of booze, how the men could fight and lick it and elevate themselves, how all of them had an inner dignity that never died, how they could lift themselves up by the power of the Christian message. "I want to ask you to believe that. I want to ask every one of you who does believe that to come down here and shake my hand."

At first, an uneasy silence held the hall as if in a timeless, motionless trance. No one moved. No one spoke. They stared at the minister. "Boys," Billy went on, stepping forward toward them, "how many of you will come down here and say, 'Billy, here's my fin. I want to live for God and be a Christian. I want to find Jesus Christ and do my best to live for him.' "[35] Still nobody stirred. More silence. Finally, a few ushers walked down the aisle to Billy. But the preacher was looking beyond them, looking into the faces of the battered men on the benches. Then a gaunt, middle-aged man with a shriveled arm and one closed eye rose slowly among the crowd from about four rows back, stumbled over several pairs of feet, reached the aisle, and walked to the evangelist. Immediately many of the others followed, grasping Billy's hand. None of the men promised to forsake the street life; there was no trailhitter card signing, or soul-wrenching confessions. They slowly passed by, some softly saying "God bless you," looking Billy square in the eye and nodding, faint smiles appearing.

That was it. And yet, when it was over, Billy called it the greatest meeting he had held in New York. It had touched him. In those faces he saw what might have been for Billy Sunday; he saw also the humanity that still remained. "I'm glad I came," he said softly."[36]

But now his car drove him north out of the Bowery, away from the grime and disease and poverty and shame. Behind, he left men like the Reverend John Callahan of Toombs Prison, whose own ministry was rooted among men from those streets. He left behind the mission-house preachers or "sky pilots" and the Salvation Army bell-ringers, men and women who worked day after day among these people. Billy hoped his own foray into the Bowery had somehow made a difference; he had no doubts about the commitment and service of those others who remained behind.

On June 17 Billy Sunday closed his ten-week New York revival. For three separate sermons on that day he filled the tabernacle. Choked with emotion after the last sermon, Billy prayed, "Oh, Jesus, thank you. Thank you for your plan of redemption, for your salvation, which I have been the poor medium to express." He had dreaded the moment of saying goodbye to New York, he said. "We say it when ships sail out, when friends depart, when the hearse drives up, but we never will say it in Heaven. We have learned to love every light in this old tabernacle."[37]

To seemingly endless cheering Billy waved and embraced friends, sharing in the warmth and fellowship. "I don't want to go! I don't want to go!" he said several times. Finally, turning to leave, swinging his arms in an embracing gesture, he uttered, "Goodbye, New York."

In sheer numbers the last day of the New York revival was the most successful in his entire career—nearly 75,000 listeners and an offering totaling almost $120,000 which would be turned over to the YMCA and the Red Cross. The records of the New York crusade for attendance and offerings dwarfed any previous revival. Nearly 100,000 trailhitters had signed pledge cards, doubling any previous campaign.

On the following day, Billy, Nell, and others in the Sunday party boarded a train at Penn Station. Crowds of admirers threw flowers and sang "Brighten the Corner Where You Are" and "God Be with You Till We Meet Again." The train headed west for Indiana.

Supporters and detractors soon traded claims and counterclaims, cited statistics, and offered personal testimonies to the success or failure of Billy's New York crusade. Some church leaders cited new figures of church membership; others claimed the Sunday revival would have no long-term effect. Prohibition advocates and opponents traded charges and insults on the effects of Billy's work, as did pro-war and pacifist spokesmen.

The New York revival, as with all the revivals throughout Billy's career, cannot be measured strictly by statistical compilations. If Billy's organization flaunted the nearly 100,000 pledge cards as proof of the crusade's mighty religious impact on the New York community, it is true that large numbers of those who signed were not new converts or were not converts at all. Indeed, the *Literary Digest* ran an article ten years after the New York revival citing statistics showing that only 200 permanent church members could be traced directly to the Sunday campaign.[38] The Sunday organization, of course, considered such studies to be error-ridden and pernicious.

But the revival was a phenomenon that affected hundreds of thousands of individuals in many varying ways, most of which are not statistically measurable. The revival was an enormous event, a happening, part church service, part political rally, part stage entertainment. Thousands trekked to the tabernacle seeking religious uplift; others were there only out of curiosity. Many trailhitters who were already church members were unquestionably strengthened in their beliefs and commitments; others who were occasional churchgoers were likely renewed in enthusiasm. And religious intensity and passion are not always reflected in later church attendance or participation. Many of those thousands of non-churchgoers who made their way to the tabernacle were certainly emotionally charged and affected, whether they subsequently joined a church or not.

To the thousands of volunteers who spent months of strenuous work in the New York revival—the ushers, secretaries, choir members, and others—the spring of 1917 may have seemed one of the most treasured periods of their lives. Indeed, several of the temporary prayer groups, choir organizations, and religious committees established for the campaign lived long after the event itself.[39]

For Billy the New York revival stands as the grandest moment in his evangelistic career. The city that had filled him with such doubt and trepidation, the city of scoffers and cynics, had given him what he saw as a great victory. At first he didn't have any ambition to go to New York. "But I did have an ambition to go where the Lord wanted me to go. . . . I was scared stiff until I got into the tabernacle, where the folk were jammed in so hard you could hear the planks creak." He found New Yorkers keenly intelligent, he said, eager to hear his message and to volunteer for campaign work.[40] The dragon was not the fearsome creature of his nightmares. "I know that many who walk the pavements of Broadway are as close to God as I am."

The massive pine tabernacle stood empty now, a great monument to a holy war; the stirring songs of an immense choir—victorious songs of struggle and conquest and prizes beyond man's dreams—were now a memory. Onward rise the hosts of God to "join that glorious train." He had crossed his Rubicon; he had survived his Waterloo. He had done it, had marshaled his troops, provided the inspiration, paved the way. And he had shown later evangelistic generals how it could be done.

Four decades later. Another famous evangelist hits Gotham. "Billy in New York," *Time* magazine headlined in 1957. Around the city, they talked about his energy, his zeal, about the evangelistic blitz he was laying on the big city, about the efficiency and dedication of his organizational team, the vanloads of recruits spreading the word, dividing the city into districts as an army preparing an assault. Reporters, city officials, and New York wags marveled at the preparation, the hoopla, the intensity and earnestness of the campaign and the preacher. Critics sneered. Catholic spokesmen attacked sharply, seeing the invader as sinister and strange, a "new junction of Madison Avenue and the Bible Belt." Under the evangelist's picture the caption read "No biz like his biz." Billy Graham was ready to take on New York.[41]

10

Joining Hands in Glory:
Billy in Atlanta

The Dixie Flyer headed toward Atlanta. It was November 1917 and from his Pullman window Billy began to see parts of the country mostly alien to him—the tobacco barns and white-picketed horse ranches of Kentucky; the farms in Tennessee manned by groups of blacks, many with heads crowned in gray and others, children, barely up to the knees of their fellow workers; the well-kept cemeteries all along the route with tiny, white, uniform tomb-stones dotting the countryside, reminders of a war less than three generations past; the cotton fields and the wooded hillsides flaming now in burnt red. As he left behind the November-bleak farmlands of the Midwest, the evangelist's mood was even more ebullient, more expectant than usual. New places, new people he would see, known before only vaguely in images of master and slave, colonels and mint juleps, white suits and grits, magnolias, and Robert E. Lee.

Billy had been in the South only a few times, as a young base-ball player in spring training; never had his revival army ventured into these lands. In the stuffy, smoke-choked confines of the Flyer, he restlessly chatted with reporters, paced, and then greeted the conductor, who assured him that Atlantans were "sure going to give him a rousing reception." Billy grinned and replied, "I expect Atlanta to come to the plate and line them out so fast the devil will have his tongue hanging out and when the game is called, the score will be one of which Atlanta will be proud."[1]

In the Chattanooga depot, Billy stood on the platform and read aloud a historical inscription about a lengendary train engine and the onlookers clapped boisterously. A trainman rushed up to the preacher and handed him a poem he had written especially for the Sunday visit, "Can a Trainman Be a Christian?" It began:

> *Can I live and be a Christian,*
> *On the railroad with its care,*
> *With its thousand frets and worries,*
> *Aggravations here and there?*

In Nashville, the widow of Sam Jones, the illustrious southern evangelist, boarded the train to shake Billy's hand. All along the route at depots and trackside, knots of people who knew of the train's famous rider waved and shouted encouragement. It was all warm and friendly.

On November 3, 1917, as the Flyer neared Atlanta after its four-day journey, Billy glowed. If Sherman had invaded Atlanta spewing fires of war, Billy would enter the city breathing the fire of the Gospel, would shower the city with the power of the Divine word, would capture the people with the promise of redemption and God's's everlasting grace. In the Pullman, the Sunday party was singing the songs that had rocked the tabernacles of the rural Midwest and those of the great metropolises—"Tell Me the Story of Jesus" and "Brighten the Corner Where You Are."

Here for all your talent you may surely find a need . . .
Brighten the corner where you are.[2]

Their corner was now Atlanta and the evangelists meant to light
this southern city with Divine incandescence. He bowed down in
the train car, his hat crushed between his knees, as all in the train
fell silent. "O Lord, may Thy spirit be upon us in this city of Atlanta
and may Atlanta feel the strength of Thy presence and be awakened to a new and better day, for Christ's sake, Amen!"

As Billy and his revival party emerged from the train at Ter-
minal Station, a great crowd pressed together to catch a glimpse of
the famous preacher from up north. As Billy's party made its way
through the Atlanta station, someone handed Nell a huge bouquet
of chrysanthemums and she beamed. To huzzahs, handshakes, and
the snapping of pictures, Billy made a triumphal march to waiting
cars. The devil, he thought, was no safer south of the Mason-Dixon
line than he had been in Iowa or New York. The Atlanta crusade
was ready to roll.

For the nation's most celebrated evangelist a trip into this section of the country had been long in coming. The delay, nevertheless, was understandable. Much of his reluctance to head south lay
in symbols and emotional sensibilities. To the son of a Union soldier who had died in the war, the Confederacy had represented
something foreign and haunting. Also, as a confirmed, unabashed
member of the Republican party, Billy had been hesitant over the
years to take his campaign organization into the section of the country
that was so overwhelmingly Democratic. The South had been the
enemy in the war; it was now the enemy of Republicans.

There was also the question of race. Billy had never been close
to blacks, either during his formative years in Iowa or as an adult.
His baseball mentor, Cap Anson, had been such an aggressive rac-
ist that he once threatened to keep his proud White Stockings off
the field if the opposing manager inserted a black player in the
lineup.[3] As a ballplayer, Billy had no black teammates and played
against no black opponents. From its earliest days, professional
baseball made segregation a powerful element of its tradition. So
did revivalism. As a preacher, Billy had seen few black faces in the

tabernacles. Religion, like baseball, was steeped in color consciousness. Indeed, the Sabbath day in the United States was the most segregated day of the week.

Billy had also met few blacks at his home in Winona Lake, Indiana. He did, however, have the opportunity to meet an influential black preacher at the Winona Lake Bible Conference a few years earlier. His name was Reverend Henry Hugh Proctor, born in Tennessee, graduate of Fisk, degrees from Yale and Clark universities. Ordained as a Congregationalist minister, Proctor was now pastor of Atlanta's First Congregational Church. Later, the black minister would move north to accept the pastorate of the Nazarene Church in Brooklyn.[4]

As early as 1908 Reverend Proctor was giving addresses at Winona Lake. He lectured at the first annual Winona Temperance Conference on the subject "The Attitude of the Colored People towards Temperance in the South."[5] Proctor had undoubtedly encouraged Billy to take his message to all the people of the country. There were black people in Atlanta, Proctor knew, who would cherish the opportunity to see the saber-rattlin' warrior of the Lord firsthand, to rock a Billy Sunday tabernacle as it had never been rocked before, with spirit and passion and choruses of hallelujah.

Billy's opinions of black people were very much in the mainstream of traditional white America at that time. From the pulpit and in answers to reporters, he pronounced blacks equal to whites in the eyes of God and equally deserving of an earned place in heaven, but they were not, he said, social or cultural equals. After a lynching and resulting race riot in Springfield, Illinois, in 1909, Billy denounced the wretched violence and said that if he had been in charge of law enforcement during the crisis the streets of Springfield would have sloshed with the blood of the lynchers, that any despicable gang members who strung up innocent blacks were foul and deserving of the most extreme punishment. But Billy, before carrying the implications of his remarks too far, backed off for an aside. The right of blacks to enjoy freedom from persecution did not carry with it an innate social equality between the races. "I don't believe there is an intelligent white man who believes in social equality or an intelligent and reasonable colored man who believes in social equality. But before God every man stands equal."[6]

When the flamboyant John Reed covered the Philadelphia Sunday revival in 1915, he asked one of Billy's lieutenants about heading south. "But you see," said the Sunday worker, "we don't know what to do about the color line. We've all been in conference several days seeking spiritual guidance. We don't know whether to have a Jim Crow tabernacle, or to alternate meetings of blacks and whites. It's very difficult."[7]

When evangelists had preached in the South in earlier years they usually treated the race question with strict deference to the social practices already in place. Dwight Moody held a few revivals in southern cities and set aside meetings devoted strictly to black audiences. Sam Jones had often preached in tabernacles strictly off-limits to blacks or in which special reserved sections had been designated. If buses and water fountains and rest rooms and restaurants offered separate facilities, why not tabernacles?

Over twenty years earlier, the U.S. Supreme Court, in *Plessy v. Ferguson*, had affirmed the so-called separate-but-equal doctrine. Enforced separation of the races, said the Court, did not abridge "the privileges or immunities of the colored man." The decision reflected much of the incendiary race hatred of the period, a growing militancy that brought over 1,000 recorded lynchings in the 1890s and a series of race riots in the new century.

Blacks found no comfort in the white-led churches and started their own. Baptists, Methodists, Presbyterians, Episcopalians—the major Protestant denominations all had separate black churches. In the South, feelings were particularly intense. The depth of those feelings can be measured by the views of Bishop Charles Galloway, a white Methodist from Mississippi. Galloway, a "moderate" on the race question, advocated segregated schools and churches, a ban on social mixing, and control by whites of all political matters. He did not, however, favor lynching.[8]

Billy's organization pondered the race dilemma for several years. Finally, they decided not to challenge tradition but to follow Moody's example and reserve special days for blacks only. With that decision behind them, and also with the realization that the mass Billy Sunday movement could not be stopped at state lines and must be truly national in scope, the evangelist threw aside his own nagging inhibitions and headed for Dixie.

Billy went armed with the results of published polls and studies indicating that the people of the South were becoming more staunchly religious and faithful churchgoers than people in other parts of the country. Indeed, at the New York revival earlier that year, Billy sounded the praises of the Southland, claiming that more than half of the people there were professed Christians, compared to a small fraction in some other states. And religious people represented American values. "There is more true Americanism south of what used to be Mason and Dixon's line," he said, "than any place in America."[9]

On November 4, 1917, the Atlanta crusade opened at the tabernacle built at Jackson and Irwin streets on the old circus grounds devastated by the city's massive fire a few years earlier. Never had Atlantans seen such a revivalist show—the huge choir; the tabernacle whose shape seemed to some observers like a gargantuan, wooden greenhouse; the massive crowd; and the preacher himself, leaping and crawling on his knees, twisting his body into corkscrew contortions, booming his message, declaiming, inflaming, leaping on chairs, pounding the pulpit, pegging the imaginary ball from deep in center field, skirmishing with the devil, spewing epithets at the satanic foe. This is what the crowd had read about in the papers, had heard about from friends and relatives who had seen him in action in other parts of the country. They, too, were quickly caught up in the frenzy, rolling with Christian punches, joining in the spirit of this extraordinary religious happening.

The state's governor, the mayor, and city councilmen and churchmen mingled with charwomen and boxing fans in the enormous arena. One reporter marveled at the size of the crowd of 12,000: "Faces—faces—faces, like a mosaic pavement as far as you could see." It was as if all the opera crowds and baseball crowds and political crowds and parades had somehow amalgamated—they all found Billy Sunday in common. Religious ardor, curiosity, a desire to be at the center of Atlanta's action on that day, whatever their particular reasons, they came.

Rivulets of perspiration flowing down his scarlet face, fists tightly clenched, Billy looked heavenward. "O God!" he pleaded, "if this city of Atlanta, pearl of the south, will fall on her knees before You and come over to Christ, then I say that this whole southland, drenched in tears of repentance, will also do as Atlanta does! Men and women of Atlanta, I hold before you the bleeding form of Jesus Christ. Take Him if you will!"[10]

The highly observant historian W. J. Cash, writing about this period in the South's history, said that people seemed to be thirsting for a new fury and passion in their religion. Ministers in the South, both urban and rural, had seemed bent on running their parishes and churches like business enterprises, like sales managers content to please boards of directors with decent quarterly sales figures and flow charts. Where was the fervor, the anger, where was the great outlet for pent-up frustrations and overwhelming fears, where was the religious zeal of the old times? It was in Atlanta in November 1917 and the people responded.[11]

As he did in all of his big-city revivals, Billy set a blistering pace—preaching, meeting with government officials and church leaders, fluttering about on side excursions. He visited the grave of Sam Jones; he took in the sights at Stone Mountain. He even learned some southern slang. When he admitted to a reporter that he had made a factual error in one of his sermons, Billy was told that he had "crawfished."

All of it was reassuring. The people appeared genuinely attracted to the famous evangelist, attuned to his manner and style. Billy took nearly every occasion to say how delighted he was to be in the South and how gracious and honest were its people. The Atlanta campaign seemed very much like Billy's other recent big-city crusades. Nevertheless, there was a difference. Ahead lay the first special evening at the Sunday tabernacle for Atlanta's black populace. How would the preacher and his workers react? How would black citizens and their own church leaders respond? Billy and his advisers worked closely with black political figures and clergy to plan for the occasion and to spread the word of the meeting throughout the community. To overcome the racial anxieties, tension, and mistrust rumbling under Atlanta's social foundation was a task that loomed mountainous.

Just over a decade before, the rumbling had broken through, the seams had fractured. On the night of September 22, 1907, a white mob, fueled by political race-baiting in a governor's election campaign, had stormed through the Decatur Street section of black Atlanta, burning businesses, assaulting blacks in bars and restaurants and on the streets, and even waiting at streetcorner stops for cars with possible new victims. Some blacks fled Atlanta; others found sanctuary on the campuses of the several black colleges in the city, especially Clark. At least ten individuals were massacred in the violence, and scores of others were seriously injured; many businesses and homes lay in burning ruins. Only after intervention by the state militia did the fury and violence end.

W. E. B. Dubois, apostle of black pride and resistance, fired off an angry and sorrowing prayer to the magazine the *Independent* which described a city in travail: "And from her loins sprang twin Murder and Black Hate. Red was the midnight; clang, crack and cry of death and fury filled the air and trembled underneath the stars when church spires pointed silently to Thee." And Booker T. Washington, who in 1896 had stood on a platform in an Atlanta auditorium at the opening of the great Atlanta Exposition and electrified a vast white audience with sweeping oratory about a new South and about the responsibilities of both races to work together for their common good, sadly lamented in 1907, "I cannot refrain from expressing a feeling of very deep grief." The horror must not discourage Atlanta's blacks, he said, but must inspire all races to come together to change the deplorable state of racial unrest.[12]

The city of Atlanta in this period had already emerged as the leading center of black higher education in the country, boasting several colleges and universities including Morehouse College, Spellman College, Clark University, Atlanta University, Atlanta Baptist College, and Fisk University. The intellectual probing and ferment in these university communities produced a number of leading spokesmen for black rights, including Professor John Hope of Atlanta Baptist and DuBois, radical writer and organizer and one of the founders of the National Association for the Advancement of Colored People, a new organization strongly advocating black resistance to social injustices. The city had also spawned the first, if only short-lived, major African-American magazine in the South in the twentieth century, *Voice of the Negro.*

Even with the growth of these institutions and movements and the ascendancy of new leaders, even though many of Atlanta's blacks had moved into an emerging professional and business class, the times were dispiriting. Ultra-racist books such as *The Negro a Beast, The Negro: A Menace to American Civilization,* and *The Clansman* circulated widely, the latter made into a motion picture adaptation as *The Birth of a Nation* in 1915. Black people were, the authors asserted, innately inferior, criminal, immoral, and generally brutish, something less than human. And they were not just happy darkies; they were a threatening and ominous force.

Although such venemous, vitriolic hatred spewed out by these publications revolted many whites, most were fearful, nevertheless, about the race question, uneasy about black aspirations and incursions, and willing to take forceful measures of control. Subjugation sank its fangs. Jim Crow railway laws, streetcar segregation laws, municipal park exclusion laws, and residential segregation ordinances all fired volleys at black rights. Lynchings remained a constant threat and a reminder of the lowly state in which black Americans languished. President Roosevelt in 1906 delivered a message to Congress asserting that lynchings were usually retribution against black men who had assaulted white women. Disenfranchisement had already been institutionalized by sundry methods, some legal and constitutional, others through intimidation and physical force. And many blacks were mired in extreme poverty. Southern black tenant farmers existed in many cases as barely more than slaves.[13]

When Billy arrived in Atlanta in 1917, racial fires still singed the city's edges. Atlanta papers recoiled at reports of near race riots in Houston, Texas, and Montgomery, Alabama, and speculated whether their effect would spread to Atlanta. Editorialists questioned whether an imminent Supreme Court decision in Washington would have any effect on an Atlanta city housing ordinance. The city law barred new influxes of blacks in city blocks now occupied by a majority of whites. At a mass meeting held on November 11 under the auspices of the Atlanta Normal and Industrial Institute, white and black politicians, businessmen, and clergy debated the role of the black worker in Atlanta society. A Coca-Cola Company official who supervised a large force of black workers at the Atlanta plant declared, "Sensible colored people who attend to their own business and work hard and save their money may have a little trouble here and there for a while, but everything will come out well in the end." The Reverend H. L. King, a black minister, talked about large numbers of blacks leaving Atlanta and the South hoping to find better conditions in the big northern cities. "Segregation, injustice and non-use of the ballot by the colored men are the causes of negro emigration and the end is not in sight," declared Reverend King.

Into Atlanta's racial chasm stepped the famous white preacher from the North, and on Monday, November 19, 1917, 15,000 black people answered his call to join him in the tabernacle. Reporters conjectured that it was the largest assemblage of blacks under one roof in the history of the South.

Billy came prepared. He had visited three black universities in the days prior to the meeting and had spoken to faculty members and students about race problems, about the hopes and aspirations of the black population. He had traveled around the city with an eye on black laborers, businessmen, and other workers and on the personal relationships between individuals of different races, their manner of communicating, their various habits and customs. Considering Sunday's relative ignorance about blacks and the race problem, this was a woefully superficial cram course in sociology. But he impressed many black leaders with his religious earnestness and sincerity and they responded. And Billy soon developed impressions and opinions and he was ready to deliver.

From all across the city and state they came this night—Sunday school classes of black youngsters, preachers, college students and their teachers, young people's organizations, black fraternal groups, soldiers from nearby Camp Gordon, and elderly individuals astonished at the chance to hear the celebrated white preacher.

With a soft rain pattering on the mammoth tabernacle roof, blacks quickly filled all the seats and ushers sat down in the aisles.

Outside, others ignored the rain and jockeyed at windows and crevices to hear the sounds from within.

Rody opened the service by asking everyone in the crowd to stand and sing "My Country Tis of Thee." Behind the choirmaster stood a chorus of 1,000 voices recruited from local black colleges and a black grammar school. In the audience sat thousands of black individuals for whom singing was a vital part of their lives, men and women who had learned the songs of freedom and salvation from parents, who had calloused their hands in cotton and tobacco fields and had found comfort in the old-time hymns of glory, who could wash away some of the pain with melodies and rhythm and could make a tabernacle quiver in sound.

They sang, one song after another, and filled the tabernacle with beats and reverberations, sounds swelling in intensity to absorb the senses. The few whites inside—Sunday lieutenants, reporters, and some ministers—said later that they never heard anything like it before in their lives. Tears rolled down faces. Even louder it grew—pounding, surging crescendos of sounds, joyously uplifting.

> *I'm going to sing and shout in Glory . . .*
> *One of these days!*

One black writer later chided the white brethren: "But listen, white folks. . . . You can make the Tabernacle rock on its foundations, and all that, but, man, when those black folks get really started . . . they don't just make that Tabernacle rock, Man—they make that old Tabernacle get up and walk about!" Another observer said that the preliminary song service was not so much a service as a "massed attack," assaulting you with glorious tones.

At one point the delegation of students from Morris Brown College broke into a swinging version of "Morris Brown Gonna Shine Tonight." Rody was so caught up in the pulsing beat and intensity of the rendition that he asked them to sing it a second and then a third time. The choirmaster then asked for "Swing Low, Sweet Chariot." A young lady from Clark University walked to the front of the platform, faced the choir, and began the old hymn.

The crowd was hushed now as the notes soared, clear and radiant, and then the chorus bore down in a melodic wave. "That kind of singing," someone said later, "I never heard anything that came close. I never expect to again—until the Atlanta black folks pack that Tabernacle again and that Old Sweet Chariot begins to swing low."

They kept singing, long into the evening, a celebration. One observer in the tabernacle later remarked that soldiers go into battle more inspired with music ringing in their ears, that Oliver Cromwell's men marched along chanting rhythmically the Hundredth Psalm, that music could somehow bring souls together, could heal, could perhaps ease long-held prejudices. Never had Billy heard one of his favorites, "Down by the Riverside," sung like this. He seemed intoxicated, lost in its energy. During one refrain, the chorus bassos stood up as one and hit a note that seemed to surface from the depths of some enormous subterranean cavern.

Rody was now flinging his arms, urging the choir on and on and they responded magnificently. "I'm not forgetting any of these songs," wrote a reporter the next day. "Nobody who heard them as sung Monday night is likely to forget them."

With the music still pulsating in his mind, the preacher walked to the pulpit. Before leaping into the text of his sermon, Billy prepared to make a number of remarks about this night, about his perception of the race problem in the South, about the religion that held the answers. He looked shaken but his voice remained steady. He talked about the tremendous advances made by blacks in the southern states since the Civil War. Those advances, he claimed, were possible only because black people in the South were living among friends, their white neighbors. Blacks and whites, he asserted, were not enemies; only the excesses and hatred of a few individuals on each side had precipitated racial disharmony.

Recounting the days during the Civil War when white fathers left their wives and children in the care of loyal, trustworthy slaves, Billy portrayed an idyllic relationship between the races almost unbelievable in its simplicity and its cordiality. It was also unbelievable in its clouding of historical accuracy. Speaking of the master-slave dynamic, this trust of the white slaveholder to leave his family surrounded by faithful slaves while he went off to fight in a war to keep them slaves, Billy remarked, "Do you think Southern men will ever forget? Never—and in your hearts, my friends, is a heritage of honor and fidelity that glows with the brilliance of the sun in heaven upon the pages of history." The white and black people of the South understood each other, he said. "They will get along together the best in the world—without any help or any advice from anybody in the North."

Billy praised Booker T. Washington's philosophy of fostering good citizenship among the black population; he lauded the industry and sacrifices of the blacks and their willingness to labor. His plea: Stay in the South; you are among friends who know your needs and problems, understand your heritage. Stay in the South in a spirit of cooperation and fellowship; do not be lured by false prophets, by wistful dreams of better fortune somewhere else in the country. With God at your side, in a spirit of goodness and righteousness, you can live peaceably and in harmony with whites and find happiness. "The South is as naturally your home as Alaska is the home of the Eskimos," he declared. "The South cannot get along without the negro, and the negro cannot get along anywhere in the world as well as he can in the South, among his friends."

Ignoring the official repression being systematically pressed upon the blacks, ignoring the extensive violence raking and intimidating the black community, the preacher served up visionary pabulum and fanciful remarks, consoling and soothing. The crowd was polite; some cheered. But the evangelist was not at his best in offering analyses of these complicated problems. He was best at his profession—preaching. Pulling off his coat, rolling up his sleeves, whipping off his collar and tie, he was now ready to go to work.

> *Text: And David said unto Nathan, "I have sinned against the Lord." And Nathan said unto David, "The Lord also hath put away thy sin; thou shalt not die."—II Samuel, xii, 13*

Unalterable truths through the ages, Divine writ for all of man; here was David, a man of God, not because he was free of sin but because he had repented. In the Blood of the Lamb, in the old-time religion, would ye find salvation, freedom from remorse, everlasting life; in the saving grace of the Lord can ye find glory.

From the assembled crowd came shouts of "Amen" and "Hallelujah" and Billy seemed charged. He painted the image of being alive in the days of the old prophets, the biblical heroes, the men of power and courage, unlike so many of the clergymen of modern America, the trimmers with their Milque-toast religion, willing to slide evil under sin-soaked rugs, unable to level with their parishioners. Amen! God commands—no man or woman can be saved until born again, until washed clean. Hallelujah!

He was taking them up Glory Mountain, this preacher from the midwestern prairie, this white preacher. For this short time he and these thousands were one, sharing the same visions of sin and salvation, of redemption and the hereafter. All the barriers seemed like wilted strands of wheat against the religious gale roaring through the tabernacle. Billy, they believed, was inspired with the feeling. When Billy asked for trailhitters they streamed down the aisles, led by the young woman from Clark who had sung the solo part in "Swing Low, Sweet Chariot." In tears, Billy clutched and patted and shook one black hand after another. He seemed profoundly moved.

The next day the *Atlanta Constitution*, echoing editorial comment in other dailies, called this night in the tabernacle "epochal." Although delivered to a black audience, Billy's remarks, the *Constitution* asserted, should be pondered and heeded by every citizen of both races. Billy had pointed the way to reconciliation. To the blacks, he had issued a challenge to make all demands for better schools, housing, and equal treatment on a foundation of equal citizenship. Upon the whites, he placed an obligation of fair play and justice. This was truth straight from the shoulder, the editorialist went on, and a prescription for the South's racial dilemmas.

A few days later, Billy and his workers, heartened by the memorable night of November 19, decided to assemble another massive black choir; this time the music would be directed at a white audience. The scene was remarkable: an immense assemblage of 1,000 black singers filling the tabernacle with the haunting, vibrant songs of Zion, songs of plantation and slavery days, the white audience astonished at their power, overwhelmed by this extraordinary musical and religious experience. "The very air," said a black minister, "was tense with excitement."[14]

Over the next two weeks, Billy's Atlanta campaign rolled on. The *Constitution* carried full texts of his sermons. A variety of civic and political leaders, clergymen, and editorialists marveled at the hold Billy seemed to command over the congregations and at the spiritual awakening which seemed to be raging through the city. People were talking and arguing religion, analyzing the revival's progress and possible long-term effects, and assessing the magic of Billy's preaching, from his tantrums to his tenacity.

Day after day at the tabernacle he prowled over the usual landscape—the war and the serpent-inspired Huns; the hellish evils of spirituous liquors; the dangers lurking in a host of human activities, from dancing to premarital sex; the inherrant truth of the Scriptures and the hope of mankind for spiritual regeneration. He was winning the hearts of those southern audiences just as he had triumphed elsewhere. One writer declared, "Billy Sunday is a human dynamo; he is as vital as life itself. He is a thoroughly modern exponent of old-fashioned religion." A woman, whose alcoholic husband had recently sat in the back of the tabernacle listening to Billy's message, wrote to the evangelist, "He since has been the best husband that a woman could want. He told me he would stop drinking. . . . Oh, Mr. Sunday, I'm so happy. I know it was your talk that got to his heart, and I pray God to bless you and your work."[15] Another Sunday admirer even felt inspired to compose a poem, one verse of which declared:

> *Mr. Sunday knoweth well*
> *where dwelleth hope and fears,*
> *He knoweth where to bat for smiles,*
> *And where to punch for tears.*

On Saturday, December 1, Billy held another mass meeting for blacks and this time he invited several black ministers to share the platform. From the African Methodist Episcopal Church came Brother I. N. Fitzpatrick who immediately called for the choir to

sing "one of the battle songs." For this black service, Billy's team
decided to reach for spiritual music's limits. They cleared the platform so that approximately 6,000 individuals could assemble into
an enormous choir, a group of veteran singers from churches all
over Atlanta—Wheat Street Baptist, Mount Olive, Mount Zion,
Big Bethel, and many others. The sounds of "Amazing Grace"
soared, seeming to penetrate every crack in the farthest rafters of
the tabernacle—"Amazing Grace How sweet the sound that saved
a wretch like me."

It was especially cold in the tabernacle this night but when the
Reverend P. James Bryant rose and began to address the crowd the
sparks from the platform made overcoats completely unnecessary.
Pastor Bryant of Wheat Street Baptist, with his celebrated white
counterpart preacher sitting nearby, slammed out his own oratorical
flourishes, telling the crowd, to a repeating chorus of "Yessir" and
"Have mercy," that many whites in the South had first learned
Bible verses from the knees of Negro nurses. Pastor Bryant then
told the story of a black man who had apparently died but had only
gone into a trance while he temporarily visited hell. When the man
awoke, he was questioned by a friend:

> *"What did you find down there?"*
> *"Found everything 'bout like it is around here."*
> *"Find any Negroes down there?"*
> *"Yes, sir, boss, found lots of 'em, and lots of white*
>   *folks, too."*
> *"What were the Negroes doing?"*
> *"Well, sir, every white man had him a nigger,*
>   *holding him twix him and de fire."*

With whoops and hollers ringing in his ears, with Billy bent up in
laughter, Bryant then made a pitch for funds. "Give me a quarter,"
he said, "to hold between the white folks and the fire." Collection
pans jingled.

Billy, his voice hampered by a severe cold, lacked his usual
power but told the assembled blacks he deeply appreciated their
interest in his meetings and their respect. The combined choir, a

sextet, and some other musical groups then took over.

Sitting in the congregation was Rheba Crawford, white, daughter of a brigadier general of the Salvation Army in the southern district. The *Atlanta Constitution* editors had asked Crawford to attend some of the Sunday rallies and to report her observations. She had been to many evangelist gatherings, had listened to the music of the Sally bell-ringers and their large choruses, and had sat in tents and tabernacles and heard the gospel effusions of many revivalists. Crawford had neither seen nor heard anything like the musical service of this night—the tempos, the swaying bodies, the piercing resonances driving out from the colossal choir. Crawford felt as if the building were rising and that she was rising with it. "Seldom have I experienced such an eerie, creepy feeling—seldom have the very depths of my emotions been stirred," she wrote. "I wanted that music to go on forever."

> *Little David was a very good man*
> *Mm—Mm—Mm—Mm*
> *He killed the old giant with the sling*
> *in his hand*
> *Mm—Mm—Mm—Mm*

"While I was gathering up my pencil and leaving the tabernacle," wrote Crawford, "the song changed once more and way down Edgewood Avenue the sweet faint strains of 'Tis the old-time religion' followed me." Crawford would later follow in Billy's path. She became an evangelist.[16]

The Atlanta campaign moved into mid-December with Billy drawing big crowds and much praise in the media. He had genuinely warmed to Atlanta's people, white and black. The tensions barely beneath the veneer were not obvious to the evangelist; the stories of racial bigotry and hatred seemed to him almost a fiction. The courtesy and soft manners of the people, the zeal of the revival services, the streams of trailhitters pledging their lives to Christ all testified to the Holy Spirit working, changing lives, filling heads and hearts with repentance and religious conviction. If the South had earlier seemed to him from his vantage point in the North as alien, almost foreboding, all those prejudices were swept away and he felt at home.

On December 20, the mellowness suddenly cracked as the Atlanta tabernacle rocked with a different form of excitement. Billy had effusively opened fire with one of his characteristic slurs upon the Germans, that "dirty bunch that would stand aside and allow a Turk to outrage a woman," when a man shoved his way through the crowd, leaped upon the platform, and rushed at the startled evangelist. Quickly reacting to the charge, Billy crouched into a boxer's stance and, without hesitation, lauched an uppercut toward his aggressor. Fending off Billy's punch, the man landed a mild blow to the preacher's chest. Unfazed, Billy ripped another upper-cut, this one landing on the chin of the assailant. By this time the tabernacle was in chaos, with men and women scrambling and swinging, overturning chairs, and surrounding Billy and his attacker. Shouts of "Lynch him" and "Kill him" screeched from the lips of a few of the tabernacle worshippers; the Atlanta mayor, who got mixed up in the scuffle, was choked by unknown hands.

The scuffle quickly abated with the aid of police, who hurried away the attacker. "It's all right," Billy assured the crowd and a few moments later resumed his sermon.

At police barracks, W. H. Beuterbaugh, a carpenter and fiercely emotional German sympathizer, posed for photographs at his book-ing, one swollen right eye the only visible sign of his confrontation with Billy Sunday. When asked about his attack, a seemingly con-fused Beuterbaugh responded, "It was the work of the Devil." No one seemed to know exactly what he meant.

The irony of Beuterbaugh's attack was that it had nothing to do with black-white relations. Although some of Billy's supporters had been uneasy about the black choirs and the nights for blacks, Atlantans accepted without violence Billy's efforts to bring the races closer together under God's banner.

The Atlanta assault was one of only a few such violent inci-dents that marred Billy's long preaching career. Considering the evangelist's unrelenting, aggressive, and, to many, offensive verbal salvos against numerous individuals, institutions, and causes, his relative immunity to such assaults seems remarkable. Yet Billy's forum was the tabernacle, his cause Christian, and preachers were not often targets of violence. Even Billy.

The Atlanta campaign drew to a close as Christmas approached. On Saturday, December 22, Billy held his last meeting for blacks. "No man who ever came to Atlanta has done as much good in so short a time in creating a better feeling between white and colored races," declared Billy's old friend Reverend Proctor of the First Congregational Church. Lula R. Rhodes, a member of the women's auxiliary of the colored YMCA and a member of the choir at one of the black services, agreed. "It's true that Mr. Sunday has brought us into closer touch with our white friends. . . . I never shook hands with as many white men and women who congratulated us on our singing and told us they were proud of us. I am an American negro, and I feel as much at home here as anyone else."

The Saturday service featured Dr. Adam D. Williams, pastor of Ebenezer Baptist, the church on Auburn Street that would, generations later, figure so prominently in the American civil-rights movement, the church of Reverend Martin Luther King, Sr., and his son. Reverend Williams turned to Billy at the beginning of the meeting, talked of the effects of the Atlanta revival and Billy's services for the blacks, and concluded: "I'm going to live a better man, sir." A soul-stirring gospel preacher in his own right, Williams told the crowd that Billy had accomplished much in Atlanta, that there seemed to be a better atmosphere on the streets. He joked that a man who had owed him money for six months had finally paid him off and that he was looking to collect other debts before the influence of the revival wore down. The Sunday campaign, he said, made him feel more confident about black-white relations.

And then the tabernacle vibrated again with the black favorites—"I'm Leaning on the Lord," "Walk Together, Children," and "Swing Low, Sweet Chariot." Billy himself asked the great choir to sing "You'd Better Live in Union." Some of the black choir leaders asked the whites to join in and said they would try to teach them the verses. One reporter who listened to the results quipped, "The turns and throbs which come so natural to colored people somehow seem to elude the Aryan thorax."

Reverend P. James Bryant of Wheat Street Baptist spoke on

behalf of the Colored Evangelical Ministers Union, representing Atlanta's black churches whose combined membership numbered 20,000. Expressing gratitude to the Sunday organization for including the special black nights in the crusade, Reverend Bryant called Billy "a hypnotic, dynamic, athletic, linguistic, spellbinding gospel expounder." The Union's resolution thanked the evangelist "for the service he has rendered our community and for the sagacious, orthodox, evangelical, ethical, and intensely practical gospel message he has delivered to us as a race."[17]

Billy walked to the pulpit and said that he would take that resolution home to Indiana and put it into a bank vault and keep it there as one of his most cherished possessions. He said that he and Nell would sit by winter fires at Winona Lake and hear again in their souls the stirring singing of the blacks of Atlanta. "I have preached all over this great country," he said, "but I shall carry the most tender recollections of any place I have ever been in away with me from Atlanta."

And then, for the last time in the crusade, the old black melodies floated and drifted through the tabernacle as the crowds lined the aisles to shake Billy's hand. The black preachers stood at the front of the platform singing with the congregation, swaying with the music. "Walk together," went the old song, "to the great camp meeting in the promised land."

Two days before Christmas, the Atlanta campaign ended with a rousing meeting before 15,000 who had pretzeled into the tabernacle long before the service. At the end, after 2,000 trailhitters had paraded through the sawdust, the great congregation stood, some on benches, and waved white handkerchiefs while the chorus led them in "God Be with You Till We Meet Again." The Atlanta campaign was over.

In the days following, the city's ministers, civic officials, newspapermen—everyone, it seemed—commented on the magnificent work of Billy Sunday. Opinion about Billy, at least in the press, did not seem to differ with race. Reverend Henry Alford Porter of the white Second Baptist Church wrote, "The Christian people of Atlanta, if wise, will take the substance of Billy Sunday and thank God for him."[18] Reverend Proctor declared, "Unconsciously perhaps, Mr. Sunday has pointed to the true method of promoting harmony between the races." Proctor talked of music as perhaps the healing balm to soothe racial divisions. "Just as David charmed Saul with his music and drove away his madness, even so the African may charm the Saxon with his songs and assuage racial asperities."[19] Billy, Proctor believed, had forged racial links, made the first great step for reconciliation, showed the South its hope for peace.

At the last service for blacks, Billy had portrayed a scene in heaven when he and his family and Rody and the various Sunday campaign workers would gather and renew their bonds with the people of Atlanta, white and black. Billy had for the first time in his life felt close to black people. Ole Cap Anson was wrong. These were honest, God-fearing Christians full of love, able to translate that love into rhythms and melodies as could no other people. Billy left Atlanta with prejudices apprently tempered, assumptions compromised.

Yet Billy's understanding of racial dissension and the plight of blacks in society remained naive. Questions and details about segregation, economic power, southern tradition, racial stereotypes, black incursions physically into white neighborhoods and economically into formerly white jobs, of lynching and torture and terror, of inner-city poverty and the lack of adequate public education and health services—all of it seemed lost to Billy, drowned in the goodwill and harmony under the tabernacle roof. He knew of racial tension but was confident that the might of the Holy Word could overcome all.

Proctor was not so uninformed or blind to the deep conflicts. Yet he envisioned in the Sunday campaign a possible revolution in racial harmony that could be wrought from common spiritual experience. He had seen the jubilance on the faces of whites listening for the first time to Negro spirituals, had himself felt a closer kinship to whites spiritually, even felt a sense of joy among his black friends. Billy and his message represented a clear path to interracial opportunity. As one of the songs at the tabernacle had proclaimed: 'Ain't Gonna Study War No More."

Shortly after attending one of the black services, Lula Rhodes wrote about the great good he had brought to Atlanta. "Mr. Sunday has knocked off more bumps, filled in more ditches, cleaned up more new ground since he has been in Atlanta than anyone else since Lincoln signed freedom."[20]

But this spirit of racial healing and charity, so apparent to so many in Atlanta, was somehow lost in the Sunday campaign shuffle. A year after the Atlanta crusade Billy was in another southern city, Richmond. The capital of the Confederacy had within its population approximately 60,000 blacks. Billy's advance organizers and Richmond's local committees failed to contact the black ministers of Richmond, failed utterly to make any provision for blacks to attend the Sunday rallies. Atlanta, it seemed, had taught nothing to the Sunday organization. The *Richmond Planet,* a black paper edited by John Mitchell, Jr., bitterly complained about the exclusion, and berated Billy's advanced workers who had thought it wise to "show only whites the way to heaven."

His campaign organization under fire, Billy intervened, offering to hold one meeting in which blacks could occupy all seats in the balcony. As much an affront as a genuine gesture of goodwill, Billy's plan infuriated the *Planet*'s editors, who called for black citizens to boycott "the unclean feast." They did. Twenty-one lonely black people sat in Billy's Richmond tabernacle on the one day they were allowed to enter.[21]

Where was the spirit of Atlanta? From the heights of those "epochal" meetings in Atlanta, the Sunday campaign drifted. Although Billy had been emotionally stirred by the Atlanta experience, he and his campaign organizers were beset by conflicting pressures. Their mission, they believed, was to spread the gospel to as many potential trailhitters as possible. An overt effort to involve large numbers of blacks in revivals around the country would have, they knew, jeopardized some of their support. They never seriously considered such an effort.

In the case of the prohibition issue, the war issue, and on matters of public morality, Billy had throughout his career played the reformer, aggressively, defiantly. He saw the issues starkly, in unadorned, simple terms of good and evil. He lined up society's transgressions in his mind and tried to shoot them down in a fusillade of holy fire. Unlike Moody and other premillennialist precursors, Billy was out to change radically the wickedness in American society, to influence personal behavior, to alter institutions. But in the case of the race issue, the vision was shaded, obscured by conflicting emotions and sensibilities and political considerations. Atlanta thus became an exceptional occurrence rather than a guidepost. Proctor's vision, whatever its practical implications, was lost with the train that took Billy north again. Billy and his people would tread softly and safely on the issue, guided by prudence and caution.

Throughout his later career, Billy did hold services for blacks in several cities such as Wichita and Kansas City and preached on occasion in black churches. He had, indeed, broken through the revivalist color barrier as few preachers would ever do. But never again would he capture the same glorious emotion of racial harmony he had achieved in Atlanta.

Where was the spirit of Atlanta? Perhaps it was best illustrated by an onlooker at the last Sunday revival meeting for blacks in that city, a white businessman not particularly known for his effusions of sentimentality. "I tell you," he said, "a sight like this makes a fellow think hard. I confess a lump came into my throat as I watched that stream of negroes pressing down the aisle. There's a tragedy in the thing somewhere, only I can't quite explain it."

11

God's Grenadier

"Am I a Soldier of the Cross?" asked the old devotional hymn. "Must I be carried to the skies / On flow'ry beds of ease, / While others fought to win the prize, / And sailed thro bloody seas?"[1]

For "God's Grenadier," as Billy styled himself, the answer resounded clearly, passionately. The belching guns, the deadly gases, the fields littered with the world's dying and maimed—they all called the Christian to action. To Billy, the First World War stood as the hour of reckoning, the challenge to God's anointed to sacrifice, to serve, to achieve glory against evil, to vanquish the forces of Satan. This was a war for righteousness, liberty, morality, for the souls of men. It was America and Christ, indissolubly linked, forging ahead in a glorious struggle.

Vance Thompson, the Georgia novelist and essayist, called Billy "the biggest force in the United States for partriotism . . . Uncle Sam's bugler." For fervor, courage, and a ringing sense of conviction, no orator in the country, Thompson said, topped the famous evangelist.[2]

Billy had not perceived the European war early on as a mighty crusade for the Lord. In 1914 he casually dismissed the collision of nations as "a lot of fools over there . . . murdering each other to satisfy the damnable ambitions of a few mutts who sit on thrones." But as the hostilities intensified in the next few years, as nation after nation fell into the growing cauldron, as stories of German atrocities and spies and treason filled newspaper columns, and as he sensed a growing belligerency in the United States against Germany, Billy was gradually swept up in the storm, his sermons now tinctured with increasingly strident attacks against the kaiser and his "Devil's hordes." And then, in Buffalo shortly before the United States entered the war, Billy declared in one of the closing sermons of the revival, "Jesus, you are surely taking a lot of back talk from the Kaiser. I wish, Lord, you would tell America to help wipe Germany off the map."[3]

In sermon after sermon the harangues sharpened, the invective grew more vicious. From the prancing, nattily dressed preacher now came waves of pejoratives, calling on America's patriots to stand up, to take on the godless, spineless, murdering Huns.

Billy now increasingly viewed the world conflict in cosmic terms, seeing it as a holy war. He had always believed that the United States was a divinely guided instrument of God's power, chosen to be settled by God's people. Here in America would be the mighty example, the proof of the covenant with God. Here would be the bastion of high morality, ethical purity, freedom, and justice. God had protected America "from the greedy eyes of monarchs 3,000 miles away," had set it aside as His land. Here, in America, man would actually progress toward a state of perfection. America would be the embodiment of a true Christian civilization, forwarding the highest values and godly order, upholding freedom against the assaults of heathen powers. Billy began to see the events on the world stage in these years as Satan's great challenge to God's plan for America.

Theology, Billy said many times, was not his long suit; he was a simple preacher offering the old-time religion. Although a pre-millennialist, Billy had never shared the aloofness displayed by many of his brethren toward things political and cultural, and, indeed, his inclination had always been to strike out against the evils he saw infecting society and governments. And now, he began to see this war as a dire threat which must be met with supreme force. "Christianity and Patriotism are synonymous terms," he declared, "and hell and traitors are synonymous."[4]

This view of America as the godly war power leading a divinely inspired mission against satanic powers was not a novel position among clerics. Across denominational lines, America's ministers overwhelmingly looked upon the war as God's stand against sin and heathenism. From a pulpit in Philadelphia, a Presbyterian minister declared with assurance, "We are fighting not only for our country . . . but for the Kingdom of God." From a Catholic prelate: "It is our sacred duty to answer with alacrity every demand our country makes upon our loyalty and devotion." From a Congregationalist writer: "Force and sacrifice are both methods of God." Back in Marshalltown, Iowa, grade-school pupils pondered the question: "How Can I Help to Win the War?" Their answers included the following:

> (1) "I can invent patents for fighting."
> (2) "I can pray to God every night that we may win in this war."
> (3) "I can feed my dog nothing but what would be thrown away."
> (4) "I can depend wholly upon God."

From church leaders to schoolchildren, Americans believed that their soldiers were going to war against God's enemies.[5]

But Billy always seemed to go further. When convinced of the efficacy of a position, when inspired to take a cause to its limits, Billy could rip and smite as no one else. From his pulpit he began to portray vivid accounts of Germans castrating hundreds of Belgians, of Germans crucifying Canadians on barn doors, of Germans raping French women, of Germans mutilating, butchering, and killing. "I lift my face to the Lord God of Hosts in heaven and I pray with all the fervency at my command 'God damn such a people.' " Billy asked God to bless the shells that screeched into the German lines. He called for President Wilson to declare war against Austria and Turkey, Germany's handmaidens. He called pacifists traitors and declared, "When the peace of the world is being assailed by armed forces, only an armed righteousness can conquer might." Billy taught schoolchildren at one of his rallies to hiss at the German flag. If Jesus Christ were on earth he would be behind the American cause in the war, would stand up for the president and his quest to make the world safe for democracy. It was Billy and Jesus, arm in arm, recruiting for the front lines, selling Liberty Bonds, admonishing cowards and trimmers; Billy and Jesus, marching side by side. "The Son of God goes forth to war," a hymnist had written, "A kingly crown to gain; His blood-red banner streams afar: Who follows in His train?"[6]

Christianity and America's fortunes in the war, Billy believed, were inextricably linked. In glorious wars such as this the church must be the servant of the state; patriotism must be an eleventh commandment. The president and editor of the *Atlanta Journal*, John Coben, wrote to President Wilson during Billy's Atlanta campaign of the evangelist's mesmerizing effects on the great crowds that jammed into the tabernacle, told of Billy's unswerving patriotic stance, his calling for volunteers to perform their Christian duty of supporting the commander in chief. "He has already proven a wonderful force in this section," Coben told the president, "in turning our people's minds away from the preachments of the cantankerous and unpatriotic, and towards the main point—the winning of the war."[7] One newspaper editorialist wrote, "Patriotism and prayer are merged at the tabernacle. The way of the cross is made the way of service and sacrifice in behalf of the nation and of humanity."[8]

If the struggle in Europe was a holy crusade, the greatest pagan was Kaiser Wilhelm. Skilled propagandists inevitably personalize their attacks. It is easier to portray a single, towering monster as a culprit, to ascribe heinous blame on a devil scapegoat, than to picture a willful mass of people acting in concert. When Thomas Jefferson drafted the Declaration of Independence he found it far more effective to place blame on the British king than on Englishmen themselves. When Billy first began his patriotic assaults, the German emperor easily became the Satanic Majesty. Metaphorically Kaiser Wilhelm was Wilhelm the Mephistopheles, enslaver, murderer, rapist, pillager, a creature vile, perverted, leader of an inferno of the damned. "The Kaiser plays no favorites," Billy declared, "he'd just as soon train his big guns upon an American woman with a baby at her breast as upon a Belgian cathedral, a Red Cross station, or a hospital; it's all the same to him."[9]

When unleashed, however, Billy found he could no longer limit the attack to the kaiser. It wasn't just the emperor or his crazed lieutenants at fault but the whole infernal horde of Huns, ancestors of Attila, sweeping across Europe massacring and torturing. The Germans of the twentieth century were the new barbarians, millions strong, madmen, placing more faith in their Krupp factories than in a God, worshipping at the idol of Nietzsche rather than Jesus Christ.[10]

At every service Billy played the Christian hero smiting the enemies of God and every service became something of a war ritual with martial music, fighting rhetoric, and searing words of· hate building up the German menace, describing the deeds and godless ideology of the enemy; and then the battle itself, breaking the neck of the lion with the awesome power of the Christian warrior. Discipline, strength, readiness—these were the qualities every good Christian must have in these times of peril. Night after night the corpses of Prussian militarism lay around Billy, slain by the mighty sword of the Almighty. He was booster, patriot, general of the Lord's troops. "I'll raise enough of an army myself to help beat the dust off the Devil's hordes."[11]

In January 1918 Billy brought his revival team to Washington, D.C. That winter had been especially harsh, the biting cold and winds crushing more gloom on a nation at war. Six months earlier General John Pershing had landed in Paris to direct the United States' overseas army. Through the year the nation's wartime industrial machine began churning out the equipment necessary to carry the fight to the Germans as millions of Americans registered for duty and were drafted. As Billy brought his revival to the nation's capital, President Wilson was preparing to issue his "Fourteen Points" address outlining a proposed basis for peace.

When the president had asked Congress to declare war he was acting, he said, "without animus, not in enmity." After the first American engagements in the war, General Pershing complained that his soldiers didn't seem to have enough hatred for the enemy, a situation he blamed on the press. Soon American draftees were given pep talks and lectures on the unspeakable atrocities apparently committed by German soldiers, were taught to "disembowel" dummies labeled "Hun" and "Fritz," and were taught that Germans were something less than human.[12]

When Billy sallied forth to his Battle of Washington, he had his own hate act well honed. On January 6, on the opening day of the crusade, at the tabernacle across from Union Station, Billy ripped into Germany with his full arsenal. "It's a whale of a job we have on our hands," he screamed to a packed tabernacle crowd of 15,000, "but we are a whale of a country, and we will not call off the dogs of war until we have that sauerkraut, weinerwurst-eating bunch of Kaiser Bill's gang on their knees." The rage that filled the Washington tabernacle that day reached an intensity unusual even for a Sunday rally. "We will bury the Kaiser and his hot-dog gang so deep that they will not hear the toot of Gabriel's horn on resurrection morn," he bellowed. "Kaiser Bill" and "his dirty bunch of pretzel-chewing, Hamburger-eating highbinders" were in for a deserved slaughter from the forces of God.

In the crowd that day were cabinet members, congressmen, senators, diplomatic envoys, and assorted other Washington notables. Whooping and shouting with each of Billy's verbal barrages, the thousands rocked the tabernacle into a delirious Allied pep rally. Exhorting them on, Billy leaped around the platform, flailing his arms, crouching low, springing into the air. Had he been there, General Pershing would have been enormously pleased.[13]

Billy's vicious anti-German vituperation had already aroused great ire among much of the German-American community. Shrugging off the criticism of his attacks, Billy offered this comment:

"I'll say what I please about the most lecherous, degenerate, hell-bound gang that every wiggled out of hell. God pity their stinking hides."[14]

After the physical assault on Billy in Atlanta, his advisers worried about more serious attacks, even possible assassination attempts. Billy's open style with the crowds, shaking hands, slapping the backs of thousands, plunging into groups of people without restraint, made him extremely vulnerable. The evangelist, nevertheless, would never back off. He was on God's mission; God would protect him from lurking evil.[15]

Shortly before the Washington crusade, an Atlanta attorney named Frank Redensleben asked the United States Attorney General whether the Justice Department could do anything to prevent Billy's anti-German slanders. An official with the Committee on Public Information responded to the attorney, "These things are not a question of law; they are, like cannibalism, a matter of taste."[16]

And now, in Washington, Billy had raised the pitch even higher. It was as if the Sunday evangelistic crusade was bent on a different kind of Great Awakening then those normally associated with revivals. The Washington event seemed primarily geared to arouse a slumbering government and its people. Here, in the center of power, among Washington's highest leaders, Billy would summon the patriotic spirit, awaken the inert, rekindle the flagging emotions, warm the cold Washington winter. "Billy Sunday is the man who put 'riot' in patriot," quipped one Washington editorialist. "He's sure all-American."[17]

Billy was soon breezily making the rounds of official Washington, visiting the White House, and meeting with the secretary of war, Newton Baker, and the secretary of the navy, Josephus Daniels. After meeting with members of Congress, he publicly declared that the "grafters and bootlickers" of past Congresses were absent from the current crop. These individuals were, he said, able and patriotic. With that kind of endorsement it wasn't long before a number of congressmen invited Billy to offer a prayer before the House of Representatives.[18]

On January 10, 1918, Billy, Nell, Rody, and several others in the Sunday party arrived on Capitol Hill for Billy's formal appearance. Greeted at 11 A.M. by Speaker of the House Champ Clark, other congressmen, and a gallery filled with spectators, Billy delivered a sizzling invocation appealing for the Lord's blessing on His chosen country and His chosen people and for the Lord's wrath against German tyranny. Like an Allied gunner razing a German infantry line, Billy blasted the kaiser and his countrymen in a startling, rapid-fire, staccato delivery that taxed the skills of the House stenographers taking it all down. The preacher was on fire, capturing the House in a rushing torrent of words. After offering thanks for Divine intervention on behalf of America and her institutions and for a government built on a foundation of faith in God, Billy declared:

> *Thou knowest, O Lord, that we are in a life-and-death struggle with one of the most infamous, vile, greedy, avaricious, bloodthirsty, sensual, and vicious nations that has ever disgraced the pages of history. Thou knowest that Germany has drawn from the eyes of mankind enough tears to make another sea; that she has drawn enough groans and shrieks from the hearts of men, women, and children to make another mountain. We pray Thee that Thou will make bare Thy mighty arm and beat back that great pack of hungry, wolfish Huns, whose fangs drip with blood and gore.*[19]

Here was vintage Sunday material, the same sentiments and coarse verbiage proclaimed in meetings across the country the previous years. The setting, however, was not a tabernacle but the United States House of Representatives. To Billy's listeners, it made no difference. As soon as the preacher uttered "Amen!" an outburst of yells, cheers, and hand-clapping swept over the chamber. Members leapt from their chairs and gathered around Billy to shake his hand. The invocation, a reporter noted, had a demoralizing effect on the regular order and decorum of the House as Billy continued to pump hands and slap backs while Champ Clark futilely banged his gavel. Billy had stormed the tabernacle of American government, emblazoning on it his unmistakable stamp of religious fury. No one in Washington could remember a prayer in the Congress ever drawing such reaction. As the *Washington Post* reported, Billy had scored another "first time in history."[20]

From the moment President Wilson had asked for a declaration of war against Germany, Billy had proffered complete loyalty to the administration and had looked for ways to play a larger role. As various war measures and recruiting drives were announced by the President and other administration officials, Billy was always on record putting in the good word—at the tabernacle, at rallies, at prayer meetings, anywhere he could find an audience. From the earliest days of the Liberty Bond drive, he delivered sales pitch after sales pitch. On one occasion he admonished his crowd not to return until they had purchased a bond. He was the honorable, fighting patriot, backing the commander in chief, extolling the virtues of the American system of government, praying for the boys in the field. When soldiers in Washington temporarily lacked sleeping quarters, he opened the tabernacle and provided cots and food. He announced his support of the conservation program of the food administrator, Herbert Hoover, and often recited "Hooverisms" as if he had written them himself. Make sure, you women of the United States, Billy instructed, to observe the wheatless days and the meatless days. On one occasion during the Washington campaign he turned the tabernacle over to the conservation division of the United States Fuel Administration so that officials of that agency could preach the need for saving coal.[21]

Billy was always there, eager, rushing to greet this official, quick to praise that one, moving from one meeting to another, one rally to another, a ubiquitous recruiter of both souls and soldiers. Driven by a powerful longing to be out front, the preacher was gritty, tough, disciplined, a battler ready to punish all enemies.

So impressive was Billy's doggedness, so admirable his dedication, that many officials in Washington enlisted his services to help solve particularly troublesome dilemmas, and Billy gladly responded. The chairman of the United States Shipping Board, Edward N. Hurley, appealed to the preacher to help persuade striking shipbuilders to return to their jobs. "One of the most helpful things you could possibly do for the nation," Hurley wrote, "would be to devote a few of your inspiring addresses to the need for shipbuilders to give the best that is in them to the construction of merchant vessels." The war effort needed the full cooperation of all; every worker who does not make his full commitment to the country is "on the same plane" with the religious slacker. "Every rivet driven is a blow at the Kaiser."

Needing to hear no more, Billy wrote back that the shipyard strike made his blood boil. "I think any bunch of men that will lift a hand to jeopardize the government's speed program in ship building are as near treason as can be." Billy said that he was known throughout the land as a champion of the man with the dinner pail, a spokesman for workingmen. Yet, "I won't tolerate for a second any move of any bunch, labor or capital, tending to delay or hamper war preparations." He agreed to help.[22]

In several sermons and other appearances he spoke out for the need of workers to put aside their selfish interests for the good of the nation. Later, after negotiations involving labor leaders such as Samuel Gompers succeeded in bringing the men back in force, Billy saw the strike as a plot hatched by the kaiser and his minions. "Germany played the trump card by trying to get the laboring men of this country to be untrue to their pledges of allegiance," he claimed. The effort had fallen flat. Thanks to such responsible men as Gompers, Billy went on, American labor would be loyal to the war effort.[23]

On February 17, 1918, Billy shook the crowd of 15,000 at the Washington tabernacle with a surprise announcement. He planned to go to France. At the conclusion of the revival campaigns in Chicago and Duluth in the spring, Billy said, his calendar was open. He promised that in the summer, "I'll be ready to go over to the trenches and see my boys." The announcement brought the crowd, including hundreds of soldiers, to their feet cheering wildly. "I'll bet," Billy declared, "that I know half the boys over there now. If General Pershing will only stake me to a rifle so that I can get a crack at that dirty German bunch, I'll be satisfied."[24]

As early as June 1917, several prominent individuals encouraged Billy to take his revival organization to Europe to inspire the troops. The editor of the nationally respected magazine *Outlook* proposed that Billy be made "Major Sunday, Chaplain-General to the American Forces." At about the same time, a member of the British war commission to the United States, General G. M. T. Bridges, suggested that Billy go to England. Billy had first shrugged off the ideas, but as he thought about them, he became increasingly enthralled—it would be Billy on the front lines, Billy rallying the troops. What better role for God's Grenadier?[25]

After several YMCA officials, some British and French military officers, members of the American General Staff, and John D. Rockefeller, Jr., all joined in encouraging the evangelist to launch his own European invasion, Billy was certain he wanted to make the trip and that Americans would stand behind him. Shortly after the announcement, the evangelist was summoned to the White House. Wilson asked him to cancel the trip. His services to the nation at home in maintaining civilian morale were desperately needed, Wilson told Billy. "We have speakers and singers and entertainers enough overseas. Not everyone here at home is doing his part like the soldiers are and you have the ears of the people and can go from city to city." Clasping Wilson's hand, Billy replied, "Mr. President, your wish is law with me."[26]

Always the patriot, always the obedient servant, always loyal to the commander in chief. To respond ungraciously to Wilson would have been unseemly, indeed unpatriotic. Billy would stay home. But he barely hid his resentment. Less than a year earlier Wilson had asked Theodore Roosevelt to give up his plans to command a special American regiment in Europe, an idea Billy had supported publicly. And now, Wilson had also asked Billy to stay clear from the action. Billy obeyed but was unquestionably hurt and angered. He wanted an official role in the war, a United States mission through which he could carry his message.

Less than four months later, Billy learned that the U.S. government planned to send representatives to Berne, Switzerland, to confer with German officials on questions regarding the exchange and treatment of prisoners of war. Billy asked Wilson to appoint him a member of the delegation. "I have been doing all in my power to encourage patriotism and back up the government in its war measures," he told the president, "but I have a strong desire to be of more effective service in some sort of work leaning directly on the war. I am sure I could help along humanitarian lines and alleviation of suffering." Once again Wilson did not accept Billy's offer. Diplomatic missions, the president undoubtedly believed, were not for evangelical revivalists, no matter how famous and influential, especially one who had recently expressed a strong interest in securing a gun to use at the front lines.[27]

As the Washington campaign drew to a close in late February 1918, Billy maintained his frantic pace. All three major newspapers covered the tabernacle activities and his other meetings extensively, the *Herald* even printing the texts of sermons. The amount of mail that flowed into the Sunday headquarters was astonishing, much more, the *Washington Times* reported, than that received by the president of the United States. From Washingtonians and from individuals around the country the letters, several hundred a day, streamed into the tabernacle post office where Fred Buse sorted and distributed. Billy continued to visit business leaders, social organizations, and political figures. Secretary of the Treasury William McAdoo, whom Billy visited shortly before leaving Washington, was now just plain "Mac" to the evangelist.[28]

On March 3, Billy closed the Washington campaign with a giant rally. Nearly 17,000 jammed inside the huge wooden building, leaving another 5,000 outside to hear only the sounds of the hymns and the crowd's reactions to the sermon. Some hearty individuals climbed on top of the building to peer down through the cracks in the ceiling; others pressed against the tabernacle sides. Many people stuffed handfuls of sawdust into their pockets for mementos.

In his long prayer, Billy asked God's continued blessing on the president, the cabinet, Congress, government departments, soldiers and sailors, newspapers, ministers, firemen, doctors at the American cantonments, the Supreme Court, and General Pershing. "I have never," he said, "been in a city that has become so tangled in my heart strings as Washington." The city, he went on, was "nearer Heaven tonight than it ever was." Billy called the nearly two-month stay "the greatest spiritual movement that Washington ever experienced."

The crusade had been held against the tense, uncertain backdrop of war, with anouncements in the newspapers of dead sons being shipped back to grieving parents, of food shortages and labor troubles, of precarious alliances and the nagging dread of what might lay ahead. Billy had brought excitement and verve to the city, with streams of people making their way daily to hear the indomitable evangelist hold forth at the tabernacle, almost within shadow's length of the U.S. Capitol. At the last meeting, Billy's old mentor, Chapman, was again on hand to introduce him, characterizing his ministerial son as "the greatest evangelist in the world today."[29]

Few would argue with Chapman's assessment. Billy was unquestionably the supreme force in American evangelism, the towering figure against whom all other preachers, past and present, would be measured. Like no other evangelist, Billy had sought to influence national public policy, had directly wedged his powerful evangelistic organization into campaigns for prohibition, war preparedness, and a host of public morality issues. In his burning quest to do the Lord's work, Billy had marched into the nation's capital more certain than ever of what was right, godly, and honorable, more convinced that he could influence national direction. The way of the country must be the way of the Lord. To save the souls of men and women, to change their lives, would be to save the soul of America, God's country.

On March 4, the fifth anniversary of the beginning of Wilson's presidency, with bold headlines in the papers announcing "Japan Prepares for War," Billy left Washington at 3 P.M. in an automobile provided by W. Bladen Lowndes, Baltimore city director of the war savings stamp campaign. At Baltimore's Lyric Theater, Billy made another of his patriotic addresses, boarded a westbound train that evening, and headed home to Winona Lake for a short rest. Chicago awaited, he knew, as did Duluth and other cities and towns along salvation's highway.[30]

He left behind in Washington a government still dodging its way through myriad problems posed by the war. He left convinced that the revival had made a difference, had brought thousands of individuals, including influential leaders, closer to God, closer to personal and national victory.

The *Washington Herald* praised the evangelist as "the greatest single instrument for good this country has ever known." Theodore Roosevelt, a year earlier, had said almost exactly the same thing.[31]

Billy had seized the mantle as the nation's foremost religious spokesman, and, at a time of national crisis and upheaval, he was there leading the flock, chastising the faithless, cajoling the timid, attacking the enemy. The way out of the morass was still the way of the Cross. The war had given him another great moral cause. Over in Europe new weapons and explosives were swallowing entire towns in hellish curtains of fire. As George Bernard Shaw lamented, soldiers could now pull strings and push buttons and "a Beethoven or a baby dies six miles off."[32] Where was all of this leading? Billy could reassure. The answers were still the same—repentance, salvation, a commitment to God's purpose; it was all simple and comforting.

Billy had reached the pinnacle of his career. But the war would change people, change countries, change attitudes and beliefs. The old world yields to the new and Billy would have to adjust. For millions, however, the Lord's warrior had helped see them through the worst of times.

On March 3, persons who passed the First Congregational Church in Washington at about the time vesper services were normally held saw a sign at the door which read:

CLOSED
ON ACCOUNT OF
FUEL ORDER

Since March 3 was quite mild with many people strolling the streets with no overcoats and since the District's fuel administrator had lifted the restrictive order weeks before, that sign seemed particularly strange. Well after ten o'clock that evening someone finally was able to reach by telephone the pastor of the church, Dr. James J. Gordon. Why, Dr. Gordon, was the sign on the church door? A sheepish voice on the other end of the phone replied, "You see, this was Billy Sunday's last night in Washington. I wanted my people to hear him."[33]

12

Fundamentalists, Take Arms!

The Armistice took effect on the eleventh hour of the eleventh day of the eleventh month of 1918. For Billy Sunday the end of the fighting represented the victory of God's forces over satanic evil. The slimy Hun had succumbed to the powers of righteousness; the land that had spawned Nietzsche and the godless attacks on the Bible from so-called higher critics had been put down. For all 100 percent Americans, for all Christians, this was a time for euphoric thanksgiving.

Just as Billy Sunday had enjoyed the crippling defeat of the whiskey gang, he now relished the demise of another great evil—the Hun. Billy had sold the Liberty Bonds, broken the whiskey bottles, cursed the kaiser and the distillers, prodded the politicians and voters, stirred masses of his followers, and he could now sip from the cup of victory. Or could he?

At the great New York and Washington revivals he had been at his career's summit. He had always been front-page, his statements cause for editorial comment, his actions scrupulously followed. But a campaign in Chicago in the spring of 1918, a meeting to which he looked forward with great anticipation, seemed to lack the fire of some of the earlier revivals, seemed anticlimactic, like a stage play losing its vitality and crispness. Millions of people across the country had by now heard the evangelist or had read his statements and sermons in the press. The Sunday revival, it seemed now, was becoming old news, dated, its power to surprise and overwhelm fading.

There is the story that Billy left the great Chicago tabernacle one day and asked a newsboy the directions to the nearest post office. Billy talked with the boy awhile, asked him the directions again to make sure, and then, turning back, called out, "Come to my meeting tonight and I'll show you the way to Heaven." The newsboy, it is said, replied, "How can you show me the way to Heaven when you don't even know the way to the post office?"[1]

The Sunday crusades were extraordinary events, sometimes sustained over several weeks, even months, requiring vast financial resources, personnel, and an intricate organization. They also required tremendous commitment on the part of individuals, churches, and civic organizations within the various communities. It would take time for each of the large cities to gear up again, to generate once more this kind of support, to find the necessary resources, to turn on the intense energy. Billy could not plan to return soon to New York or Philadelphia or Atlanta or the other major cities for new mammoth crusades. After such religious explosions there needed to be time for the emotional debris to settle.

And now, with his power in decline, Billy faced the twenties. For the famous preacher the cultural changes of this period seemed almost too cataclysmic to understand. Ranging over almost every area of American life—from the growing dominance of the cities to consumerism to moral standards—it was as if a devil's whirlwind was enveloping the country, twisting and turning people's minds and behavior. Here was a new age of advertisers, consumer credit, speculators, motion pictures, radios, gambling, fads, fashions, hot dances, a growing national mania for automobiles, jazz, flagpole sitters, Hollywood film depravity, flappers, bootleggers, speakeasies, "petting" and "necking," women smokers, moonshiners, racketeering, mob violence, strikes, industrial violence, Bolsheviks, Communists, race troubles, and black Zionism. On and on and on. The Honorable Lindsay Blanton, Texas congressman, Sunday school teacher, and prohibitionist, decided one day in 1921, for no reason apparent to anyone except perhaps Blanton, to insert dirty words into the *Congressional Record*. He was censored formally by his colleagues. Postwar America was to Billy increasingly bewildering.

But it was bewildering also to almost everyone else. From the point of view of intellectuals, radicals, and other enemies of Billy Sunday, the era of the twenties was hardly a time of glory. The Red Scare, the rise of nativism, the deportation of radicals, the failure of reform movements, the ascendancy to power of Republican conservatives—for the left, the twenties represented a time of repression and apathy.

But the assault on the liberals and radicals did not translate into a rise in religious commitment. Indeed, American religious leaders in the 1920s observed that belief and religious commitment seemed to be withering under the assault of cynicism, scientism, humanism, and scholasticism. Postwar America seemed tired of sobering crusades for moral righteousness, weary of the demands of evangelical religious dictates. Theologian Reinhold Niebuhr talked about a "psychology of defeat" gripping organized religion. Welcome to the twenties, Billy Sunday![2]

As no other preacher before him, Billy Sunday had carried revivalism out of the sectarian and into the secular, had splashed the popular culture with tabernacle excitement, promotion, business acumen, and personal charm. But the old act was competing with newer diversions and enticements. The tabernacle, to many Americans now, seemed a less compelling attraction.

The evangelist no longer could hold out for large cities or demand tabernacles. Seldom did the revivals attract extensive press coverage or sweep up communities in excitement and fervor. The

Cincinatti crusade, held over a two-month period in 1921, drew impressive crowds and daily newspaper coverage, but many of the revivals were now smaller and shorter and were often held in armories, warehouses, and churches. But the evangelist, sixty years old in 1922, kept up the frantic pace despite his age and increasing health concerns. There were still thousands out there wanting to hear the Word, he said, people to be saved, the Lord's work to be done. And at times it seemed that the power to turn on crowds was still as strong, the evangelical weapons still as devastating. After a one hour and twenty minute sermon on Americanism in Charles Town, West Virginia, preached to thousands who had been brought to the small town in special trains, Billy wrote, "It was the most patriotic audience I ever addressed as I turned my guns on socialism and radicalism. They raised the roof." He was still a man on a mission, a disciple, and he simply refused to quit.[3]

In the twenties Billy would hit cities such as Richmond, Knoxville, Louisville, and Memphis, but he would also hit such places as Bristol, Virginia; Fairmont, West Virginia; Morristown, Tennessee; Cape Giraroleau, Missouri; and Aurora, Illinois. There would always be calls for the evangelist; there would always be the Sunday magic and the adoring crowds. But it would never be as before.

The geographical focus of the Sunday campaigns shifted dramatically in these years. Not until the Atlanta revival in 1917 did he venture into Dixie. But in the twenties the predominant area of his work was in the South with its Methodist and Baptist evangelical orthodoxy and its strong fundamentalist bent in both religion and politics. As no other area in the country, the South was still receptive to Billy's old-time religious message. But, even here, he struggled to draw the kinds of crowds as years before.

It did not help that the nation was now awash in evangelists trying to be like Billy. Hundreds of preachers in all parts of the country had begun to imitate Billy's slam-bang style and mannerisms and his organizational methods—from the advance workers and guarantee fund and wooden tabernacles to the trailhitting, society meetings, and the wooing of various delegations. From relatively successful evangelists such as Rodney "Gypsy" Smith and William Biederwolf to scores of small-time preachers such as the "Railroad

Evangelist" and the "Cowboy Evangelist," they all dreamed the big dream—of duplicating the enormous success of the master evangelist. None came close. Indeed, many were woefully cheap imitators—some left towns without paying off their debts; others tried the acrobatic maneuvers and merely looked silly; others so insulted their audiences that they were often close to being lynched. Some were unabashed liars or, more politely, false advertisers. One evangelist, for example, claimed that he had "converted a whole town in Oklahoma."[4]

As the new decade began, Billy seemed cocky and confident. Keep battering the enemy, he cried, keep up the pressure, wipe out the infidels from decent society. The anarchists, the whiskey boys—kept after their tails.

In early January 1920 on his way to Norfolk, Virginia, Billy took time to lavish praise on the Justice Department and its raids on left-wing radicals around the country. "I would stand every one of the ornery, wild-eyed I.W.W.'s, anarchists, crazy Socialists, and other types of Reds up before a firing squad and save space on our ships," he declared. He would later pronounce his own sentence on Nicola Sacco and Bartolomeo Vanzetti, Italian anarchists convicted of murder in 1921: "Give 'em the juice. Burn them if they're guilty. That's the way to handle it. I'm tired of hearing these foreigners, these radicals coming over here and telling us what we should do." At one rally hundreds of listeners hurled their hats into the rafters and tossed hymnbooks on the sawdust when the evangelist called for the government to close the mouths of those who preached "their dirty European doctrines in the land of the free and the home of the brave." Scour the country clean![5]

And as for the liquor interests, Billy had a special cure. Norfolk, Virginia, Saturday, January 16, 1920, one day before Prohibition officially began. At one o'clock, a black, twenty-foot-long coffin encasing the "corpse" of John Barleycorn rolled out of Union Station on a carriage attended by twenty pallbearers dressed in costumes. They included a masked, bright-red devil in the rear of the procession seemingly in deep mourning and anguish. Down the streets of Norfolk the parade progressed through cheering crowds until it reached the 15,000-seat wooden tabernacle.

Once inside, the pallbearers carried the coffin down the sawdust aisle to the sounds of a funeral dirge and the approving shouts of the enormous congregation. At the tabernacle platform stood a man who had fought ole John B. for many years and was eager to perform the burial rites. The congregation sang "John Barleycorn's Body Lies a Mouldering in the Clay." In the center section of the crowd sat several hundred members of the Woman's Christian Temperance Union. Three small girls carried bunches of white roses and carnations and presented them to Billy.

Once into his funeral oration, Billy abandoned most of the levity and hurled the old slams and rebukes against the liquor dealers and their ilk, telling the old stories of men, great men, brought to their knees by the devil's drink. Following the sermon, Billy announced that, given the special occasion, he and Nell would sing a duet of a song he had written that morning. Billy's musical abilities, much like his handling of curveballs had been in the majors, were limited, and so this was something of a surprise. To the laughter and shrieks of the crowd, the two got through one verse:

> *John was a murderer,*
> *Last night he died.*
> *Toll the bells for John is dead—*
> *Darn his drunken, filthy hide.*

Billy then grabbed an American flag and climbed atop the pulpit. As the crowd sang the doxology, Billy waved the flag and his voice, although discordant, could be heard above almost everyone else.[6]

But Billy's battles with the demon did not abate with the advent of Prohibition. In the era of speakeasies and hip flasks ole John fought back. Colonel John Baker White, superintendent of the Law and Order League of Kanawha County, West Virginia, soon despaired that the upper classes as well as the poor were flaunting their disrespect for the Eighteenth Amendment. Thus, "we have bootleggers on every corner, gamblers, thieves, murderers, and your women are insulted and debauched . . . our best citizens are breaking the law without compunction." Society, in Colonel White's view, was tumbling down the hellish slope to perdition. When the country's best citizens were casually asking their friends "Who's your boot-legger," the country itself was swirling in lawlessness and anarchy.[7]

Down in Savannah, Georgia, the city's mayor was also lament-ing a society gone berserk. "An immense amount of moonshine and very inferior liquor is being sold," he said, "which is burning up the insides of the population." The "best citizens" break the Prohibition laws, he continued, echoing the words of Colonel White in West Virginia. Judges, for God's sake, were drinking whiskey.[8]

During the Cincinnati campaign, a little more than a year after John Barleycorn's burial, an impassioned Billy charged that the whiskey interests had gone too far—they had defaced the grave of his mother, who had died five years earlier. Billy told the crowd how he had taken his mother's body home to the old family farm and had made the tombstone himself, how some "godless, whis-key-soaked degenerates" had recently broken down the fence around the graveyard, knocked over the tombstone, piled brush over the grave, took pictures, and then claimed that Billy had so little respect for his mother's memory that he allowed her gravesite to deterio-rate.

"So help me God!" Billy cried out, "if I had been there I would have shot them where they stood. Oh yes, I would. I'd have filled them so full of shot that the undertaker could have essayed the whole bunch for lead and thought he was striking the mother lode." When Billy finished the very personal, emotional attack, a thunderous applause erupted from the thousands in the taber-nacle.[9]

Those demonstrations of support charged the Sunday motor, convinced him, against increasing evidence to the contrary, that he still held the same kind of magnetic spell over Americans as before. And as the 1920 presidential election neared, various rumors floated throughout the political community and the press about the possi-bility of Billy Sunday entering politics, at the highest level. The preacher/politician idea, Billy for president or vice-president, intrigued a number of wags who relished the thought of Billy as stump orator on the political trail. With his large following and the sheer physical energy he could bring to a campaign, it was enough to make some political advisers salivate.

The spicy tidbits of gossip moistened Billy's palate, and in March he announced, somewhat jocularly, that he would be ready to accept the Republican nomination for president if it were offered. He vaulted even further in the arena, listing some of the individuals he would place in various cabinet positions: attorney general, Judge Kenesaw Mountain Landis; secretary of war, General Leonard Wood; postmaster general, Herbert Hoover; and secretary of state, Henry Cabot Lodge or Nell Sunday.

In July Billy's name gained credence in serious discussions by leaders of one political group—the Prohibition party. As the delegates to the party convention gathered in Lincoln, Nebraska, W. G. Calder-Wood, chairman of the Prohibition National Convention, declared that he would be satisfied only with a ticket headed by William Jennings Bryan and Billy Sunday. A *New York Times* editorialist was enchanted with the idea. "One cannot build even in the wildest dreams of imagination a ticket more eloquent, more indomitable, richer in genius, than the one that has been suggested," said the writer playfully. For a small, eager party brimming with gusto and zeal, could there be any more able spokesman than Misters Bryan and Sunday!

But in August the ticket never materialized at the party convention. The day before the convention opened in Lincoln, Nebraska, Billy announced from Hood River that he was satisfied with the Republican nominee, Warren G. Harding. He thus took himself out of the running for the Prohibition ticket. Bryan was formally nominated but declined to accept, preferring to stay in the Democratic party for which he had toiled so long.[10]

If Billy entertained dreams of political office, if he remained publicly upbeat about his own career and his ability to influence masses of people, disillusionment loomed. The war within the Protestant community continued to blaze hot in the twenties—the fundamentalists vs. the modernists, the battle between the orthodox and the liberal, the Bible and its "higher critics." This internecine struggle, which had been growing more divisive through the years, would serve to make mass evangelistic revivals even more difficult in the twenties. Billy had always counted on a relatively united Protestant community in the various cities to ensure success and the controversies of the twenties hopelessly fragmented that community.

Fundamentalist orthodoxy rested on a number of beliefs: a divinely inspired, errorless, completely authoritative Bible; the miraculous Virgin Birth of Christ; the bodily resurrection; Christ's second coming; and substitutionary atonement, the belief that Christ died for man's sins. There were other elements but these were the primary areas in which scholars and laymen and ministers of all denominations were waging a mighty quarrel.

The theological positions of the modernists, just as those of the fundamentalists, varied among the leaders but the modernists generally claimed that the Bible was not miraculously inspired and, indeed, contained legend and myth; that the Virgin Birth was a questionable occurrence (Jesus himself never talked about it and St. Paul never did either); and that belief in the literal bodily return of Christ as King is not scripturally sound. Some modernists rejected entirely Christ's divinity. Many modernists in influential Protestant seminaries and churches, and others in leadership positions in several denominations, had also blended into their theology some of the theories of Charles Darwin. To Billy, the monkeymen, as he had asserted for many years, had a special place in hell.

The two sides had powerful, colorful leaders. Among the fundamentalists were William Bell Riley, president of the Interdenominational Fundamentals Association, who once declared that "thinking men have not given up Genesis"; Reverend J. Frank Norris, a vigorous campaigner who, almost single-handedly, succeeded in ousting several professors from Texas universities because they taught evolution heresy; Professor J. Gresham Machen of Princeton Theological Seminary, New Testament scholar and author of the impressive work *Christianity and Liberalism,* who once declared, "if Catholicism is a perversion of Christianity, Modernism is not Christianity at all."

Among the modernists were Dr. Harry Emerson Fosdick, professor at Union Theological Seminary and preacher at New York's First Presbyterian Church, who called the entire theological dogma of fundamentalism "false in fact and pernicious in practical result"; Glenn Frank, editor of the *Century,* who called for a religion of

Jesus, not a religion about Jesus; and Dr. Percy Stickney Grant, an Episcopalian who rejected completely most of the beliefs of Protestant orthodoxy including the divinity of Christ. Reverend Leon Birkhead of Kansas City, Missouri, a former Methodist turned Unitarian, once declared that the Bible was a "gravely overrated book." Men such as these were in Billy's eyes traitorous scum. How could so-called religious leaders and scholars reject the Son of God?

The apostle of manliness, Billy saw his modernist adversaries in the pulpits, seminary classrooms, and administrative offices as cowardly and devious, like intellectual rapists stalking "our boys and girls." To Billy the American liberal/modernist was a "wishy-washy, sissified sort of galoot that lets everybody make a doormat out of him." The American sissies had fallen prey to the heinous views of German sissies, who had replaced Christ with Darwin and Nietzsche. They had bought it all and were now the proselytizers of evolution, attacking all things equated with Christian salvation—"decency, patriotism, and manliness."

As the views of modernists began slowly to influence seminaries and churches around the country, most of the leaders assumed they were spearheading a successful theological revolution which would gradually displace legend and antiquated belief with reasoned, learned philosophy. Most were surprised at the ferocity with which the fundamentalists fought back. From pulpits and revival platforms, from organizations such as the Moody Bible Institute, with its publishing houses and correspondence courses, and the Milton Stuart Evangelistic Fund, which circulated a publication called "Jesus Is Coming," and in such periodicals as the *Sunday School Times*, the fundamentalists had forums and dynamic leaders with which to wage a formidable war.[11]

For a decade the most cited source for fundamentalist theology had been a series of pamphlets containing ninety essays entitled *The Fundamentals*. Founded in 1909 by businessmen Lyman and Milton Stuart, who called themselves, "Two Christian Laymen," the project drew such figures as Amzi C. Dixon, Baptist minister and pastor of the Moody Memorial Church; Reuben A. Torrey, dean of the Bible Institute of Los Angeles; and Elmore Harris, president of the Toronto Bible Institute. Written by over

sixty-four authors, the articles in the pamphlets ranged in subject
from biblical authority to evangelism. They argued for scriptural
inerrancy, the miracle-working power of Christ, the Virgin Birth,
and other traditional doctrines now under scrutiny and attack by
some scholars. More than three million of the pamphlets were distributed free to ministers and students across America.[12]

If fundamentalists needed a doctrinal defense of the infallibility of the Scriptures, they could turn to scholars such as Charles
Hodge and B. B. Warfield. They argued that biblical authors, through
God's inspiration, recorded truth in every word, reference, quota-
tion, and even statistic. The orginal autograph manuscripts were
inerrant in every instance. Only man's misunderstandings, distor-
tions, prejudices, and error have raised apparent contradictions. If
scholars were able to re-create every text as written and have
understanding of every word and phrase, the full truth would be
obvious.[13]

In late May 1919 over 6,500 fundamentalists from around the
country gathered in the Music Hall in Philadelphia. For a week,
the conference filled the hall and several nearby Philadelphia auditoriums and after all the speeches and forums and caucuses and
planning sessions, there emerged the World's Christian Fundamentals Association. Led by William Bell Riley, the organization
was dominated by millenarian thinkers. They stood for the exor-
cism of modernism and all its assorted evil notions. Although Riley
was an effective trooper for the organization, it collapsed, mired in
dissension and a lack of clear, strategic planning. But other organizations followed, spawned by the titanic issue of evolution.[14]

The fundamentalist organizations attempted to influence legislation; trumpeted the anti-evolution banner in meetings, newspapers, and magazines; and attempted to rouse God-fearing, patriotic
Americans to action. In 1926 Edward Clarke, former "Sir Knight
Supreme of the Knights of the Kamelia" of the Ku Klux Klan,
founded the Supreme Kingdom. Clarke modeled his new organization much like the Klan itself with sovereigns and prime ministers and princes. A number of former Klan members joined as did
Fred Rapp, a one-time business manager for Billy. Although the
Kingdom's initial growth was rapid, it fell into dissolution after rev-

elations about Clarke's financial misdealings and profit-skimming hit the papers.

Gerald Winrod of Kansas created the Defenders of the Christian Faith in 1926. In addition to assailing evolution and modernism, the Defenders also propagated right-wing race and religious prejudices. Winrod recruited a number of speakers who toured the Midwest and called his troops the "Flying Fundamentalists." Winrod's Defenders remained in business long after Clarke's Kingdom. Billy addressed the Defenders' World-Wide Congress in 1930.

There were others—a plethora of organizations designed to fight off the anti-Christ, to cling to the traditional ways and the old faith in the Bible: the Research Science Bureau, an organization which issued a barrage of pamphlets designed to prove that man had not splashed up from the primeval swamp; the Anti-Evolution League, an organization influential in the South whose periodical was called, appropriately, *Conflict;* the School-Bag Gospel League, whose mission was to distribute books of the Bible nationwide; the Bryan Bible League, founded by California evangelist Paul Rood, a man who claimed that God in a vision had told him to form the organization; the Interdenominational Fundamentals Association; the National Association for the Promotion of Holiness; and the Victorious Life Testimony. Riley said, "Fundamentalists hold that the world is illumined and the Church is instructed and even science itself is confirmed, when true, and condemned when false, by the clear teachings of the open Book."[15]

Much like the McCarthyite purges would seek to accomplish three decades later, fundamentalists in the twenties demanded that seminary professors and clergymen pass public tests of orthodoxy; they attempted to oust church journal editors who displayed liberal-modernist tendencies; they petitioned church memberships to seek out and remove modernists who held denominational office. They also sought to ban the teaching of evolution in public schools and to prevent the use in the classroom of any books which discussed evolutionary theory.[16]

There were skirmishes in communities across the country over the teaching of evolution. In a school district in Jewell County, Kansas, fundamentalists won a rousing victory against the local board of education. Their target: *The Book of Knowledge*, an encyclopedia geared for young readers which contained an entry on evolution. At a Christian Endeavor meeting in Denver, a minister from Kansas City hailed the victory over the offensive publication, declaring that rape-fiends were saints compared to teachers of evolution and modern science. "Worse than an assassin who kills the body is he who shatters the faith of youth."

For Billy such direct action against evil men and their evil writings was part of the holy war. The anti-Christ was in the Sanctuary. False prophets, heretics, infidels—they must be rooted out, replaced by right-thinking defenders of the faith. For Billy the evolution issue was an extension of World War I—the need to rescue civilization from the hellish influence of the German skeptics and their anti-Christ, superman theology that had so polluted American religious life. [17]

In this war, Billy would have a special ally—his old friend William Jennings Bryan. Bryan's new crusade was anti-evolution and he vigorously took to the hustings, speaking in great halls and from small-town pulpits, organizing campaigns and committees, cajoling legislators. So involved in religious matters did Bryan become in the early 1920s that he even ran for moderator of the Presbyterian General Assembly in 1923, a race he lost on the third ballot. It was Bryan's last election defeat. But the populist warhorse became the most nationally visible of the fundamentalists simply because of his background and zeal.

Bryan and Billy both saw the theory of evolution as a creature invading hearts and minds, destroying faith, perverting educational institutions, churches, legislatures, and the media, attacking the soul of America. Bryan once said that all of the nation's ills, all of them, could be traced back to this single cause, the teaching of evolution. Better to burn all books ever written, said Bryan, and save the book of Genesis, Verses 1 through 3.

Professor E. G. Conklin, one of those egghead intellectuals so despised by Bryan, Billy, and the other fundamentalists, quipped about the Great Commoner's anti-evolution campaign, "Apparently Mr. Bryan demands to see a monkey or an ass transformed into a man, though he must be familiar enough with the reverse process."[18]

Billy went so far as to pronounce that Charles Darwin was now in hell (Billy, of course, assigned that residence to a number of historical figures). All ministers and scholars who teach evolution, said the evangelist, were stinking skunks and liars and all scholarship supporting the idea of evolution was pure "fal-de-rot."

Between 1921 and 1929 nearly forty anti-evolution bills landed in the hoppers of over twenty state legislatures. If the dreaded demon liquor could be bottled up in legislative action, so could the cursed evolution creature. In some states the anti-evolutionist troops made inroads; in others it was hopeless. When a bill was introduced into the Delaware legislature to forbid the teaching that man emerged from lower species, it was referred to the Committee on Fish, Game, and Oysters.[19]

The controversy between fundamentalists and modernists had implications far beyond religious debate. The fundamentalist movement involved a whole system of belief and prejudice encompassing politics, social systems, race, and philosophy. And much of the movement can be seen clearly in the views of Billy Sunday.

Billy believed that America was the one true Christian nation in the world, that God was using this country to restore faith. Linking both Bolshevism and the German menace with religious liberalism and its evolutionists, higher critics, and egghead theorists, he drew up lists of individuals he thought dangerous to the security of the country. Mistrusting foreigners and immigrants, he lamented the growth and power of the cities and the waning influence of the country's heartland; he stood for the rural ethos against the sin-stenched morality of the metropolis, was suspicious of social reform movements, and stood four-square for "100% Americanism," an old-fashioned patriotism of flags and fireworks and lemonade on the Fourth of July. He stood for capitalism against newfangled theories of government, considered radicals fit for the noose or firing squad, fiercely resented what he saw as the decline of morals in society, and stood for tradition and order, the agrarian ideal, and the Bible.

The world in Billy's mind was in danger of tilting on its axis and all around were evidences of a nihilistic jungle of unbelief, rebellion, and anti-Americanism. It must be stopped cold for if the liberals, radicals, and evolutionists were to prevail the laws of nature might themselves be suspended. As he said half seriously in Cincinnati, oil and water would mix perfectly, turtle doves would mate with turkey buzzards, cats would bark, and yesterday would follow tomorrow. It was all so confusing, disturbing, and dangerous to trusted patterns of American faith and piety.[20]

But for Billy there were also the personal concerns, family problems, burdensome and heavy. Throughout his career, much of the public felt personally close to the evangelist, had felt he was one of them, that he shared their common roots and private travails. In November 1923, the human frailties of the Sunday family were revealed to the public as never before. The *New York Times* ran a headline, "Sunday's Son Tries to Die." The short account talked of an unconscious George Sunday in the bedroom of his Los Angeles home, found with a tube from a nearby gas jet leading to his mouth. In Charleston, South Carolina, Billy received a telegram from George's brother, Billy, Jr.: "Pay no attention to newspaper report concerning George. Absolutely false."

In Los Angeles police and investigative reporters began to weave together the tangled threads of what the *Los Angeles Times* preferred to call a "mystery." Four hours after police reports called the incident an attempted suicide, George told reporters that it was his brother, Billy Jr., now in his early twenties, who had been on the floor stricken by illness and that he had recovered.

Reverend John Ely, pastor of the Wilshire Presbyterian Church, met reporters and also denied that George had attempted to take his own life. "George Sunday is an officer in my church," said Reverend Ely. The minister remarked that George was suffering something in the nature of a nervous breakdown but had not filled his home and mouth with gas.

Hours later George appeared outside his home, still claiming it was Billy, Jr., and not he who had been found on the floor. "An unfortunate occurrence," he said. "You know how accidents happen. Poor Billy . . ."

George's Swedish chauffeur then offered his own account. Also denying the gas report, he mumbled something about somebody falling down the stairs. Inside the home, the police and reporters found Billy, Jr., lying on a couch, lifting a limp hand in salute as the guests entered. "Had a touch of gastritis," said Billy, Jr. He claimed he had contracted ptomaine poisoning from a fish dinner.

In wrapping up the story, the *Times* reported, "Whatever the extent of the illness either or both of the brothers had suffered, its effects had practically disappeared that night." Unfortunately, the effects of this story as well as many others in the papers about George and Billy, Jr., would not disappear and for their father the stories and tension and pain increased with the years.

All his life Billy Sunday had preached against the excesses of liquor and yet George often drank heavily, as did Billy, Jr. The evangelist had always preached morality and family values and yet both George and Billy, Jr., cavorted with numerous women. Both sons married, divorced, and remarried. Throughout these years, Billy was alternatively angered, saddened, remorseful, and forgiving of his sons. He had wanted them to follow an evangelistic career.

Indeed, George had once been part of the Sunday team, for a time acting as an advance man. But later, he decided to attempt a career on his own, establishing a real estate business in Los Angeles. His father helped finance that business. A few days before the suicide incident in 1923 police had found George's name on a bootlegger's list in a raid in Hollywood and federal agents were preparing to question all individuals on that list.

Through all of the stories in the press about the evangelist's wayward sons, Billy publicly remained stoic. Privately, nevertheless, he was tormented, fearful that the publicity was wrecking all the good that his crusade had accomplished through the years. In 1921 he had written a despairing, vengeful letter to Nell after a story appeared about Billy, Jr.'s philandering and drinking. "The name Sunday God has made famous with his cause and I would die before I would dishonor it and I would rather the boy die than disgrace it. Ma and I have kept it clean and bequeathed it to our children and I pray God they keep it clean."

At other times he was tender: "I love you same old way and

have for 35 years or more and I love the boys same old way I have since they were born." He took much of the blame for his children's difficulties on himself, often remarking that his career had robbed them of the time they should have had with their father. Burdened with guilt, Billy lavished money on them, trying to make up for what he felt he had not given them as children.

He worried not only about George and Billy, Jr., but about his daughter, Helen, the oldest of the children. She had married a man named Mark Haines, editor and publisher of the *Sturgis Journal* in Michigan, and Billy had helped finance part of their business. In 1918 they had a son they named Paul after her other brother, the youngest child of Billy and Nell. Charming and warm, Helen was often ill. Over succeeding years she became increasingly weak and tired, and doctors later realized she had contracted a debilitating degenerative disease. She often fell into deep depression and worried about her mental stability. Shortly before the birth of her son she had written to her mother that she longed for oblivion: "Life's just calamity, turmoil, and dread . . . nothing ahead but more misery. I am sick to death of the struggle."

For Billy the family's increasing struggles took an enormous toll. On the road he began to feel the utter exhaustion overwhelming him. He wrote to Nell, "I guess I am getting near the end of the rope. These long campaigns are a big strain on me tho the smaller towns are not so hard." On another occasion he wrote, "I long to be with you but this is war and all must pay a price."[21]

The Sundays were also beginning to feel another concern—a strain on their finances. With the revivals bringing in far less money than before, as they began to provide money to the children in ever-increasing amounts, and with the continued offers to charity, the family's cash situation was, at times, precarious. When John D. Rockefeller, Jr., sent Billy a $5,000 check, a jubilant evangelist wrote to Nell, "Hurrah—hurrah!" He kept going, kept up the grueling evangelistic life convinced he was following God's will. "God will help me won't he Ma."[22]

In the summer of 1925 the little town of Dayton, Tennessee, near Chattanooga, became the site of a showdown. Suddenly, here in this tiny place, were swarms of reporters almost as thick as those

pesky gnats and, to some people, just as annoying; here were political wags and pundits, celebrities, crowds and emotional fervor and
pitchmen hawking souvenirs and people carrying placards with such
messages as "Be Sure Your Sins Will find You Out" and "You Need
God in Your Business." This national spectacle condensed for a
few weeks the whole evolution debate into a gladiatorial joust of
wit and oratory. It was Clarence Darrow, eminent attorney for the
defense, versus William Jennings Bryan, prosecuting attorney for
the Holy Word; monkeys versus man; science versus belief. It was
all here for a brief time, played out like some comic opera in the
sweltering confines of a small but soon to be significant southern
courtroom.

The case involved a textbook entitled *Civic Biology* written by
George Hunter, a work that had been in use in Tennessee schoolhouses since 1909. On March 13, 1925, the General Assembly of
Tennessee passed a law entitled "An Act Prohibiting the Teaching
of Evolution Theory." During debate over the law, a member of
the state senate implored his colleagues, "Save our children for
God!" A teacher in Dayton, John T. Scopes, responded to an
advertisement issued by the American Civil Liberties Union to put
the Tennessee law to a test case. Scopes continued to use *Civic
Biology* and was arrested for violating the new state act.

Into Dayton came Darrow, hired gun for the ACLU, spokesman for academic freedom and freedom of thought. Into Dayton
came Bryan, defender of the faith, apostle of biblical inerrancy. For
Bryan the issue was simple: John Scopes had violated the law. The
people of Tennessee had a right to prevent the use of their tax
dollars for the teaching of precepts which a majority of citizens
considered repugnant and abhorrent. For Darrow, it was also clear—
the freedom to learn and teach, the right to express opinions without censure, and the responsibility of the educational system to
probe all areas of human inquiry, from the sciences to philosophy.

Although the prosecution asked a number of fundamentalist
ministers to assist in the case, none of them made the trip to Dayton. J. Frank Norris, T. T. Shields, William Bell Riley, John Roach
Straton, J. C. Massee, J. Gresham Machen, P. H. Welshimer—all
were otherwise occupied; all sent Bryan their regrets and their

encouragement. Bryan would face Darrow without benefit of religious scholars or fundamentalist leaders. It had been twenty-eight years since he had been in a courtroom.

Bryan wrote Billy on June 23, 1925, asking whether the evangelist would be available as a witness in the case against evolution and asking also for any suggestions in the prosecution of the trial. On July 3, the *Louisville-Courier Journal* reported that Walter White, superintendent of schools at Dayton, had also invited Billy to assist in the prosecution. Billy was on the road when the Associated Press contacted Hood River. When asked about the offer made to her husband, Nell said, "I know he won't do it."

On the Fourth of July, Billy wrote Bryan from Hood River, "Thank God for W. J. B. Sorry I cannot be there." Billy jotted down some random thoughts about evolution, "some ideas that may suggest a line of thought." He quoted Daniel Webster, referred to the Mayflower Compact, equated atheism with evolution and called them both a public enemy, quoted Wendell Phillips, declared that man cannot be an evolutionist and a Christian at the same time, and denied that species, once begun, could change into other species. He said that in a reef in Florida scientists found the remains of insects thousands of years old, the same kind of insects found there in 1925. "All the believing world is back of you in your defense of God and the Bible," Billy wrote Bryan.

The scrappy evangelist, never one to back off from a fight, was reluctant to enter this one in Dayton. He was bone tired, having just completed long campaigns in Newport News, Virginia, and Winston-Salem, North Carolina. He was consumed by the continuing problems with his family and needed time to rest and reflect.

In addition, although he and Bryan shared common ground in their fights for temperance and in their attacks on evolution, Billy was a bedrock Republican, Bryan a staunch Democrat. And perhaps most important, Billy's talents were not suited to the intellectual thrust and parry of the courtroom. He would be hopelessly out of his element and he, to some degree, undoubtedly realized it. He would sit this one out.

Bryan and other fundamentalists saw before them the specter of their children being misled by teachers and diverted from Christian faith, and their strident attacks against the teaching of evolution in the schools were a defense of home and family. Bryan declared that "no teacher paid by their money should rob their children of faith in God and send them back to their homes skeptical, infidels, agnostics, or atheists." Bryan felt he was in Dayton on behalf of the majority of God-fearing Americans defending their rights against the arrogant, elitist intellectuals, acting the part of both the good Democratic populist and the old-fashioned preacher. He saw the contest in cosmic terms. If evolution triumphed in the Dayton battle, Christianity would decline. But, he said, in "an open fight the truth will triumph."

Henry L. Mencken of the *Baltimore Sun*, the scribe wielding perhaps the most acid-dripped pen in the journalism business, covered the trial. He had consulted with Darrow weeks before and told the renowned lawyer that making a fool out of Bryan could discredit the forces of ignorance and darkness, the fundamentalist boobs and buffoons holding back progress and enlightenment.

Upon arrival, the Sage of Baltimore contemptuously growled that he could find no local resident in Dayton who doubted "so much as the typographical errors in Holy Writ." If a man were accused of being a doubter in this part of the country, he wrote, it was almost akin to being accused of cannibalism. The Scopes trial, through the influence of Mencken and other reporters, was being played in a larger courtroom than the steaming little building in Dayton, Tennessee, and both sides knew it. Carried on radio to various stations around the country, hyped up in the press like a championship prizefight, the trial lasted for eleven days. For Bryan, ill, overweight, and suffering from the intense heat, those eleven days seemed interminable, especially with the brilliant Darrow on the attack.

When the cagey lawyer manuevered Bryan to the witness stand and fired at him a withering barrage of questions about miraculous biblical events, Bryan stumbled into a web of illogic. Although he countered with an impassioned plea for religious belief and biblical infallibility, the fundamentalist general at times appeared confused and foolish. When Darrow finished with Bryan, the old Democratic orator must have felt as if he were the one in the belly of the bib-

lical fish. Asked about historical calculations regarding the Great
Flood, Bryan said, "I do not think about things I don't think about."
Darrow: "Do you think about things you do think about?" Bryan:
"Well, sometimes."

Although John Scopes was declared guilty of the charge against
him and given a token fine, his cause stood triumphant nationally.
To pundits, the warrior from Nebraska had become an object of
ridicule and so had his cause. Bryan died only a few days later of
what doctors called "apoplexy." Mencken later said of Bryan, "Well,
we killed the son of a bitch."

For Billy the trial and Bryan's death were yet more blows add-
ing to his sense of loss. But Billy and other fundamentalist leaders
did not retire from the battlefield. The loss of Bryan, one of the
great warriors, fueled their determination to carry on, and the rhetoric and bitterness of Billy and his allies intensified.

One fundamentalist leader vowed to take back the country
and the government from the city-slicker atheists and return them
to the people who "still believe two plus two is four, God is in his
Heaven, and the Bible is the Word." And Mencken, the acerbic
basher of what he saw as country yokels, hicks, bumpkins, and
village ignoramuses, knew the battle was not over. Throw an egg
out of any Pullman window, he said, and you're likely to hit a
fundamentalist; they were everywhere.[23]

In 1926 one of Mencken's least favorite fundamentalists, a
certain ex-ballplayer preacher, was on the attack. The editors at
Collier's thought it would be good sport to pit Billy, the fire-eating
evangelist bulldog, against a Unitarian minister in a written debate
on two questions: "What will our children's children believe?" and
"Which way are the spiritual winds blowing?" Billy had not shown
up in Dayton, but he showed up in the pages of *Collier's*.

Billy's opponent was the Reverend A. Wakefield Slaten, minister of the West Side Unitarian Church of New York City and a
graduate of William Jewell College, a Baptist institution in Liberty,
Missouri. Dr. Slaten had also studied in universities in Glasgow
and Leipzig.

Side by side in the magazine the men's responses to the questions appeared, along with pictures of the combatants—Billy, arms

outstretched, left leg lifted, looking as if he had just completed a complicated dance step; and Slaten, appearing serious and dignified.

Billy versus an evolutionist, a Unitarian yet. Unlike in Dayton, there would be no cross-examination, no matching of wits in real debate. The arena here was mere magazine column space, one shot at reaching the people, hitting the right philosophical tones.

Slaten's response was much like his picture, serious and dignified. Our grandchildren, he said, will be liberated from the shibboleths of old, will be freed from beliefs in flat earths, demons, and heaven and hell. Our grandchildren will revere the mighty processes of nature, will lead lives of sacrificial social service, will find truth, beauty, and courage, not in superstition and myth but in the light of science and reason. Fears of the supernatural and death will vanish in knowledge and understanding. The world is living, said Slaten, in the last stages of Christianity and the noise we hear is the death rattle of ancient, misguided faith. In the advance of science, religions such as Christianity become anachronistic. In evolution, in scientific determinism are the secrets of the universe, not in outmoded faith in the divinity of Jesus Christ. Jesus was a man, a great man, but only a man. He was exalted in the minds of other men because they needed a spiritual crutch, and our grandchildren will need no such crutches. They will know God as nature, as a "controlling force in the vast process of cosmic evolution."

Billy's response: To science and rationalism, to the purveyors of infidel erudition, to highbrow religious journals and religious institutes dispensing blasphemous rot, the evangelist had one word—"BLAH." To jazz and cubism and lascivious plays and experimental theologies and evolutionists and birth-control advocates and higher critics he had another word—"BUNK." Our grandchildren will stand by the faith of the apostles, will stand by Martin Luther and Dwight Moody. We are passing through a period of groping, a time of "idiotic, asinine, topsy-turvy, neurotic, insane scramble after the unusual." This was true in art, music, literature, science, and government, and especially in religion. But our grandchildren will overcome the atheists and the bunco modernists and psychoanalysts, and they will accept the Bible as truth, every word of it, believing what has stood the test of the ages. "Let me tell these loud-mouthed, big vocabulary, foreign-lingo slinging, quack-theory preaching bolsheviki in the pulpits and colleges that I'll put what I preach to the test any time against what they preach." And the grandchildren will listen and will believe in the Cross, in salvation, in a God who can work miracles, and they will be saved.[24]

In this short essay in *Collier's*, Billy packed almost the whole arsenal of arguments, prejudices, and instincts on which his old-time religion, his Americanism, and his fundamentalism rested— premillennialist theology, the inerrancy of the Scriptures, rejection of evolution, and an abiding antipathy for radicals, intellectuals, philsophical and scientific meddling, foreigners, and modernist preachers and teachers.

During a short stay in Atlanta months later, Billy was still on the offensive, remarking that modernist Dr. Harry Emerson Fosdick and his "Pack of pretentious, pliable, mental perverts" were dedicated to the destruction of the Christian religion. He then called upon Columbia University to expel its president, Nicholas Murray Butler, another "mental pervert." Billy was still the master of invective, still dealing out the body blows. But the evangelist in these years was absorbing some crushing shots of his own.[25]

Billy had read many times in the *Gospel According to St. Luke* the story of the prodigal son who had spent money given to him by his father in riotous living and who had lived with harlots. As Billy anguished over the excesses of his own boys, as he learned of the womanizing and the drinking, as he frequently paid off the costs of those excesses, he must have thought often about that biblical story.

In September 1929 the wayward sons were again in the news. A week after Billy, Jr., was sued for divorce by his second wife, newspapers announced that George's wife, Harriet, accompanied by private investigators, had broken into George's apartment and found her husband with a Hollywood model. When police arrived with a warrant accusing George and his lover of immoral relations and criminal infidelity, neither could be found. Bail was set at $10,000.

In November 1929, police arrested George in the Santa Cruz Mountains and he now faced an additional charge—grand theft. He had rented a car in Oakland and not returned it. After spinning a long tale about his domestic troubles, George gave a check to Santa Cruz authorities for his bail and left town. The check bounced. A bad-check charge was now added to an ever-growing list.

Harriet soon gained a divorce in Los Angeles Superior Court. During the proceedings, she claimed that George had beaten her and was a philanderer and a drunk. She testified in court that George kept an apartment away from their home to carry on his liaisons. "Did he drink more before prohibition or after?" asked the judge. "Oh, much more after it," she replied. "He didn't follow the example of his father very closely, eh?" remarked the judge. "I should say not," Harriet agreed.[26]

Meanwhile, with George on the lam and a sheaf of warrants awaiting his capture, Billy, Jr., was enmeshed in his own personal odyssey. He had already married and divorced twice and on October 19, 1929, he took another wife, this time in Mexicali, Mexico. The marriage occurred even before the divorce from his second wife had become final in the United States.

Shortly after Billy, Jr.'s marriage in Mexicali, George was spotted in Winona Lake in December 1929 but managed to elude the police. But three months later, a Chicago patrolman picked up a man weaving unsteadily along Wells Street and arrested him on drunk-and-disorderly charges. Although the man gave his name as Johnson, the cards in his wallet told otherwise—he was George Sunday.

California authorities immediately began proceedings to retrieve the elusive fugitive. Over the next several days, however, the charges were dropped. One newspaper account summed it up: "No one ever knew why but the wiseacres spoke knowingly of the wide influence of the saddened father, who ever has stood loyally by his sons through all their troubles."[27]

Weary from the road, exasperated by the continuing turmoil into which his sons seemed inevitably drawn, emotionally drained by worry over illnesses to Nell and Helen, concerned over personal financial problems, Billy harbored deepening fears and anxieties. Behind the public ebullience, the stage bravura, the evangelist battled doubt and depression. When his other son, Paul, admitted he was seeing a divorced woman, Billy wrote to Nell of the constant public embarrassment over his children's behavior. More of it, he said, "will become known and people will laugh at me." He talked about quitting, giving in to circumstances and the hardships of old age. If he did quit, he said, "we will also have to stop handing out money to the boys."

To earn that money, Billy journeyed to those small towns, speaking in Lion's Clubs and Rotary Clubs for small donations. He even found it worthy to note in a letter to Nell that the Aurora Laundry paid him back $5 after destroying two of his shirts. The evangelist king had turned in his robes for a host of miseries common to many of his countrymen. He wrote to his wife, "I am amazed that I can preach as I do with this on my back."

Billy deeply regretted that the boys had not followed in his path. George, he said, could have become his best advance man, if only he had not succumbed to the world of destructive lures— women, liquor, and bad investments. Of Billy, Jr.'s female companions Billy used these descriptive adjectives: "damnable, gold-digger, lazy, useless dolls." Billy fretted, complained, and despaired but continued to hand over the money to his sons. If disgusted by their lives he was not able to refuse their demands. Parental guilt, fear of additional revelations leaking to the press, genuine concern over their well-being—all of it crushed down. "It almost floors me," he said, "but I struggle on." [28]

The strains and trials of the twenties also took their toll on Billy's relationship with Rody who was now on the road with other evangelistic teams. In 1929 Rody wrote a long letter to Billy expressing his love for the evangelist and dedication to his work but also telling Billy straight out that certain things had to change. Billy had become, said Rody, so desperate over money that it was almost embarrassing to see him before the revival crowds demanding more and more. Billy had become more isolated, less willing to make important social contacts in the towns and cities to cultivate support, more self-absorbed, and more preoccupied with the personal problems which seemed to overwhelm him. Somehow, the effervescent personality and the drive had been submerged in a torrent of demons stalking the preacher. Even his sermons had become increasingly long and rambling. "Whether you believe it or not," said Rody to his friend, "this letter has been written after careful consideration and with a great love in my heart for you and your work and the greatest possible sympathy for the troubles you have been having."[29]

Billy remained on the road, pounding out as best he could his fundamentalist message. The cultural winds had so shifted, Billy knew, that he was up against a rising tide of secularism and godlessness. Billy's cry was desperate—how to turn the country around, how to bring back the old faith, how to fight the purveyors of the anti-Christ. This was more than a quest to preserve religious dogma and tradition. In his ultra-nationalism, demands for censorship, frantic crusades for morality, and paranoia of foreigners, cities, and intellectuals, Billy, as many other fundamentalists, was embroiled in the deepening politics and cultural battles of the modern world.

The fundamentalists would regroup. They would establish networks of missions, institutes, Bible schools, and conferences; would start newsletters and periodicals; would form interdenominational groups to proselytize the conservative call. Their fight and his were not over; they would not surrender to the Darrows and Menckens and the other intellectuals and big-city pundits; they had not abandoned the quest to restore America to its traditional roots. Their people were still out there, still as rock-solid in their beliefs as ever and still willing to fight. And although he would not lead their resurgence, an old warrior still had his guns drawn.

On November 6, 1930, Billy appeared for one night in New York's Broadway Temple Methodist Episcopal Church at Broadway and 174th Street. A crowd of 1,000 packed into the auditorium and several dozen more gathered around a loudspeaker outside. But over thirteen years earlier, at the massive tabernacle in Washington Heights, Billy had preached to many thousands nearly every day for thirteen weeks. It had all changed.

The national election a few days earlier had just swept into the United States Congress additional members favoring repeal of Prohibition. Billy reminisced about his battles over the years with

King Alcohol, how he had been vilified, how he was proud of that vilification. And this night Billy was still defiant: "They will never repeal the Eighteenth Amendment. The American flag will never again wave over a licensed saloon."[30]

With that prediction, Billy left New York. He did not head for big campaigns in Washington, D.C., or Chicago; he headed for a five-week stint in Hutchinson, Kansas.

13

Amen!

Still combative, preaching as always the uncompromising message of repentance and salvation, fighting with all his energy the enemies of righteousness as he saw them, Billy carried on. Sometimes the going got so rough that he wondered if he could keep at it. A tangled thicket of family concerns and national worries littered his path but he struggled along, convinced of his role as God's messenger, certain of the soundness of his views, determined to strike damaging blows against the forces of evil.

If the great days of the big-city crusades were only memories and scrapbook clippings, he didn't forsake the cause. Long after most evangelists had given up the traveling circuit, Billy stubbornly packed his grips, climbed aboard those Pullmans, and pushed his aging body to more towns. Nell encouraged him. This was the work they had been called to do and they persevered.

In May 1930, in Mt. Holly, New Jersey, Billy held his last citywide tabernacle revival. Billy, Nell, and song leader Harry Clarke now conducted small, localized revivals in churches, existing tabernacles, and auditoriums. Some were one-night engagements. Not until the crusades of Billy Graham and others two decades later would mass urban revivalism rise again.

The tide of national affairs in these years dealt crushing blows to the things Billy held dear. In 1932, their political fortunes strangled by the Great Depression, the Republicans were swept from the White House, much to Billy's disgust. As Franklin Roosevelt and the Democrats launched the New Deal, Billy beheld in his mind a guerrilla war of the left, the specter of a Bolshevik state. In his sermons and public comments, he slashed at the National Recovery Administration and other agencies which, he believed, threatened traditional laissez-faire capitalism and individual liberties. The Roosevelt administration represented dangerous centralized authority, he said, and was legislatively steamrolling toward the abyss. It won't be long, he quipped, until a man can kiss his wife only after legislative action.[1]

With the leftist menace taking over, Billy feared an Armageddonal crisis of magnitude, and he looked wistfully back to the glory days a decade earlier when the nation gave to the radicals what they deserved. "I remember the day (And it was a high day for the country, too) when we chucked Alexander Berkman, Emma Goldman . . . and . . . other Reds into a transport and shoved them off in the dark toward the country that spewed them out on the world in the first place."[2]

There were those who were still listening, still applauding Billy's anti-leftist venom. On December 20, 1932, in Long Beach, California, the Ancient Order of the Supreme Council of Independent Patriots, in solemn conclave, conferred on Billy the title of "Sublime Patriot."[3]

On the other side, however, were people like Ben B. Lindsay, eminent California Supreme Court judge, expert on juvenile delinquency, and advocate of liberal judicial reforms. Judge Lindsay said that Billy was still living in the sixteenth century and was still chasing devils. Billy retorted, "The Judge is an old fool."[4]

Mostly the news was bad and most devastating of all was the assault on Prohibition. The wet forces had clearly gained ascendancy; the country was tiring of its experiment in moral enforcement. To Billy, who had played such a robust role in the temperance wars for over two decades, the turn of events was demoralizing. He just couldn't understand why Americans were yielding to the devil's brew.

In March 1930, Billy was still publicly confident, telling a revival audience in Philadelphia that the wet forces in the country would have as much chance of repealing the Eighteenth Amendment as they would have of "wrecking Gibraltar with a bombardment of green peas." Looking back at the last presidential election as a referendum on Prohibition, he claimed that wet influence was strong only in the big cities. Thank God, he said, for rural America.[5]

But after the 1932 election Billy could see the national trend; it was raining green peas. He joined a prohibitionist group in Chicago whose members included a University of Chicago professor and future United States senator named Paul Douglass. The group futilely attempted to hold back the anti-prohibitionist tide in Illinois after the *Chicago Tribune* had come out in favor of repeal. Billy called the *Tribune*'s staff "the most lecherous crowd this side of Hell."[6]

Although federal officials had by 1929 made over 500,000 arrests for violation of Prohibition, it was apparent that enforcement could not begin to keep pace with the lawbreaking. Bootleggers became so commonplace in many communities that law enforcement officials gave up arresting them. The pressures on Congress to end Prohibition mounted.

It had been clear for some time that Prohibition fostered networks of criminal industry. And now, with the tentacles of the Great Depression strangling America's economic and social systems, anti-Prohibition forces argued persuasively that the effort to legislate away the evils of alcohol was too costly, was misguided, gave government odious license to invade personal lives, and deprived the country of a great revenue potential—a tax on liquor.

Thus, less than four months after the Democrats' victory in 1932, Congress approved an amendment repealing Prohibition and directed that the public be given the opportunity to vote directly on the question. Congress also allowed the sale of beer with an alcohol content of 3.2 percent. By December 1933, ratification of the Twenty-first Amendment restored King Alcohol's crown. A few states, mostly southern, retained state prohibition until the 1960s; others resorted to a ban on liquor by the drink, an attempt to prevent the operation of saloons. But the days of the speakeasy were over.

For Billy, bottoms were, indeed, up. He called the repealists the "worst crowd of God forsaken cut throats this side of Hell." And if he were God, he continued, they wouldn't be this side.[7]

There were signs everywhere that the millennium must be drawing near. Even to some left-wing observers, it all seemed apocalyptic. Edmund Wilson, literary critic, described the stock market crash as something like "a rendering of the earth in preparation for the Day of Judgment." Billy concurred. The Second Coming, he declared, was closer than ever. To Billy the nation's ills were Divine retribution for its disregard of God's will. The Almighty was knocking America on its knees "before she became too chesty."[8]

In October 1932, Billy was on a tour of the state of Michigan on behalf of temperance forces there. After he spoke in Detroit on October 12 at a Methodist church, he and Nell were awakened in their room at about 2 A.M. by the phone call parents most fear. Their daughter Helen had died of pneumonia. They managed to find a friend in Detroit in the early-morning hours who arranged to drive them to Sturgis, Michigan, Helen's home. Billy broke down completely, Nell said later. She and son-in-law Mark Haines took care of the funeral details. On the day of the burial the stores of the small town closed for two hours in tribute. Afterward, on the way to catch a train for Chicago, Billy turned to his wife and told her he didn't think he could go on preaching. Nell asked him what he wanted to do and Billy couldn't answer. He kept his next speaking engagement in Waterloo, Iowa.[9]

Several months later, as Billy was delivering a sermon at the

First Federated Church in Des Moines, his speech pattern suddenly faltered and he began to appear disoriented. Singer Harry Clarke rushed to his side and led him slowly off the stage, Billy protesting all the while that he wanted to continue. "Don't let them go," Billy muttered. "They're lost." After an ambulance arrived, the doctors carried the stricken evangelist on a stretcher through the church and Nell remembered later the intense silence of the crowd. After the ambulance left, most of the crowd stayed. Led by Clarke, the folks remained in their pews for several hours, some until 4 A.M., praying that God would not take Billy Sunday that night.[10]

With Nell constantly at his side for several weeks, Billy slowly recovered from the heart attack. Billy, Jr., wrote to his mother, "This scare may prove a blessing in disguise in that it will force him to realize a man in his seventies can't do the work that would burn up a man half his age."

The heart attack didn't stop him. Soon he was back on the road—Millbrook, New York; Erie, Pennsylvania; Evansville, Indiana. Billy, Jr., later wrote, "Why can't Dad quit and rest the rest of his life? Even working as hard as he does the collections are so small it hardly pays for the strain he has to exert."[11]

Recovering in 1933, Billy granted a reporter named A. B. Macdonald of the *Kansas City Star* a bedside interview more reflective and personal than perhaps any he had ever given. Weak and gaunt, Billy had barely won his scrap with death only a few weeks before. Although trying to be upbeat and chatty, Billy pensively looked back over the years as if trying to understand the driving forces and values which had given shape to his life. He was prepared to die, he said, and had been prepared for forty-five years. But he felt he still had work to do, service to give for the unsaved, the Lord's work. Cheered by the hundreds of letters and telegrams arriving each day from around the country, letters from big cities and small towns, from the educated and the nearly illiterate, from preachers, from men and women who had been converted in Sunday rallies, people whose lives had been deeply touched by the evangelist from Iowa, Billy vowed to preach again.

After a physician interrupted the interview with a quick examination and orders to give his heart a long rest, Billy lifted up his hands and looked at them. "Think of how many have shaken these old hands of mine," he said softly. He had led his life, he said, so that all the world would know that he was a man of Christ, that he was honored to preach the word. Refusing to bow and scrape to the world, he had remained true to the biblical commands as he understood them, had shunned amusements, worked to the limits of his strength, had been a faithful warrior. "I fell fighting on the field of battle," he said of his last tabernacle appearance in Des Moines.

Lamenting the tidal wave of licentiousness and crime and godlessness which seemed to grip America, he said that the country needed new revival shock troops, a fresh infusion of the blood of the Cross. The revival had always been God's way of cleansing, of bolstering the church; it had been that way since Peter and Paul. The revivalist could touch masses of people that the churches never reached, he said. In those tents and tabernacles, where people from all walks of life wedged together in religious community, God reached out. It had been Billy's mission to be God's spokesman and to that cause he was totally committed.

As the interview ended, Nell said, "Our lives have been closer together than most married persons, I believe." She was grateful, she said, to have been part of the great work for God.

Another fifteen years of preaching lay ahead for him, the evangelist predicted. He had played life's game according to biblical rules, made sacrifices, and now awaited "orders form the Great Umpire of the Universe." Unswerving, uncomplicated faith, simple faith, a complete confidence about life's calling, clear direction—Billy held fast.[12]

On September 7, 1933, less than a year after the death of Billy's daughter Helen, the evangelist, conducting a series of revival meetings in Portland, Oregon, received another devastating phone call. George Sunday had been gravely injured in San Francisco from a fall out of an apartment window.

Suffering from serious financial reverses and from alcoholism, George had recently begun to use morphine and had quarreled violently at his home with both his second wife, Renee, and with his mother, who had traveled to San Francisco from Hood River to try to help him out of his difficulties. After striking his wife and ordering Nell from the house, George, alone in one of the rooms of the fourth-floor apartment, plunged seventy-five feet to the ground in an apparent suicide leap. At Central Emergency Hospital he told his wife he had fallen accidentally while attempting to raise a stuck window.

A few days later, during an operation to reset some of the fractures sustained in the fall, George, forty years old, died. Billy and Nell had lost another of their children. Nell later remembered Billy somberly staring out at Winona Lake shortly after George's death and uttering remorsefully, "Ma, where did I go wrong?"[13]

The Sundays did their best to help various family members weather financial difficulties in these dark times. They helped Billy, Jr., whose dry-ice business in California had gone bankrupt; they helped pay off the *Sturgis Journal* building for Helen's husband; they gave money to George's wife who told the Sundays that she was receiving only 75¢ a week from government relief. "I know that you would like to forget about me altogether but even with all of that I don't think you would like or let me go hungry," she wrote. Billy also helped build a house for George's first wife, Harriet, and her two children and pledged to pay monthly expenses for the children until they reached age twenty-one. "That's why I have to go to these little places," he said. "I ought to have rest, but I can't."[14]

In 1934 Billy was in New York to speak at Calvary Baptist Church. "I have got just as much ginger and tabasco sauce for God as ever," Billy shouted. Still as natty as ever in striped trousers, frock coat, and pearl stickpin, Billy went after the devil with the usual flourishes. One reason that sin was on the upsurge, said Billy, was because clergymen treated it "like a cream puff, a charlotte russe, instead of a rattlesnake."[15]

In addition to what he saw as an ineffective clergy, Billy could see the indignities American revivalism was suffering at the hands of various upstart preachers. Aimee Semple McPherson of Los Angeles, who managed to charm thousands at the Angelus Temple, once staged her own kidnapping. A Tennessee evangelist called Sister Smothers proved the power of prayer by allowing herself to be bitten by a diamondback rattlesnake. A California preacher won notice by playing "Rock of Ages" on the circus calliope, saxophone, and xylophone, all to the background sounds of 360 sleigh bells. An Ohio evangelist was arrested on bigamy charges. There was no evidence he was a Mormon.[16]

In these hard times, Billy kept exhorting his audiences to return to the old beliefs in sin and salvation, return again to Pentecost, to Apostolic truth, back to the courage of the Fathers, back to a time when people were gloriously saved. If Billy's message was muted in these years, the evangelist's fervid belief never wavered. If he kept plugging, kept up the pace, pushed with everything he had, perhaps he could turn it all around. Like the Old Testament prophets, he must remain steadfast, must keep up the campaign for the Lord, the urgent work to save a world on the brink of catastrophe.

If mass tabernacle revivalism was now in national decline, there was emerging a new technology holding great promise for evangelists, a technology which could make an enormous difference. It was called radio. On January 2, 1921, station KDKA in Pittsburgh, which had been in operation for two months and had broadcast election returns for the first time in American history, now added another momentous inaugural—it carried a church worship service.

In the years following, as Americans eagerly bought up the new crystal sets and infant commercial stations hurried to the airwaves, some American religious figures soon realized the tremendous possibilities of this new invention to bring souls to Christ. In 1922 Paul Rader, pastor of the Chicago Gospel Tabernacle, set up his own once-a-week station with the call letters WJBT ("Where Jesus Blesses Thousands"). Rader became one of the giants in gospel broadcasting.

In 1923 R. E. Brown, founder of the Omaha Gospel Tabernacle, became the first preacher to broadcast a nondenominational religious service. By the 1930s, Brown's Radio Chapel Service reached an estimated 500,000 listeners a week and the preacher became known as "the Billy Sunday of the air."

From the Moody Bible Institute's WHBI in Chicago to small stations in St. Louis, Denver, Cincinnati, Richmond, and many other cities, radio gospel pioneers appeared across the country. In the thirties, with the emergence of commercial networks, radio preachers reached audiences from New York to California. Walter Maier's *The Lutheran Hour,* Charles Fuller's *Old Fashioned Revival Hour,* T. Myron Webb's *Bible Fellowship Hour,* and Glenn Tingley's *Radio Revival* joined on the air other national shows such as *Heaven at Home Hour, Back to the Bible,* and *Back to God Hour.*

On a foggy San Diego beach in 1934, a drunken man named Paul Myers, a prominent radio broadcaster from Hollywood, was awakened by the clanging of a ship's bell. Later, when he opened a Gideon Bible in his cheap hotel room, the despairing Myers was soon a changed man. He returned to his family in Hollywood and embarked on a worldwide radio ministry. As Myers's program opens, audiences hear the clanging of ship's bells, whistles, and a quartet singing, "I've anchored my sail in the Haven of Rest . . ." The pipe organ swells its sounds and a voice triumphantly declares, "Ahoy, there, shipmate! Eight bells and all's well . . ." And then on comes First Mate Bob and with him the crew of the Good Ship Grace "coming from the harbor called 'Haven of Rest' in Hollywood, California."

The advent of radio opened up evangelism to a new dimension. At the height of Billy's career during World War I, he often filled tabernacles holding 20,000 people or more. He had been the most successful evangelist in American history in attracting massive crowds over weeks and months in individual cities. Radio paled those numbers. The Columbia Broadcasting System estimated that *The Lutheran Hour* reached an average of several million listeners in each broadcast in 1935. Charles Fuller in 1939 reached more than ten million each Sabbath night on the Mutual network. Although the medium was entirely different, with radio listeners unable to participate in the religious service in the same ways as congregations, the numbers were astonishing.[17]

Billy saw clearly the tremendous potential of radio and began to use it; he appeared on *Haven of Rest* and other programs. Letters arrived from Tennessee, Boston, New York, Virginia, and Canada, all testifying to the power of his message on radio.

Before one of his broadcasts in 1934 in New York's Grace Gospel Church, Billy talked of the day when electronics could revolutionize American evangelism. To be effective, he said, a radio ministry must employ the combination that made tabernacle evangelism exciting—a preacher with spark and verve; inspiring music; a cheerful, bright atmosphere; pleasant fellowship. "Radio has scarcely scratched the surface of its usefulness," Billy perceptively observed. Many new applications in the medium await the imaginative bearers of the Gospel, he said. Billy, the master of drawing crowds, saw the new age ahead.[18]

Several individuals in the radio industry suggested that Billy give up the road appearances and launch his own national radio series. A New York radio station offered Billy a weekly revival service that would reach several million listeners and Rody also urged Billy to begin a regular national evangelistic radio program. But Billy never could make the leap. Even though he wore himself out on the revival trail, even though he complained at times to Nell about the grinding pace, the road was in his blood, was his place—not seated in a small room before a microphone but on his feet, before those crowds, looking into their eyes, watching them laugh and cry, bringing them to God.[19]

But Billy, the preacher who had, as no other before, popularized the institution of revivalism, was reaching the end of his career. He had helped give urban revivalism its organizational shape, had perfected techniques for gathering masses of people to its banner, had made it big tent, center stage, top billing. He had infused it with a scorching, firebrand fundamentalism. He had, as no other religious figure of his time, convinced Americans to stand fast to traditional biblical teachings.

If his immediate evangelistic predecessors had avoided the rough and tumble of sectarian, doctrinal disputes and the welter of external problems plaguing the country, if they preferred to wait it out until the millennium, Billy had plunged into the cauldron headlong. The hideous libertinism and godlessness and moral decay demanded a counterassault and the evangelist had delivered with both fists. He helped uproot urban revivalism from its premillennialist shell. He still believed deeply in the Second Coming, still considered himself a premillennialist, but he was too much a fighter to allow Satan's forces to roam about the nation's field without a struggle. His crusades were about preserving spirituality, morality, decency, and scriptural study. He helped develop the revivalist institution and demonstrated how to develop parachurch organization. The evangelists of a later generation would pick up Billy's armor and forge ahead.[20]

But now he fended off the phantasms, the lurking demons. Tincturing his sermons in these last years with references to the dangers of occultism and its séances, Ouija boards, and dark cabinets, he also warned of the dangers of vegetarianism and companionate marriage. He scorned, with more hysterical vengeance than ever, the Bolsheviks, those Reds flitting about "like wharf rats." He struck personally at men like Bertrand Russell and H. L. Mencken, men of poison, luring the youth, hoodwinking gullible Americans, and turning much of the country into a land of barnyard ethics.

Some of his sermons now were foreboding, despairing, with allusions to world dictatorships, wrecked governments, collapsing economic systems, the ascension of the anti-Christ, and the mark of 666 as prophesied in the book of Revelation. Billy was a tired warrior.[21]

In May 1935, in Chattanooga, his heart felled him once again. This time he rested for half a year, spending time in Winona Lake and Hood River, and visiting his two sons, Billy, Jr., and Paul, in Los Angeles. In October, Rody asked him to preach in Mishawaka, Indiana. Against the advice of Nell and instructions from his physicians, Billy accepted. Over forty converts came forward to accept Christ at the service on October 27 and Billy was joyous. But later, when Nell asked him how he felt, he said, "I feel like the power is off." A few days later he died at the home of his brother-in-law in Chicago.[22]

Tributes came in to his widow from the famous as well as the lowly. "I am and always have been plain Billy Sunday trying to do God's will," he once said. But millions of Americans knew that they had lost someone special.[23]

Tragedy loomed in the years ahead for others of the Sunday family. In 1938 Billy, Jr., was killed in an automobile accident.

Paul, the last surviving of the Sunday children, died in 1944 in an airplane crash. Nell had buried her husband and all four children.

But she carried on with remarkable commitment and energy after Billy's death, addressing revival meetings and youth groups, raising money for the Winona Lake Assembly and other religious organizations, and encouraging younger evangelists. She told a writer in 1950, "The Lord has kept me busy."[24]

The links were strong between Billy Sunday and his successors. Charlotte, North Carolina, 1924. A young boy sits among a throng of tabernacle worshippers at a Billy Sunday crusade, frightened at the shouts of fiery invective thundering from the pulpit, at the ferocity and combustion of emotion that warned of cataclysm. The boy's name is Billy Graham.[25]

A young boy in Lynchburg, Virginia, hears a woman relative attempt to persuade his alcoholic father to give his life to Christ. The woman is a friend of Billy Sunday. The boy's name is Jerry Falwell.[26]

Links. Billy was a trustee of Bob Jones College, an ultraconservative, fundamentalist Bible school in Cleveland, Tennessee. Later moved to Greenville, South Carolina, the college was interdenominational and thoroughly "100% American," from its strict moral codes imposed on the students to its superpatriotism, its old-time religious orthodoxy, and its rejection of dissent. At Cleveland, Tennessee, on May 29, 1935, Bob Jones College confers on Billy an honorary doctor of laws. Shortly thereafter, Billy Graham enrolls in the college.[27]

Many years later, at Oral Roberts University in Tulsa, Oklahoma, radio station KORU carries the religious program broadcast from a venerable institution in Chicago's tenderloin—the Pacific Garden Mission.

In 1952 Billy Graham warns a young man that his excessive drinking may cost him his life. The man is Paul Haines, son of Helen Haines, grandson of Billy Sunday.[28]

At Pacific Garden Mission's 109th anniversary in October 1986, an evangelist calls himself a "great-great grandson of the Mission." Pacific Garden, he said, had led Billy Sunday to Christ, who had "led Fred Donnelson to Christ, who led Paul Donnelson to Christ, who led Jerry Falwell to Christ."[29]

In testifying to the debt that modern evangelists owe to the career of Billy Sunday, Oral Roberts speaks of three things—Billy's uncompromising, tireless commitment to his ministry; his example in establishing sound business methods in the field of revivalism; and his courage in trying new approaches to reach the people, from the wooden tabernacles to the sawdust, the music, and the preaching style. He was, says Oral Roberts, an innovator and, to those who followed and learned from him, "virtually a prophet."[30]

The crusades of the Billy Graham Evangelistic Association became mighty echoes of the Sunday revivals of thirty years before—the legions of advance workers, the extensive involvement and support of local churches and civic organizations, the formidable publicity, the magnetic charm and oratory of the evangelist, the great choirs and the prominent role of the chorister, the participation of various delegations attending en masse, the call for converts and the march down the aisles to the preacher, and the follow-up activities. Indeed, about the only technical difference between a typical Sunday rally in the years of the First World War and a Graham revival was the advanced microphone and loudspeaker system. If Graham's personal style was less vaudevillian, he had learned much from his revivalist forebear. As part of his early training, Graham preached at the Winona Lake summer conference. Links.[31]

Oral Roberts, Billy Graham, Jimmy Swaggart—the great figures of late-twentieth century evangelism all emerged from the revivalist tradition. Revivalism had become a structured American institution, pitched as much toward morality and virtue as toward doctrinal religion. Appealing to popular culture, using sales and promotion strategies straight from corporate boardrooms, the American revivalist was now following ordered processes. This was not the spontaneous, soul-ripping wave of hysteria of the days of Jonathan Edwards. This was carefully planned orchestration, rational and deliberate.

By the mid-1950s Graham, who began to carry his revivals on radio and television, was well on his way to becoming a world figure; Oral Roberts had brought faith healing to television audiences; Rex Humbard had launched his media industry; and Robert Schuller had established his ministry at a drive-in church in Garden Grove, California, preaching atop a snack bar. By 1981 Schuller had completed his Crystal Cathedral at a cost of $16 million.

The entreprenurial success of men like Roberts and Schuller paved the way for others such as Jim Bakker, who parlayed old-time religion into massive corporate structures, into preaching empires. They all had taken Billy Sunday a step further.[32]

Billy presaged the televangelists in many ways—in his militant superpatriotism, his uncompromising social and political discourse, his rigid fundamentalism, and his Christian activism. To listen to Pat Robertson decry the moral laxity of modern America, to hear Jimmy Swaggart warn of the devil's mischief, and to watch other evangelists transfix crowds and call for the redemption of sin-stained souls is to catch today something of Billy's tabernacle message.

Detractors of television ministries argue today that the institution is a perversion of traditional religious forms, that television (and radio) revivalism is a debilitating force in truly bringing souls to Christ. Supporters of televangelism, on the other hand, argue that the medium offers a tremendous stimulus upon which the established churches must build, that it can reach the hearts of millions of lost and wavering individuals and stir them to religious commitment. The same arguments and counterarguments had thundered about mass urban revivalism in the days of Billy Sunday. Revivalism, Billy always argued, could bring souls to Christ in great numbers; it was up to the ministers to use the intensity and power of the revivals to sustain that enthusiasm.

Billy had preached a masculine fundamentalism, a message that the effeminate Christians of the new theology must stand aside, that Christ was tough and wanted any follower to be tough also, "not a sissified sort of galoot that let everybody make a doormat out of him." Decades later, hear Jerry Falwell: "Christ wasn't effeminate. . . . The man who lived on this earth was a man with muscle. . . . Christ was a he-man!" No meek, wimpering Christ was this, no sissified sort. Echoes of Billy.[33]

In the late twentieth century the new term for the anti-Christ became "secular humanism." Much as Billy had done a half century before, fundamentalist preachers castigate the liberal, egghead ethos, the erosion of Christian values at the hands of the godless elite, and the sweeping away of traditional moral values in a torrent of abortions, sexual aberration, drugs, and lawlessness. Much like Billy had done, they battle for spiritual regeneration, seek to purge liberals from positions of authority, and marshal their followers in crusades for moral uplift.

The battles among America's Protestants over fundamentalism continue well over half a century after Billy's death. At the 1990 Southern Baptist Convention two news editors of the Baptist Press were ordered to resign because their reporting, according to the executive committee, was biased against fundamentalists, who were in a majority at the convention. In Texas, a pastor of one of the state's most influential churches attacked the leadership for its betrayal of historic religious principles such as freedom of belief and separation of church and state. The controversy rolls on.[34]

The fundamentalist fight against the anti-Christ takes on new enemies and new conspiracies through the years. But somehow it all has a familiar ring. If Billy Sunday in his day lamented the satanic curses of licentious music and close dancing, the pagan theater, and birth control, modern preachers excoriate the National Endowment for the Arts for sponsoring obscene work, push for censorship in the recording and motion picture industries, and zealously make war on abortion.

The message is still the same—God, country, family, clean living, born-again redemption, millennial expectancy, and civic responsibility. The enemies are still the same—radicals, perverts, the dangers of alien and foreign influence on American society and culture, and left-wing political ideology. Yes, the ACLU, as in the twenties, is still the enemy.

But now the fundamentalist arsenal has formidable weapons not available to Billy Sunday. Television, computers, direct-mail technological innovations, advanced techniques of mass persuasion and public opinion sampling—all of the sophisticated tools of advertising and image-making employed by big business and political organizations have been marshaled by the religion industry in ways Billy would have admired.

If some of the evangelists who followed Billy to the revival spotlight were undoubtedly con artists and pitchmen using the new technologies for primarily entrepreneurial motives, others believed they were on Divine missions; Sunday himself had certainly believed that. Long after the tabernacle had ceased to bring him financial wealth Billy had plugged ahead, believing in his soul that he was performing God's will. On the revival stage he had employed all the innovations he and his team could muster—from the twenties' version of klieg lights to circus giants acting as ushers. The slick, multi-media barrages of the later evangelists would have made perfect sense to Billy; use all the tools available for the Lord's cause.

In the power of television, fundamentalists found an especially sophisticated means to enlarge their following and solicit the dollars. From the tin pails of the Billy Sunday revivals we now have dial-a-pledge—credit cards, checks, or cash accepted.

H. L. Mencken and Clarence Darrow left Dayton, Tennessee, in the summer of 1925 hoping they had conquered the fundamentalist beast. Public opinion polls over sixty years later reveal a remarkably different unfolding of American national life. Eighty percent of Americans believe God will judge them for their sins; a healthy percentage believe in Divine miracles; over 90 percent say they pray at least once a week. Around 40 percent of Americans attend church each week, almost four times the rate of attendance in Britain and France. And 40 percent of the population calls itself "born again." If Billy could see these statistics, he would belt out a joyous whoop.

The Lord's battle rages on. Many of the people touched by Billy's preaching became part of that battle. Throughout his later years, in the times that had brought him so much pain and remorse, he had been comforted by many letters from those people across the country, men and women, remembering when they had first seen him taking on the devil, testifying to how much Billy's ministry had meant in their own lives. One woman remembered that when she was a small girl she had been in the Boston tabernacle on the final day of the campaign in 1919. Thirty thousand were inside, she said, with as many others outside, surrounding the building. "Never listened to such a powerful sermon," she said, "never saw such activity on a platform, and never heard singing like it, as that multitude sang 'We're Marching to Zion.' "[35]

From the Billy Sunday Club of Winston-Salem, North Carolina, came a letter from its secretary, W. F. Vaughn, reporting that during the past ten years the club had conducted many meetings where hundreds of people had accepted Christ as their personal savior. "We shall be ever grateful for the great work which you started in our city."[36]

Fern Johnson of Bellville, Ohio, wrote to the evangelist on March 13, 1933, soon after he had suffered his heart attack in Des Moines. She had heard of Billy's troubles and decided to tell him of the impact he had made on her life. When she was eleven years old she attended one of the children's meetings at the Erie, Pennsylvania, revival. She remembered Billy trying to speak over the roar of the railroad engines nearby, remembered the heat inside the tabernacle on a midsummer day, and the feeling she had on the streetcar leaving the tabernacle with her mother and others who were all crying as they still heard voices singing "God Be with You Till We Meet Again."

Johnson was thirty-three years old when she wrote that letter to Billy. The revivals, she said, had changed her life completely. She later attended the Moody Bible Institute, sang in church musical groups, and married a Presbyterian minister. In January 1933, they asked a Methodist minister to assist them in some of their services. The minister told them that he, too, had been converted at a Billy Sunday revival. Johnson also remembered that at one of the classes at the Moody Bible Institute, each student was asked how he or she had come to know Christ. Most testified that they had been converted at a Billy Sunday crusade. She wrote, "So tonight as I am thinking of you, perhaps a little heartsick, I am praising my Heavenly Father for leading you and giving you the power . . . to win precious souls."[37]

Johnson and others like her who had been to Billy Sunday revivals never forgot them—the low-slung, sprawling, wooden tab-

ernacle; the smell of the sawdust shavings in the aisles; the crowds
streaming in from all directions to find places on the long benches;
the huge choir assembled on the platform ready to send forth shock
waves of sound; the chorister, dapper and engaging, armed with
that trombone, uttering witticisms; the ushers and other workers
hurrying about performing assorted duties; the reporters taking it
all down in their best prose; the delegations from the factories and
clubs and fraternal organizations massed in groups; and the evangelist, natty, sprightly, face beaming, ready to bounce into one hell
of a sermon. This was big-time evangelism; this was a big-time
preacher.

Hallelujah! Amen!

Notes

CHAPTER 1: Prairie Days

1. *Wichita Beacon*, November 23, 1911; Record Group (RG) 94, Records of the Adjutant General's Office, Compiled Military Service Records, William Sunday, and RG 15, Records of the Veterans Administration, Civil War Pension File, Mary Jane Stowell Family, Cert. No. 653177, National Archives, Washington, D.C.; William G. McLoughlin, *Billy Sunday Was His Real Name* (Chicago, 1955), 1; Billy Sunday (B.S.), "The Sawdust Trail," *Ladies' Home Journal* (September 1932), 82; draft of autobiographical sketch, Sunday Papers, Roll 16; William T. Ellis, *"Billy" Sunday: The Man and His Message* (Philadelphia, 1914), 22–24.

2. Karen Gullen, *Billy Sunday Speaks* (New York, 1970), 208; Elijah P. Brown, *The Real Billy Sunday* (New York, 1914), 15.

3. RG 15, Records of the Veterans Administration, Mary Jane Stowell Pension File, National Archives.

4. Marriage and guardian documents and other affidavits from the Iowa Circuit

Court and the U.S. Bureau of Pensions are in the Mary Jane Stowell pension file, National Archives.

5. Gullen, 208–209; McLoughlin, 3; RG 29, Records of the Bureau of the Census, Ninth Census, 1870, Iowa, Vol. 9, National Archives.

6. *Atlanta Constitution,* November 8, 1917.

7. Quoted in Gordon Langley Hall, *The Sawdust Trail* (Philadelphia, 1964), 129.

8. B.S., "The Sawdust Trail" (September 1932), 81–84.

9. Stowell Pension File, National Archives; Earl S. Fullbrook, "Relief Work During the Civil War," *Iowa Journal of History and Politics* (April 1918), 257–266.

10. B.S., "The Sawdust Trail" (September 1932), 84.

11. Ibid. (October 1932), 12.

12. Ibid., 12–13; McLoughlin, 3; Hall, 130–131; *First Album of the City of Davenport, Iowa* (Davenport, 1887), 14–15; *History of Mills County, Iowa* (Des Moines, Iowa, 1881), 199–200.

13. B.S., "The Sawdust Trail" (October 1932), 13; McLoughlin, 4; Hall, 131; clipping, "How Billy Sunday Became a Famous Ball Player, as related by 'Ma' Sunday to Fred Lockley." *Baseball Magazine* (June 1920), 319, copy in Chicago Historical Society.

14. Stowell Pension File, National Archives.

15. *Des Moines Register and Leader,* April 5, 1914; B.S., "The Sawdust Trail" (October 1932), 99; "How Billy Sunday Became a Famous Ball Player," 319; Brown, 26–30.

16. B.S., "The Sawdust Trail" (November 1932), 12.

17. Quoted in Gullen, 211.

18. Ellis, 25.

CHAPTER 2: From Sandlots to Sawdust

1. *Chicago Inter-Ocean,* July 11, 1886; *Chicago Tribune,* July 11, 1886; *Detroit Evening News,* July 11, 1886.

2. Billy Sunday (B.S.), "The Sawdust Trail," *Ladies' Home Journal* (November 1931), 16; William G. McLoughlin, *Billy Sunday Was His Real Name* (Chicago, 1955), 4–5; J. A. Swisher, "Billy Sunday," *Palimpsest* (August 1930), 345.

3. B.S., "The Sawdust Trail," (November 1931), 17; McLoughlin, 4; clipping, Sunday Papers, Reel 9; Irene Fosness, *Marshalltown: A Pictorial History* (Rock Island, IL, 1985), 72, 92.

4. *A Baseball Century: The First 100 Years of the National League* (New York, 1976), 24–25; Hy Turkin and S. C. Thompson, *The Official Encyclopedia of Baseball* (New York, 1970), 5th ed., 5–6; *Pittsburgh Dispatch,* May 11, 1888.

5. *New York Times,* May 31, 1888.

6. Henry Chadwick Scrapbook, Vol. 2, A. G. Spaulding Collection, New York Public Library; Bill James, *Historical Baseball Abstract* (New York, 1988), 36.

7. Harvey Frommer, *Primitive Baseball* (New York, 1988), 97–101; *A Baseball Century,* 29; John Durant, *The Story of Baseball in Words and Pictures* (New York, 1973), 30–33; David L. Porter, "Cap Anson of Marshalltown," *Palimpsest* (July/August 1980), 103.

8. B.S., "The Sawdust Trail," (February 1932), 110; clippings, "How Billy Sunday Became a Famous Ball Player, as related by 'Ma' Sunday to Fred Lockley," *Baseball Magazine* (June 1920), 320, copy in Chicago Historical Society.

9. *Chicago Tribune*, May 23, 1883; *Chicago Inter-Ocean*, May 23, 1883.

10. "How Billy Sunday Became a Famous Ball-Player," 320; Elijah P. Brown, *The Real Billy Sunday* (New York, 1914), 33.

11. Clippings, Sunday Papers, Reels 6, 26; clippings, National Baseball Hall of Fame and Museum, Inc., Cooperstown, New York; *Chicago Inter-Ocean*, September 13, 1885; *The Baseball Encyclopedia: Bicentennial Edition* (New York, 1976), 1372.

12. *Chicago Inter-Ocean*, August 21, 1885; clipping, National Baseball Hall of Fame; George S. May, "Outfielders McVey to Lindell," *Palimpsest* (April 1955), 140.

13. *Chicago Tribune*, July 24, 1886.

14. *Hearst's Sunday American*, October 28, 1917; sermon, Sunday Papers, New York Revival File, Reel 10; Karen Gullen, *Billy Sunday Speaks* (New York, 1970), 213–214; Samuel P. Wilson, *Chicago and Its Cesspools of Infamy* (Chicago, 1910), 185–191; Brown, 36–40.

15. *Hearst's Sunday American*, October 28, 1917.

16. B.S., "The Sawdust Trail," (February 1932), 87; McLoughlin, 6; Brown, 65.

17. *Chicago Tribune*, July 11, 1886; *Chicago Inter-Ocean*, July 11, 1886; *Detroit Evening News*, July 11, 1886; clippings, National Baseball Hall of Fame.

18. Peter Levine, *A. G. Spaulding and the Rise of Baseball* (New York, 1985), 40–41; *Sporting News*, March 5, 1887; clippings, Spaulding scrapbooks, Spaulding Collection, New York Public Library.

19. Levine, 41–43; David Q. Voigt, *American Baseball: From Gentleman's Sport to the Commissioner System*, 1966, 110–111.

20. *The Baseball Encyclopedia*, 1372.

21. Quoted in Brown, 49; McLoughlin, 7; *Sporting News*, February 4, 1888.

22. Gullen, 216.

23. *Sporting News*, February 4, 1888.

24. B.S., "The Sawdust Trail," (February 1932), 87; W. A. Nimick to B.S., March 23, 1888, National Baseball Hall of Fame.

25. Frederick G. Lieb, *The Pittsburgh Pirates* (New York, 1948), 11–13.

26. Clipping, Sunday Papers, Reel 6.

27. Preston Orem, "Baseball from the Newspaper Accounts" (Altadena, CA, 1967), 479–480, unpublished copy in the Library of Congress.

28. *Pittsburgh Dispatch*, May 4, 1888.

29. *The Baseball Encyclopedia*, 1372.

30. *Chicago Herald*, June 3, 1888.

31. B.S. to Helen Thompson (H.T.), March 19, 1888, Sunday Papers, Reel 6.

32. B.S. to H.T., May 9, 1888, Sunday Papers, Reel 6.

33. B.S. to H.T., May 8, 1888, Sunday Papers, Reel 6.

34. B.S. to H.T., May 17, 1888, Sunday Papers, Reel 6.

35. B.S. to H.T., June 1888, Sunday Papers, Reel 6.

36. B.S. to H.T, June 1888, Sunday Papers, Reel 6.

37. Clipping, Sunday Papers, Reel 6.

38. *Pittsburgh Dispatch*, September 4, 1888.

39. B.S., "The Sawdust Trail," (February 1932), 87; *Chicago Inter-Ocean*, September 6, 1888.

40. B.S., "The Sawdust Trail," (February 1932), 87.

41. B.S. to H.T., May 12, 1888, Sunday Papers, Reel 6.

42. Clipping, *Little Rock Gazette*, November 8, 1935, copy in Sunday Papers, Reel 24.

43. Orem, 438; Lieb, 17–18; Albert Spaulding, *America's National Game* (New York, 1911), 272–279; Adrian Anson, *A Ball Player's Career* (Chicago, 1900), 291–293; Harry Palmer, *Stories of the Base Ball Field* (Chicago, 1890), 142–157.

44. Lieb, 17–18; clipping, Sunday Papers, Reel 26.; Lowell Reidenbaugh, *100 Years of National League Baseball* (St. Louis, 1976), 28; clipping, National Baseball Hall of Fame.

45. Voigt, 168; *Pittsburgh Dispatch*, November 21, 1890.

46. Lieb, 20–21.

47. William T. Ellis, "Billy" Sunday: The Man and His Message (Philadelphia, 1914), 37; McLoughlin, 8; B.S., "The Sawdust Trail," (February 1932), 87.

48. Frederick J. Haskin to P. E. Clemmen, June 9, 1925, Martin Luther King Public Library, "Biographical File," Washington, D.C.

49. McLoughlin, 8; Ellis, 37–38; B.S., "The Sawdust Trail," (February 1932), 89.

50. B.S., "My All-Star Nine," *Colliers* (October 18, 1913), 19.

Chapter 3: Revivalist

1. Sermons, Sunday Papers, Reel 10; Billy Sunday (B.S.), "The Sawdust Trail," *Ladies' Home Journal* (February 1933), 88.

2. Karen Gullen, *Billy Sunday Speaks* (New York, 1970), 75.

3. William T. Ellis, *"Billy Sunday: The Man and His Message* (Philadelphia, 1914), 52–56.

4. Quoted in William G. McLoughlin, *Billy Sunday Was His Real Name* (Chicago, 1955), 8.

5. Sermon, Marshalltown campaign, Sunday Papers, Reel 21.

6. B.S., "The Sawdust Trail," (February 1933), 90.

7. Quoted in Douglas Frank, *Less than Conquerors* (Grand Rapids, MI, 1986), 173.

8. Bernard A. Weisberger, *They Gathered at the River* (Chicago, 1966), 231–233, 238.

9. Elijah P. Brown, *The Real Billy Sunday* (New York, 1914), 74–75; Weisberger, 245.

10. Sermon, New York campaign, Sunday Papers, Reel 12.

11. Clipping, National Baseball Hall of Fame, Cooperstown, New York.

12. Brown, 75–76; clipping, Sunday Papers, Reel 1.

13. B.S., "The Sawdust Trail," (February 1933), 90.

14. William G. McLoughlin, *Revivals, Awakenings, and Reform* (Chicago, 1978),

45–58; Jerald C. Brauer, *Prostestantism in America* (Philadelphia, 1965), 47–62; Jeffrey Hadden and Anson Shupe, *Televangelism: Power and Politics on God's Frontier* (New York, 1988), 96–100; George Marsden, *Fundamentalism and American Culture* (New York, 1982), 86–87.

15. Weisberger, 55–56.

16. Brauer, 53; Mark A. Noll, ed., *Religion and American Politics: From the Colonial Period to the 1980's* (New York, 1990), 110.

17. Brauer, 108–112; Noll, 99–101.

18. Quoted in Weisberger, 72; Lyman Beecher fathered another famous theological figure, Henry Ward Beecher, called by many his generation's most accomplished preacher.

19. McLoughlin, *Revivals*, 113–114.

20. Weisberger, 101–102.

21. Brauer, 121.

22. Marsden, 86–87; ibid., 150; Frank, 25.

23. McLoughlin, *Revivals*, 127–128.

24. Brauer, 203; Marsden, 32.

25. Joseph Collins, "Revivals Past and Present," *Harper's Monthly Magazine* (November 1917), 858.

26. Martin E. Marty, *Modern American Religion* (Chicago, 1966), 209–210; Razelle Frankl, *Televangelism: The Marketing of Popular Religion* (Carbondale, IL, 1987), 43–50; Timothy P. Weber, *Living in the Shadow of the Second Coming* (Chicago, 1987), 52–53; McLoughlin, *Revivals*, 140–145; Brauer, 201–205; Frank, 169–170; Hadden and Shupe, 98–99; for a detailed examination of different views of the millennium see Robert G. Clouse, *The Meaning of the Millennium: Four Views* (Downers Grove, IL, 1977).

27. B.S., "The Sawdust Trail," (February 1933), 90; McLoughlin, *Billy Sunday Was His Real Name*, 11; Frank, 173; Brown, 79–80; Ellis, 58; *Hancock Signal*, January 15, 1896, copy in Sunday Papers, Reel 1.

28. *Sigourney News*, January 23, 1896.

29. Ibid., January 29, 1896.

30. Ibid., February 6, 1896.

31. B.S., "The Sawdust Trail," (February 1933), 90.

32. Ibid.; quotes from Brown, 84–87.

33. Olivia L. Spenser to B.S., March 28, 1895; Reverend S. T. Davis to B.S., March 7, 1901, Sunday Papers, Reel 1.

34. "Billy Sunday Campaign Souvenir," Spokane, Sunday Papers, Reel 9.

CHAPTER 4: The Man, the Method, the Team

1. Lindsey Denison, "The Rev. Billy Sunday and His War on the Devil," *American Magazine* (September 1907); William G. McLoughlin, *Billy Sunday Was His Real Name* (Chicago, 1955), 47–48.

2. Lyle W. Dorsett, *Billy Sunday and the Redemption of Urban America* (Grand Rapids, MI, 1991), 83–88.

3. Clipping, Marshalltown, Sunday Papers, Reel 21.

4. *Philadelphia Ledger*, March 8, 1915; quote in McLoughlin, 159; *Boston Globe*, November 10, 1935; Vincent Gaddis and Jasper Huffman, *The Story of Winona Lake* (Winona Lake, IN, 1960), 72.

5. Clipping, "My Impressions of Billy Sunday," Mrs. J. S. Edwards Scrapbook, Archives Collection, Atlanta Historical Society; *Detroit News*, September 17, 1916.

6. *Wichita Beacon*, December 1, 1911; clipping, Atlanta, Sunday Papers, Reel 21; Theodore T. Frankenberg, *Billy Sunday: His Tabernacles and Sawdust Trails* (Columbus, 1917), 128.

7. Clipping, Atlanta, Sunday Papers, Reel 26; Gaddis and Huffman, 25–31.

8. *Wichita Beacon*, December 5, 1911.

9. Helen Sunday to Nell Sunday, 1911, Sunday Papers, Reel 7.

10. *Wichita Beacon*, December 8, 1911.

11. Joseph Collins, "Revivals Past and Present," *Harper's Monthly Magazine* (November 1917), 863–864; Marshall Frady, *Billy Graham: A Parable of American Righteousness* (Boston, 1979), 234.

12. Denison, 399.

13. *Boston Globe*, November 10, 1935; Robert Gambone, *Art and Popular Religion in Evangelical America, 1915–1940* (Knoxville, 1989), 41–42.

14. *New York Times*, May 24, 1915.

15. "Billy Sunday in the Big Cities," *Literary Digest* (April 4, 1914), 761–762.

16. Ned B. Stonehouse, *J. Gresham Machen: A Biographical Memoir* (Grand Rapids, MI, 1954), 222–224; George Seldes, *Witness to a Century* (New York, 1987), 31–33; *Philadelphia Ledger*, March 15 and 22, 1915.

17. William L. Coleman, "Billy Sunday: A Style Meant for His Time and Place," *Christianity Today* (December 17, 1976), 14–17; clipping, New York, Sunday Papers, Reel 24; *Des Moines Register*, April 5, 1914.

18. Homer Rodeheaver, *Twenty Years with Billy Sunday* (Nashville, 1936), 107; *Wichita Beacon*, December 2, 1911.

19. McLoughlin, 19.

20. "Billy Sunday Campaign Souvenir," Spokane, Sunday Papers, Reel 9; McLoughlin, 67–68, 80–88; Rodeheaver, 119–120.

21. Mary Berenbaum, "The Greatest Show that Ever Came to Town," *Niagara Frontier* (Autumn 1975), 54–55.

22. *Detroit News*, September 11, 1916.

23. Clipping, Atlanta, Sunday Papers, Reel 26.

24. Clipping, Detroit, Sunday Papers, Reel 29.

25. Clipping, Atlanta, Sunday Papers, Reel 26.

26. Clipping, Marshalltown, Sunday Papers, Reel 21.

27. Clipping, National Baseball Hall of Fame, Cooperstown, New York; clipping, Pittsburgh, Sunday Papers, Reel 21; McLoughlin, 82–83; Rodeheaver, 75–81; Gambone, 48.

28. John Reed, "Back of Billy Sunday," *Metropolitan Magazine* (May 1915), 9–12, 66.

29. *Wichita Beacon*, November 27, 1911, and December 7, 1911.

30. Ibid., December 7, 1911.

31. *New York Times*, April 17, 1915.

32. Clipping, National Baseball Hall of Fame.

33. Clipping, Marshalltown, Sunday Papers, Reel 21.

34. Clipping, Pittsburgh, Sunday Papers, Reel 21.

35. *Wichita Beacon*, December 22, 1911.

36. "Billy Sunday," *New Republic* (March 20, 1915), 173–174; Rodeheaver, 35.

37. Thomas P. Riggio, ed., *Dreiser-Mencken Letters: The Correspondence of Theodore Dreiser and H. L. Mencken, 1907–1945* (Philadelphia, 1986), Vol. 1, 225; *Philadelphia Ledger*, March 12, 1915; "Making Religion Yellow," *The Nation* (June 11, 1908), 527–528.

38. *Springfield Journal*, February 27, 1909; McLoughlin, 64.

39. William Jennings Bryan to Billy Sunday, January 12, 1914, Bryan Papers, General Correspondence, Library of Congress.

40. *Washington Evening Star*, January 19, 1915.

41. *New York Times*, March 10, 1915.

42. "The Greatest Man in the United States," *American Magazine* (October 1914), 63–64.

43. Joseph Odell, "The Mechanics of Revivalism," *Atlantic Monthly* (May 1915), 591.

CHAPTER 5: Furies of Change

1. *Victorious Service Songs: Rodeheaver's Combination Song Book for All Services* (Chicago, 1925), 90.

2. William G. McLoughlin, *Revivals, Awakenings, and Reform* (Chicago, 1978), 150–156; George Marsden, *Fundamentalism and American Culture* (New York, 1982), 19–24, 107–108, 122; Bernard A. Weisberger, *They Gathered at the River* (Chicago, 1966), 166–167.

3. William Woodring to Washington Gladden, December 8, 1914, Gladden Papers, Ohio Historical Society.

4. Marsden, 33.

5. Martin Marty, *Pilgrims in Their Own Land* (New York, 1984), 316.

6. Marsden, 134.

7. *Victorious Service Songs*, 147.

8. Sermon, Sunday Papers, Reel 15; "Making Religion Yellow," *The Nation* (June 11, 1908), 527; *Wichita Beacon*, December 8 and December 14, 1911; scrapbook, 1916–1921, Sunday ephemera collection, Archives of the Billy Graham Center, Wheaton College.

9. Sermon, Sunday Papers, Reel 15; Charles Aked to Washington Gladden, September 11, 1915, and George Merrill to Gladden, August 27, 1913, Gladden Papers, Ohio Historical Society, Reel 11.

10. Martin Marty, *Modern American Religion*, Vol. 1: *The Irony of It All, 1893–1919* (Chicago, 1986), 17–22.

11. Sermon, Marshalltown, Sunday Papers, Reel 21; sermon, New York, Sunday Papers, Reel 10.

12. Marty, *Modern American Religion*, 38–41.

13. Charles Chauncey, *Seasonable Thoughts on the State of Religion in New England* (Boston, 1743), 249.

14. Marty, *Modern American Religion*, 216; Richard Hofstadter, *Anti-Intellectualism in American Life* (New York, 1963), 133.

15. Clipping, Buffalo, Sunday Papers, Reel 24.

16. Sermon, New York, Sunday Papers, Reel 11; *Wichita Beacon*, November 22, 1911.

17. Clipping, Detroit, Sunday Papers, Reel 29; sermon, Marshalltown, Sunday Papers, Reel 21.

18. Karen Gullen, *Billy Sunday Speaks* (New York, 1970), 12–13.

19. Ibid.,, 18–19; sermon, Marshalltown, Sunday Papers, Reel 21; clipping, Pittsburgh, Sunday Papers, Reel 21.

20. Washington Gladden, "Samples of Modern Evangelism," *Independent* (May 23, 1912), 1102.

21. Walter Rauschenbusch, *Christianity and the Social Crisis* (New York, 1907), 287.

22. Quote in Marty, *Modern American Religion*, 288.

23. Gary Arnold, ed., *The Washington Gladden Collection: An Inventory to the Microfilm Edition* (Columbus, 1972); this guide is an excellent finding aid to the Gladden writings, correspondence, and sermons, a collection representing one of the best sources for material on the Social Gospel movement.

24. Marty, *Modern American Religion*, 294–295; Marty, *Pilgrims*, 350–354; Marsden, 91–92.

25. Hofstadter, 121; Marsden, 91–92; Marty, *Pilgrims*, 352; William G. McLoughlin, *Billy Sunday Was His Real Name* (Chicago, 1955), 138; *New York Times*, May 2, 1917; George Parkinson to Washington Gladden, February 17, 1914, Gladden Papers, Ohio Historical Society, Reel 10.

26. Sermon, New York, Sunday Papers, Reel 9.

27. Billy Sunday, "The Second Coming of Christ," in *Winona Echoes: A Book of Sermons and Addresses Delivered at the Nineteenth Annual Bible Conference* (Winona Lake, IN, 1913).

28. Sermon notes, Sunday Papers, Reel 27.

CHAPTER 6: Up with the Dukes, Devil!

1. *Victorious Service Songs: Rodeheaver's Combination Song Book for All Services* (Chicago, 1925), 126.

2. See Richard McBrien, *Caesar's Coin: Religion and Politics in America* (New York, 1987), 106–107; "Social Conflict in an Urban Industrial Society," in Richard Leopold, Arthur Link, and Stanley Coben, eds., *Problems in American History* (Englewood Cliffs, NJ), 65.

3. Quoted in William G. McLoughlin, *Billy Sunday Was His Real Name* (Chicago, 1955), 131.

4. "Billy Sunday Campaign Souvenir," Spokane, Sunday Papers, Reel 9.

5. Dale Soden, "Billy Sunday in Spokane," *Pacific Northwest Quarterly* (January 1988), 13; clipping, Philadelphia, Sunday Papers, Reel 23; Richard Hofstadter, *Anti-Intellectualism in American Life* (New York, 1963), 119; clipping, scrapbook, 1916–1921, Archives of the Billy Graham Center, Wheaton College.

6. *Toledo News-Bee*, April 17, 1911; on Sunday's role as evangelical hero see Douglas Frank, *Less than Conquerors* (Grand Rapids, MI, 1986), 244–266.

7. Sermon, Marshalltown, Sunday Papers, Reel 21; quote in *Newark Evening News*, April 14, 1915.

8. *Des Moines Register*, April 5, 1914; quote in Charles Hesselgrove, "Billy Sunday," *Independent* (February 1915), 161.

9. Elijah P. Brown, *The Real Billy Sunday* (New York, 1914), 133; Frank, 185; *Wichita Beacon*, November 13, 1911.

10. Ray Rensi, "The Gospel According to Sam Jones," *Georgia Historical Quarterly* (Fall 1976), 251–257.

11. Irwin Cobb, "Sunday as Cobb Saw Him," *Literary Digest* (June 16, 1917), 1873; *Wichita Beacon*, December 9, 1911.

12. Clipping, Sunday Papers, Reel 17; sermon, Marshalltown, Sunday Papers, Reel 21; "Princeton's Thrust at Billy Sunday," *Literary Digest* (April 24, 1915), 960; sermon, New York, Sunday Papers, Reel 11.

13. Karen Gullen, *Billy Sunday Speaks* (New York, 1970), 93; *Kansas City Times*, May 15, 1916.

14. *Toledo News-Bee*, April 17, 1911; sermon, Marshalltown, Sunday Papers, Reel 21; *Detroit News*, March 4 and March 5, 1917.

15. Clipping, Atlanta, Sunday Papers, Reel 26; *Toledo News-Bee*, April 17, 1911; McLoughlin, 132–133; clipping, Marshalltown, Sunday Papers, Reel 21.

16. Scrapbook, Sunday ephermera collection, Archives of the Billy Graham Center, Wheaton College; sermon, Marshalltown, Sunday Papers, Reel 21.

17. Gullen, 92; *Wichita Beacon*, December 4, 1911.

18. William T. Ellis, *"Billy" Sunday: The Man and His Message* (Philadelphia, 1914), 215–216; sermon, New York, Sunday Papers, Reel 11; Gullen, 110.

19. Denison, 397.

20. Rupert Hughes, *George Washington: The Human Being and the Hero, 1732–1762* (New York, 1926), 26–29.

21. Soden, 14–17.

22. Joseph Odell, "A Revivalist Judged by Results," *Outlook* (April 11, 1914), 804.

23. *Des Moines Register*, April 5, 1914.

24. Frederick Davenport, "The National Value of Billy Sunday," *Outlook* (June 9, 1915), 312; quote in William G. McLoughlin, *Revivals, Awakenings, and Reform* (Chicago, 1978), 147; *Detroit Journal*, March 3, 1917.

25. Hesselgrove, 161.

26. "The Problem of Billy Sunday," *Literary Digest* (June 14, 1913), 1336.

27. Edmund Merrian, "Sunday, the Modern Juvenal," *Watchman Examiner* (April 12, 1917), 450.

28. John Reed, "Back of Billy Sunday," *Metropolitan Magazine* (May 1915), 10.

29. Soden, 10–11.

30. "Princeton's Thrust at Billy Sunday," 959–960.

31. A. P. Watts to Washington Gladden, October 7, 1917, Gladden Papers, Ohio Historical Society, Reel 12.

32. "Poll of the Religious Press on Billy Sunday," *Literary Digest* (June 12, 1915), 1404–1405.

33. Alfred Isaac to Washington Gladden, March 23, 1911, and R. W. Atcheson to Gladden, March 4, 1912, Gladden Papers, Ohio Historical Society.

34. "Evangelism as a Means to Reform: Some Results of Sunday's Campaigns in Columbus and Erie," *Missionary Review of the World* (June 1913), 437.

35. Gullen, 34–35.

36. Sermon, New York, Sunday Papers, Reel 11.

CHAPTER 7: Away, John Barleycorn!

1. Herbert Asbury, *The Great Illusion: An Informal History of Prohibition* (New York, 1950), 105; Henry Lee, *How Dry We Were: Prohibition Revisited* (Englewood Cliffs, NJ, 1963), 14–15.

2. John Kobler, *Ardent Spirits: The Rise and Fall of Prohibition* (New York, 1973), 16–18.

3. Kobler, 20; Asbury, 10–12; Norman H. Clark, *Deliver Us from Evil: An Interpretation of American Prohibition* (New York, 1976), 7–9; David Kyvig, *Prohibition: The 18th Amendment; The Volstead Act; The 21st Amendment*, milestones documents in the National Archives series (Washington, D.C., 1986), 2; K. Austin Kerr, *Organized for Prohibition: A New History of the Anti-Saloon League* (New Haven, CT, 1985), 16.

4. The pamphlet was published in Trenton, New Jersey. See copy on microcard in the Early American Imprint Project of the Readex Microprint Corporation and the American Antiquarian Society. Clifford K. Shipton and James C. Mooney's *National Index of American Imprints through 1800, the Short Title Evans* (Worcester, MA, 1969), 2 vols., acts as a bibliographic tool for this material.

5. Kobler, 32–37; Asbury, 26–29; Stewart H. Holbrook, *Dreamers of the American Dream* (New York, 1957), 61–62.

6. Quoted in Asbury, 32; Randall Jimerson, Francis Blouin, and Charles Isetts, eds., *Guide to the Microfilm Edition of Temperance and Prohibition Papers* (Ann Arbor, MI, 1977), 2. Any study of the rise and fall of prohibition must include the examination of the papers of numerous temperance organizations, of leaders such as Ernest Cherrington and Francis Scott McBride, and various temperance newspapers such as *American Issue*. The Ohio Historical Society, the Michigan Historical Collections, and the Woman's Christian Temperance Union collaborated to gather and publish in 1977 a massive microfilm collection of these papers. The Jimerson et al. volume is a guide to that edition.

7. Holbrook, 63–64; Asbury, 38–45; Kobler, 32–34; John Allen Krout, *The Origins of Prohibition* (New York, 1925), 127–131.

8. Krout, 176.

9. Kerr, 35; see advertisement in Kyvig, 3.

10. Jimerson et al., 12; Kerr, 82–89; Holbrook, 97; John S. Blocker, *Retreat from Reform: The Prohibition Movement in the United States, 1890–1913* (Westport, CT, 1976), 154–171.

11. Kobler, 118–119; Ray Rensi, "The Gospel According to Sam Jones," *Georgia Historical Quarterly* (Fall 1976).

12. Lawrence Levine, *Defender of the Faith: William Jennings Bryan: The Last Decade, 1915–1925* (New York, 1965), 108.

13. See Edward Berkowitz, "Public History, Academic History, and Policy Analysis: A Case Study with Commentary," *Public Historian* (Fall 1988), 48.

14. William G. McLoughlin, *Billy Sunday Was His Real Name* (Chicago, 1955), 232; McLoughlin, *Revivals, Awakenings, and Reform* (Chicago, 1978), 149.

15. Quoted in Douglas Frank, *Less than Conquerors* (Grand Rapids, MI, 1986), 260.

16. Sunday Papers, Reel 12; Karen Gullen, *Billy Sunday Speaks* (New York, 1970), 51–77.

17. *American Issue*, Ohio edition, December 27, 1913.

18. *American Issue*, August 1910.

19. Ibid., March 1911.

20. Billy Sunday (B.S.) to Nell Sunday, 1908, Sunday Papers, Reel 7; *American Issue*, Ohio edition, January 4, January 25, March 1, and July 19, 1913; "Billy Sunday's Greatest Campaign," *Literary Digest* (March 15, 1913), 576–577.

21. "Billy Sunday Campaign Souvenir," Spokane, 1908–1909, Sunday Papers, Reel 9; *American Issue*, Ohio edition, December 30, 1913; Joseph Odell, "A Revivalist Judged by Results," *Outlook* (April 11, 1914), 804.

22. *American Issue*, October 1913.

23. J. S. Caster to B.S., December 20, 1905; F. M. Vagan to B.S., February 10, 1912; J. M. Murdock to B.S., February 25, 1914; Frank Taylor to B.S., March 6, 1915; "An Admirer," to B.S., April 9, 1917; poem entitled "Billy Sunday's Water Wagon," Sunday Papers, Reel 1; Bruce Barton, "Billy Sunday—Baseball Evangelist," *Colliers* (July 26, 1913), 8.

24. Bernard A. Weisberger, *They Gathered at the River* (Chicago, 1966), 261–262.

25. Quoted in Ferdinand Iglehart, *King Alcohol Dethroned* (Westerville, OH, 1917), 300; Blocker, 227–229.

26. Kerr, 1–3; *American Issue*, January 1915; Lee, 38–39.

27. *Philadelphia Ledger*, March 1, 1915; William T. Ellis, *"Billy" Sunday: The Man and His Message* (Philadelphia, 1914), 84–85; Frank, 263; *Victorious Service Songs: Rodeheaver's Combination Song Book for All Services* (Chicago, 1925), 147; John Reed, "Back of Billy Sunday," *Metropolitan Magazine* (May 1915), 12.

28. *Philadelphia Ledger*, March 7 and March 8, 1915.

29. Ibid., March 16, 1915: *Philadelphia Inquirer*, March 16, 1915; *New York Times*, March 16, 1915.

30. *Philadelphia Ledger*, March 16, 1915.

31. *American Issue*, October 30, 1915, May 6 and September 2, 1916.

32. Larry Engelmann, *Intemperance: The Lost War against Liquor* (New York, 1979), 21–22; *Detroit News*, September 9, 1916; *Detroit Journal*, September 9 and October 16, 1916.

33. Larry Engelmann, "Billy Sunday: 'God You've Got a Job on Your Hands in Detroit,' " *Michigan History* (Spring 1971), 9–10; *Detroit News*, September 9, September 10 and September 11, 1916.

34. *Detroit News*, September 11, 1916; songbook, Sunday ephemera collection, Archives of the Billy Graham Center, Wheaton College.

35. *Detroit News*, September 17, 1916.

36. Engelmann, "Billy Sunday," 14–16.

37. *Detroit News*, September 24, 1916; clipping, October 8, 1917, Sunday Papers, Reel 25.

38. *Detroit News*, October 16, 1916.

39. *American Issue*, October 21, 1916; Engelmann, "Billy Sunday," 18.

40. *Detroit News*, October 5 and October 31, 1916; Engelmann, "Billy Sunday," 17.

41. *Detroit News*, November 6, 1916; clippings, Sunday Papers, Reel 29; Homer Rodeheaver, *Twenty Years with Billy Sunday* (Nashville, 1936), 51.

42. Engelmann, "Billy Sunday," 20–21; *American Issue*, November 8, 1916, and February 10, 1917.

43. Frank, 237–238; Ellis, 83.

44. Ellis, 352.

45. George Mills, *Rogues and Heroes from Iowa's Amazing Past* (Ames, 1972), 122.

46. Clipping, Marshalltown, 1909, Sunday Papers, Reel 21; clipping, New York, May 2, 1917, Sunday Papers, Reel 25.

47. "Billy Sunday's New York Campaign," *Literary Digest* (June 30, 1917), 1998; William L. Coleman, "Billy Sunday: A Style Meant for His Time and Place," *Christianity Today* (December 17, 1976), 16.

48. Sermon, New York, 1917, Sunday Papers, Reel 10.

CHAPTER 8: Red Emma Et Al.

1. See Emma Goldman, *Living My Life* (New York, 1977); Candace Falk, *Love, Anarchy, and Emma Goldman* (New York, 1984); Richard Drinnon, *Rebel in Paradise* (New York 1976); Paul Avrich, *Anarchist Portraits* (Princeton, 1989).

2. *Mother Earth*, Vol. 12 (July 1917), 129.

3. Eugene Debs to W. S. Valkenbourgh, January 15, 1926, Tamiment Library, New York University.

4. *Mother Earth*, Vol. 10 (May 1915), 100–101; Drinnon, 99; Leslie Fishbein, *Rebels in Bohemia* (Chapel Hill, 1982), 119.

5. Joyce Kornbluh, *Rebel Voices: An I.W.W. Anthology* (Ann Arbor, MI, 1972), 197–226.

6. E. Dawe to Billy Sunday, August 23, 1930, Sunday Papers, Reel 2; *New York Times*, April 17, 1915.

7. *New York Times*, April 18, 1915.

8. Ibid., April 21, 1915; *Newark Evening News*, April 21, 1915; *Mother Earth*, Vol. 10 (May 1915), 97–98.

9. *New York Times*, April 21, 1915.

10. *Newark Evening News*, April 21, 1915.

11. Goldman, 554–555.

12. *New York Times*, May 24, 1915.

13. Richard Hofstadter, *Anti-Intellectualism in American Life* (New York, 1963), 121–122.

14. Sermon notes, Sunday Papers, Reel 27.

15. Sermon notes, Sunday Papers, Reel 15.

16. The poem first appeared under the title "To Billy Sunday," *The Masses,* Vol. 6 (September 1915), 11. Upon its reprinting the title was changed; Richard Crowder, *Carl Sandburg* (Boston, 1964), 47.

17. Harry Golden, Carl Sandburg (New York, 1961), 65; Herbert Mitgang, ed., *The Letters of Carl Sandburg* (New York, 1968), 108–109.

18. Irvin Wylie, "The Socialist Press and the Libel Laws: A Case Study," *Midwest Journal,* Vol. 4 (Summer, 1952), 72–79.

19. Fishbein, 178–179; Charles Erskine Scott Wood, *Heavenly Discourse* (New York, 1927), 62–66.

20. Robert L. Gambone, *Art and Popular Religion in Evangelical America, 1915–1940* (Knoxville, 1989), 42–48.

21. Sermons, Sunday Papers, Reel 15.

22. Fishbein, 117–125.

23. Sermons, Sunday Papers, Reel 9.

24. Undated newspaper clipping, Sunday Papers, Reel 24.

25. Revival Files, New York campaign, Sunday Papers, Reel 10.

26. Ibid.

27. Martin Marty, *Pilgrims in Their Own Land* (New York, 1984), 352–353.

28. Edward Robb Ellis, *Echoes of a Distant Thunder: Life in the United States, 1914–1918* (New York, 1975), 447; Nick Salvatore, *Eugene Debs: Citizen and Socialist* (Urbana, IL, 1978), 288; Record Group 65, Records of the Department of Justice, FBI Reel 647, OG 234939, Tom Clifford to Newton Baker, August 24, 1918, National Archives.

29. Ray H. Abrams, *Preachers Present Arms* (Philadelphia, 1933), 217.

30. Douglas Frank, *Less than Conquerors* (Grand Rapids, MI, 1986), 262.

31. *Victorious Service Songs: Rodeheaver's Combination Song Book for All Seasons* (Chicago, 1925), 198–199.

32. Frank, 213.

33. Sermons, New York campaign, Sunday Papers, Reel 11.

34. David L. Calkins, "Billy Sunday's Cincinnati Crusade," *Cincinnati Historical Society Bulletin,* Vol. 27 (Winter 1969), 295–296.

CHAPTER 9: Of Rubicons and Waterloos:
Billy in New York

1. A large portion of the material used in the chapter is from several New York newspapers—the *American, Globe, Times, Tribune, World,* and *Herald.* Except for specific quotes, I have not provided every citation to the material because most of it is repetitive, the same general information from each day of the campaign appearing in most of the papers. Some of the material is from a collection of clippings in the Sunday Papers, Reels 9, 24, and 25 of the microfilm publication. The hymn "Soldiers of the Cross," verses of which appear several times in the chapter, is from *Victorious Service Songs: Rodeheaver's Combination Song Book for All Services* (Chicago, 1925), 288.

2. Undated clipping, Sunday Papers, Reel 24.

3. Theodore Roosevelt to Billy Sunday, January 14, 1917, Roosevelt Papers, Library of Congress.

4. "The New York William A. Sunday Evangelistic Campaign—April, May, June 1917," revival report, Sunday Papers, Reel 9; William G. McLoughlin, *Billy Sunday Was His Real Name* (Chicago, 1955), xxiii; Francis Hackett, "Billy Sunday, Salesman," *New Republic*, Vol. 10 (April 28, 1917), 371.

5. New York revival report, Sunday Papers, Reel 9; Jean C. Noble, "Billy Sunday's New York City Campaign: 1917," unpublished thesis, Barnard College, 1977, 24–26.

6. Sermons, New York campaign, Sunday Papers, Reel 11.

7. Undated clipping, Sunday Papers, Reel 24.

8. *New York World*, April 8, 1917.

9. *New York American*, April 8, 1917.

10. *New York Herald*, April 19, 1917.

11. Ibid.; Irwin S. Cobb, "Sunday as Cobb Saw Him," *Literary Digest*, Vol. 54 (June 16, 1917), 1870–1874.

12. *New York Herald*, April 19, 1917.

13. Ibid.

14. Ibid.

15. Ibid.

16. Sermons, New York campaign, Sunday Papers, Reel 9.

17. Undated clipping, Sunday Papers, Reel 25.

18. Ibid.

19. *New York American*, April 20, 1917.

20. Sunday Evangelistic Campaign report, Sunday Papers, Reel 9; Noble, 26.

21. *New York World*, April 16, 1917.

22. "Billy Sunday Assailed by Leaders of Three Denominations," *Current Opinion*, Vol. 62 (May 7, 1917), 543; J. B. Warren, "Tabernacle Evangelism," *Presbyterian*, Vol. 87 (September 27, 1917), 10–11; Henry Jones Mulford, "Our Children and 'Billy Sunday,' " *Outlook*, Vol. 115 (April 18, 1917); Joseph Collins, "Revivals Past and Present—Reflections on Some of Their Psychological Aspects," *Harper's*, Vol. 135 (November 1917), 862; *New York Times*, May 2, 1917.

23. Undated clipping, Sunday Papers, Reel 25; "Why Billy Sunday Does Not Appeal to Roman Catholics," *Current Opinion*, Vol. 63 (July 1917), 44–45.

24. *The Masses* (June 1917), 13.

25. Bernard A. Weisberger, *They Gathered at the River* (Chicago, 1966), 258.

26. "Billy Sunday and the War," *Outlook*, Vol. 115 (April 18, 1917), 687.

27. *New York Evening Mail*, April 19, 1917.

28. Sermons, New York campaign, Sunday Papers, Reel 9.

29. Ibid.

30. Clipping, April 27, 1917, Sunday Papers, Reel 25.

31. Clipping, April 21, 1917, Sunday Papers, Reel 25.

32. Ibid.

33. *New York Tribune*, April 26, 1917.

34. *New York Evening Mail*, June 14, 1917.

35. Ibid.

36. Ibid.

37. Clipping, June 18, 1917, Sunday Papers, Reel 25.

38. "Abjuring the Sawdust Trail," *Literary Digest*, Vol. 95 (October 8, 1927), 32.

39. McLoughlin, xxviii–xxix; Noble, 51–56.

40. "Billy Sunday's New York Campaign," *Literary Digest*, Vol. 54 (June 30, 1917), 1998.

41. "Billy in New York," *Time*, Vol. 69 (May 20, 1957), 104.

CHAPTER 10: Joining Hands in Glory:
Billy in Atlanta

1. Quoted in Franklin Garrett, *Atlanta and Environs* (New York, 1954), 710. Unless otherwise indicated, the material for this chapter is from the extensive newspaper coverage of the Atlanta campaign in two major dailies: the *Constitution* and the *Georgian*. Some of the newspaper clippings of the campaign are available in the Sunday Papers, Reel, 26.

2. *Victorious Service Songs: Rodeheaver's Combination Song Book for All Services* (Chicago, 1925), 46.

3. Daniel Okrent and Steve Wulf, *Baseball Anecdotes* (New York, 1989), 21–22.

4. Herbert Aptheker, ed., *The Correspondence of W. E. B. DuBois* (Amherst, MA, 1973), Vol. 1, 462.

5. *Winona Year Book and Programs* (Winona Lake, IN, 1908), 23.

6. William G. McLoughlin, *Billy Sunday Was His Real Name* (Chicago, 1955), 272–273; *Illinois State Register*, March 5, 1909.

7. John Reed, "Back of Billy Sunday," *Metropolitan Magazine* (May 1915), 12.

8. Martin Marty, *Modern American Religion*, Vol. 1: *The Irony of It All, 1893–1919* (Chicago, 1986), 98–106.

9. Sermon, New York campaign, Sunday Papers, Reel 9.

10. Garrett, 711.

11. W. J. Cash, *The Mind of the South* (New York, 1941), 298.

12. W. E. B. DuBois, "A Litany of Atlanta," *Independent* (October 11, 1906), 856–858; Louis Harlan and Raymond Smock, eds., *The Booker T. Washington Papers* (Urbana, IL, 1980), Vol. 1, 74–85.

13. August Meier, *Negro Thought in America, 1880–1915* (Ann Arbor, MI, 1969), 91, 161–164; Penelope Bullock, "Profile of a Periodical: The 'Voice of the Negro,'" *Atlanta Historical Bulletin* (Spring 1977), 95–113; Webb Garrison, *The Legacy of Atlanta* (Atlanta, 1987), 60–64.

14. "Billy Sunday as a Peace Maker between the Races," *Current Opinion* (March 1918), 201.

15. Mrs. J. S. Edwards Scrapbook, clipping, Atlanta Historical Society.

16. Clipping, 1935, "Billy Sunday Biographical File," Martin Luther King, Jr., Public Library, Washington, DC.

17. Colored Evangelical Ministers Union resolution, December 1917, Sunday Papers, Reel 1.

18. Mrs. J. S. Edwards Scrapbook, clipping.

19. "Billy Sunday as a Peace Maker," 201.

20. Lula R. Rhodes testimonial on Atlanta campaign, 1917, Sunday Papers, Reel 1.

21. McLoughlin, 273–274.

CHAPTER 11: God's Grenadier

1. *Victorious Service Songs: Rodeheaver's Combination Song Book for All Services* (Chicago, 1925), 246.

2. *Atlanta Georgian*, October 17, 1917.

3. William G. McLoughlin, *Billy Sunday Was His Real Name* (Chicago, 1955), 255–257.

4. *Ibid.;* 131; George Marsden, *Fundamentalism and American Culture* (New York, 1982), 142.

5. Ray H. Abrams, *Preachers Present Arms* (Philadelphia, 1933), 71–75.

6. Sermons, Sunday Papers, Reel 15; undated clipping, Atlanta campaign, Sunday Papers, Reel 26; *Atlanta Georgian*, November 26, 1917; undated clipping, Los Angeles campaign, Sunday Papers, Reel 25; Edward Robb Ellis, *Echoes of a Distant Thunder: Life in the United States, 1914–1918* (New York, 1975), 423; *Victorious Service Songs*, 244.

7. John Coben to Woodrow Wilson, November 23, 1917, Papers of Woodrow Wilson, Case #4453, Microfilm Reel 367, Library of Congress.

8. Clipping, Papers of William L. Daley, Library of Congress.

9. Sermons, Sunday Papers, Reel 15.

10. Sermon notes, Sunday Papers, Reel 28.

11. McLoughlin, 257.

12. Ellis, 423–424.

13. *Washington Post*, January 19, 1918.

14. Clipping, Atlanta campaign, Sunday Papers, Reel 26.

15. *Atlanta Georgian*, December 21, 1917; *New York Times*, December 21, 1917.

16. Frank Redensleben to Attorney General, December 19, 1917; Director, Division of News, to Redensleben, January 11, 1918, Record Group 60, Records of the Department of Justice, Mail and File Division, #189296, National Archives.

17. *Washington Herald*, January 11, 1918.

18. *Washington Post*, January 10, 1918.

19. *Congressional Record*, 65th Congress, 2nd Session (Washington, D.C., 1917), LVI, 761.

20. *Washington Post*, January 11, 1918; Billy Sunday (B.S.), "The Sawdust Trail," *Ladies' Home Journal* (February 1933), 92; *Washington Times*, January 11, 1918; *Washington Herald*, January 11, 1918.

21. *Washington Post*, January 9 and February 9, 1918; David Morgan, "The Revivalist as Patriot: Billy Sunday and World War I," *Journal of Presbyterian History*, Vol. 51 (Summer 1973), 206–212.

22. Edward N. Hurley to B.S., February 14, 1918; B.S. to Hurley, February 16, 1918, Record Group 32, Records of the U.S. Shipping Board, Subject-Classified General Files, 1917–1920, National Archives.

23. *Washington Times*, February 25, 1918.

24. Ibid., February 18, 1918.

25. Morgan, 213; *Washington Post*, February 18, 1918.

26. B.S., "The Sawdust Trail" (February 1933), 92.

27. B.S. to Woodrow Wilson, June 29, 1918, Wilson Papers, Reel 366, Case #4362, Library of Congress.

28. *Washington Times*, March 4, 1918.

29. *Washington Post*, March 4, 1918; *Washington Herald*, March 4, 1918; *Washington Times*, March 4, 1918.

30. *Washington Post*, March 5, 1918; *Washington Herald*, March 5, 1918; *Washington Times*, March 5, 1918.

31. *Washington Herald*, March 4, 1918; Theodore Roosevelt to B.S., January 14, 1917, Roosevelt Papers, Library of Congress.

32. Ellis, 383.

33. *Washington Post*, March 4, 1918.

CHAPTER 12: Fundamentalists, Take Arms!

1. Archie Robertson, *That Old-Time Religion* (Boston, 1950), 78.

2. See especially George E. Mowry, ed., *The Twenties: Fords, Flappers, and Fanatics* (Englewood Cliffs, NJ, 1963); Richard Shenkman and Kurt Reiger, *One Night Stands with American History* (New York, 1982), 213; Robert T. Handy, *The American Religious Depression* (Philadelphia, 1968), 8–12.

3. David Calkins, "Billy Sunday's Cincinnati Crusade," *Cincinnati Historical Society Bulletin* (Winter 1969), 293–303; Billy Sunday (B.S.) to Nell Sunday (N.S.), March 26, 1922, Sunday Papers, Reel 7.

4. William G. McLoughlin, *Billy Sunday Was His Real Name* (Chicago, 1955), 261–264.

5. *New York Times*, January 4, 1920; E. Digby Baltzell, *The Protestant Establishment* (New York, 1966), 266; Calkins, 298.

6. *New York Times*, January 17, 1920; *Virginian-Pilot and Norfolk Landmark*, January 17, 1920.

7. Colonel John Baker White to B.S., 1922, Sunday Papers, Reel 2.

8. *New York Times*, March 5, 1922.

9. Ibid., April 18, 1921.

10. Ibid., March 12, July 17, July 21, July 22, and July 23, 1920.

11. See especially George Marsden, *Fundamentalism and American Culture* (New York, 1982); *New York Times*, December 16, 1923; Willard Gatewood, ed., *Controversy in the Twenties: Fundamentalism, Modernism, and Evolution* (Nashville, 1969), 22–26, 116; Martin Marty, *Pilgrims in Their Own Land* (New York, 1984), 373–382; Sean Wilentz, "The Trials of Televangelism," *Dissent* (Winter 1990), 44; Leo P. Ribuffo, *The Old Christian Right* (Philadelphia, 1983), 85.

12. Ernest Sandeen, "Towards a Historical Interpretation of the Origins of Fundamentalism," *Church History* (March 1967), 77–79; Jeffrey Hadden and Anson Shupe, *Televangelism: Power and Politics on God's Frontier* (New York, 1988), 107–108.

13. Sandeen, 75.

14. Sandeen, *The Roots of Fundamentalism: British and American Millenarianism, 1800–1930* (Chicago, 1970), 238–247; W. B. Riley, "The Faith of the Fundamentalists," *Current History* (June 1927), 435.

15. Norman F. Furniss, *Fundamentalist Controversy, 1918–1931* (Hamden, CT, 1963), 66–71; Ribuffo, 80–87; Riley, 436.

16. Erling Jorstad, *The Politics of Doomsday: Fundamentalists of the Far Right* (Nashville, 1970), 26.

17. Marsden, 169–170; Harbor Allen, "The Anti-Evolution Campaign in America," *Current History* (September 1926), 896.

18. Maynard Shipley, *The War on Modern Science* (New York, 1927), 251–255; Charles Russell, *Voices of American Fundamentalism* (Philadelphia, 1976), 180–181; *New York Times*, March 5, 1922.

19. William Leuchtenburg, *The Perils of Prosperity* (Chicago, 1983), 219.

20. Jorstad, 24–25; Marsden, 221.

21. B.S. to N.S., 1918 and 1921, Sunday Papers, Reel 7; *New York Times*, November 19 and November 20, 1923; *Los Angeles Times*, November 19, 1923; clipping, 1933; Chicago Historical Society; Helen Sunday to NS, February 14, 1918, Sunday Papers, Reel 7; B.S. to N.S., September 22, 1921, and March 2, 1925, Sunday Papers, Reel 7.

22. B.S. to N.S., 1921, Sunday Papers, Reel 7.

23. For an account of the Scopes trial see especially Ray Ginger, *Six Days or Forever? Tennessee v. John Thomas Scopes* (Chicago, 1969); Russell, 184–185; William Jennings Bryan to B.S., June 23, 1925, Sunday Papers, Reel 2; *Louisville-Courier Journal*, July 3, 1925; *Chattanooga Daily Times*, July 6, 1925; *New York Times*, July 4, 1925; Gatewood, 342–343; Richard Hofstadter, *Anti-Intellectualism in American Life* (New York, 1963), 126–127, 132; Lawrence Levine, *Defender of the Faith: William Jennings Bryan: The Last Decade, 1915–1925* (New York, 1965), 339; *Chattanooga News*, July 11, 1925; Loren Baritz, *The Culture of the Twenties* (Indianapolis, 1970); Hadden and Shupe, 109; Garry Wills, *Under God: Religion and American Politics* (New York, 1990), 108–114.

24. B.S., "Back to the Old-Time Religion," and A. Wakefield Slaten, "The Old-Time Religion Is Dying," *Collier's* (July 10, 1926), 8 and 34.

25. *Time Capsule / 1927* (New York, 1968), 193.

26. *New York Times*, November 25, 1929, and April 23, 1930; *San Francisco Examiner*, November 25, 1929; *Los Angeles Times*, April 22 and November 26, 1929.

27. Clipping, 1933, Chicago Historical Society; *New York Times*, March 27, 1930.

28. B.S. to N.S., 1927, Sunday Papers, Reel 2; B.S. to N.S., 1929, Sunday Papers, Reel 7.

29. Homer Rodeheaver to B.S., October 20, 1929, Sunday Papers, Reel 2.

30. *New York Times*, November 7, 1930.

CHAPTER 13: Amen!

1. Clipping, Martin Luther King Public Library, Washington, D.C., biographical file.

2. Clipping, Sunday Papers, Reel 27.

3. Certificate, December 20, 1932, Sunday Papers, Reel 2.

4. *New York World Telegram*, November 7, 1935.

5. *New York Times*, March 24, 1930.

6. *Chicago Tribune*, December 26, 1982.

7. David Kyvig, *Prohibition: The 18th Amendment; The Volstead Act; the 21st Amendment*, milestones documents in the National Archives series (Washington, D.C., 1986), 5–7; Larry Engelmann, *Intemperance: The Lost War against Liquor* (New York, 1979), 214.

8. Leo P. Ribuffo, *The Old Christian Right* (Philadelphia, 1983), 3; William G. McLoughlin, *Billy Sunday Was His Real Name* (Chicago, 1955), 288.

9. *Minnesota Tribune*, November 7, 1935; *Detroit Free Press*, October 13, 1932.

10. Helen A. (Nell) Sunday, *"Ma" Sunday Still Speaks: Transcription of Tape Recording Made in 1954* (Winona Lake, IN, 1957), 28–33; McLoughlin, 291–292.

11. Billy Sunday, Jr., to Nell Sunday (N.S.), February 27, 1933, and May 17, 1935, Sunday Papers, Reel 8.

12. *Kansas City Star*, February 26, 1933.

13. *San Francisco Examiner*, September 12 and September 13, 1933; *New York Times*, September 8 and September 12, 1933; clipping, Chicago Historical Society; quote in Lyle W. Dorsett, *Billy Sunday and the Redemption of Urban America* (Grand Rapids, MI, 1991), 132.

14. Mauryne Sunday to N.S., 1934; Sunday Papers, Reel 8; *Minnesota Tribune*, November 7, 1935.

15. "Billy Sunday's War on the Devil in New York," *Literary Digest* (January 27, 1934), 21.

16. Charles Stelzle, "The Evangelist in Present Day America," *Current History* (November 1931), 228; *San Francisco Examiner*, September 11, 1933.

17. Ben Armstrong, *The Electric Church* (Nashville, 1979), 19–43.

18. *New York Times*, October 28, 1934.

19. Robert Wood to Billy Sunday (B.S.), May 26, 1933, and Homer Rodeheaver to B.S., December 7, 1931, Sunday Papers, Reel 2.

20. Jeffrey Hadden and Anson Shupe, *Televangelism: Power and Politics on God's Frontier* (New York, 1988), 46.

21. See numerous sermon notes in Sunday Papers, Reels 27 and 28.

22. Helen (Nell) Sunday, 33–38.

23. McLoughlin, 293.

24. "Ma Sunday at 82," *Newsweek* (November 27, 1950), 72.

25. Marshall Frady, *Billy Graham: A Parable of American Righteousness* (Boston, 1979), 51, 78.

26. Jerry Falwell, *Strength for the Journey: An Autobiography* (New York, 1987), 76–77.

27. Certificate, May 29, 1935, Sunday Papers, Reel 2.

28. Mark Haines to N.S., November 8, 1952, Sunday Papers, Reel 8.

29. Dorsett, 152.

30. Karen Gullen, *Billy Sunday Speaks* (New York, 1970), 1–4.

31. See especially two major biographies of Graham: Frady's *Billy Graham* and William McLoughlin's *Billy Graham: Revivalist in a Secular Age* (New York, 1960).

32. Razelle Frankl, *Televangelism* (Carbondale, IL, 1987), 73–74.

33. Sean Wilentz, "The Trials of Televangelism," *Dissent* (Winter 1990),42–48.

34. *Washington Post*, September 1, 1990; Garry Wills, *Under God: Religion and American Politics* (New York, 1990), 16–17.

35. George Gallup, Jr., and Jim Castelli, *The People's Religion: American Faith in the 90's* (New York, 1989), 4, 33, 45, 93; Billie Beaton Rinsmer to B.S., 1934, Sunday Papers, Reel 2.

36. W. F. Vaughn to B.S., June 5, 1935, Sunday Papers, Reel 2.

37. Fern Johnson to B.S., March 13, 1933, Sunday Papers, Reel 2.

Selected Bibliography

Any study of the life and career of Billy Sunday must begin with the large collection of personal papers of the evangelist and his wife. In 1977, twenty years after Mrs. Sunday's death, the collection was placed in the Library of Grace Theological Seminary. Through the cooperative efforts of the Seminary and the Billy Graham Center of Wheaton College, the records were microfilmed under the direction of Robert Shuster, the Center's Director of Archives. Shuster's *The Papers of William and Helen Sunday: A Guide to the Microfilm Edition*, published along with the microfilm in 1978, is an excellent introduction to the 29 published reels of film. Personal and family correspondence, sermon notes, revival files, newspaper clippings, photographs, scrapbooks—the collection covers the range of Billy Sunday's work and interests. Although the microfilm edition, now available for purchase from Scholarly Resources, Inc., Wilmington, Delaware, includes most of the Sunday collection, there are some additional materials at the Billy Graham Center Archives, including documents in the papers of other evangelists, additional press clippings, and oral history tapes of individuals who worked with the evangelist and knew him personally. The Center has done a marvelous job making the collection accessible for research.

Several other archives and manuscript repositories hold materials on Sunday. The National Archives has pension records relating to claims made by Sunday's mother which give much early biographical information on the family. The National Baseball Hall of Fame in Cooperstown, New York, has biographical files on Sunday and some of his teammates. The Chicago Historical Society has some clippings on Sunday and his career as well as records of the White Stockings organization. The New York Public Library has in its manuscript division the Albert Spalding Collection, a rich source of information on early baseball, especially the scrapbooks of Harry Chadwick. The William Jennings Bryan Collection at the Library of Congress has extensive material on the prohibition and anti-evolution movements as well as some correspondence between Bryan and Sunday. Sunday material also appears in the papers of presidents Theodore Roosevelt, Woodrow Wilson, Calvin Coolidge, and Herbert Hoover at the Library of Congress. The major source of documentary material on the temperance movement is in a 416-reel microfilm edition of papers in the custody of the Ohio Historical Society, Michigan Historical Collections, and the Woman's Christian Temperance Union. The edition was published by the University of Michigan in 1977. The Washington Gladden Papers at the Ohio Historical Society are an excellent source of material on a prominent Social Gospel advocate and bitter critic of Sunday. The papers are available on microfilm in 52 reels.

At the Martin Luther King Public Library in Washington, D.C., is a helpful biographical file on Sunday which contains not only clippings but some letters relating to the evangelist's later career. The Moody Institute in Chicago, the Duke University Library, East Carolina University Library, the University of Michigan's Bentley Library, the Southern Illinois University Library—all have material on Sunday. The Presbyterian Historical Society in Philadelphia has several collections documenting the fundamentalist-modernist battles.

This book makes much use of newspaper coverage of Sunday's campaigns in the various towns and cities across the country. The publicity generated by the Sunday organization was unprecedented in the history of American evangelism and is reflected in the amount of copy that made its way into newspaper print. Indeed, in major cities such as New York, Washington, Chicago, and Philadelphia several newspapers extensively covered the events surrounding the revivals and some even ran daily transcripts of Sunday's sermons.

The best recent biography is Lyle Dorsett's *Billy Sunday and the Redemption of Urban America*, published by Eerdmans in their new series of biographies. William McLoughlin's *Billy Sunday Was His Real Name*, published by the University of Chicago Press in 1955, is still quite valuable. Several contemporary biographies, some authorized by Sunday, are helpful for anecdotal offerings and sermon material, especially William T. Ellis's *Billy Sunday: The Man and His Method* and Elijah Brown's *The Real Billy Sunday*.

The selected bibliography that follows lists articles and books consulted in the writing of this work.

Abbott, Ernest, "Billy Sunday: An Impression," *Outlook* (May 19, 1915), 141.

"Abjuring the Sawdust Trail," *Literary Digest* (October 8, 1927), 32–33.

Abrams, Ray. *Preachers Present Arms: A Study of the War-Time Attitudes and Activities of the Churches and the Clergy in the United States, 1914–1918*. Philadelphia: doctoral thesis, Round Table Press, Inc., 1933.

Allen, Frederick Lewis. *Only Yesterday: An Informal History of the 1920's*. New York: Harper & Row, Perennial Library Edition, 1939.

Allen, Harbor. "The Anti-Evolution Campaign in America," *Current History* (September 1926), 893–897.

Anderson, Scott. "Billy Sunday, Prophet or Charlatan," *Overland Monthly* (January 1918), 75–80.

Anson, Adrian. *A Ball Player's Career*. Chicago: Era Publishing Company, 1900.

Armstrong, Ben. *The Electric Church*. Nashville: Thomas Nelson Publishers, 1979.

Asbury, Herbert. *The Great Illusion: An Informal History of Prohibition*. New York: Doubleday & Co., 1950.

Balmer, Randall. *Mine Eyes Have Seen the Glory: A Journey into the Evangelical Subculture in America*. New York: Oxford University Press, 1989.

Baltzell, E. Digby. *The Protestant Establishment: Aristocracy and Caste in America*. New York: Random House, 1964.

Baritz, Loren, ed. *The Culture of the Twenties*. Indianapolis: Bobbs-Merrill Educational Publishing, 1970.

Barrett, Marvin. *The Jazz Age*. New York G. P. Putnam's Sons, 1959.

Barton, Bruce. "Billy Sunday—Baseball Evangelist," *Collier's* (July 26, 1913), 7–8.

A Baseball Century: The First 100 Years of the National League. New York: Macmillan Publishing Co., 1976.

The Baseball Encyclopedia. New York: Macmillan Publishing Co., 1976.

Berenbaum, May. " 'The Greatest Show that Ever Came to Town'—An Account of the Billy Sunday Crusade in Buffalo, New York, January 27–March 25, 1917," *Niagara Frontier* (Autumn 1975), 43–63.

Betts, Frederick W. *Billy Sunday: The Man and Method*. Boston: Universalist Publishing House, 1916.

"Billy in New York," *Time* (May 20, 1957), 104.

"Billy Sunday," *Outlook* (March 21, 1914), 608–609.

"Billy Sunday," *New Republic* (March 20, 1915), 173–175.

"Billy Sunday and the War," *Outlook* (April 18, 1917), 687.

"Billy Sunday as a Peace-Maker between the Races," *Current Opinion* (March 1918), 201.

"Billy Sunday Assailed by Leaders of Three Denominations," *Current Opinion* (May 1917), 341.

"Billy Sunday in the Big Cities," *Literary Digest* (April 4, 1914), 761–762.

"Billy Sunday's Greatest Campaign," *Literary Digest* (March 15, 1913), 576–577.

"Billy Sunday New York Campaign," *Literary Digest* (June 30, 1917), 1998.

"Billy Sunday's Results," *Literary Digest* (April 25, 1914), 990.

"Billy Sunday's Telling Exhibit," *Union Signal* (February 22, 1917), 14.

"Billy Sunday's War on the Devil in New York," *Literary Digest* (January 27, 1934), 21.

"Billy Sunday Sympathetically Interpreted," *Current Opinion* (May 1914), 369–370.

"Billy Sunday Under Fire," *Literary Digest* (April 18, 1914), 907.

Blocker, Jack S. *Retreat from Reform: The Prohibition Movement in the United States, 1890–1913.* Westport, CT: Greenwood Press, 1976.

Blum, John. "Nativism, Anti-Radicalism, and the Foreign Scare, 1917–1920," *Midwest Journal* (Winter 1950–51), 46–53.

Brauer, Jerald C. *Protestantism in America: A Narrative History.* Philadelphia: Westminster Press, 1965.

Brown, Elijah P. *The Real Bill Sunday.* New York: Fleming H. Revell Co., 1914.

Bruns, Roger. *The Damndest Radical: The Life and World of Ben Reitman, Chicago's Celebrated Social Reformer, Hobo King, and Whorehouse Physician.* Urbana: University of Illinois Press, 1987.

Bullock, Penelope L. "Profile of a Periodical: The 'Voice of the Negro,' " *Atlanta Historical Bulletin* (Spring 1977).

Burtt, Richard. *The Pittsburgh Pirates: A Pictorial History.* Virginia Beach, VA: Jordan & Company, 1977.

Calkins, David. "Billy Sunday's Cincinnati Crusade," *Cincinnati History Society Bulletin* (Winter 1969), 292–303.

Carpenter, Joel A. "Fundamentalist Institutions and the Rise of Evangelical Protestantism, 1929–1942," *Church History* (1980), 62–75.

Carter, Paul. *The Twenties in America.* Arlington Heights, IL: AHM Publishing Corporation, 1975.

Cash, W. J. *The Mind of the South.* New York: Alfred A. Knopf, 1941.

Chieger, Bob. *The Cubbies: Quotations on the Chicago Cubs.* New York: Atheneum, 1987.

Cobb, Irwin S. "Sunday as Cobb Saw Him," *Literary Digest* (June 16, 1917), 1870.

Coben, Stanley. "A Study in Nativism: The American Red Scare of 1919–1920," in Robert Marcus and David Burner, eds., *The American Scene: Varieties of American History.* New York: Appleton-Century Crofts, 1971.

Coleman, William L. "Billy Sunday: A Style Meant for His Time and Place," *Christianity Today* (December 17, 1976), 14–17.

Coleta, Paolo E. *William Jennings Bryan,* Vol. III: *Political Puritan, 1915–1925.* Lincoln: University of Nebraska Press, 1969.

Collins, Joseph. "Revivals, Past and Present," *Harper's Monthly* (November 1917), 856–865.

Creel, George. "Salvation Circus," *Harper's Weekly* (June 19, 1915), 580–582.

The Cubs: The Complete Record of Chicago Cubs Baseball. New York: Collier Books, 1986.

Davenport, F. M. "The National Value of Billy Sunday," *Outlook* (June 9, 1915), 31.

Denison, Lindsay. "The Rev. Billy Sunday and His War on the Devil," *American Magazine* (September 1907), 451–468.

Dorsett, Lyle W. *Billy Sunday and the Redemption of Urban America.* Grand Rapids, MI: William B. Eerdmans Publishing Co., 1991.

"Dramatizing Billy Sunday," *Literary Digest* (October 2, 1915), 713.

Drinnon, Richard. *Rebel in Paradise: A Biography of Emma Goldman.* New York: Harper & Row, 1976.

DuBois, W. E. B. "A Litany of Atlanta," *Independent* (October 11, 1906), 856–857.

Eckhouse, Morris, and Carl Mastrocola. *This Date in Pittsburgh Pirates History.* New York: Stein and Day, 1980.

Ellis, Edward R. *Echoes of Distant Thunder: Life in the United States, 1914–1918.* New York: Coward, McCann & Geoghegan, 1975.

Ellis, William T. *"Billy" Sunday: The Man and His Message.* Philadelphia: L. T. Myers, 1914.

———. "In the Light of Billy Sunday," *Outlook* (March 24, 1915), 677–680.

Englmann, Larry. "Billy Sunday: 'God, You've Got a Job on Your Hands in Detroit,' " *Michigan History* (Spring 1971), 1–21.

———. *Intemperance: The Lost War against Liquor.* New York: Free Press, 1979.

"Evangelism as a Means to Reform: Some Results of Mr. Sunday's Campaigns in Columbus and Erie," *Missionary Review of the World* (June 1913), 433–441.

Fackre, Gabriel. *The Religious Right and Christian Faith* (Grand Rapids, MI: William B. Eerdmans Publishing Co., 1982.

Falk, Candace. *Love, Anarchy, and Emma Goldman.* New York: Holt, Rinehart and Winston, 1984.

Falwell, Jerry. *Strength for the Journey: An Autobiography.* New York: Simon and Schuster, 1987.

First Album of the City of Davenport. Davenport, IA: Huebinger's Photographic Art Gallery, 1887.

Fishbein, Leslie. *Rebels in Bohemia.* Chapel Hill: University of North Carolina Press, 1982.

Fosness, Irene. *Marshalltown: A Pictorial History.* Rock Island, IL: Quest Publishing, 1985.

Frady, Marshall. *Billy Graham: A Parable of American Righteousness.* Boston: Little, Brown and Company, 1977.

Frank, Douglass. *Less than Conquerors: How Evangelicals Entered the Twentieth Century.* Grand Rapids, MI: William B. Eerdmans Publishing Co., 1986.

Frankenberg, Theodore T. *Billy Sunday: His Tabernacles and Sawdust Trails.* Columbus, OH: F. J. Meer Printing Company, 1917.

———. *The Spectacular Career of Rev. Billy Sunday: Famous Baseball Evangelist.* Columbus, OH: McClelland, 1913.

Frankl, Razelle. *Televangelism.* Carbondale: Southern Illinois University Press, 1987.

Frommer, Harvey. *Primitive Baseball: The First Quarter Century of the National Pastime.* New York: Atheneum, 1988.

Fullbrook, Earl. "Relief Work during the Civil War," *Iowa Journal of History and Politics* (April 1918), 257–267.

Furniss, Norman. *The Fundamentalist Controversy, 1918–1931.* Hamden, CT: Anchor Books, 1963.

Gaddis, Vincent, and Jasper Huffman. *The Story of Winona Lake.* Winona Lake, IN: Winona Lake Christian Assembly, 1960.

Gallup, George, Jr., and Jim Castelli. *The People's Religion: American Faith in the 90's.* New York: Macmillan, 1989.

Gambone, Robert. *Art and Popular Religion in Evangelical America, 1915–1940.*

Knoxville: University of Tennessee Press, 1989.

Gatewood, Willard B., ed. *Controversy in the Twenties: Fundamentalism, Modernism, and Evolution*. Nashville: Vanderbilt University Press, 1969.

Ginger, Ray. *Six Days or Forever? Tennessee v. John Thomas Scopes*. Chicago: Quadrangle Books, 1969.

Gladden, Washington. "Samples of Modern Evangelism," *Independent* (May 23, 1912), 1103–1104.

Gold, Eddie, and Art Ahrens. *The Golden Era Cubs, 1876–1940*. Chicago: Bonus Books, 1985.

Golden, Harry. *Carl Sandburg*. Cleveland and New York: World Publishing Co., 1961.

Goldman, Emma. *Living My Life*. New York: New American Library, 1977.

"The Greatest Man in the United States," *American Magazine* (October 1914), 63–64.

Greeley, Andrew. "In Defense of TV Evangelism," *TV Guide* (July 9, 1988), 4–7.

Gullen, Karen. *Billy Sunday Speaks*. New York: Chelsea House Publishers, 1970.

Hackett, Francis. "Billy Sunday, Salesman," *New Republic* (April 28, 1917), 370–372.

Hadden, Jeffrey, and Anson Shupe. *Televangelism: Power and Politics on God's Frontier*. New York: Henry Holt and Company, 1988.

Hall, Gordon L. *The Sawdust Trail: The Story of American Evangelism*. Philadelphia: Macrae Smith Company, 1964.

Handy, Robert T. *The American Religious Depression, 1925–1935*. Philadelphia: Fortress Press, 1968.

Harbor, Allen. "The Anti-Evolution Campaign in America," *Current History* (September 1926), 893–897.

Harlan, Louis, and Raymond Smock, eds. *The Booker T. Washington Papers*, Vols. 4, 9, 10, 11. Urbana: University of Illinois Press, 1975–81.

Harrell, David, ed. *Varieties of Southern Evangelism*. Macon, GA: Mercer University Press, 1981.

Hays, Samuel P. *The Response to Industrialism, 1885–1914*. Chicago: University of Chicago Press, 1957.

Hesselgrove, Charles. "Billy Sunday," *Independent* (February 1, 1915), 160–162.

Hicks, Granville. *John Reed: The Making of a Revolutionary*. New York: Macmillan, 1936.

History of Mills County, Iowa. Des Moines: State Historical Co., 1881.

Hofstadter, Richard. *Anti-Intellectualism in American Life*. New York: Alfred A. Knopf, 1963.

Hudson, Winthrop S. *Religion in America*. New York: Charles Scribner's Sons, 1965.

Hunter, James D. *Evangelicalism: The Coming Generation*. Chicago: University of Chicago Press, 1987.

James, Bill. *Historical Baseball Abstract*. New York: Villard Books, 1988.

Jimerson, Randall; Francis Blouin; and Charles Isetts, eds. *Guide to the Microfilm Edition of Temperance and Prohibition Papers*. Ann Arbor: University of Michigan, 1977.

Jorstad, Erling. *The Politics of Doomsday: Fundamentalists of the Far Right.* Nashville: Abingdon Press, 1970.

Ketchum, Ralph M. "Faces from the Past," *American Heritage* (August 1961), 38–39.

Kornbluh, Joyce. *Rebel Voices: An I.W.W. Anthology.* Ann Arbor: University of Michigan Press, 1972.

Kyvig, David. *Prohibition: The 18th Amendment; The Volstead Act; The 21st Amendment.* Washington, D.C.: National Archives and Records Administration, 1986.

———. *Repealing National Prohibition.* Chicago: University of Chicago Press, 1979.

Lacour, Lawrence L. "Study of Revival Methods in America, 1920–1955, with Special Reference to Billy Sunday, Aimee Semple McPherson, and Billy Graham." Unpublished Ph.D. thesis, Northwestern University, 1956.

Lee, Henry. *How Dry We Were: Prohibition Revisited.* Englewood Cliffs, NJ: Prentice-Hall, 1963.

Lender, Mark E. *Dictionary of American Temperance Biography.* Westport, CT: Greenwood Press, 1984.

Leopold, Richard; Arthur Link; and Stanley Coben, eds. *Problems in American History, Vol. II: Since Reconstruction.* Englewood Cliffs, NJ: Prentice-Hall, 1966.

Leuchtenburg, William E. *The Perils of Prosperity, 1914–32.* Chicago: University of Chicago Press, 1958.

Levine, Lawrence W. *Defender of the Faith: William Jennings Bryan: The Last Decade, 1915–1925.* New York: Oxford University Press, 1965.

Levine, Peter. *A. G. Spalding and the Rise of Baseball.* New York: Oxford University Press, 1985.

Lewis, Sinclair. *Elmer Gantry.* New York: Harcourt, Brace & Company, 1927.

Lieb, Frederick. *The Pittsburgh Pirates.* New York: G. P. Putnam's Sons, 1948.

Lippmann, Walter. *American Inquisitors: A Commentary on Dayton and Chicago.* New York: Macmillan, 1928.

"Making Religion Yellow," *The Nation* (June 11, 1908), 527–528.

Marsden, George. *Fundamentalism and American Culture: The Shaping of Twentieth-Century Evangelicalism, 1870–1925.* New York: Oxford University Press, 1982.

Marty, Martin. *Pilgrims in Their Own Land: 500 Years of Religion in America.* New York: Penguin Books, 1984.

———. *Religion and Republic: The American Circumstance.* Boston: Beacon Press, 1987.

"Mass Conversions," *Christian Century* (May 29, 1957), 677–679.

"Ma Sunday at 82," *Newsweek* (November 27, 1950), 74.

Mathews, Shailer. "Ten Years of Protestantism," *North American Review* (May 1923), 577–593.

May, George S. "Outfielders McVey to Lindell," *Palimpsest* (April 1955), 140–141.

McBride, Joseph. *High and Inside: The Complete Guide to Baseball Slang.* New York: Warner Books, 1980.

McBrien, Richard. *Caesar's Coin: Religion and Politics in America*. New York: Macmillan, 1987.

McLoughlin, William G. *Billy Graham: Revivalist in a Secular Age*. New York: Ronald Press Company, 1960.

———. *Billy Sunday Was His Real Name*. Chicago: University of Chicago Press, 1955.

———. *Revivals, Awakenings, and Reform*. Chicago: University of Chicago Press, 1978.

Meier, August. *Negro Thought in America, 1880–1915*. Ann Arbor: University of Michigan Press, 1969.

Merrian, Edmund. "Sunday the Modern Juvenal," *The Watchman-Examiner* (April 12, 1917), 459.

Mills, George. *Rogues and Heroes from Iowa's Amazing Past*. Ames: Iowa State University Press, 1972.

Mitgang, Herbert, ed. *The Letters of Carl Sandburg*. New York: Harcourt, Brace & World, 1968.

"Modern Evangelism: Its Strength and Its Weaknesses," *Presbyterian* (February 8, 1917), 8–9.

Moody, William R. *The Live of Dwight L. Moody*. New York: Fleming Revell Company, 1900.

Mordden, Ethan. *That Jazz! An Idiosyncratic Social History of the American Twenties*. New York: G. P. Putnam's Sons, 1978.

Morgan, David T. "The Revivalist as Patriot: Billy Sunday and World War I," *Journal of Presbyterian History* (Summer 1973), 199–215.

Mowry, George. *The Twenties: Fords, Flappers, and Fanatics*. Englewood Cliffs, NJ: Prentice-Hall, 1963.

Muhlbach, Robert. "Billy Sunday, Evangelist," *Baseball Research Journal* (November 1980), 5–7.

Mulford, Henry J. "Our Children and 'Billy' Sunday," *Outlook* (April 18, 1917).

"The New Attitude toward Evangelism," *Current Literature* (February 1906), 163.

"New Evangelism," *Outlook* (July 3, 1909), 546–547.

"The New Evangelist," *Time* (October 25, 1954), 54–60.

Newton, Joseph F. *River of Years*. New York: J. B. Lippincott Co., 1946.

"Observations and Comments," *Mother Earth* (May 1915), 99–101.

Odell, Joseph. "The Mechanics of Revivalism," *Atlantic Monthly* (May 1915), 585–592.

———. "Revivalist Judged by Results," *Outlook* (April 11, 1914), 804–805.

Okrent, Daniel, and Steve Wulf. *Baseball Anecdotes*. New York: Oxford University Press, 1989.

Oliver, Robert T. *History of Public Speaking in America*. Boston: Allyn and Bacon, 1965.

O'Neill, William L. *The Last Romantic: A Life of Max Eastman*. New York: Oxford University Press, 1978.

"Opinions about Billy Sunday," *Outlook* (May 9, 1917), 57–58.

Orem, Preston D. "Baseball from the Newspaper Accounts." Altadena, CA: 1967. Unpublished copy in Library of Congress.

Palmer, Harry. *Stories of the Base Ball Field*. Chicago: Rand, McNally & Co., 1890.

Peterson, Harold. *The Man Who Invented Baseball*. New York: Charles Scribner's Sons, 1973.

"Poll of the Religious Press on Billy Sunday," *Literary Digest* (June 12, 1915), 1404–1405.

Porter, David L. "Cap Anson of Marshalltown," *Palimpsest* (July / August 1980), 100–107.

"Princeton's Thrust at Billy Sunday," *Literary Digest* (April 24, 1915), 960.

"The Problem of Billy Sunday," *Literary Digest* (June 14, 1913), 1336–1337.

Reed, John. "Back of Billy Sunday," *Metropolitan Magazine* (May 1915), 9*ff.*

Reichley, A. James. *Religion in American Public Life*. Washington, D.C.: Brookings Institution, 1985.

Reidenbaugh, Lowell. *100 Years of National League Baseball*. St. Louis: The Sporting News, 1976.

"Religion with a Punch," *The Nation* (March 19, 1914), 287.

Rensi, Ray. "The Gospel According to Sam Jones," *Georgia Historical Quarterly* (Fall 1976), 251–261.

"A Revival of Religion," *Century* (April 1910), 951–952.

Ribuffo, Leo P. *The Old Christian Right: The Protestant Far Right from the Great Depression to the Cold War*. Philadelphia: Temple University Press, 1983.

Riley, William B. "The Faith of the Fundamentalists," *Current History* (June 1927), 434–440.

Robertson, Archie. *That Old-Time Religion*. Boston: Houghton Mifflin Company, 1950.

Rodeheaver, Homer. *Twenty Years with Billy Sunday*. Nashville: Cokesbury Press, 1936.

Rosenburg, John. *The Story of Baseball*. New York: Random House, 1962.

Rosenstone, Robert A. *Romantic Revolutionary: A Biography of John Reed*. New York: Vintage Books, 1981.

Russell, Charles A. *Voices of American Fundamentalism*. Philadelphia: Westminster Press, 1976.

Sandeen, Ernest. *The Roots of Fundamentalism: British and American Millenarianism, 1800–1930*. Chicago: University of Chicago Press, 1970.

———. "Towards a Historical Interpretation of the Origins of Fundamentalism," *Church History* (March 1967), 66–83.

Seldes, George. *Witness to a Century: Encounters with the Noted, the Notorious, and the Three SOBs*. New York: Ballantine Books, 1987.

"Sensational Evangelists Rebuked," *Literary Digest* (November 23, 1912), 963–964.

Shipley, Maynard. *The War on Modern Science*. New York: Alfred A. Knopf, 1927.

Shirer, William. *Twentieth Century Journey: The Start: 1904–1930*. Boston: Little, Brown and Company, 1976.

Simpson, Jeffrey. "Utopia by the Lake," *American Heritage* (August 1972), 76.

Sizer, Sandra. "Politics and Apolitical Religion: The Great Urban Revivals of the Late Nineteenth Century," *Church History* (1979), 81–98.

Slaten, A. Wakefield. "The Old-time Religion Is Dying," *Collier's* (July 10, 1926), 8, 34.

Soden, Dale. "Billy Sunday in Spokane," *Pacific Northwest Quarterly* (January 1988), 10–17.

Southwestern Iowa Guide. Works Project Administration, Federal Writers' Project, 1936.

Spalding, Albert G. *America's National Game*. New York: American Sports Publishing Company, 1911.

Stelzle, Charles. "The Evangelist in Present-Day America," *Current History* (November 1931), 224–228.

Stonehouse, Ned. *J. Gresham Machen: A Memoir*. Grand Rapids, MI: Eerdmans Publishing Co., 1954.

Sunday, Billy. "Back to the Old-Time Religion," *Collier's* (July 10, 1926), 24.

———. "My All-Star Nine," *Collier's* (October 18, 1913), 19.

———. "The Sawdust Trail," *Ladies' Home Journal* (serialized between September 1932 and April 1933).

Sunday, Helen A. *"Ma" Sunday Still Speaks: Transcription of Tape Recording Made in 1954*. Winona Lake, IN: Winona Lake Christian Assembly, 1957.

Swisher, J. A. "Adrian Anson," *Palimpsest* (November 1922), 374–387.

———. "Billy Sunday," *Palimpsest* (August 1930), 343–354.

Terkel, Studs. *Talking to Myself: A Memoir of My Times*. New York: Pantheon Books, 1973.

Turkin, Hy, and S. C. Thompson. *The Official Encyclopedia of Baseball, Fifth Revised Edition*. South Brunswick and New York: A. S. Barnes and Company, 1970.

Voigt, David Q. *American Baseball: From Gentleman's Sport to the Commissioner System*. Norman: University of Oklahoma Press, 1966.

Weber, Timothy. *Living in the Shadow of the Second Coming: American Premillennialism, 1815–1925*. New York: Oxford University Press, 1987.

Weisberger, Bernard. "Pentecost in the Backwoods," *American Heritage* (June 1959), 26.

———. *They Gathered at the River: The Story of the Great Revivalists and Their Impact upon Religion in America*. Boston: Little, Brown, 1958.

"Welcome Old Man Gloom," *The Historic New Orleans Collection Newsletter* (Summer 1988), 6–7.

"Why Billy Sunday Does Not Appeal to Roman Catholics," *Current Opinion* (July 1917), 44–45.

Wiebe, Robert H. *The Search for Order, 1877–1920*. New York: Hill and Wang, 1967.

Wilentz, Sean. "The Trials of Televangelism," *Dissent* (Winter 1990), 42–48.

Wills, Garry. *Under God: Religion and American Politics*. New York: Simon and Schuster, 1990.

Wilson, Richard. "Sam Jones: An Apostle of the New South," *Georgia Historical Quarterly* (Winter 1973), 459–473.

Wilson, Samuel Paynter. *Chicago and Its Cesspools of Infamy*. Chicago: Samuel Paynter Wilson, 1910.

Winona Echoes: A Book of Sermons and Addresses Delivered at the Nineteenth Annual Bible Conference. Winona Lake, IN: Committee on Publication, 1913.

Winona Year Book. Winona Lake, IN: Winona Assembly, 1908 and 1909 editions.

Wood, Charles Erskine Scott. *Heavenly Discourse.* New York: Vanguard Press, 1927.

Wylie, Irvin G. "The Socialist Press and the Libel Laws: A Case Study," *Midwestern Journal* (Summer 1952), 72–79.

Index

The University of Illinois Press
is a founding member of the
Association of American University Presses.

University of Illinois Press
1325 South Oak Street
Champaign, IL 61820-6903
www.press.uillinois.edu